LEAP BEFORE YOU LOOK

LEAP BEFORE
YOU LOOK

A Memoir

AIDAN CRAWLEY

COLLINS
8 Grafton Street, London W 1
1988

William Collins Sons & Co. Ltd
London · Glasgow · Sydney · Auckland
Toronto · Johannesburg

BRITISH LIBRARY CATALOGUING IN PUBLICATION DATA

Crawley, Aidan
Leap before you look.
1. Crawley, Aidan 2. Authors, English –
20th century – Biography
I. Title
823'.914 PR6053.R375/

ISBN 0–00–217950–4

First published 1988
Copyright © Aidan Crawley 1988

Photoset in Linotron Ehrhardt
by Wyvern Typesetting Ltd

Made and printed in Great Britain by
T. J. Press (Padstow) Ltd, Padstow, Cornwall

In memory of Virginia

CONTENTS

CONTENTS

ILLUSTRATIONS

Between pages 94 and 95:

My father as Canon of Windsor in 1935
My mother in the early thirties
Archbishop Cosmo Lang, with me and my elder
brother Cosmo, 1925
Six Crawleys at Harrow, 1922
With brothers Cosmo and Kenneth, 1929
With John Cowdray, 1931
Going out to bat for Oxford, Lords, 1929

Between pages 222 and 223:

With the tiger I shot, Bhopal, India, 1934
One of the gates of Peking, 1934
Esmond Rothermere, 1965
Camp breakfast, Jerusalem, 1937
Camping in Jerusalem, 1937
My younger brother Kenneth and myself, 1939
East Compound, Stalage Luft III, 1943
With Virginia at our wedding, 1945
A victory group of Labour Party helpers, 1945

Between pages 350 and 351:

Kingsbridge, Bucks, our home from 1948 to 1962
Virginia and I with our children, Kingsbridge, 1951
With a patrol in Malaya, 1951
Filming in Texas, 1954
Farnborough Air Show, 1951
Farnborough Air Show, 1951
With Virginia and Harriet in Parliament Square
on the way to take my seat, 1962

PREFACE

Millions of words have been written this century by men and women who felt their lives of sufficient interest or importance to warrant memoirs. My life has not been important but it has touched the lives of some people who were and many who thought they were; it has been lived against many different backgrounds: the Church, sport, journalism, films, politics, television and two world wars. It spans the century, minus a decade at either end. My childhood memories are of men in top hats, women in wide-brimmed hats and veils, horses and carriages. I have lived to see the space shuttle and feel the threat of Chernobyl. I shall not live to see 'The Orient Express' or 'Hotol', the air-cum-spacecraft now on the drawing boards in America and Europe, but am confident that my children will fly from London to Tokyo or Sydney in less than two hours.

A young and beautiful authoress who read my manuscript expressed regret that I had not described any of the women with whom I had been in love. When I explained my objection she said I ought to mention it in the foreword. All my life I have been susceptible to women and think them in most ways superior to men. They are often more courageous, less selfish, more sympathetic and quite as intelligent. Their physical attraction is the most thrilling thing in life. But a relationship between a man and a woman, even a youthful flirtation, has always seemed to me essentially private and I have never wanted to talk about it in detail. I am grateful when a woman is attracted to me, but however much I enjoy remembering her, I feel she may not want to be reminded of our relationship. The bond of an old love can be intimate and charming but it can also revive painful memories. I know that to some readers this will make these reminiscences less interesting, but I do not apologize for it.

Nevertheless there can only be one valid reason for remembering any part of the sort of life I have led and that is that I enormously enjoyed it and hope that others may get pleasure from recalling the things we did together or being reminded of their own similar experiences. If that happens, then I shall feel rewarded for the effort of recollection which has been spread over several years and involved much reading and research.

AIDAN CRAWLEY, 1988

ACKNOWLEDGEMENTS

My thanks go first to my younger son, Randall, and to Professor Hilde Himmelweit, who both read the manuscript in its earliest stages and made fundamental and valid criticisms; to Philip Ziegler, who not only read the finished version but agreed to edit it; and to Mrs Judith Mooney, whose word processor was capable of absorbing limitless corrections.

Air Commodore Henry Probert, MBE, and his staff at the Historical Branch of the Air Ministry, the staffs of the Foreign and Commonwealth Library, the Lambeth Palace Library and the London Library were tirelessly helpful, as was the Curator of the Library in Lord's Pavilion and the staffs of the MCC and the National Cricket Association. I bothered several friends to check certain passages and ask their forgiveness if, in reducing the book to a length commensurate with its commercial prospects, the fruit of their labours has had to be cut out.

I

A Forest of Gaiters

It must have been early May because I had only recently changed from my blue serge sailor suit with brown canvas gaiters to the white trousers and tunic of the summer uniform, worn with a wide-brimmed straw hat. My mother always wanted me to wear the brim turned down, which got in the way of my eyes. Whenever she was out of sight, I turned it up. This morning I had taken the hat off and thrown it on the grass.

I was playing on the steps of the Palace. The steps were ideal because they were broad, smooth and shallow, whereas the Palace drive was pebbly and the wheels of my new wooden steam engine, a present for my fifth birthday a few weeks before, would not run on them. The steps began against the Palace wall, jutted out into the drive for ten yards or so, then turned at right angles and ran right across the front of the Palladian portico before turning back into the wall again. Because the engine had to be pulled by a string, each rectangular corner had become a station at which the train stopped. I then lifted the engine round the corner and started off again.

I had just negotiated a corner when I suddenly noticed a change. I had been alone, concentrating on keeping the engine straight. Suddenly I was surrounded by a forest of black gaiters. I looked up and saw that the steps were crowded by what I rightly took to be bishops. The Archbishop, whom I knew well, was standing near me. He came and put his hand on my head and said, 'Well, Aidan, are you going to be a bishop when you grow up?'

'Oh, no,' I replied instantly, 'I'm going to be a saint,' and went on with my game.

I had been called Aidan because at the time of my birth my father had been reading about Saint Aidan and the community at Iona. I can just remember being carried across the sands to Lindisfarne to see the chapel where Saint Aidan prayed in the seventh century. On the way back the tide had come in and everyone had to padde. My retort to the Archbishop, therefore, came naturally. But it delighted him and he often used to tell me, as I grew up, that however witty I might think myself I should never make a more brilliant repartee than I had at the age of five.

The Archbishop's name, although I did not then know it, was Cosmo Lang. My father was his chaplain and also vicar of Bishop-thorpe, the village where the Archbishop lived four miles south of York. For the next thirty years 'the Arch', as we called him, loomed large in the background of my life. As I first remember him, he had dark, almost black hair which was already receding, dark, very bright eyes, a broad forehead and sharp features. But it is his voice I remember most clearly. It was not particularly deep – he used to describe his singing as 'baritone' – but resonant and wonderfully musical. Although he could still speak with a Scottish accent if he wanted to, Oxford and Cuddesden (the Anglican College for can-didates for ordination) had polished this away. When he spoke to us children his voice was always gentle; but when I heard him preach in York Minster I was struck by its strength. Nowadays loudspeakers, hanging from each of the great pillars down the nave, can make even the most feeble preacher audible. At that time there were none, yet the Archbishop had not the slightest difficulty in making his voice carry to the farthest corner of the great cathedral.

The Bishops' Conference was an annual event. They came from all over the north of England and from anywhere else which was within the province of York, like Wales or Scotland, although Anglican bishops were thin on the ground in those parts. It was a time when our house, the vicarage, was full of guests, and children were expected to keep out of the way. This was not difficult. The vicarage had a large garden and the Palace one even larger, and we had the run of both. The Yorkshire Ouse ran down one side, but it was so dirty and its banks so muddy that we never played there. But there were endless bushes where we could hide and there was the weeping willow tree on the vicarage lawn where Nanny and the nursery maid used to take the 'little ones' in their prams and, if it was fine, have tea. The willow's branches swept the ground and made lovely alcoves which my elder sister and I used to pretend were the rooms of our house. I had also one or two favourite places of my own: a large box hedge which was hollow but also so damp and dirty that no one else wanted to go there, and the yew trees at the bottom end of the vicarage lawn, which were easy to climb but made one's hands and clothes filthy. In summer, when bed time approached, I used to go to the top of one of those trees and hide.

My constant companion was Janet, two years older, about the same height as me with long brown hair and very large brown eyes. We fought every day, but it was a recognized convention that, although she could pull my hair, I could not pull hers; it would have been too easy. Once, when we were playing at the far end of the vicarage garden, she got so furious with me that she picked up a spade and swung it at my head. Fortunately, although she could run a little faster, the effort of swinging slowed her down and I just managed to reach the shelter of the house without being hit. Then there were the little ones, Anstice, three years younger than me, and Kenneth, two years younger still. In fact Kenneth did not arrive until the autumn of 1913, the year I was found playing on the steps.

The routine of our lives proceeded serenely. Each day began with family prayers in the dining room. At eight-thirty a bell would peal through the house and Janet and I, dressed and waiting, would go downstairs followed by Nanny and the nursery maid. In the hall below, the entire household would be assembling, the butler, the parlourmaid, the cook and kitchen maid, the two housemaids and my mother's maid. Janet and I went straight into the dining room and took our places next to Mother on a row of chairs with their backs to the window. Anyone staying in the house sat next to us. Then, on some unseen signal, the butler would lead in his colleagues, marshalled in an order of pre-cedence which they had settled among themselves. First came the cook, then Mother's maid, then the head housemaid, and so on. They sat in a row of chairs facing us. My Mother would say, 'Good morning all,' and was answered by a 'Good morning, ma'am,' said in unison, after which my father came in carrying a prayer book and a Bible and stood in front of a lectern which had been brought in from his study and placed at one end of the room. He at once began reading the Collect of the Day. (The dining room table must have been moved to one side because I remember there was nothing between us and the servants who sat facing us and I was never quite sure whether to look at them or away from them.)

For me, the highlight came a little while after the Collect. If anyone in the village or the family needed remembering in our prayers, Father would then say, 'This morning I would like you all to remember so-and-so, who is ill [or going to have a baby]. Let us also pray for the Queen and all members of the Royal Family and for the Archbishop and all who serve him.' He would then turn and kneel at his lectern with his back to us. This was the signal for everyone else to turn round and kneel, leaning their elbows on the seat of the chair they had just been sitting on. By looking behind me, underneath my arm so that no one could notice, I could then contemplate the row of bottoms which stretched across the opposite side of the room. The cook's was massive, swathed in dark red bombazine stretched so tightly across her buttocks that the whole looked like one of those rounded hills in the South Downs whose gentle curves make one of the most appealing skylines in Britain. The kitchen and nursery maids also wore the red uniform and their bottoms were round and plump. The housemaids and the parlourmaid wore black, and had behinds which were rather skinny. (Over their uniforms all the maids wore white aprons and white mob caps edged with lace.) Mother's maid didn't wear a uniform at all and for some reason this made one pass over her, perhaps because one didn't feel she was really a servant. Yet it was the butler who held my interest for longest. His trousers shone in the light of the window and were so tight that I wondered whether they would not split. They were striped and, as I learned later, were an old pair of my father's which had been given to the butler to go with his short black coat. But the expected never happened and the butler's strong voice led the responses and was the first to say 'Our Father' in the Lord's Prayer. When prayers were over everyone trooped silently out and we waited in the hall for the table to be laid for breakfast.

From the time of Kenneth's arrival, Janet and I had been allowed to breakfast in the dining room. It was not exciting. Father ate his porridge standing because, he said, that was the way the Scots ate it and they invented the dish. He also took salt rather than sugar for the same reason. With our porridge we had milk but never cream. After that we gobbled up eggs and bacon, or sausages, kidneys or mushrooms, whichever Cook had decided upon for the day. We always ended with toast and marmalade. While Father read the paper and regaled Mother with the news, we would ask if we might 'get down' and slipped out to continue whatever we had left off doing the night before. Governesses

18

must already have arrived on the scene because I remember that I often used to get a quarter of an hour at a jigsaw puzzle before lessons began.

Governesses came and went. The only one I can remember was called Miss Dillon, who rapped our knuckles with a ruler. After she had done this once or twice Janet and I simply ran away into the garden. Miss Dillon left. The part of the morning I looked forward to most was 'the break' which came at about half-past eleven. Either I would take a tennis racket and see how often I could hit a tennis ball, first bounce, up against a wall in the back yard or, if it was summer and I was lucky, my father or mother would come and bowl at me. A cricket net with short sides was always put in front of the oak tree at the bottom of the vicarage lawn in April, before my elder brother went back to school. It was here that I would set up the stumps and wait hopefully.

If Father was not 'having trouble with a sermon' – dread phrase in my childhood – he would come out, take off his coat and bowl to me in his braces. He used to dance up to the wicket with little steps and then half throw, half bowl very slow off breaks. There was plenty of time in which to play them but they were difficult because their normal bounce came at the height of my head or chest. It was only when a half-volley or a full pitch came along that I could really let go. Still, Father bowled overhand and that was important. Mother on the other hand, who had had five brothers older than herself, was a splendid bowler. She had a strong underhand action and kept the ball low enough for me to hit it comfortably; and she bowled very straight. How many hours she spent at the net I cannot imagine, but I never had enough and, if the weather was fine, she would sometimes come out three or four times a day.

2

Life at the Vicarage

I would like to try to paint a picture of my father. He was only five feet eight inches tall but well proportioned, with classical features, dark hair and blue eyes. As a young man he had not only played games well but had won the 'hundred yards' and 'high hurdles' at Harrow. My mother told me he was a beautiful dancer. To his children he was gentle and encouraging. I never saw him lose his temper, but could sense his anger at untruth or injustice. We were not afraid of him, but we had to summon up our courage to enter his study, which smelled of smoke, because we felt that there we were unwelcome. He would always stop what he was doing and listen to what we wanted, but in the study he did not lift us on to his knee or play with us. We were an interruption. Occasionally he would reprove us – when I kicked a football through his study window he took the ball away – but he never lectured. The only swearword I ever heard him use was 'damn', and that very occasionally. He considered the use of bad language a confession of failure in self-expression.

I can barely remember my grandmother, but have been told that she was a strong character and very devout. It was largely because of her that my father went into the Church. Father had been at Magdalen College, Oxford, when Cosmo Lang became Dean of Divinity and, like many others, had come under his influence, but it was Mrs Pringle who kept the flame alive in the ensuing few years. Although my mother often used to say that he should never have become a parson, I do not think he regretted it. His belief was profound and he read widely in theology, keeping abreast of the thought of contemporaries such as Dean Inge and Canon Streeter. His difficulty lay in assimilating their thoughts and drawing his own conclusions. When I was living with him at Windsor just before the Second World War, he used to ask me to read his sermons in manuscript (he had beautiful writing). I found that he often lost his thread and became prolix: he would generally accept my criticism and rework what he had written. It was because of this awareness of his own shortcomings that he found preaching such a burden. Nevertheless, in his last years at Windsor his sermons became quite a feature in St George's Chapel; I have seen a letter from Sir Owen Morshead, the Queen's Librarian at that time, thanking him for the inspiration and challenge he had given his congregation.

In Church matters, Father was an Anglo-Catholic, believing in the apostolic succession of Anglican bishops; but he followed Cosmo Lang in his efforts to restore unity to all Christian churches and would have preferred disestablishment after the rejection of the Revised Prayer Book in 1928 to the acceptance of rule 'by a lot of atheists in the House of Commons'. He resented having to marry or bury people who had never been to church and would often try to arrange that other parsons with more flexible views performed the ceremony. Politically he was Conservative, partly from upbringing but also because he thought that socialism might too easily lead to tyranny; he mistrusted the Marxist thread in the Labour Party, yet would always discuss politics and sympathized with much that the Labour Governments of 1945 and 1951 were trying to do. My father is often in my mind and I am aware when I do or say something of which he would have disapproved. Whether he loved life, I am not sure; he was apt to hope too much and suffered disappointments in people, but when he was doing something he enjoyed, he added greatly to the fun of foxhunting, dinghy sailing, picnicking, sight-seeing, or playing any game. I do not think of him as witty, but he loved to laugh. He would have deprecated it had he known, but many people spoke of him as a saintly man.

In winter the routine of our lives varied. I had apparently had two bouts of pneumonia when little and this had earned me the reputation of being delicate. Fresh air and exercise in all weather were prescribed and, as a result, I had a daily ride on a pony called Teeny. Teeny was short, round and lively. Radenbury, the groom, used to put me on a leading rein and ride to Acaster, a small Saxon church about three miles down the road to Selby. I hated the leading rein. No doubt I could not have managed Teeny without it, but it made him turn his head towards Radenbury's horse so that there was space in front of me where the head ought to have been. And as the grass verge either side of the road was cut with little drainage ditches every thirty yards or so, I was always afraid that Teeny, unable to see where he was going, would put his foot in one and throw me over his head. Later, when I was allowed to go solo, I used to love the ditches and rode Teeny over them as fast as I could.

On some afternoons Father or Mother would take us out with them. This meant a ride in the pony cart (Father always called it a pony trap) either to visit friends or to see parishioners. Teeny was too small to pull the cart. This was done by a short-tailed cob which my father also sometimes rode. The cob went at a spanking trot and from a very early age I learned to hold the reins, sitting on my mother's or father's knee.

Occasionally we went out with the Archbishop. Father had a carriage, but 'the Arch's' was much grander. It was low slung, with four big wheels, the tops of which came above the sides of the carriage, and when it was open you could see everyone who was in it quite plainly. Usually there were four men, all in black clothes and black top hats, sitting opposite each other in pairs; but there were sometimes ladies wearing wide-brimmed hats, each with a large veil which went over the top of the hat and was tied under the chin. The Arch's top hat had black strings stretching from the brim to the crown as if to hold the two together and a black rosette on the front of the hat band. I was told more than once what the origin of the strings was, but I can never remember. Often the Arch went to York and back, a distance of eight miles in all, but if he was going nowhere in particular and happened to see Janet and me playing in the Palace drive, he would stop and ask us if we wanted to jump in. The coachman would get down from the box, let down the steps at the side of the carriage and in we would get, taking it in turns to sit on the Arch's knee and play with the gold cross which hung on his chest.

Evenings were formal. When Mother or Father were at home, we children had to be dressed in our best clothes to go down to the drawing room after tea. We never questioned this rather chilling performance. I do not know what is considered the earliest age at which an adult can recollect, but I know that my first memory is of reaching up for the china knob of the drawing room door. I was dressed in a white frock with a dark blue sash of which I was particularly proud. On entering the drawing room certain things were always the same. The tea things were set on a round table before the fireplace. The teapot was fat and silver and the hot water (for second cups) was in another rather flat silver pot hanging in a silver frame over a paraffin lamp. Hot scones were in a silver dish with a cover, cucumber sandwiches and very thin bread-and-butter on plates. There were cakes in what my father called the 'dumb waiter', a tall triangular wooden contraption which stood to one side of the table.

As soon as we came in Mother would ring for the tea things to be taken away. (We did not like hot scones and the sandwiches were too thin and messy. It was only if there was currant bread or a good solid currant cake that we would grab something before it went.) On the sofa, opposite the teapot, sat my mother, dressed in a red velvet teagown with a square neck edged in gold, looking very elegant. Her shiny brown hair was done in a sort of circle with a round bun on top. In the other corner of the sofa sat a man. If it was 'the Arch' he would be dressed either in purple or black with gaiters and cummerbund, according to whether it was a Sunday or saint's day or just an ordinary weekday. But it might be an uncle or one of 'the Arch's' chaplains – perhaps Edward Gibbs, my mother's cousin, who laughed in a very loud voice; or Uncle Reggie Merivale, who was nearly a great uncle, lived in Australia and had a sovereign case full of gold coins on his watch chain. Once the tea things had gone we would play games, Dumb Crambo, Hunt the Slipper, anything which would get the grown-ups, the Arch included, down on their knees or even lower. This was fun while it lasted and because we were small and agile we had a great advantage. Then back upstairs to bed.

Goodnights were rather formal too. However much Nanny had scolded us during the day, she always forgave us when she came to say goodnight. She was a squat, dumpy figure with a wrinkled face and thinning hair who looked very like pictures of Queen Victoria. In the evenings she wore a black dress through which one could see outlined the top of her corsets. She had not an 'h' to her name and could barely read or write, but she was the centre of our lives. She did not hold with the spoiling of children. She often made us stand in the corner, and, when we still had meals in the nursery, would make us sit at the table until we had finished what was in front of us. 'There are lots of people who would be grateful for half of what you get,' she would say. I remember winning one such battle because every time I tried to swallow a mouthful of vermicelli pudding, which by then was cold and congealed, I was sick. Nanny did not relent but, by sheer luck, my mother came in and saw what was happening. Very tactfully she put an end to my ordeal.

But Nanny's eyes were always kind and when she bent over us to say goodnight she would call us 'darling' – something she never did during the day – and give us a kiss. Later, when we were half asleep, my mother would come in, bend over our beds holding her long necklaces against her chest, and kiss us also. It was not until I was a year or two older that I realized that, since I had last seen her after tea, she had changed her clothes again.

It was much later that I realized that Mother was beautiful. Her pictures show an oval face with cleanly cut features, brown hair, usually piled high on her head, brown eyes, clearly marked arched eyebrows and a lovely complexion. All her life she must have been a centre of attention. The Archbishop, who admired pretty women, always paid court to her and wrote to her regularly over the years. Having been brought up in a large, well-to-do family, she fell easily into the role of acting as his hostess, both at Amen Court when he was Bishop of Stepney, and at Bishopthorpe when my father was his chaplain.

For years I never thought of her except as a mother, loving, finding time to read to or play with us, gently exercising discipline and only occasionally resorting to reproof. Even when home from Oxford I used to go and sit on her bed when saying goodnight and, while my father turned over and went to sleep, would tell her my troubles and talk about the girl or girls of the moment. If she saw I was worried, she would reciprocate and tell me about her early loves. Once she admitted that after her marriage she had fallen in love with an actor and for a wild moment had actually thought of running away with him. The romance would never have lasted; she lived for my father.

Sadly my relationship with her changed as I grew older and began to recognize her limitations. She was downright, warm-hearted and possessed great charm but very little intellect. She tried to keep abreast of the topics of the day but had no real curiosity. It was impossible to discuss a subject with her: her views on most things were those she had inherited and she saw no reason to question or even to defend them. I began to think that when she asked me or my father to explain reports in the newspaper, she did it only so that she could hold her own at a dinner party, rather than through any genuine interest. My father noticed that I sometimes got irritated by her questions and told me that the time when a son or daughter begins to see their father and mother as real people instead of as parents is one of the most difficult. He urged me to be patient and hold on to my affection until I could accept my mother for what she was instead of wishing her to be different. It is one of the regrets of my life that I was too self-centred to act on his advice and allowed my intimacy with my mother to fade. In her old age, other people appreciated her more than I did. I saw her regularly but always slightly resented her pose of the *grande dame*. Even in her eighties I felt she was still more interested in herself than in what went on around her.

There were no family prayers on Sundays because Father and Mother went out early to Holy Communion. Breakfast was later, about nine-fifteen, and at ten we went upstairs to get ready for church. We were dressed in our best. The way to church led through the Palace garden, across the York Road and up the path leading to the vestry. We would pass Father putting on his surplice in the vestry on our way to the pew under the pulpit. In the pew the most important things were the footstools. There were two sizes, one thin, which meant one had to go right down to the floor when one knelt, and the other fat, about nine inches high and covered in red felt, on which we could put our knees and still sit on the edge of the seat. The first thing Janet and I did, therefore, was to shuffle the footstools until we got the ones we wanted. Then, as we could not see over the top of the pew, we would carry on a whispered conversation in a world of our own. We were always taken out before the sermon.

The age of seven was a watershed. After our seventh birthday we had to listen to the sermon and quite often help the churchwarden with the collection. We would leave our pew, walk down to the font at the back of the nave to get the collection trays – flat wooden bowls, the bottom of which was lined with red velvet so that the coins would not clink – then walk up the aisle and begin collecting at the front pews, moving steadily down the church. We always knew who might put in a pound or ten-shilling note and watched carefully to see if they did. If not, we knew they didn't approve of the cause for which we were collecting. 'Missions to Seamen' was the most frequent, and because it came so often, no one gave more than ten shillings. An earthquake or a mine disaster brought several notes. And at Easter there were even cheques. We didn't know that Father was supposed to keep the Easter money for himself or we would have been thrilled. Mother once told me, however, that he always gave it away. I was made to promise never to tell anyone. We also knew the people who would pretend to put in a coin and never did. They were not the poor people, either. I once asked my father about them. 'They probably forgot to bring any money with them,' was the answer. I did not believe it. The same people forgot too often.

*

Holidays were heaven. They meant, first, that my elder brother Cosmo came home from his school at Farnborough. Partly through the enthusiasm of my mother, who had had years of welcoming older brothers home, the day of Cosmo's return was approached with mounting excitement. The gardener would put up two tall posts either side of the gate leading into the vicarage drive and Janet and I would spend days decorating them with laurels, holly, flowers – whatever was appropriate to the season. Then we would embroider a great banner with the words 'Welcome Home' and string it between the tops of the posts. Mother would give us Union Jacks to wave.

Farnborough was in Hampshire and it took nearly a whole day for Cosmo to reach York by train. Father went to meet him in the carriage, dressed in a top hat and the long black frock coat which clergymen wore with their dog collars. 'How young and handsome he looks!' Mother would exclaim. The train arrived in the afternoon and Janet and I would hang around the gate looking down the road for the carriage. When it came in sight we would rush and tell Mother. Then, all armed with flags, we would stand by the door waiting. When the carriage turned into the drive we would break into screams and rush to open the doors. Cosmo, in a top hat and an Eton suit, took it all very grandly. He would kiss us quickly, give Mother a hug and disappear into the house while Radenbury took his school trunk down from the box.

Cosmo's presence changed everything. He was four years older than me and I was his shadow. In term time, at the age of five, I would sleep in an iron cot at the foot of Mother's and Father's bed. It was fun, because Mother had a hip bath in her room and the housemaid used to bring lovely copper cans full of hot water and put them by the side of the bath so that Mother could top it up after she had got in. If I had been good, I was sometimes allowed to pour the last little can round her legs myself. But I was also sometimes frightened because in winter there was a fire in the bedroom and the shadows of the furniture, flickering against the wall, used to make me think the sofas and chairs were lions and tigers. I would stare, petrified. When I could stand it no longer, I would rush out of bed and go screaming along the passage to the nursery.

With Cosmo home I put all such things behind me. I then slept in his room. We were never allowed a fire in our bedroom and the window was always open so that, in winter, it was extremely cold. I would be sent to bed first and would lie awake for Cosmo. We would then talk in whispers until we could keep awake no longer. He taught me to pillow fight. Unfortunately, one night the pillows burst and covered the room with so many feathers that we could not hide them. That sport came to an end. He also taught me how to 'fox': pretend to be asleep when I wasn't. This greatly enlarged the scope of our activities. Mother or Father would look in quietly after dinner to make sure we were asleep and happily go downstairs. Then the night began. When it was warm, Cosmo would climb out of our window and take me up on to the roof. Fortunately it had a parapet and we could roam around quite safely. As far as I can remember, we were never caught. Once, on a very hot night, we shinned down a drainpipe into the back yard and went out into the garden. But climbing back was hard on the feet and we did not do it again.

Cosmo broadened our horizons by day as well as by night. We would follow his bicycle up the village street where he would buy us sweets with the pocket money Father had given him, or take us out to the level crossing to watch the express trains roaring off to London. In summer we would visit farms or go and watch the village play cricket. Father was captain. We used to lie at the bottom of the hedge at the end of the field until he had made ten and then emerge proudly and sit by the scorer. Cosmo sometimes used to put up the tin number plates of the 'tellywag'. Our best bowler was Stanley Johnson, the organist who also sang the tenor solos in church. Sometimes Cosmo would get him to bowl at him on the edge of the field.

Cosmo added a new dimension to my own cricket. In his first year he had played for his school and was already a useful bowler. Because Father had so little spare time, I was the only batsman against whom Cosmo could practise. When I first came in he would bowl gently and show me how to make strokes, but as time went on he would get bored and start his bowling run further and further away until he reached the single stump which marked the full length of the pitch. Then, flattering me by saying that he thought I was now ready to play his ordinary bowling, he would take his full run and hurl the ball down at what seemed to me terrifying speed. I would stand my ground unless the ball came straight for me; then I would try to get out of the way. If it hit me, Cosmo was most solicitous. He would come and dry my tears, tell me I was already a better player than most of the boys he bowled against at school, and end by suggesting that the ball had not hurt as much as I had thought at first. Although I knew that his chief anxiety was to prevent me running into the house and telling Mother or Father that he had been bowling too fast, he invariably succeeded in pacifying me. A mixture of hero worship and vanity kept me at the crease. I relished Cosmo's praise and was prepared to go through a considerable degree of physical and mental torture to win it. And when, in the evening, I heard him tell my father how well I had played, it made it all worthwhile. In retrospect, I believe this trial by ordeal to have been beneficial. Certainly no bowler I subsequently played, however fast, frightened me half as much as Cosmo did when I was five years old.

3

Forebears and Clerics

It was E.F. Benson who wrote somewhere that he came of 'a long line of well-ascertained persons all of them entirely undistinguished'. Much the same might be said of the Crawley family. Cuthbert Headlam, who wrote a memoir of his brother-in-law, my Uncle George, described them as 'unostentatious gentlefolks who lived worthily – did faithful and useful service in whatever profession or calling they happened to be engaged'. However, the Crawleys developed certain proclivities. They were strong churchmen, they married members of the Gibbs family every three or four generations, they went to Harrow School, and over the last hundred and fifty years have been good games players.

My grandfather, George Baden Crawley, began a family tradition by playing cricket for Harrow in 1850 and 1851, followed by his brother Francis in 1853 and 1854. Rather curiously, while still at Harrow, George was asked to play for the Gentlemen of England, the highest cricketing honour available at the time, but the headmaster, Dr Warre, refused to allow it. Francis went into the church.

My grandfather was an enterprising man. It was the high noon of Victorian expansion and he became a contractor, specializing in the building of railways. There is a story that, when building a viaduct in Mexico, he and his party were attacked by bandits. The only means of escape lay in crossing the half-finished viaduct and so, driving his workmen and his wife before him and making them jump from sleeper to sleeper with a drop of several hundred feet below, they got away. My grandfather had made a large fortune by the time he was forty and was going from strength to strength. But his energy and curiosity were his undoing. While watching some railway lines being loaded into a ship he had chartered, he was struck by a crane and knocked on to the iron lines in the hold below. He was killed instantly. He was then forty-five years old; his wife had already borne him ten children, six sons and four daughters, two of whom died young. The extent of his fortune can be judged by the fact that he not only left his widow a rich woman but left each of his children, the youngest of whom was my father, a considerable sum. My father then succumbed to the family tradition. He played cricket for Harrow, went into the church and married a Gibbs.

The Gibbs family had fared better than the Crawleys. They too had a long history, coming from yeoman farmer stock round Exeter. But in the early 1800s one Antony Gibbs founded what is now known as a merchant bank. If not the first, it is certainly one of the three oldest such banks in England. Banking may not have been as exciting as contracting, but in the end it proved more lucrative. The Gibbs family flourished and, in the twentieth century, reaped their harvest by achieving three separate peerages for different types of public service.

The ecclesiastical tradition within the Gibbs family was every bit as strong as among the Crawleys. My great-grandfather, William Gibbs, not only restored many churches and endowed others, but was one of the founders of Lancing College, whose students were originally taken from clerical families, and of Keble College, Oxford, which had a similar tradition. By a curious chance, the scholarship examination which I took at Oxford in 1926 was held at Keble. When I sat down in Hall for my first paper I found myself looking at a portrait of my great-grandfather on the wall opposite. I did not go to Keble, but the omen proved favourable.

That a country parson and his wife could live on the scale my parents did was not unusual. As the Bishop of Lichfield wrote in a survey of the clerical income of his diocese before the First World War: 'The property of the Church is still being maintained by the private means of the clergy.' He noted that in many of his archdeaconries the private income of the clergy exceeded their public income. The tradition in many well-to-do families that the eldest sons went into the army or navy and the younger into the church still held in many parts of the country and, of course, money then went a long way.

I remember asking my mother, years later, how much she had paid the servants at Bishopthorpe. Her reply was that it was not really the pay that mattered. All the servants lived in the house. The young ones shared bedrooms, the elder had rooms to themselves. They ate much the same as we did. Their uniforms and a 'walking out' suit or dress were bought for them. They also had first choice of any clothes the family discarded. They had one afternoon off a week and their railway fare to their homes was paid when they went on holiday, which they did once a year for a week. Actual pay was very small. An under-housemaid, kitchen maid, scullery maid or nursery maid got five shillings a week pocket money to start with, doubled if she stayed a year. I do not believe that either the butler or the groom earned more than two pounds a week and the others got correspondingly less. If either butler or groom was married, he had a free cottage. At that time a good ready-made suit cost only thirty shillings, ready-made shoes from five to ten shillings.

When all living expenses were paid for, as they were if you were in domestic service, a man or woman with two pounds a week to spend may well have been better off than their counterparts today with a hundred pounds. Travel played only a small part in most people's lives. The gentry went long distances to visit each other but might then spend several weeks free of charge as guests. Ordinary folk lived in their towns and villages and went 'abroad', if at all, once a year. In 1931, with my brother-in-law, Edward Woodall, I rode on horseback from Oxford to Exeter, travelling mainly along the downs and staying wherever we happened to find ourselves around seven o'clock in the evening. Not only did every inn at which we spent the night still have stables and fodder for a horse but, more astonishing to us, most of our hosts had never been more than twenty miles from their homes.

Higher up the income scale, the prices people like my father and mother paid for the things they wanted seem ridiculously low today. Hunting boots could be specially made for less than ten pounds, for which sum you could also buy a pony. If, like my father, you had friends among those who kept hounds, you could often buy horses from the hunt stable which had broken down in some way, for twenty or thirty pounds. After a year out to grass they would often recover completely so that in the end you had a perfectly schooled hunter for a quarter of its market price.

Nevertheless, although Father and Mother managed to do most of the things they wanted to do, they never thought of themselves as rich. The family observed that convenient Victorian taboo which decreed that it was vulgar to talk about money (convenient because it only applied to those who had plenty) yet we were aware that there were many things 'we' could not afford. Certain things, like Tiptree's jam and real cream, were 'too expensive' for the nursery. Their absence never bothered us; except when we went out to tea and ate them in other people's houses, we never thought about them. Yet, no doubt because of some Freudian reflex, Tiptree's Little Scarlet Strawberry Jam has always been one of the luxuries of my adult life.

It also seemed perfectly natural that I should wear nothing but my elder brother's clothes. All Cosmo's clothes were carefully put away when he grew out of them, to be given to me as soon as I was the right size. They looked new to me and I was just as excited putting them on for the first time as if they had come from a shop. When I grew out of them they were put away again for my younger brother, Kenneth. I did not actually wear a new suit until I was seventeen. I had just been given an 'allowance' which also meant having my first cheque book, and I ordered the suit from the Harrow tailor. The colour was a rather violent steel blue with a faint pale pink stripe running through it. I wore it first at Winchester, where I had gone to watch the Eton v. Winchester cricket match, and felt rather proud when I noticed, as I walked round the ground, that my appearance attracted attention. That some mothers and daughters giggled as I went by I put down to feminine stupidity. It was not until my own mother and sisters told me what they thought of the suit that it occurred to me there might have been another reason.

Of course, Father and Mother knew that they were better off then most other parsons. Father often used to go to other parishes to preach on Sundays and would afterwards stay to lunch or supper with the vicar. I used to hear him describe to Mother how cold and bare their houses were and how he wished they had not made such an effort to entertain him when he knew they only ate meat once a week. Hundreds of 'livings' were worth less than two hundred pounds a year; a few less than one hundred. Vicarages with twenty or more rooms, large gardens and out-buildings might cost a thousand pounds a year to maintain. Parsons often clung to their freeholds when they were too old to carry out their duties because otherwise they had nothing. My parents were lucky in having money of their own but, even so, it was something of a struggle to keep up with the Joneses.

Horses were a case in point. I could tell that Mother often envied the horses of some of our neighbours. They were not only beautifully turned out but were faster than hers. Father, on the other hand, used to take pride in the fact that, when it came to a hunt, his 'old crocks' often did as well, if not better than others. He was an accomplished horseman, light enough to ride even a pony, and there were few horses that would not go well for him. He also had an unerring eye for the sort of horse he wanted and was constantly surprising us by returning from some ecclesiastical function riding a new animal which he had 'managed to pick up'. His purchases became a recurring source of adventure for the entire family.

Once, when he was looking for a hunter for Janet, he noticed that the mare pulling the Archbishop's mowing machine had certain good points which its unkempt appearance could not conceal. The mare was obviously getting on in years and had a hollow back; but she also had an intelligent head and strong quarters. One summer evening, after the mowing was finished, Father went quietly round to her stall with a saddle and bridle, took her out into the fields and 'popped her over' one or two fences. He found that she jumped perfectly. A week or two later I overheard the following conversation:

Father: 'By the way, Archbishop, I have taken the pony which pulls your mowing machine.'

Archbishop: 'Have you indeed. And may I enquire why?'

Father: 'I thought it looked rather too good for the job, so I tried it out. It will do perfectly as a hunter for Janet.'

Archbishop: 'I would not dream of depriving Janet of her hunter. But what is to happen to my lawns?'

Father: 'Oh, I'll find another pony. I'll give you a tenner for this one. That ought to cover it.'

Archbishop: 'Stafford, you are incorrigible. You ought to have been a horse coper, not my chaplain.'

When Janet rode the mare to hounds for the first time – now a very smart-looking chestnut – the Master came up to her and said, 'Where on earth did you find that mare? She used to be the favourite of our hunt stable, but she broke down. I thought she had gone to the knacker.' Janet told him, and the story spread. Mowing the archi-episcopal lawns had given the mare just the rest she needed. She would jump anything and never turned her head. Janet hunted her for four seasons.

Not all Father's purchases were quite so successful. When I was ten or eleven years old and we were living at Tewkesbury, his eye was caught by the butcher's pony which used to deliver meat all over the town. It was a very strong-looking bay, about fourteen hands (much larger than anything I had ridden) and trotted fast and tirelessly throughout the day.

'That pony might just do for you, Aidan,' he said one day as the butcher's cart rattled past our gate. I looked at it dubiously.

Within forty-eight hours he had tried the pony out and bought it for something under twenty pounds. To make sure it would be all right for me, he took it out hunting the next day with the Ledbury, the local pack of hounds. He came back delighted.

'It is as good a hunter as I have ridden for years,' he said. 'Very strong and plenty of courage. Take it out into the fields tomorrow and see how you get on.'

If Father had a fault it was that he was apt to assume that anything he could do, others could do as well or better. That a son of his should not be able to manage a pony which he had pronounced suitable was unthinkable. I took the pony out next morning, walking it up Tew-kesbury High Street and out to the water meadows beyond. The meadows were usually flooded in winter, but that happened to be a dry year. They stretched for about a mile and a half on one side of the road, quite flat and covered in short cropped grass. Without being actually frightened, there was something about that pony that made me uneasy. Its neck muscles felt like iron and it had danced sideways the whole way up Tewkesbury High Street. When we got to the meadows I kept it at a slow trot until we reached the far end. Then I turned.

As soon as it faced home, the pony set off. Within fifty yards it had detected my inadequacy as a rider and had settled into a steady gallop. My efforts to slow it down were ineffective. As we neared the town the pony saw the meadow narrowing; the river on our right turned in towards the road to pass under a bridge before the houses began. Of its own accord the pony went up the bank on our left, on to the road. The feel of firm tarmac under its hooves gave it a new lease of life. This was what it was used to. We entered the High Street, which the pony knew so well, at full gallop. The butcher's shop was on our right and as we passed it, the butcher came to the door and waved at us delightedly. He had misunderstood the situation. I was rigid with fear and fatigue but, pull how I might, I made not the slightest impression. The pony had a mouth of iron. We missed a bus by inches and nearly collided with a pram, but on we went. At last we came to the leftward bend off which led the entrance to the Abbey House where we lived. I had assumed that the pony would make for home, but I had forgotten how recently he had changed owners; home for him was anywhere within the butcher's round and he was plainly enjoying making that round without tiresome halts or a cart to slow him down. With sparks flying and the pony's hooves slipping sideways under him, we swept round the bend just as my father came through the gate on to the road. He stopped dead, while we went on. It was not for another mile, when we were well out into open country, that the pony began to tire and eventually came to a stop. By then I was in tears. Father on a bicycle met me walking back down the road.

'What happened?' he asked kindly, falling in by the pony's head.

I told him.

'You should not pull at him so,' he said when I had finished. 'The more you pull at a horse the more he pulls at you.'

'Yes,' I replied miserably. 'But then how do you ever stop him?'

'You must never let him get out of control. You coax him, pull a little, give a little. You must humour him.'

I was silent because what he said made no sense. I might just as well have tried to humour a rhinoceros. The pony was far too strong for me. Father continued to hunt him in the hope that I might 'grow into him' in a couple of years. But by then we had moved to a new parish.

*

I have jumped ahead. On April 10th 1914, still at Bishopthorpe, I was six years old and was given a new cricket bat. It seemed to me to provide the acme of bliss. Events might be casting shadows before them, but no one in our world seemed to bother. It must have been in April or May of that year that Uncle Ernest, a brother ten years older than my father, came to stay, travelling from London – not by train, but in a new

Sunbeam motor car. Amazingly he arrived without a breakdown. We were all thrilled.

It was the first car I had seen at close quarters. It had a shiny brass bonnet, huge brass headlamps and brass handles to the doors. The hood was of canvas, only to be put up when it rained. Two long straps ran from the front of the hood down to the mudguards to hold it down. In rain the driver had to open the top half of the windscreen so as to be able to see ahead and to wear goggles to keep rain out of his eyes. The car went faster than Teeny could gallop.

Very soon afterwards the Archbishop got a car as well, a Wolseley. Its body was oblong and tall with large glass windows running along each side like a hearse. It was painted black and the headlamps were not of brass but silver coloured, probably of steel. Fortunately, as we drove out in the Sunbeam or the Wolseley, no one had the slightest inkling of what was to come. By the time Father had a car himself we had lived through a holocaust and the Western world had been transformed, not only by a terrible war, but by the Russian revolution.

4

World War I

I remember clearly the day war was declared. Cosmo and I had been playing cricket on the lawn and had just come into the house. I was putting my new bat away at the back of the hall. Mother was talking to Father, whose study door led out of the hall to the right of the grandfather clock; Cosmo was walking upstairs. Suddenly a friend of Father's called Colonel English came through the open front door and said without any greeting, 'We have declared war on the Germans.'

There was a moment's silence, then Father said, 'Thank God! We should never have been able to hold up our heads again if we hadn't.' He meant, of course, that having guaranteed Belgium's neutrality we were in honour bound to go to her assistance when the Germans crossed her frontiers.

Cosmo, who was halfway up the stairs, came running down again saying excitedly, 'Shall we win?' No one answered, so when he reached his mother's side, he asked again, 'Shall we win, Mummy?'

'Of course, darling. But don't ask any more questions now.' The grown-ups went into the drawing room and Cosmo and I went upstairs.

Nothing changed immediately. Some time before, Father had agreed to act as 'stand-in' while a Scottish minister went on holiday, so we all went to live in his manse for the rest of August. It was my first visit to Scotland and on subsequent visits I have experienced the same thrill as I felt as a child at waking up in the morning and seeing the heather and the moors. We happily dammed burns to make paddling pools and I received my first lesson in fishing from a neighbouring pastor.

It was only after we returned to Bishopthorpe that we noticed the differences the war had made. There was no butler and no Radenbury and in the stables only Teeny, the cob and one carriage horse. Radenbury had gone to join the Yorkshire Hussars and was soon on his way to France. He had been a silent, kindly man, but he did not like children hanging about the stables. I never saw him again. The ponies were turned out into a field and Mother taught us how to catch them with a halter and a bowl of oats, and then how to groom and saddle them.

One day Mother appeared in a nurse's uniform, grey with pink piping. There was a sort of sham cloak over her shoulders and she wore a starched white collar and belt and a white scarf over her head tied behind her neck. A badge bearing the letters VAD was on the front. I remember thinking how small her waist was. She used to go to training classes in the village hall and later worked in a hospital in York, but her nursing can only have been part-time as she was never away from home for long. Her main war work was looking after her five children.

No doubt khaki uniforms did appear in the village, but I do not remember seeing any. I do remember Mother pointing out to me a rather pale, weedy young man, a farmer's son, who was riding a horse down the village street, and saying in a low voice that he had received several 'white feathers' because he had refused to join up. Until conscription was introduced in March 1916, there was quite an epidemic of white feathers, usually sent by people who knew nothing of the victim's personal circumstances. In the end the young man pointed out by my mother left the village.

Whether it was during that first winter that we began to eat maize cakes and potato scones I'm not sure. Neither were very good, but at least they did not make me sick like vermicelli. However, food had suddenly become serious. Janet and I began to knit great thick scarves on wooden frames which the government provided; we knew the scarves went to the men in the trenches and rather enjoyed it.

Then one night – it must have been during the winter because it was cold – Mother woke me up and said there was a Zeppelin and I must come and look. She wrapped me in an eiderdown and we all went to Cosmo's empty bedroom where the window looked out northwards towards the Palace. There, not very high in the sky and looking bright silver in the searchlight, was the Zeppelin moving very slowly away from us, just the other side of the river. Suddenly there was a thud and the windows shook.

'It must be following the river,' said Father. 'It's probably the only thing they can see.'

I noticed all the lights were out, even the street light outside the gate. Then came another thud.

'It's dropping its bombs the other side of the river, in the open fields. York must be in darkness.' It was Father speaking again.

I asked what a bomb did.

'It explodes and kills people,' Mother replied.

'But there aren't any people in the fields.' No one replied. I tried another tack. 'Could it come through a roof?'

'It could, but it won't come back here tonight. Let's hope it doesn't hit any roofs in York.' We watched silently as the Zeppelin moved away, past the trees by the Palace and then gradually out of sight. There had been several more thuds but they had got further and further away. Then Father picked me up and carried me back to bed.

Not long after the Zeppelin had passed out of sight it was hit by a shell and caught fire. Half Yorkshire must have watched it burning as it slowly descended on to Skipton Common. Everyone in it was burned alive. I remember trying to imagine what the pain would be like and wondering what one would do as the flames surrounded one. But no one was sorry for the crew because they had been bombing 'helpless' civilians and that was horrible and unfair. In fact none of the bombs had done any real damage; four had fallen in the fields just across the river, the nearest about a half-mile away. The Zeppelin was my only sight of the enemy.

*

In the spring of 1915 things really began to happen. Unknown even to Mother, Father had been badgering the Archbishop to let him go to France as a chaplain to the forces. In April or May, it must have been, the Arch consented. No doubt we were told, but it was not until Father suddenly appeared in a khaki uniform, still in a dog collar but with three black stars on his shoulder straps (chaplains were given the rank of captain), that we realized he was going away. He left next day. Mother was wonderfully controlled and sent Janet and me on our bicycles down to the level crossing to wave to him as his train went by. The line runs straight from York to Selby and we could see the train coming a long way off. Then we saw Father's head out of the window and we waved and shouted. He waved back until he was out of sight. The train was going very fast. Mother so seldom cried that it never even occurred to us to wonder whether she had broken down in our absence.

We knew we might not see Father again, but Mother said it was worse for other people. I asked what chaplains did in the war and whether Father would shoot any Germans. She said he would not carry a gun, which she thought was safer. If any Germans got close to him and saw he was a parson, they might not shoot him. Chaplains, she said, held services before battles and looked after the wounded. She thought Father stood a better chance of survival than an ordinary infantry officer. He had not told her much, probably because he did not know much himself.

In the summer came the news that Mother's brother Eustace, whom we had never seen, had been killed in one of the many battles of Loos. She went down to her old home at Tyntesfield near Bristol for the memorial service. A few weeks later she was in London again. One of Father's brothers, also called Eustace, a great athlete and Gentleman Rider, had had his head blown off by a shell when far behind the front line. Years later I met the man who had been with him at the time. 'It was a lovely summer day and we were sitting on a wall together watching the larks rising into the sky. There was a whining noise and suddenly Eustace was not there. I found his headless body in the field behind me. The shell had never exploded and buried itself in the ground,' he told me. He added that had they known more about shell fire they would have thrown themselves on the ground as soon as they heard the whine. Mother went to London to be with Aunt Vitie, Eustace's widow. I had a black arm band on the sleeve of my coat, which I thought rather grand. In church I noticed a lot of the older men were wearing similar arm bands. Mother said they had all lost some member of their family. She would talk to many of them, but I doubt if she ever discussed the war. It was a subject to be avoided.

Then we left the vicarage. The Archbishop had said that although it did not matter much whether he had any chaplains, it did matter that Bishopthorpe should have a vicar. He had appointed a man to take Father's place and had offered Mother a home in the Elizabethan wing of the Palace while Father was away. Mother was greatly relieved and we moved over during the summer. The wrench of leaving home was lessened by the fact that the Palace was so close and also because we had always used the garden there as if it had been our own. Curiously enough, although the vicarage was only a few hundred yards away and I am sure we should have been made welcome, I never remember going inside its gates again. The house was no longer ours and we did not want to see it.

The Elizabethan wing was the prettiest part of the Palace. It was built of red brick and shaped like an 'E' without the centre. One side looked out on the garden and the other on the broad drive. The rooms were larger than in the vicarage. Father, when he was home, had a lovely panelled study and Mother her own boudoir which was all windows and faced south. They also had what seemed to us an enormous bedroom which had once been slept in either by Queen Victoria or Queen Elizabeth, or perhaps by both. We children inhabited the Common Room, so-called because during the Bishops' Conferences or Ordinations it was used by all the visiting clergy. It was a large room with a door into the garden. On the whole Janet and I approved of the change. Nanny was still there and also Gertie, round-faced and pink-cheeked, the one nursery maid we loved who stayed for many years. Teeny must have gone, but the cob came over to the Archbishop's stables with the pony trap. This and bicycles became our only means of transport. Mother drove us regularly into York for dancing classes, shopping, the dentist and occasionally for a pantomime. We also saw our first play: Fred and Ellen Terry in *The Scarlet Pimpernel*. I can still see the French inn-keeper wiping the dirty plates on the seat of his trousers and putting them back on the table.

Mother used to read us parts of Father's letters. I remember thinking how dull they were. Mother kept them all and, reading through them again today, I think I was partly right. As a whole, the letters do convey a feeling of the war, the discomfort, dirt, endless funerals in the open. And I see now that the dullness was deliberate. Being a highly sensitive man, Father felt the horror and waste of war so intensely that he was determined to convey as little as possible to my mother. Indeed, whenever he mentioned he had been under shellfire we could tell that it made her nervous. When he came home on leave he never talked about the war and it was only when his hair began to fall out and he was sent home on sick leave that we realized the strain he was under. But Mother always told us not to ask him about it.

Officially Father was a chaplain in the Guards Division. But although he was assigned to a company and reported regularly to his company commander, as a chaplain he really had to make his own life. Apart from holding services on Sundays, wherever and whenever he could, and officiating all too frequently at burials, his real job was to get to know the men and officers and help them in every possible way. Because he was a parson (called 'padre' in the army for some reason) they would often talk to him in ways they would not dream of talking to each other. Young officers who lacked the confidence to lead, officers and men who were scared stiff and nearing breakdown, men who hated each other, men who simply wanted to get out of it all and go home, would pour out their feelings to him, knowing that not a word would ever be repeated. Sometimes his Company Commander or even the Colonel would ask him to have a chat with some man about whom they were worried; in those cases Father had to use his discretion as to what he should repeat and what not. In many ways it was like ministering to a parish, but a parish so closely knit that everyone knew everyone else's business. It was rewarding because, at some time or other, almost every man wanted to see and talk to him.

He told me one harrowing story. It was, I think, on the Somme, sometime in 1916. The weather was appalling, wet and often foggy, and the war was at its worst. Men were spending far too long in the front line, casualties were persistent and desertions becoming so frequent that Commanding Officers had been ordered to make an example of anyone straying from his unit. One day Father was sent for to see a young man who had been condemned to be shot. He found a nice-looking boy of eighteen who had only just come out from home. It was his first action and, after he had gone over the top with his platoon, the mist came down and he got lost. Eventually he found his way back to our lines, but to the wrong unit about half a mile away from his own.

Father cross-examined him, then checked his story with other members of his platoon. They all agreed that the same might easily have happened to them. It was only through experience that they had managed to keep together. No one had really known where they were. The more Father talked to the boy the more convinced he became that he was telling the truth. He was composed and, although he hated the thought of dying in that way, he understood the position. To Father he seemed unusually brave. Father went to the Commanding Officer and put the boy's case as strongly as he could. The Colonel was sympathetic and agreed to do his utmost. He went personally to urge a reprieve at Brigade Headquarters. The matter was taken to Division. The answer came back that if this boy were let off, it might lead to a rash of similar cases. Father had to return and tell the boy he could do no more. When it came to writing to the boy's parents, Father simply lied, saying that their son had been killed in action. It was, he said, his worst experience in the whole war, and it haunted him for the rest of his life.

The war began to tell on Father. Once or twice he got home leave and spent a week with Mother in London. But she told me that he never really enjoyed himself; he could not shake off the thought of what he was going back to and of the men he had left behind. Then his hair began to fall out. He had caught alopecia, a disease which is partly nervous, and he was sent home. In the end he went quite bald and then his hair began to grow again – white at first and then its original dark colour. Mother had taken a house for the summer on the edge of Lord Lansdowne's estate at Bowood, between Calne and Chippenham, so as to be nearer some of her own relations. It was a nice house with two tennis courts and several clumps of pampas grass in which bees and hornets had their swarms. Cosmo had been given an air gun and when he came home for the holidays he started shooting into the hornets' nests. The result justified the old adage about letting sleeping dogs lie for we virtually had to stay in a locked house until someone came to gas them. Father came there and rested. When his hair had grown again he went back to France.

In the winter we were again at Bishopthorpe, skating for weeks on end. It was the following year, 1917, that the Yorkshire Ouse froze solid. The river was deep and dangerous, but several people ran across it. Londoners roasted an ox in the middle of the Thames. But by then our lives had changed again. So as to be ready for Father's leaves, which came unannounced, Mother took a house in London for the summer. I do not remember where it was, but I do remember going to school at Miss Ironside's, 2 Elvaston Place.[1]

Soon Mother was to get a pleasant surprise. After their defeat at Caporetto, the Italians asked for help. General the Earl of Cavan was sent out with two divisions to reconstitute their line. Cavan, or 'K' as everyone called him, had married Father's eldest sister, Inez. I can just remember her, short, rather fat, but tremendously energetic. She was always asking us what we wanted and seeing that we got it. She died in 1920. Uncle Cavan asked Father to go with him as his headquarters' chaplain; by leave of the Guards Division, he went, sometime in the summer of 1918.

It may be my imagination, but I seem to remember Mother becoming altogether different, as if some terrible headache had suddenly cleared. She laughed and played with us as she had done before the war. Of course there was fighting in Italy, but Father was only occasionally sent up to the front line and even then only on some errand for 'K'. And the front line itself was along the crest of a glorious mountain and not in Flanders mud. His letters were suddenly real and interesting, for he had nothing to hide. By then, however, my life had changed yet again, although this time it had nothing to do with Father. I was sent to join Cosmo at school in Farnborough. I was nine and a half years old.

5

Farnborough School

The story of Farnborough School could have been the plot for a Somerset Maugham novel. The headmasters, Edward North and Robert Ingram, had been friends at Oxford and had gone into partnership when they went down. They bought Farnborough School, a neo-Georgian house built in stucco and grey brick in the reign of Queen Victoria, and settled down to what both believed would be a useful and agreeable life.

They were a well-matched pair. North was a scholar and although the well-known classical textbooks by North and Hilliard were mainly written by his brother, he himself had produced some which he continued to revise. His room at Farnborough was often full of galley proofs. North was a fine-looking man, tall and dark and of a build which had made him a useful forward in his college rugger team. Ingram was the exact opposite: fair, of medium build, with slightly curly brown hair, a small mouth and very small neat feet. He had been a soccer blue and later had played for the Corinthians, the amateur team which for many years took part in the FA Cup. He was also musical, with a pleasant tenor voice.

All went well to begin with and the school began to attract quite a distinguished clientele. Then North married. From that moment things began to go wrong. Even as a small boy I wondered what he had seen in her; perhaps she had once had sex appeal. She was dark, with rather fine eyes, but by the time I saw her she was getting plump, so that she bulged in all the wrong places. She had thick lips, the upper one garnished not only with a moustache but with a large black wart which was riveting. She spoke with a faintly disguised Cockney accent. Ingram had thought that his friend had married beneath him and disliked Mrs North from the beginning. The two friends began to drift apart.

45

Decades of the air display have made Farnborough famous. Few of today's spectators gazing up into the sky know that the grass on which they are standing used to be the playing fields of a school. They covered some twenty acres, and were reached by going through a tunnel under the road. During the First World War, the Royal Flying Corps established a test centre on Farnborough Heath and the War Ministry requisitioned the Farnborough School playing fields to incorporate them into the airfield. North and Ingram were still complaining about the pitiful compensation they had received when I arrived. We used to be taken to see the entrance to the tunnel, now blocked up.

I never liked any school. I remember the first day I arrived at Farnborough thinking how bleak and ugly everything was. The passages had stone floors, whitewash was peeling off the walls; chairs, desks and tables were hard and hideous. In the part of the house inhabited by the boys there was not a picture or a bowl of flowers. The dormitories looked like hospital wards. When I was invited or summoned into the private part of the house, the immediate impression was of re-entering civilized life. After being dismissed I used to linger in the hall for the pleasure of walking on a carpet and looking at the grandfather clock.

My school was in the middle of Farnborough, yet it was not until years later, when I took my family to an air display, that I ever really saw the town. And by then the school had disappeared. Almost the only time we were allowed through the gates was in the bus which took us to play matches against other schools. Occasionally, 'Ingie', as we called him, used to take my cousin Charles and me out in his car, but he was always in such a hurry to reach the Hertford Bridge Flats that we rushed straight through the town. The Flats are crossed by a long, straight stretch of road with only one bend in it. Ingie had an Austin 20 of which he was immensely proud. Once on the Flats he would put his foot down and then, urging the car on by moving backwards and forwards in his seat, breathing heavily all the time, he would see how fast he could make it go. If we had reached fifty by the bend, then we knew there was a chance of the needle just touching sixty miles an hour. Charles and I used to enter the spirit of his race, telling him exactly what the needle read while he kept his eyes on the road.

The other master we revered was Mr Cumberbatch, the 'Mr Chips' of our school. He had been headmaster before North and Ingram and still lived in a house in the grounds. He was an old man and not always well, but when he felt up to it he would come in on a Sunday evening, gather the Upper School in the library, turn out the lights and tell us a ghost story that lasted at least half an hour. No doubt the stories came from various anthologies, but he never had a note and his soft, slightly husky voice, getting softer and more tense as he neared the climax, held us spellbound. I do not believe any boy voluntarily missed one of his evenings and it became a regular punishment to be forbidden to attend.

The other memory which has survived is of the chapel services. I had a good treble voice and in my third and fourth years used to sing the solos. Whether the masters were picked for their voices as well as their academic qualifications I do not know, but all except Mr North, who listened in disdainful silence, could sing a part. As a choir, therefore, we had quite a large repertoire, regularly singing services by Stainer and Purcell, anthems and oratorios by Handel. Since a boy's voice is like a bird's and emerges without training, it was all sheer pleasure.

It must have been after he had come back from the war that Father once took me to sing in York Minster. The organist, who was also choir master, was a friend of his. He made me sing Mendelssohn's 'Hear My Prayer' and 'Oh, For the Wings Of a Dove'. There was no one about except for a few tourists, and I stood in the choir stalls and sang my heart out. I remember listening to the sound of my voice echoing up through that vast tower and wishing I could sing there regularly.

My first year at Farnborough was dominated by the war. I had a daily copy of *The Times* and in the morning break would study the little map of the Western Front which was always placed in the centre of the main report of the fighting. The wavy front lines would vary from week to week, a bulge appearing or disappearing as we or the Germans made a minor advance. In the spring of 1918, the German bulge became larger and larger. I plied everyone with questions but a sense of doom seemed to pervade the school. Ever since I could remember, or so it seemed, those lines had been there, roughly in the same place. Now we were being pushed back to the sea. No doubt I had read about the American entry into the war and I must have followed the great counter-attacks of the Allies in August of that year; but as we were then on holiday in Scotland, these events obviously had not made the same impression. When I returned to school in September I resumed my daily study of the maps. Until then, the idea that the war might come to an end had never occurred to me.

One morning in November during break we were all summoned into the dining hall to find that not only North and Ingram but Mrs North and the entire staff were there, a sure sign of some momentous event. Mr North read out the communiqué announcing the Armistice. He stressed that it was only an Armistice and that we must not take it for granted that the war was over. Nevertheless, we were all given Union Jacks to wave and were taken out on to the playing fields where we were paraded in forms, and then marched round and round the ground singing 'Land of Hope and Glory', 'Tipperary', 'Pack Up Your Troubles in Your Old Kit Bag', and 'There's a Silver Lining'. This went on until lunch time. A half-holiday was announced for the afternoon. It took a little time to realize that an underlying dread, which had permeated most of one's life, had vanished, and that, unbelievably, we had won.

6

Cricket and Country Houses

It is clear from my father's letters to my mother that he wanted to stay on with the army after the war. He had loved the camaraderie of the front, and found it inspiring to be holding services attended by a thousand men, a hundred or more of whom would take communion. But few of my mother's letters to him have survived. He stayed on in Italy until the summer of 1919, and when he returned home accepted an offer, no doubt on the Archbishop's recommendation, to become secretary of the Diocesan Association, an administrative job which would be a change from parish work and release him from the duties of being a chaplain. This change meant living at Tewkesbury in Gloucestershire and at the end of that year we went to the Abbey House, next door to the great Norman Abbey.

The house was reached through the old Abbey gateway; one end of it had been part of the Abbey buildings. A windowless passage, which was said to be haunted by some of the three hundred soldiers who had been killed in the battle of 1471 which raged round and within the Abbey itself, led to a side door in the west end of the nave. It was dimly lit, and whenever Janet or I used it to come home from a church service, we would run through it at full speed. A beautiful cedar tree stood in the middle of the lawn.

For us children, Tewkesbury was an interlude in my father's ecclesiastical pilgrimage, because he did not have to preach sermons every Sunday. He had never evolved a method which made them less of a chore and his whole spirit lifted when the effort no longer had to be made. But the Diocesan Association never caught on and after two years he returned to a parish, this time at East Meon in Hampshire. It was a lovely parish, including several miles of downland which allowed him to do a lot of his visiting on horseback. If we were not at school, he would usually take Janet and me with him and while he went into a

49

farmhouse or cottage or walked round the hamlet, we would be left to hold the horses – a simple enough task until they started stamping their feet or raising their heads with impatience. Father never knew how glad we were to see him when his visit was over and we could gallop once more across the downs.

It was at East Meon that I began to play village cricket. Our blacksmith, who bore the inspiring name of Hobbs, was a fast bowler in the best village tradition. Of massive girth and shoulder, he took only five or six paces to the wicket and hurled the ball down to an immaculate length. What happened when it hit the ground was not really his affair. The wicket was 'natural', which meant it received a good mowing the day before a match and a few minutes' treatment with a limestone roller just before the game began. It received a generous amount of fertilizer from the cows which continued to graze the field while the game was in progress. Long grass grew on both sides of the pitch within ten yards of the stumps. Father captained the village team and so long as he got 10 or 15 runs and Hobbs was available to bowl, the result was usually in our favour.

The occasion I particularly remember was a game in which Father had collected his own side to play against the village. His team included several Crawleys and a friend or two from Harrow and Oxford. As usual, Father opened the batting and he was nearing 20 when a well pitched up ball from Hobbs rose steeply and broke his nose. It poured with blood and Father was unable to continue. While Mother kept winding blocks of ice in cloths and putting them either side of his face, he sat in a chair by the pavilion gate and gave us advice as we went out to bat. When my turn came I remember murmuring something about feeling nervous, to which he replied, 'Don't be silly. The ball doesn't come nearly as fast as you expect. Just watch it and hit it.' I believe I got into double figures, mainly by singles, but I made one unorthodox stroke. Hobbs had hurled one just outside the off-stump. I did not move my feet but executed a scythe-like motion towards the ball which hit the back of the bat, cleared the slips and landed on a cow. It then disappeared. Four or five fielders went to look for it and it was finally found trodden into the ground beneath a thick tuft of grass. Meanwhile we had made 4. When I returned to the crease, the wicket-keeper said to me, 'I wish I could learn to do that shot. I never know how to play them when they pitch close to me.'

*

The pleasures of village cricket, which is the game's foundation, are exceptional. It is the act of a community. Seventy years ago (and I expect it is much the same today) the pavilion locker in a country village contained an assortment of stumps, bats, pads and sometimes one or more pairs of boots. The pads did not necessarily match and some of the bats were the colour of mahogany, seasoned heavily with linseed oil, on which no ball made any dent however hard it was hit. Batsmen seldom wore batting gloves; helmets and even 'boxes' were unheard of. The umpire was either the next man in to bat or a former player who liked to keep in touch with the game. Nobody expected complete impartiality but decisions which were too blatantly one-sided invited retaliation. When the game was finished everyone flocked to the pub and lived it over again.

One of the villages in which I frequently played was Charlton in Oxfordshire, where the first Lord Birkenhead lived. His son and I were together at Oxford. The ground must once have been a gravel pit because the outfield was full of lumps and hollows in which a fieldsman almost disappeared. One year, playing against the village, I was hit on the head by a ball which rose from a good length and was knocked out. The bowler was sixteen-year-old Chris Loggins, the son of a farmer who lived less than a mile away and whom I knew well. His father gave him a dressing-down while I was lying on the ground. I met Chris again in 1985 when he was playing in the annual Charlton tennis tournament. He remembered the incident well and told me that it was in 1964. 'My father was quite angry and told me to pitch the ball up,' he said. 'But it *was* well pitched up; the trouble was the pitch. We had had a hot, dry summer . . .' I agreed with him. Then, as if to prove his innocence, he added, '. . . and you got up and went on batting.'

In an evening match for Charlton against a neighbouring village – Somerton, I think – we found when we arrived a well-shod Clydesdale pulling the lightest of stone rollers up and down the pitch, leaving huge hoof-marks which no roller could obliterate. We batted second and it was nearly nine before our last man came in; we still had a few runs to make. Someone asked the umpire if he thought there was enough light; a pale moon had risen behind the bowler's end. He looked round, saw

it and said, 'Aye, t'moon's up, ye can play all night.' I am pleased to say
we won.

Club cricket has a shorter history.[1] Lords and Commons Cricket,
which has never been a club although it boasts a tie, was founded in
1845, the same year as another famous peripatetic team, I Zingari
(Wanderers). The players are drawn from either House of Parliament,
near relations of Members, officials of the Palace of Westminster and
police whose duty it is to guard both Members and the Palace.

In the years immediately after the Second World War, Lords
Ebbisham and Hawke, both very slow right-arm bowlers, were still
playing, the former always putting at least five men on the boundary,
hoping against hope that one would hold a catch. Lords Home and
Nugent occasionally turned out and others, many of whom have held
office, such as Tom King, Lord Orr-Ewing, Patrick Gordon-Walker,
Gwylm Lloyd George, Jim Prior, Cranley Onslow, Henry Usborne and
James Johnson, all made runs, bowled or kept wicket. Neville Ford,
whose first wife was Member for County Down, played well into his
seventies and with Nick Scott was one of our most consistent bats.
Walter Bromley Davenport and Patrick Wolrige-Gordon were slow
left-arm bowlers. Charlie Mott-Radclyffe, the Member for Eton and
Slough, was for many years Captain. Denis Howell, once Minister for
Sport, was always prepared to umpire and we took it in turns to score.
Dr John Rae, the headmaster of Westminster for many years, discovered that before the First World War the School had always given
the Lords and Commons a champagne lunch and generously revived
the custom.

Perhaps the greatest triumph of the Lords and Commons took place
at the Oval in 1956 when they defeated the last Egyptian touring side to
visit this country. It was a victory in which I played an unusual and
slightly controversial part, making few runs but taking six wickets
including a hat-trick with my in-swingers. The wind was in the right
direction and the ball moved a long way in the air. In the hat-trick each
batsman was given out l.b.w.; I still believe all three decisions were
correct, but the fact that the octogenarian umpire usually officiated for
the Harrow Wanderers enabled envious colleagues to raise doubts.
The Egyptians, who had perfect manners, never gave the slightest
indication of being dissatisfied with the verdicts.

Some club matches acquired something of the character of the legendary country house cricket of Edwardian days. For example, there were regular cricket weeks at Welbeck Abbey in Nottinghamshire, the home of the Duke of Portland. I was asked to play in one such in 1927 or 1928. The matches lasted two days and the teams included the Harrow Wanderers, Free Foresters and I Zingari; among our opponents were the Nottinghamshire Gentlemen. I knew Morven Bentinck, the Duke's youngest son, and when he saw my name on the first day's match card he asked me to stay. I told him that I had brought nothing except my cricket clothes but he said he was sure one of the footmen would lend me a dinner jacket and he would lend me anything else I needed. There was a large house party and besides playing cricket we played lawn tennis in the evenings, golf on the Duke's private course on the Sunday, sailed on the lake and danced through the night to Morven's piano playing.

Life at Welbeck was impressive. I remarked on the number of grass tennis courts spread round the house and Morven explained that at one time there had been fourteen grass courts, each angled so that the sun need not be in one's eyes at any hour of the day. Now the number had been reduced to seven. There were also four excellent *en-tout-cas* hard courts in a sunken garden. Welbeck was so large that it needed a small railway in the basement to carry the food the quarter of a mile from the lifts up to the dining room. Some of the trolleys had special heating, others special ice packs. They were pushed by hand. I was taken downstairs before dinner to watch the railway work.

The room in which we dined had a very high ceiling and on the wall behind the Duke's chair were stretched the skins of his two most famous stallions, St Simon and Donovan. On plaques beneath the skins were recorded their winnings and perhaps the winnings of their progeny. I cannot be sure because, although Lady Anne Cavendish Bentinck, the sixth Duke's granddaughter, remembered the skins and the plaques, neither she nor anyone of whom she enquired knew what had happened to them. In my mind is a total figure of seven hundred thousand pounds between the two horses, a useful addition by the values of the turn of the century, even to the Portland income.

The Duke himself, a small, grey-haired figure, had succeeded a distant cousin. His wife, Winifred, had been a Miss Yorke. She was still a beautiful woman and seemed to me in my twenties all that one could expect of a duchess, tall, graceful, welcoming and full of fun. I had driven to Welbeck in an old Dodge car, painted in the colours of the Bullingdon Club – sky blue and white – which I shared with three friends at Oxford. I had two or three gallons of petrol left as I parked it in what was once the stable yard, but when I went to collect the car before leaving I found that the petrol tank was quite full. I asked one of the chauffeurs how much money I owed and he said, 'Nothing at all.' Apparently the custom of refuelling visitors' cars was a tradition handed down from coaching days; since visitors' horses had always been stabled and fed, the same rule applied when the horses changed into motor cars.

A house whose hospitality rivalled Welbeck's was Arundel Castle. Bernard Norfolk had succeeded his father and become the sixteenth Duke of Norfolk in 1917 at the age of nine. In the years following the war he decided to bring the cricket ground back into use. The ground had been cut out of the side of a hill to the north-west of the Castle and was of the same dimensions as the Oval. Around one end and half a side was a steep grass bank where spectators could sit, and above it a wood full of rhododendrons. There were, and still are (for the ground is in constant use) beautiful trees all round, and on the south-eastern side one caught glimpses of the Castle. Cricket actually began again in 1921, and by 1927, when I first went to play there, there was a considerable fixture list. The Duke himself loved the game and for many years captained his own side. Quite often the members of both teams would stay at the Castle with wives or girlfriends and one would sit down fifty or more to dinner in the Great Hall. There was always someone who could play the piano for the rest of us to dance and sing.

From 1956 onwards, Arundel became the ground where every visiting Test Match team plays their first game. Since the Duke died in 1975, his widow, Lavinia, Duchess of Norfolk, has carried on the tradition of Arundel cricket with wonderful enthusiasm and, with the help of the Friends of Arundel Cricket, has made the ground one of the cricket attractions south of the Thames.

7

Quintus at Harrow

Cricket has bedevilled my chronology. In the year that I first played for a village at East Meon, I also went to Harrow. It has been said that if you stand on the church tower at the top of the famous hill and look east, there is no higher elevation until you reach the Ural Mountains. According to the atlas this line would have to run across Holland, the north German and Polish plains, the Pripet Marshes, pass below Minsk and Moscow and on to Kazan. It might have to jink a little to the south of Moscow, but it seems possible that the saying is true. As boys, however, we normally looked no further than south-east over London or westwards where, on a clear day, we could see Windsor Castle and Eton College Chapel. It was a challenging view.

In the early 1920s, members of several family clans were at the school. There were seven Barclays, eight Buxtons and six Crawleys. I was Crawley Quintus and my cousin Charles was Crawley Sextus. We were all at a house called The Park under an amiable but not very forceful housemaster. On the whole we enjoyed life. I had a retentive memory so examinations were never a bogey. I loved games and history, disliked the Officers' Training Corps which in the aftermath of war took far too much of our time. Scenes flit across my mind. Cecil Beaton, wearing a high-winged stiff collar and fur-lined gloves, walking proudly down the middle of the High Street with an umbrella; he used to play the female parts in all our dramatic productions and was very popular. A small round-faced boy called Terence Rattigan, whose father had been a cricketer, and who became my fag. After I had left the school he attained his first literary distinction with a letter to *The Times* protesting against the amount of time and effort boys were forced to spend on the Officers' Training Corps, which was supposed to be voluntary. His letter was taken up by the Prime Minister, Mr Baldwin, himself an Old Harrovian, after which the tyranny of the military

55

minded was significantly reduced. Lastly the scene outside Chapel on a Sunday evening when the boys waited to see if the mothers and sisters of their friends were pretty. The most beautiful among them was called Mary Thynne, remote and worthy of a stained glass window. I never spoke to her.

I must confess I hardly noticed the supposed terrors of a public school. One took fagging in one's stride and learned how to do the minimum. I was aware that some boys had homosexual tendencies, but if one did not reciprocate it seldom became a problem. Indeed, only once, in my fourth year, were the placid waters of Harrow life seriously disturbed and that had nothing directly to do with sex. Reggie Butterworth, a boy a year older than me and a fine athlete, became Head of my House and Captain of the School Cricket XI during the winter of 1924–25. He confided to me that he thought he had a good chance of becoming Head of the School. The headmaster, the Revd Lionel Ford, was a devout churchman and Reggie thought he had discovered the way to his heart. He used to go along in the evenings two or three times a week to the headmaster's study and read the Bible with him. I knew Reggie was not in the least religious and I could not believe that Ford would be taken in, but it was an audacious scheme and Reggie was extremely plausible. I was sworn to secrecy and every now and then Reggie would report progress. He could not hide his pleasure at hoodwinking Lionel Ford, who was rather a portentous figure. One day he came back in high spirits. His plan had worked and Ford had told him that he intended to make him Head of the School. Reggie added that he knew that this was against the advice of every house-master including our own.

Ford was as good as his word and Reggie fulfilled his new duties with authority and style. But I was apprehensive, for I was one of the very few who knew that Reggie and two or three other boys were engaged in a secret adventure which, if discovered, would mean their instant expulsion from the school. All of them were seventeen or eighteen years old and, finding the restrictions of school irksome, they had organized regular nocturnal visits to London. With the help of a shopkeeper, they hired a Daimler which waited in a side street after dark. Each of them then climbed out of a window in their different school houses and made their way to the car. Reggie was the only member of the party who lived in our house, The Park, and the window

56

with the shortest drop to the ground into what we called 'the bottom passage' was mine. So every now and then during the winter and Lent terms, Reggie would come into my room after lights out, climb through the window as quietly as possible and disappear. I never knew how he re-entered the house, but it cannot have been until after six a.m. when the doors were unlocked and people were getting ready for early school. All ran smoothly for so long that I began to think the boys would get away with it. Then the blow fell. A young master, who also apparently found life at Harrow frustrating, went to a night club known as 'The 43' and there saw Reggie and the other boys. He reported the fact to the headmaster. Ford was understandably outraged and sacked all of them immediately. There was no formal announcement but the story was picked up by the newspapers; I do seem to remember a sort of hushed atmosphere until a new Head of the School was appointed.

Not long afterwards my housemaster sent for me. He said he had something to tell me which he was afraid might disappoint me. In view of Butterworth's departure the members of the Cricket XI who had won their 'flannels'[1] had met to choose a successor and they had chosen me. The three masters in charge of cricket had endorsed their decision which had then been reported to the headmaster. But Ford had refused to appoint me because I was too young (I would be seventeen in April of that year, 1925) and had appointed his own son, Neville Ford, who was a year older. My housemaster added that, as Neville was staying on for the following summer, this meant that he would be Captain for two years and I had no chance of being Captain myself unless I too stayed on until I was nineteen. I told him at once that I had no intention of doing so. My housemaster was a kindly man and I could tell that he was not only disappointed for me but angry at what, as I learned later, he considered the blatant nepotism of Lionel Ford. I think he felt it more strongly that I did. Neville was and has remained a friend, and although when I thought about it I could muster some indignation, I never really harboured any resentment. The thing was done and I accepted it. I do, however, remember feeling that the headmaster might exert too great an influence on Neville's captaincy, and when at Lord's that summer Neville failed to make Eton follow on, I certainly blamed his father.

My time at Harrow ended in minor glory. In the Lent term of 1926 I won the top History Scholarship at Trinity College, Oxford, to go up in

October of the same year. My success was due almost entirely to the History master at Harrow, Leonard Henry, who was a dedicated and provocative teacher. In the months leading up to the examination he would invite me to his house after supper and discuss whatever subject we were studying over a glass of port. He treated me as an adult and encouraged me to form opinions and defend them. He became a friend. In his reports he used to describe my work as 'thorough'; if by that he meant that I was able to reproduce in my essays a high proportion of what he had told me, then perhaps it was true.

During my last term he behaved as if I had already left the school, letting me sit at the back of the sixth form and read whatever I liked. As my housemaster also allowed me to keep a car (which my father kindly provided) so that I could go to Lords and watch cricket any afternoon, I had an agreeable time. These visits had the right effect, because I made 87 against Eton in July in an innings described by 'Plum' Warner as one of the best he had seen in the years he had been watching the match. The Eton and Harrow match was still one of the great fashion parades of the London Season. That day there were said to be twenty-five thousand spectators, all dressed in their best. Whole families came together, boys and girls all wearing dark or light blue buttonholes or ribbons. The arbours round the nursery ground and behind the pavilion were booked a year in advance for family picnics. A long line of coaches was driven on to the ground at the nursery end to provide sumptuous alfresco lunches for those sitting on top. At the lunch and tea intervals the spectators covered the whole playing area except the pitch, which was roped off. Every man and boy wore a top hat.

I am grateful to Harrow. Some friends I made there were enduring, and in a hundred different situations in later life the fact that one had known the man one was dealing with when he was a boy turned out to be helpful. Both my sons were to play cricket for the school.

8

Trinity, Oxford

Until I left Harrow I had led a protected life. My chief friends were my many cousins, both Gibbs and Crawley, whom we visited in the holidays or had to stay at home, and our neighbours in Yorkshire and elsewhere. I had met few people who came from a different background to that of my parents. In the villages in which we had lived I knew many people, but always from a vicarage standpoint. As a child I once made a friend of a farmer who gave me warm Jersey cream to drink straight from his separator; but when it was discovered that he did not go to church I was gently discouraged from seeing him too often. I realize now that had we children become regular visitors it would have given offence to other farmers who supported the church.

At Oxford I grew up. I was lucky in my college: Trinity, in Broad Street, is central. Across the road from the great blue iron gates stands one of the most striking groups of buildings in the University, the old Ashmolean Museum, the Sheldonian Theatre, the Old Clarendon building and, visible behind them, the Bodleian Library with the dome of its reading room, the Radcliffe Camera, rising above it. Many undergraduates had bicycles but I always preferred to walk and from Trinity was within ten minutes of all that was most beautiful in the city. When you live in Oxford you absorb its beauty through the pores of your skin; its magic never leaves you.

My rooms were in the New Buildings, where I had a large sitting room and two bedrooms. A 'scout' called Lynes looked after the three undergraduates who were on that one staircase. One could always lunch in one's room with two or three guests and could also have dinner there if one ordered it a day in advance. Male friends could sleep in the spare room at any time. Lynes looked after us all. To me the most exciting thing was being grown up. Younger dons called me by my Christian name and expected me to do the same to them. One called nobody 'sir'. Food in college was good and cheap. I seem to remember lunch in Hall costing two shillings and sixpence. The only spartan touch were the baths, two quads and several stone passages away. When the snow was on the ground one was apt to wash only when mud from the football field had made it essential.

And I could entertain and be entertained. I remember waking up one morning and realizing that from now on life was what one made it. If one liked people, one cultivated them. It did not matter whether they were in the same college or not. One walked round to see them in the morning, lunched together at a club or in college, played games in the afternoon and dined with some other group. The work for the preliminary examination at the end of the first year was not exacting. It was necessary to read a few special books but the rest was familiar ground. I set about enjoying myself.

In *Brideshead Revisited* Evelyn Waugh has drawn a picture of life at Oxford in the 1920s, much of which rings true. It was an age when 'tolerance' was an undergraduate watchword. The First World War, only eight years behind us, had broken many shibboleths, and the notion that some things were not done was laughed at. People must do what they liked and every opinion had at least to be entertained. Preconceived ideas of behaviour fell away. Homosexuals were not shunned as they had been at Harrow. Several members of a group known as 'the Aesthetes' were amusing and talented. Beverley Nicholls had gone down but used often to come and stay with friends and play the piano in the evenings. So did Rex Colclough and Richard Sykes, although they were not part of the Aesthetes. Of the group perhaps Brian Howard was the most memorable. Dark, emaciated and pale with a malicious tongue but considerable charm, Brian was at every party and never in a hurry. He was interested in painting and contemptuous of the Surrealists. It was said that one day, in a fit of indignation, he had hired a gallery in Bond Street and spent the next twenty-four hours painting and concocting pictures, one of which was a boiled shirt with an ink pot attached and spilt ink smeared all down the shirt front. On the day of the exhibition Brian dressed up as an old man with a beard and was pushed in a wheelchair around the gallery by a friend, listening to the comments. His day was made when Lytton Strachey, the historian, bought one of the pictures for fifty pounds.

A blue-blooded coterie of men like Michael Ross, a charming Irish earl, Henry Weymouth (now the Marquess of Bath), Sydney Herbert, then heir to the Earl of Pembroke, Mark Ogilvie-Grant, Richard Sykes, son of Edward VII's friend Mark Sykes and owner of Sledmere in Yorkshire, would have fitted in with the Brideshead circle. A few had special accomplishments – Richard Sykes, for example, was a brilliant pianist and organist – but all possessed the talent to enjoy and amuse. A group of rich Americans added to the extravagance of some of the parties. Jock Whitney and 'Bob' Coe, both later to be American Ambassadors, Henry Rogers, whose sister Millicent was one of the beauties of her generation, Bradley Martin, an international polo player, John Schiff, scion of a merchant banking family whose father owned a famous library, were all at Oxford in the twenties, having already taken degrees at American universities. They gave parties which sometimes lasted two or three days and drank inordinate quantities of champagne at which we did our best to help them.

As Cambridge men are never tired of observing, compared to the Pitt Club, whose comfort equals that of the best clubs in London, Oxford club-land is a desert. Perhaps our clubs were rather small and dowdy, but they showed great variety. The Gridiron, which was then on the first floor of one of the buildings at Carfax crossroads, demanded no special qualifications and was popular. Vincents, known as 'The Club' to its regulars, was mainly for Blues past and present, some of the latter of whom consumed astonishing quantities of beer; at the 'Union', which fathered the Oxford Debating Society, you met a wide cross-section of Oxford life, and a narrower but no less lively one at the OUDS, which nurtured future actors, playwrights and pro-ducers. Many colleges had dining clubs of which the best, in my partisan opinion, was 'the Trinity Claret Club', whose dinners were still being held in the Garden Quad where the club's founder, the elder Pitt, had rooms. In my year as President, we were drinking Château-Margaux 1904 and laying down vintages of 1920 and 1921.

But the club of which I made most use was the Bullingdon, whose small rooms were above Adamson's, the tailor, in High Street. The Bullingdon had had a chequered history. At the turn of the century its members had been forbidden by the University authorities to accept an invitation by the Duke of Marlborough to a ball at Blenheim Palace. In retaliation, the club members are alleged to have broken every window in Peckwater Quad in Christ Church and were consequently banned from the University. The ban was lifted some years later but the club had no premises and its annual dinner had to be held outside the city, usually in a village barn. It had little to offer, therefore, except a certain snob value because it had always included in its ranks several members of the aristocracy. Its members had the right to wear a particularly elegant evening dress: dark blue tail coat with a velvet collar, white silk facings, gold buttons and yellow waistcoat. The Bullingdon tie was sky-blue and white stripes. Fortunately, in the year before I went up to Oxford the club secretary had not only received a licence to have rooms but had obtained an ideal suite. There were only about twenty-five members, and a sitting and dining room with a caretaker were all that were required. Launchbury, who looked after the club, was an excellent cook and would serve omelettes, mixed grills, steaks, herrings and baked potatoes at any hour of the day up to midnight. In winter his high teas after football or a day with the drag-hounds became famous.

History then began to repeat itself. The Duke of Marlborough gave another ball and invited the Bullingdon. This time we were not only allowed to go but Roger Chetwode, our President, was asked to organize a torchlight procession of undergraduates which would wind its way across Blenheim Park and end up in the main courtyard. Everything went perfectly. The night was fine, the torches burned bravely, the procession moved slowly and reasonably quietly. Inside the Palace, proceedings were formal, but the organ in the great ballroom was played in the intervals between dances and we could wander through the whole ground floor of the house and the gardens. No window panes were broken either at Blenheim or at Oxford that night. It was an evening to remember.

For the next decade the Bullingdon flourished. It ran an annual point-to-point, which made a little money for the club. It had its annual dinner in the village barn, to which every member invited a guest. It organized a fancy-dress flat race on Port Meadow and its members wore their evening coats at London dances and hunt balls. Of those who played cricket for the University, nine were members of the club. With the addition of Peter Carlisle, George Hyde and Taffy Landale, who all played for Eton or Harrow, it would have fielded a formidable club side. Two members of the club took first class honours in finals: Peter Fleming and Frank Pakenham. Peter Fleming, who read English, was soon to embark on an expedition to South America in search of Colonel Fawcett, who had disappeared in the Matto Grosso looking for a hidden civilization. Peter's first book *Brazilian Adventure* describes his journey hilariously. He went on to write several more books in which his role was part explorer, part historian. After master-minding an escape operation in Crete he survived the war and died while shooting grouse in 1975. He was married to Celia Johnson, the famous actress. I first got to know Peter when he wrote about me for the Oxford magazine *Isis*, which regularly published a satirical profile of some Oxford personality under the title 'The Idol'. We met on and off throughout our lives and he once suggested my accompanying him on one of his expeditions, but plainly changed his mind as in the end he never asked me. Once or twice I played cricket for his eleven against the village of Nettlebed in Oxfordshire.

Frank Pakenham, later Lord Longford, who got a first in Modern Greats, was then a bushy-haired, blond eccentric who was to become one of the most controversial figures of our time. Frank later became a lecturer in politics at Oxford, joined the Economic Research Department of the Conservative Party, but then 'crossed the floor' (as I was to do later in the opposite direction) and joined the Labour Party. We were colleagues in Parliament for many years and Frank was to hold important ministerial posts in Attlee's government. Frank and I were both friends of another club member, Freddy Furneaux, the first Lord Birkenhead's son, and used to go frequently to play tennis and dine at Charlton, near Banbury, where his father, 'F.E.', had turned three cottages into one.

'F.E.' was the famous barrister F.E. Smith, who became Lord Chancellor and later Secretary of State for India. Some writers have suggested that he was a malign influence on young men and that he encouraged Freddy's friends to drink with disastrous results. That was not my experience. Of course champagne flowed, but no more than at many Oxford parties. The dinners were exciting because 'F.E.' liked to shine and always had Ashmead Bartlett, a famous journalist or some Cabinet Minister to act as a foil to his wit. And he would encourage us to express ourselves. Heavy drinkers, like Basil Dufferin, Balliol's Brackenbury scholar, had formed their habits quite independently of 'F.E.'. Balliol was next door to Trinity and Basil used to ask me to go and drink port with him in the middle of the morning. I sometimes

63

went, but my stomach was unequal to the challenge. More than once Basil drove me out to Charlton in his Sunbeam sports car and, more remarkably, drove me back. But the dinners at Charlton included dons and people like Frank Pakenham and Quintin Hogg, who drank sparingly, if at all. I have always thought that if people drink to excess they can blame no one but themselves.

Freddy not only read widely but had a memory which allowed him to recite poems or passages of prose after reading them only two or three times. One of his favourite satirical poems was Dryden's 'Absolom and Achitophel', verses from which he loved to repeat to friends to whom he felt they applied. 'Bankrupt of life yet prodigal of ease,' one would hear him chortle as one lay in a deck-chair by the swimming pool into which he would immmediately perform a jack-knife dive. Freddy had hoped to get a first, but his father died just when he was preparing for his finals in 1930 and he became involved in the winding up of an encumbered inheritance. This altered his life, for he once admitted to me that he had really wanted to become a don; he would have been an inspiring teacher. As it was, he immediately had to start earning his living and embarked upon the first of a series of biographies with a 'life' of his father.

When Freddy married Sheila Berry, the first Lord Camrose's daughter, in 1935, I was his best man. I had ascertained from a member of the family that the wedding at St Margaret's, Westminster, was to be at two-thirty p.m. After lunching at the Ritz, Freddy and I there-fore strolled across St James's Park. When we reached Parliament Square, we were surprised to see a beribboned Daimler containing Sheila and Lord Camrose motoring slowly round. We waved but got no response. When we reached the vestry we saw the Archbishop of Canterbury, Cosmo Lang, who was to perform the ceremony, sitting in full regalia with his mitre, waiting. As we approached, he said, 'Freddy, you go on in, but leave me Aidan for a moment.' He then turned to me and began, 'Aidan, it is not customary to keep the Archbishop of Canterbury waiting for a quarter of an hour . . .' Mercifully I forget the rest of his reproof. Buns Cartwright, one-time assistant to Freddy's father and a good cricketer, was offering odds, as he ushered the guests into their seats, that Freddy had forgotten about the wedding altogether and gone off to play golf. In fact everything went smoothly and Freddy and Sheila embarked on a marriage that survived every hazard and brought both of them profound happiness.

Occasionally an 'undergraduette' would leave her punt on the Cherwell and come to watch cricket in the Parks; otherwise one seldom saw women except at lectures or examinations. There were no mixed colleges and we were essentially a male community. Girls were reserved for vacations, picnics on the Cherwell or 'Commemoration' balls. However, there were signs of change. In my first year a female Idol appeared in the *Isis* for the first time. She was Elizabeth Harman, the beautiful daughter of a Harley Street surgeon, who in 1931 was to marry Frank Pakenham.

Some dons made a point of getting to know undergraduates. Philip Landon of Trinity had evenings when anyone could go and have a drink in his rooms, which overlooked the garden. It was a great meeting place. 'Sligger' Urquhart in Balliol, Roy Harrod in Peckwater Quad and 'J.C.' Masterman, also at Christ Church but with rooms in Tom Quad, were each as hospitable in his own way. There were many others equally generous whom I did not know.

In the winter I sometimes played soccer for the college, real tennis in the court in Merton Street and rode horses. A livery stable under the sourly genial management of a Mr Macpherson would hire one a horse for two pounds a day to go hacking or hunting. They were not very good horses but at least one was able to go out with the Oxford Drag or with hounds. The Masters of the Bicester, Waddon Chase, Warwickshire or Berkshire hunts were so welcoming to undergraduates that they seldom charged us a 'cap', which for ordinary visitors varied from two to five pounds a day; if the hunt secretary asked us for anything it would be ten shillings. One could also buy a horse comparatively cheaply.

My partner in all to do with horses was Peter Cazalet. We had first met when playing on opposite sides in the Eton and Harrow Match of 1926 and from then onwards remained close friends until he died in 1975. Although a strict disciplinarian in his profession as a trainer of steeplechasers, he was by nature one of the gentlest of men. Peter's father, William Cazalet, who had seen his business destroyed by the Russian Revolution, had become something of a recluse and seldom left his lovely home at Fairlawn near Tonbridge in Kent. Peter's eldest brother was killed in the First World War and as the next eldest, Victor, and his sister Thelma (both of whom were Members of Parliament for many years) had their own houses, Peter inherited Fairlawn when his father died in 1939. It was a lovely estate with about three thousand acres of first-class farmland, woods and a large park which was filled with splendid Turkey oaks. One building, on the edge of a large walled garden, housed a real tennis court and an indoor swimming pool under the same roof. There were three grass tennis courts, terraced down a slope out of sight of the house, a conservatory which became a loggia, and large stables. Peter was a beautiful games player. He could always beat me at both forms of tennis and I could never win at racquets. In 1926 we went in first together for Oxford and were given our 'blue' on the same day in 1927. He did everything thoroughly. When I persuaded him to learn to ride he went to a riding school at Camberley and never looked back. After his first year he gave up cricket and took up riding seriously. I accompanied him in 1930 to his first steeplechase which he won on an old horse called Horse Marine, riding in the snow at Towcester. For the next ten years he was one of the leading amateur jockeys.

Later Peter turned to training and converted the Park at Fairlawn into a series of schools and gallops. To begin with, his great friend Anthony Mildmay was his chief client and jockey; later Peter became trainer to Queen Elizabeth the Queen Mother. Although successful as a trainer, Peter was twice the victim of phenomenally bad luck. Anthony Mildmay rode Davy Jones in the Grand National of 1936. He jumped the last fence at least twenty lengths in front and seemed to have the race in his pocket. But somehow both reins had got to one side of the horse's neck and Anthony could not steer him. On the run-in Davy Jones, still galloping strongly, left the course and never finished. Twenty years later an even odder event deprived Peter of what again looked like certain victory. The Queen Mother's horse, Devon Loch, was leading comfortably in the straight when, with only a hundred yards to go, the horse suddenly spread-eagled its legs – as if it had seen a ghost – and almost stopped. By the time it reached the winning post several other horses had passed it.

At Oxford, Peter used to buy race-horses out of selling plates for a hundred pounds or less and we used to school them over fences belonging to an Irishman called Charlie Kelly who had a stables close to Bicester aerodrome. Our best buy was from one of Charlie's friends who had a one-eyed chestnut which could gallop and, provided its good eye was pointing in the right direction, jumped fast and well. One morning after some gallops Charlie asked us if we would like to buy the horse. He had brought his friend over and they were sitting in his car ready to drive away. The friend said he would take twenty pounds. We offered five pounds and they drove away, but soon returned in reverse. After this exercise had been repeated several times, we finally settled for nine pounds ten. I won a race on the horse at one of the 'Grinds', as our point-to-points were called, and started a hot favourite for the members' race at the Bullingdon meeting. We got to the first fence well in front but at the last minute the horse turned its blind eye towards it. As I lay on the ground on the far side, the entire field of twenty runners, most of them hirelings, came over me. I was untouched.

In our second year, Bill Astor became Master of the Drag, and Peter, Henry Douglas-Home and I were enlisted as whippers-in. A drag is a form of hunt in which hounds follow not the scent of a fox but a trail laid by a bag of linseed, dragged along the ground by a man on foot who chooses a line of country – with the co-operation of the farmers concerned – which has plenty of fences, posts and rails, a stream or two and sometimes perhaps a locked gate. Long-distance runners training for cross country races used to welcome the chance to 'lay a drag line'. They were instructed to make a gap in the trail at about the halfway mark by carrying rather than dragging the bag of linseed for a couple of fields so that the hounds and horses would have a check; linseed has such a strong scent that otherwise the leading hounds would have galloped away from the field and finished without any followers. The Master was told in advance where to pick up the scent again and meanwhile the whips had time to collect hounds that had strayed after hares or rabbits. On one occasion they went after a fox but fortunately never caught it or we should have had to apologize to the local Master of Fox Hounds. The hounds, usually unruly cast-offs from some pack, were chosen for speed. A 'line' was between four and five miles long and was laid an hour or two before the hunt assembled. From then on the whole proceeding was over in a couple of hours.

The following year, John Cowdray became Master and the whips remained the same. John enjoyed the Drag so much that he endowed it with a sum of money that would ensure that kennels, a pack of hounds and a kennel huntsman could always be maintained. Thanks to him the Oxford Drag continues to this day.

9

The MCC

In the summer I played cricket. Many Oxford colleges have lovely cricket grounds but the most beautiful of all is the University ground in the Parks with the River Cherwell running along one side and a great variety of trees chosen by successive curators of the Botanical Gardens forming a distant background. Both pitch and outfield were good. Spectators sat in deck-chairs or simply stood or walked around. The pavilion was old fashioned with primitive changing-rooms in the basement, but an attractive long room with high windows, whose walls were panelled with the names of all former Oxford teams, looked out on to the ground. It was used for a plentiful but unimaginative lunch. On fine evenings we migrated to the river after the game was over and picnicked on its banks. Sometimes girls came down from London to join us.

I had been given my blue in 1927 and was elected Secretary for 1928. This meant going to Lords in the winter to meet all the county secretaries and arrange the fixtures for the following year. I felt that we did not meet enough good counties and managed to persuade ten of them to play the University the following year, including Yorkshire and Lancashire, the latter never having been to Oxford before. Because Maurice McCanlis was taking his finals and did not play at all during the term, I had to act as Captain as well as Secretary until we went on tour after the term was over. We had quite a good season and I scored 1,000 runs before the Varsity match, apparently the first Oxford batsman to do so, although several have done so since. At one point I scored centuries in four consecutive matches, and when I got o in the second innings against the MCC at Lords there were banner headlines in the *Evening Standard*: 'CRAWLEY OUT FOR o'. Against Cambridge I ran myself out in the second innings just when I had got going; infuriating. I was picked for Gentlemen against Players at Lords and got my fifty by hitting 'Tich' Freeman over the stand at the nursery end behind mid-off. A few balls later I tried to hit him into the grandstand on the leg-side but got a top edge and was caught by Frank Woolley running back from fine-leg. Back in the pavilion, Percy Chapman, our Captain, said to me, 'What a pity. I thought you had just got going.'

In the winter term, when the Oxford team came to elect the Cricket Captain for 1929, they voted 6 to 5 for Alan Barber instead of me; I had not been aware of any criticism but was told afterwards that they felt I had not given a fair trial to several good college players and had not liked the way I handled the bowling. To the first criticism I might have answered that almost everyone I chose had done well; to the second I could only bow. I was the more disappointed because I knew that as Secretary I had done a good job, particularly in improving the fixture list. But Alan was a friend and by the time the next season came round I had put it behind me.

1929 brought a tantalizing opportunity. At the beginning of the summer term I got a letter from Bill Astor saying that he was not coming up to Oxford as he had intended, but had already sent four polo ponies with his groom to a stables in the town. Would I play them for him when I could? It was difficult to fit in polo with cricket, but by slipping away from the Parks after I had batted and if the side was doing well, I managed to play several games on Port Meadow and some at Datchet, where the Household Brigade had a ground. John Cowdray, who was captain of the polo team, told me he would like me to play against Cambridge if I could find a little more time to practise. Unfortunately, I had the Oxford cricket tour in front of me and no free days; in any event the University polo match took place on one of the days of the cricket match at Lords. It would have been fun to have been able to do both.

I did have one piece of good luck. There was a ball at Magdalen College at the end of the summer term and both Alan Barber and I went to it. Neither of us went to bed afterwards, and I picked him up at Queen's College at nine o'clock next morning to drive in my snub-nose Morris to Wellingborough where we were to play Northamptonshire on the school ground. It was a grey morning and we prayed either that it would rain or that Alan would lose the toss. Unfortunately he won it, but it did rain so we got some sleep before a delayed start at two-forty p.m. We went in first together and for half an hour missed almost every ball at which we played. Albert Thomas and Austin Mathews in particular missed our stumps several times by a fraction of an inch. Then we had a conference in the middle of the pitch. I suggested to Alan that we chance our luck and have a go. He agreed. Alan got out, but the Nawab of Pataudi stayed with me. By the close of play I had scored 204 and hit ten sixes; 'the Noob' as we called him, had got 60. We were especially hard on Valence Jupp, the Northamptonshire Captain who bowled slow off-spinners and played several times for England.

The following week my name was among twelve picked to play for England against South Africa at Lords. Then my luck ran out. Tom Killick, who was then going in first for Cambridge, was also among the chosen twelve. On the morning of the match the four selectors who were at Lords were divided equally between Killick and me. They cabled the fifth, who was playing in a county match and he voted for Killick, so I was twelfth man. Just after the decision had been taken, Killick came up to me and said he wished they had chosen me because he had flu and was feeling unwell. When Jack White, the England Captain heard this, he also came up and said that if only Killick had told him earlier, he would have gone to the selectors and told them he wanted me. But now it was too late. The names of the team had been given already to the South Africans. Killick, who was a fine player, made 0 and 1 in the match. Later he became a parson and died tragically young.

I should really have left Oxford in 1929, but Trinity College generously extended my scholarship for a year on condition that I played no cricket until after the final examinations. I had a respectable number of 'alphas' in my papers but did badly in the viva-voce and only got a second. 1930 was the year of the Australian tour of England and as a spectator I watched Clarence Crimmett make havoc of the Oxford batting on the Christ Church ground.[1] I did not join the side until Oxford went on tour but played more games than usual for Kent in July and August.

Against Essex at Gravesend, I played the best innings of my life. Nichols and Farnes, who were opening the bowling for England at that time, also opened for Essex. Farnes, who was truly fast, got me out for 25 in the first innings, but in the second I made 176 and at one time both Nichols and Farnes had four men in the deep field, one of whom was my cousin Leonard. I hit two sixes over his head and he waved delightedly at both. Lord Harris, a great Kent figure, then in his eighties, was watching. Leonard kept the ball we had used and had engraved on a silver band which still surrounds it the remark Lord Harris made to him after the match: 'Surely one of the most remarkable innings ever played.' I was even more flattered when Frank Woolley said that it was some of the finest hitting of fast bowling he could remember.

'Bodyline' did not become an issue until after I had ceased playing, but as I batted against Larwood several times, including an occasion at Canterbury when he beat me by sheer pace and knocked back my offstump, perhaps the experience is worth recording. Going in first in a Gentlemen and Players match or a Test Trial one usually had to face Larwood at one end and Maurice Tate at the other. I always preferred playing Larwood. With a new ball he swung so far to the off that one rarely had to play more than two or three balls an over, whereas Maurice Tate would not only swing both ways but might go either way off the seam when the ball bounced. He always bowled at the stumps and had such pace off the pitch that mentally one thought of him as the faster of the two. It was different when the shine was off the ball. Then Larwood would be very accurate, his balls often cutting in from the off with a tendency to rise about heart high. When he had three or four men close to the wicket on the leg side, he greatly restricted one's stroke play. I remember thinking that if such a field-placing became common it would spoil the game. Larwood only occasionally dropped one short and although he attained speeds of around ninety miles an hour, I never felt it was impossible to hook or get out of the way provided one kept one's eye on the ball.

When the England team returned from the 'bodyline' tour in Australia, I asked Leslie Ames, whom I had got to know well playing for Kent and who kept wicket for England throughout the tour, whether he thought that Larwood's bowling had been in any way dangerous. Leslie himself was an extremely good player of fast bowling. He thought for a minute and then said, 'It was dangerous if the batsman made a mistake.' He went on to explain that Larwood was faster in Australia than in England, so that if a batsman hesitated he was more likely to get hit. On the other hand, the ball kept lower out there. 'To give you an idea of the speed,' he went on, 'I used to wear a slab of raw meat inside my gloves and stood more than twenty yards back, yet by the end of an Australian innings my hands would be quite sore.'

Except for a few games later on for Kent, the year 1930 saw the end of my serious cricket. I had been asked at Lords that summer whether I would be available to tour South Africa in the winter, but said regretfully that I had to start earning a living. To be truthful, the regret was not overwhelming. I loved cricket and continued to play for village clubs and the Lords and Commons until I was over seventy, but I always regarded it as a game; at the end of three months, even at Harrow, I felt I had had enough. There were so many other things one wanted to do.

Having had so much fun out of the game, it was a pleasure in later life to be able to repay a little of it as an administrator. In the 1960s I became Chairman of the National Cricket Association, responsible for fostering all forms of cricket other than the first-class game. With Jim Dunbar, an assistant secretary of the MCC, I started a coaching scheme which now covers most of the country. We also helped to launch the National Village Cricket Competition, now run by the *Cricketer* magazine, and the Young England Cricket XI from which come so many of our Test cricketers. Perhaps because of this, in May 1972, Freddie Brown, then President of the MCC, nominated me as his successor. Walter Monckton once said that of all the public offices he had held, none gave him as much pleasure as the presidency of the MCC. I was soon to understand what he meant. The office only lasts for a year, but during that year the President is more than a figurehead; he is Chairman of the MCC Committee, which is still responsible for the laws of the game, and of the International Cricket Conference, which has considerable influence throughout the cricket world. On general policy, for instance over apartheid, the President is the voice of cricket. When an England team tours abroad, the President accompanies it for at least one Test match. In my year as President, we went to India. We had a truly royal time. The cricket ground at Bombay holds seventy-five thousand people and for the Test match was filled to capacity. Most of the spectators sat behind a steel mesh partition, but this in no way dampened their excitement. As Chandrasekar, their star bowler, who had suffered from polio in his youth, loped slowly to the wicket; the crowd, beginning in a whisper, increased the volume of their encouragement with every stride until it became such a roar as the bowler reached the wicket that one felt the batsman must be distracted. However, Tony Greig, who made 148 for England, positively enjoyed it and deliberately played up to the crowd. Meanwhile in the enclosure, bookmakers offered odds on every ball and members passed their betting slips from hand to hand over the heads of their neighbours. Such enthusiasm is infectious. In the mornings before play began, as many as five thousand people would pay to watch the players at the nets. In the evenings, as one walked across the Maidan, one passed literally hundreds of games of cricket, all played by men and boys in white trousers and shirts. As an Indian remarked, 'In the days of the Raj, cricket was an aristocratic sport; now it is the game of the people.'

My year as President of MCC had a sequel. Having been more than once to Australia, but never having seen a cricket match there, my wife Virginia and I decided to go for the Centenary Test Match in 1978. A few years previously, I had presented a picture of Sir Donald Bradman to his wife Jessie in the Long Room at Lords. Now we not only dined with the Bradmans, but I spent two days as 'the Don's' guest watching a Sheffield Shield match in the pavilion at Adelaide. Bradman was a fascinating companion. There was no name in cricket I could mention about whom he did not know something interesting; whenever he was uncertain about a fact or figure, he would get up, disappear into the recesses of the pavilion, which houses one of the best cricket libraries in the world, and come back with a piece of paper on which the necessary information or reference was written. I had seen the film of Gary Sobers' great innings of 254 against Australia in the World Series in 1972 for which Sir Donald had done the commentary. He repeated to me what he had said then, that it was the greatest innings he had ever seen, but that no schoolboy should be allowed to watch the film. Sobers was a genius and played too many unorthodox strokes.

10

'The Arch'

In the autumn of 1924, when I was in my third year at Harrow, my father had returned to Bishopthorpe, not as vicar but as a Canon of York and Cosmo Lang's chaplain. Since our old home was occupied by a new vicar, we lived once more in the Elizabethan wing of the Palace. We lived at Bishopthorpe until the autumn of 1928. I think of it as a carefree form of country house life. We set up tennis courts and a cricket net in the Archbishop's garden. Gubby Allen was among those who came to stay and we persuaded him to bowl to us. One day the Archbishop said that he had a bishop staying at the Palace who had been an Oxford cricket blue; he thought he would love a net. The bishop, who was tall and thin, turned up in a dark suit. He removed his coat but not his dog collar, put pads over his trousers and batted for half an hour with great elegance. I have always believed that his name was Thesiger and that his diocese was Chelmsford, but Crockford's tells me I am wrong, so he must remain anonymous.

In November 1928 the Archbishop was translated from York to Canterbury on the retirement of Randall Davidson. He asked my father to come with him and bring the whole family. To my mother Lang had once written: 'You are almost the only friend whom I allow even to think that they manage me.' She had been his hostess for so many years that he was bound to miss her; we had become very much his family. 'I love all the boys and the two girls as if they were my own,' he wrote to her, lamenting his departure from Bishopthorpe. But although the Archbishop was achieving his life's ambition, my father felt that it was time to make a break. He became Canon of St Albans and we went to live at Praewood, a house on a hill just outside the town.

During the next two or three years I used to stay with the Archbishop at the Old Palace in Canterbury whenever I played cricket for Kent there. Once or twice he came briefly to watch the game. Breakfast at the Palace was interesting. The Archbishop used to take it with two chaplains: Mervyn Haig, who later became Bishop of Winchester, and Alec Sargent, who became Archdeacon of Canterbury. I suspect they found it difficult to get decisions from him about many domestic and administrative problems and resented any break in serious conversation. I could feel their irritation when the Archbishop cross-examined me about the cricket score and my own performance on the St Lawrence ground.

He did not even mention his favourite diversion but used to make an assignation with me privately. The Archbishop loved speed. Knowing this, I once borrowed an Alvis sports car from Anthony Winn with whom I was sharing a flat in London. I would fix a time for an evening spin with the Archbishop, depending on the weather and the state of the game. The Archbishop, having dismissed his chaplains, would retire to change and reappear dressed exactly like Sherlock Holmes in a tweed suit with a tweed cape and a matching deer-stalker hat. We would then slip out of a back door and go to the spot where he had told me to leave the car. Traffic was not as dense as it is today and there were usually two stretches on the Dover Road where I could let the car out. He was happy when we reached eighty miles an hour.

Every summer the Archbishop used to go for a few weeks to a little house called Ballure on the Mull of Kintyre belonging to the Macdonald family who lived at Largie. Jock Macdonald had been at Magdalen when the Archbishop was Dean, and his wife Daisy (a widow by the time I met her) was perhaps the woman of whom the Archbishop was thinking when he implied to my mother that there might be another whom he allowed to think she 'managed' him. Twice I went up to stay with him. It was a small, square house with a little portico and might well have been a manse. The Archbishop loved his native land and we used to go for long drives, sometimes with a girl he had asked me to invite, sitting three together on the back seat of the old Wolseley, covered in rugs. He loved gossip and was full of anecdotes. It was on one of those drives that he told me that when he was at the Bar, in his late twenties, his leading QC had died. His solicitors were approached by many other QCs who hoped to capture some of his practice, but their reply was always the same: 'We are sorry to disappoint you, but all our business is being reserved for young Mr Lang.' Nevertheless, within six months he had decided to leave the Bar and go into the Church – with the overt intention, as some of his colleagues said, of becoming head of it.

One part of his life at Ballure one could only share at a distance. There was a little chapel in the house and every morning, quite early, the Archbishop used to enter it alone to pray. A small lectern stood in front of the altar and he would kneel at it in an upright position which he would maintain for hours. The door was always left open and I would tiptoe in and sit behind him. He made no sound and he scarcely moved. The physical effort alone must have been enormous. He told me he seldom knelt for less than three hours.

There was no subject one could not discuss with him, but I did not ask him directly what he thought about when praying. It came out in other ways. I remember once inveighing against the number of church services I had had to attend as a boy. He looked at me sharply. 'And what do you think I feel, having to attend them day after day?' I was taken aback. 'I suppose you think it is part of my job,' he continued. 'But that doesn't make it any easier.' I do not remember how the rest of the conversation went, but it was a subject to which I returned.

At some time I must have said that I thought church-going a waste of time and that parsons would be better employed doing voluntary work. 'I see,' he said. 'You are a muscular Christian, a follower of Thomas à Kempis, perhaps?' He paused, but no doubt guessing that I had never read Thomas à Kempis, then asked, 'Have you any idea of the meaning of worship?' I do not remember my exact answer, but it must have been that I had never really understood it, other than as a ritual. Very gently he explained that of all mental disciplines, worship was the most selfless and perhaps the most exacting. He told me that during those long hours on his knees in his chapel he repeated to himself parts of the Bible and prayers; he contemplated his own shortcomings. I took that to mean that he did not even ask for forgiveness, but he accepted God's judgement. When, a few years later, the Archbishop was widely criticized for the stand he took over Edward VIII's desire to make Mrs Simpson his Queen, I felt for him instinctively. Unless he was to betray his position, how could he give any other advice to the constitutional head of his Church, the King, than to forego such a marriage?

In a letter to my mother, written just after his retirement in 1942, the Archbishop said, 'The only thing that does trouble me is that my life-work is over and I have done so little with it.' He was always his own most severe critic and, remembering his hopes and ambitions, there was something in this self-accusation. The Revised Prayer Book, of which as Archbishop of York he had been an ardent champion, had twice been rejected by the House of Commons and many people felt that the Church should have severed its connection with the State by accepting Disestablishment and asserting its right to revise its own forms of worship and frame its own laws on spiritual matters. The Archbishop preferred to wait for the public mood to change. His biographer, J.G. Lockhart, says the mark made on the history of the Church by Cosmo Lang's thirty-four years as Archbishop was comparatively small.[1] His greatest contribution 'not only to the Church of England but to Christendom' was the advance of Christian Reunion which resulted in a qualified recognition by the Orthodox Churches of the Anglican priesthood and a rapprochement, which still stops short of full intercommunion, with the non-Episcopal churches throughout the world and the Non-Conformist churches in Britain.

Yet, as Lockhart also points out, a surprisingly large number of those who met or served Cosmo Lang spoke and wrote of him as 'a great Archbishop'. This was due first to his exceptional powers of advocacy and oratory, which were often compared favourably with those of his contemporary, F.E. Smith, and were so persuasive that his opponents in an argument sometimes came to feel that he used them unfairly; next, to his 'inhuman' capacity for work, attested by all his chaplains; and finally, to his gift for entering other people's lives to an extent which was marvellously encouraging but carried with it the danger of making them think too highly of themselves.

Sir William Orpen, who painted him, said that in Lang he saw seven Archbishops and chose to portray the 'proud prelate', an aspect which the Archbishop recognized but which pleased him not at all. Certainly, he saw himself as an actor on a great stage, and was even a snob in the sense that he liked the company of those who held prominent positions or had great possessions. He enjoyed playing the part of statesman, revelled in beautiful places like Oxford, cathedrals like York or Canterbury, great houses like Bishopthorpe. At the same time, as he showed when vicar of Leeds and Portsea, or as Bishop of Stepney, he had genuine sympathy not only for the poor but for people who were down on their luck, or who had simply gone wrong. He was a regular prison visitor in his parishes, and in his diaries are many stories of criminals, prostitutes and petty thieves whom he befriended. In his personal habits he was spartan. One of his chaplains once spent a night in his room and vowed never to do it again. There was no carpet, only one small table and an upright chair, a jug of cold water and a basin. The bedstead was of iron with a chain mattress covered only with a blanket and a sheet. The chaplain was so uncomfortable he spent the night on the floor.

Lord Hugh Cecil (later Lord Quickswood) described him as one of the best speakers he had ever heard and praised in particular his many-sidedness, the 'effortless ease' with which he found the right word, and his effectiveness in furthering the object he had in view. With others, he felt that the Archbishop was better on a platform or in the House of Lords than in a pulpit, although there were many occasions when his sermons had a profound effect on those who heard them. Politically the Archbishop described himself as a liberal conservative and was fearless in his denunciation of Russian and Nazi terrorism and of all forms of tyranny. He could understand pacifism but never shared in it, believing that the Church must support a just cause even if it meant war. Yet he hated the extremes of bitterness and hysteria which war provoked.

He was reviled again for his speech following the abdication of Edward VIII. The Archbishop had played hardly any part in the events leading up to the abdication, being asked only once for his opinion, which concurred with that of the Prime Minister, Mr Baldwin, who handled the whole affair. But two days after the King made his farewell speech, the Archbishop was invited by the BBC to broadcast to the nation. I listened to his speech. His theme was the tragedy of the situation. He recalled the King's charm, his 'genuine care' for the poor and the unemployed. Seldom, if ever, he said, had any British sovereign come to the throne with greater natural gifts or been welcomed with more enthusiastic loyalty in assuming his 'high and sacred trust'. Yet by his own will he had surrendered that trust. If the Archbishop had left it at that, there could scarcely have been any criticism. But he went on to regret that the King had sought his private happiness in a manner 'inconsistent with the Christian principles of marriage and within a social circle whose standards and ways of life are alien to all the best instincts and traditions of his people.' This circle now stood 'rebuked by the judgement of the nation'.

It was this reference to the social circle which was particularly resented. Even some of those who agreed with everything else the Archbishop had said felt it had been gratuitous. Later, when I asked him about it, he replied that he thought the people with whom the King spent most of his time had been a very bad influence and bore considerable responsibility for what had happened. He felt it right to say so publicly. Remembering that the Archbishop was the chief executive of the Church of which the King was to become the head at his coronation, I feel now as I felt then, that he was both courageous and correct. In the letters he received, many people agreed with him and expressed their gratitude.

Having been away for almost the whole war I did not see him again until 1945. I had married Virginia at the end of July and been elected to Parliament in the same month. I took her to see him at King's Cottage, Kew Green, a 'Grace and Favour' house which the King had granted him. We talked and I hoped that she would sense something of what he had meant to me; but I think she saw him simply as a gentle and graceful old man. Before we left he made us kneel in front of him in the little hall and blessed us. Virginia was embarrassed; today I like to think that his blessing helped hold us together for the next forty years.

11

A Career in Journalism

I went into journalism by accident. The University Appointments Board had suggested several jobs and I was considering an opening in Unilever which would mean going to North Borneo, when I received a letter from Esmond Harmsworth, the only surviving son of Lord Rothermere who owned the *Daily Mail*, asking me to go to see him. A mutual friend had suggested that I might be the sort of young man he was looking for. He explained that if I liked the idea and proved satisfactory, he would want me to learn the whole business of newspaper production and spend some time in each department. It sounded an exciting prospect and I accepted.

My journalistic career began at the *Daily Mail* office in Tudor Street near Blackfriars Bridge on October 5th, 1930. It happened to be the day that the airship R101 crashed in France; the accident occurred at about ten-thirty in the morning. The newsroom emptied at once and I was left alone. Then the Assistant News Editor came out and told me that Sir Sefton Brancker, who had been Director of Civil Aviation and had died in the crash, had had a mistress called Miss Auriel Lee, an actress. I was to go and interview her. He gave me six addresses in London and I tried them all but thankfully she was not at home.

The reporters' room in Tudor Street was a lively place, dominated by two massive figures: Montague Smith, a veteran crime reporter, and Stan Mellor, a foreign affairs reporter who seldom went abroad, but in whose large, bald and domed head lay all the essential details of any country likely to be in the news. Everyone had his or her own desk and typewriter and we all sat in the same room without any partitions. The News Editor's door was always open and his minions were constantly drifting in and out of our room to hurry up a story or send someone out on a fresh one. There were several women reporters, of whom the cleverest was Margaret Lane, a great beauty with fair hair and very blue eyes whose name still appears at the head of book reviews. There were certain hardy annuals on which cub reporters used to break their teeth: Cruft's Dog Show at the Crystal Palace, the Trooping of the Colour, the University Boat Race, the Lord Mayor's Show, the crowd at the Chelsea Flower Show, and so on. I covered them all, some more than once. I nearly got myself into trouble over the Boat Race. Having thought myself recently quite a figure at Oxford, I used to dread having to go and interview the crews as they came to the boat house. None of them recognized me, but as I knew nothing about rowing, my interviews were puerile and I was amazed that anything got printed. The second or third time I had to cover the race, I skipped the interviews and tried to write something about the people who were watching. I never went to the boat house at all. When I got back to the office the News Editor sent for me and said he hoped I would build my story around the flood which had covered the boat house jetty and the tow path. He looked crestfallen when I said there was no flood on the banks of the river where I had been, so I rushed to the evening papers and concocted an amalgam of the accounts of the difficulties the crews had had in launching their boats. The news room seemed quite pleased with it.

At some point in 1931 or 1932, I became assistant to Jack Broadbent, the lobby correspondent in the House of Commons, and was given a lobby ticket. Lobby correspondents have the right not only to go into the press gallery to listen to debates but to enter the Lobby through which Members themselves enter and leave the Chamber. There, or more often in the passages leading to the Lobby, they waylay Members and try to find out what is really going on behind the scenes. The relationship between correspondents and Members, whether Ministers or back-benchers, is intimate and delicate. Members want publicity for their pet causes and Ministers want a good press for the bills they are proposing. The Opposition front bench is always on the lookout for ammunition with which to berate the Government, and its Members are not above swapping titbits with well-informed journalists. It is a process of give-and-take which depends on mutual trust. Members and Ministers will often talk freely to journalists on the understanding that they are not to be quoted and it is a golden rule among lobby correspondents not to attribute a remark to a Member without permission. On the whole, the system works well and Jack

Broadbent was a trusted and good-natured man who understood his business. I learned a lot from him.

Faces and incidents stand out in my memory like photographs in an album. Victor Cazalet, Peter's elder brother and Member for Chippenham, gave a lunch in the House for Margot Asquith, widow of the former Prime Minister, and made me sit next to her. She so dominated the table from the moment we sat down that I was never able to address a remark to her. In the Chamber Lloyd George made several long speeches, particularly upon agriculture. He looked sage and elegant and used pince-nez, which hung round his neck on a black ribbon, as a prop rather than to help him with his notes, at which he hardly glanced. His voice was mellifluent, but although the House stayed to hear him, nobody any longer cared about what he said. Ramsay MacDonald's voice also had magic. I had met him once or twice, first when he came to visit the Archbishop at Bishopthorpe in 1924 or 1925, just after he had proudly claimed the recognition of the revolutionary Soviet Government as one of the first Labour Government's finest achievements. He had brought his daughter, Ishbel, who was shy and silent, whereas her father's Scottish brogue reverberated through the passages, much to the delight of his host, Cosmo Lang, a fellow Scot. Later I saw him being lionized at a ball at Londonderry House in Park Lane. A few years later MacDonald committed political suicide by courageously agreeing to form a national government in coalition with the Conservative leader, Stanley Baldwin, so as to carry through the measures necessary to save the pound from collapse and the country from ruin. The Labour Party never forgave him. When I first listened to him in the House, he was still Prime Minister and his brogue was still in evidence, but his mind was wandering and his speeches had become embarrassing.

I also heard Winston Churchill make his first speech after leaving office as the Chancellor of the Exchequer. It must have been in 1929 or 1930, before I became a lobby correspondent. He had been out of office for some months and had lain low, but the word had gone round that he was to speak that day and I must have been there as a visitor, or perhaps Jack Broadbent had taken me. Winston came in and climbed the gangway to sit on the very highest bench with his back against the wall. When the Speaker called him he began, looking round as if in alarm: 'Unaccustomed as I am to these dizzy heights . . .' and the

House roared with laughter. For a fallen Cabinet Minister it was an irresistible way to begin his comeback, but he was to spend another ten years on the back benches, and, but for Hitler, might never have left them.

*

The daily routine of reporting was occasionally interrupted by a trip abroad. In 1931, Mr George Lane, Margaret Lane's father and Editor of the *Sunday Dispatch*, to which I had been transferred, sent me to write about the battlefields in France. I visited the Somme and all the war graves around Ypres. The trenches on Vimy Ridge were on either side of the crater which had been formed by the explosion of a land mine and one could easily hear the voices of fellow visitors in what was once the German front line forty yards away. A member of the staff of the War Graves Commission took me across a shallow little valley covered in poppies to try and explain to me the battle of Loos. 'The first time I crossed this valley,' he said, 'I trod on nothing but human bodies, half covered in mud.' I noticed that all the trees were still saplings.

The most moving moment came at the Menin Gate at Ypres. A week or two before, in the course of some extensive road repairs a few hundred yards outside the Gate, workmen had discovered an old dug-out several feet under the ground. It had obviously been sealed by some major explosion. When the workmen first uncovered it they saw several men in uniform lying in their bunks as they had been when the explosion occurred. In just a few seconds the bodies had dissolved into dust. I was shown the spot just before sunset, and then asked to wait. As the sun went down, two men in mufti, carrying bugles, emerged from the Menin Gate, walking on either side of the road. They stopped, turned towards Passchendaele, which rose gently across the fields in front of them, and together played the Last Post. Then the two war veterans slowly turned and walked back whence they had come. I am told that exactly the same ritual is still performed every day.

For two winters I became the *Daily Mail*'s hunting correspondent. It was a miraculous assignment and meant that I could hire a horse to ride with any pack of hounds in the country and have all expenses paid. Instead, therefore, of hiring cheap horses, as I had at Oxford, I hired the best and chose my own time and place. To my surprise, even some of the old hands in the news room liked the hunting reports. They said it added something entirely fresh to the paper. In the end I found I had hunted with sixty-six different packs of hounds, not quite half the total number in the country.

My base for all this activity was a flat in Reeves Mews, just behind the Connaught Hotel. It belonged to John Cowdray who had succeeded his father as Viscount in 1933 and lived nearby at 54 Mount Street. The flat cost eight pounds a week and consisted of two bedrooms and a servant's room, a sitting room, dining room and kitchen. A succession of friends came to share it with me between 1931 and 1936. My salary had begun at the minimum for a journalist, four hundred pounds a year, but this could be augmented by the occasional paragraph for gossip columnists like Charles Graves or Lord Donegal, and generous expenses. Soon after I had joined the *Daily Mail*, an elderly reporter saw me making out an expense sheet and sat down beside me. 'You don't want to waste time on these works of fiction,' he said. 'Let me explain.' He told me that it was impossible to keep track of all the little items for which one could reasonably charge and that this was well understood. So long as you were reasonable, no one asked questions. Working on any story you would have to take taxis, sometimes buy drinks for the people you were interviewing, and pay for your own meals, hotels and transport outside London. These were the basics. The total varied according to the work you had done, but could amount to twenty or thirty a pounds a week for a junior reporter and seldom came to less than ten pounds, and you received your expenses in cash from an expenses cashier on Friday afternoons. I do not suppose we actually made money on our expenses, but the cash was tax-free and kept us going. Life was cheap. Two grilled herrings in any pub or lunch bar cost around three shillings and beer was sixpence a pint.

During the London Season one seldom paid for a dinner. There were innumerable dances, almost all of which were given in private houses. If you were lucky enough to get on the list of young men which hostesses circulated among themselves, you lived in a white tie and tailcoat four evenings a week. A lady giving a dance for her daughter arranged for you to dine, either with her or with one of her friends. There were a few 'musts'. You always asked your dinner hostess to dance and the lady giving the dance, if you knew her. You also asked the girls next to whom you sat at dinner. You were supplied with programmes on which the dances were numbered one to twenty, and you found you had soon filled in the first six with the little pencil that hung from the programmes on a ribbon. After that you felt free. Quite often you had invitations to more than one dance on the same evening. Once, I remember, there were four dances in Berkeley Square, to each of which the inhabitants of Reeves Mews had been invited. It was a lovely night and, having done our duty dances, we wandered round looking for our favourite girls. Many of the houses were not very large and the dancers 'sat out' on the stairs. Occasionally a host or hostess would make their way past the couples to go to their bedroom and find a young couple in occupation. The culprits were turned out of the house forthwith and were unlikely to be asked to that or many other houses again.

Dances were not an unmixed pleasure. Bands varied, as did partners. Not all the girls were pretty or good dancers; the men were often shy and gauche. There have been many descriptions of the agonies girls went through when they were without partners and had to keep each other company in the cloakroom; the men were luckier in that they could spend some time talking to each other by the bar or stand in groups at the edge of the dance floor, pretending they were looking for some special friend. My worst experiences occurred in America, where the habit of 'cutting in' meant that no sooner had you found one of the few girls you knew than some other man took her away from you. You had to be very brave, or brash, to cut in on a girl you had never seen before, and she might refuse to dance with you. One of my hosts on Long Island was John Schiff, an Oxford friend whose father had collected a famous library. Many of the books had been sold, but during the dance I found my way to the library and sat reading until I felt I could respectably go home. It was at this dance that I first saw Virginia Cowles, dancing with Roger Chetwode with whom I had shared my flat in London and who now lived in New York, but I was not introduced and did not speak to her.

Occasionally I went down to Mereworth, Esmond Harmsworth's house in Kent, built in imitation of Palladio's famous villa, the Rotunda, at Vicenza in Italy, and played lawn tennis. Esmond regularly played in the doubles at Wimbledon and often invited some of the stars to Mereworth for the weekend.

Charles Kingsley, who was England's number one in the Davies Cup for many years, was a regular visitor, and one weekend Brugnon, one of the famous French quartet of the 1930s, came to stay. Several

85

times I played with Kingsley against Esmond and the Frenchman. It was the highest-class tennis in which I ever took part.

*

In 1932 Esmond Harmsworth sent me to work in the provinces. Northcliffe Newspapers were nearing the end of a long war against another chain, Allied Newspapers, owned by Lord Kemsley. Both proprietors aimed at eliminating their rival in cities where each had a newspaper, but after several years' struggle neither had won. In the end, which came when I was working for Esmond's chain, they reached a compromise whereby each would sell his paper to the other in cities where the 'war' had proved it could not be won. Honours were about even, but it meant that several long-established evening newspapers disappeared. On the other hand, those which survived could look forward to a stable future. The agreement ushered in an era when provincial papers became so profitable that they were often able to carry the parent company's national daily.

When my colleagues on the *Daily Mail* heard that I was leaving for the provinces they said I was very lucky; one learned far more about newspapers on a local daily than in a large London office. They were right. During the next year I worked successively in Bristol, Swansea, Gloucester, Leicester, Derby and Manchester. Except in Manchester, which printed a northern edition of the *Daily Mail*, I was working on evening newspapers, not just as a reporter: I worked in advertising, distribution and circulation. I became a sub-editor, leader-writer, features editor and did a short stint as a police court reporter. I made many new friends and got to know many parts of England better than if I had lived in them.

I spent longest in Swansea and Bristol. The Editor of the *Swansea Evening Post* took me under his wing. I sat in on the morning conferences, worked at the sub-editor's table, watching the paper being printed and packed, and finally went out with the vans which distributed it in the valleys in the early mornings. Strangely, the packers provided the most glamour. As they folded and tied the bundles of papers and threw them in a human chain to the waiting vans, they would sing the Bach chorales in parts and keep their movements in time with the music. Welsh voices are like no others and when the

86

drivers and anyone else in the packers' shed joined in, they formed a splendid choir.

Out in the valleys our van moved fast through the villages, as we threw the labelled bundles on to the doorsteps of the village news-agents; but when we reached Neath, Llanelly or other towns, the tempo would slow down. By six a.m. the queues had started forming, not to buy newspapers but to collect the dole. In 1932 there were 2,750,000 people out of work in the United Kingdom, a high proportion of whom had been so for more than a year. Several of the men had been joining the queue since 1930. They squatted on the pavement and sat silently waiting while the van did the round of agents in the town. I used to give them a few copies of the paper and talk to them. Few were bitter; they had simply lost hope. Some of the younger men said they had walked all over England looking for jobs.

I was to meet just such a man a few weeks later. Driving back to Windsor late one Friday night I saw a figure stumbling along on the left-hand side of the road. I stopped and gave him a lift. I could tell from his accent that he was Welsh. He said he had walked all over the West Country and was now on his way to London; he was in a bad way and kept falling asleep in the car from exhaustion. I took him home. My father had just become Canon of Windsor and lived at 4 The Cloisters, just behind St George's Chapel. I had a lovely room at the top of the house, overlooking Eton College Chapel. We got the young man upstairs and on to my younger brother's bed in the room next door to mine. He fell asleep immediately. We undressed him but his feet had swollen so badly that we had to cut off his boots. He smelt. Next day we let him sleep while I found some old clothes that would fit him and bought him a new pair of boots. He had a bath and ate a huge lunch, but nothing would make him stay another night, nor would he accept the rail fare to London. He kept saying that in London he knew he would find work. Before he left he asked for only one favour: a postcard of Windsor Castle on which I marked the window of the room in which he had slept. Otherwise, he said, no one would believe him when he told them.

The dole queues in the valleys of South Wales, and above all the memory of that young man, changed my life. What struck me most was his indomitable courage. He never complained, he hated the idea of being a charge on his fellow men and was reluctant even to accept a pair of boots as a gift. He was unshakeable in his belief that he could stand on his own feet and was determined to find a job. Moved by his spirit I started thinking seriously about what could be done to help such people and began reading the books I had neglected at Oxford: Maynard Keynes' *General Theory of Employment, Interest and Money*, Marx's *Das Kapital*, Evan Durbin's *Democratic Socialism*, G.D.H. Cole, Harold Laski and other writers of the Left Book Club. Had Professor Popper finished his great study *The Free Society*, or Walter Bagehot been available in paperback, I should probably have devoured both and my conclusions might have been different. As it was, I was veering towards socialism, but the final decisions still lay ahead.

The Editor of the *Bristol Evening World* was 'Blos' Lewis, a former cartoonist who still doodled in the same vein. He was short, on the heavy side, with a round face obscured by spectacles but enlivened by a permanent twinkle. He was enjoying the battle with the *Bristol Evening Post*, a respectable tabloid belonging to Allied Newspapers. He was determined to win and spent half his time trying to anticipate his competitor's next circulation gambit, whether a quiz, a 'give-away', or a vicious attack on the *World*. He would frequently meet the opposition Editor at lunches or other functions and come back chortling with delight at his complaints. Blos was immensely helpful to me.

Knowing I had been a reporter, he made me start as a sub-editor, a function which entails taking reporters' stories, which may run to half a column or more in length, and cutting them to the two or three column inches the chief sub-editor prescribed, keeping the essence of the story as far as possible. Usually it was possible. Subbing is a discipline to which every reporter should be subjected. It teaches him economy in the use of words and discrimination in assessing what any story is worth.

The *Evening World*'s chief sub-editor, a Welshman named Emrys Jones, was a delight to work with. If he thought I had emasculated a story, he would ask to see the original and spot at once where I had gone wrong. After some weeks he and Blos decided I should have a fortnight as chief sub-editor myself. This meant not only deciding which news stories should be used but deciding the length and position of each, planning the layout of each page, including the advertisements, choosing the typeface for the headlines, and finally going upstairs to the compositors' room and 'putting the pages to bed' in the frames containing the metal type from which the stereotype plates were cast for the presses. This last phase entailed learning to read the metal type upside down. During my fortnight Blos and Emrys hardly ever interfered but were always there to consult. At the end they gave me a dinner and told me some of the things they would have done differently.

A settlement with Allied Newspapers was reached before I left Bristol and plans were made to expand the *Evening World*. But by then I was back in London. In 1933 Mr Lane sent me to the United States to report on the New Deal. I began in Washington where I had a letter to Sir Willmott Lewis, *The Times'* correspondent who was also the doyen of foreign correspondents in the capital. Franklyn Roosevelt had been elected President a few months before and Lewis took me to one of the President's press conferences, at which he asked several questions, mainly about the National Reconstruction Administration (NRA). The atmosphere was electric. It was clear from their questions that many American journalists believed that Roosevelt had given General Hugh Johnson, the administrator of the NRA, such powers that he was bound to run foul of the Constitution (which he duly did) and bring about the collapse of the whole of the New Deal. But the spirit of hope which permeated the NRA overcame all obstacles. Aided by the massive inflation generated by Government and the banks, a recovery began. Roosevelt was said to be familiar with the work of Maynard Keynes; if so, he certainly chose the ideal moment at which to apply Keynes' theories and did so with greater success than any other statesman.

This was the high point of Roosevelt's career. The stock market crash of 1929 had undermined the self-confidence of millions of Americans. Everyone had been involved in it, from the highest to the lowest. Being still a nation of pioneers they enjoyed a gamble and suddenly what had seemed a harmless flutter had become a catastrophe. Roosevelt refused to allow remorse and lifted his people back on to their feet. His speeches, and particularly his slogan, 'The only thing we have to fear is fear itself', were as inspiring to Americans in 1932 as Winston Churchill's speeches were to the British in 1940. I was caught up in an extraordinary enthusiasm. A decade later, when Roosevelt's powers were declining and he was coming under influences many of which I thought malign, I used to remind myself of the occasions when I saw him at his best. For ten years he had been one of the greatest of Americans and the British will always have many things for which to be grateful to him.

Through Willmott Lewis I met General Johnson, robust and cheerful in the face of constant criticism; Henry Wallace, a justly famous Minister of Agriculture who helped farmers without giving way to their extreme demands; and Henry Morgenthau, a young but rising star in the Treasury. What surprised me was the ease with which Lewis arranged the appointments. In England, a young and inexperienced journalist would have had no chance whatever of seeing any senior Minister. But Wallace and Morgenthau in particular let me fire at them every question in my head, and answered patiently. I do not think this meant that the press was more powerful in the United States than in Britain (there were after all no national newspapers) but Americans in public life knew far better how to handle the press than their British counterparts.

After I had visited various employment centres, someone in New York told me that if I wanted to meet young people who had made original use of the Depression, I ought to visit one of the nudist camps. Tens of thousands of Americans had been living in these camps all over the country for the last two or three years, the most enterprising moving from one to another, keeping fit and following the sun. I rang up an address I had been given near Poughkeepsie, up the Hudson River in New York State, explained that I was writing articles for an English newspaper and asked if I might come for a weekend. The voice at the other end was friendly, said that so long as I obeyed their rules they would be delighted if I came, but added that they would prefer it if I brought a lady. I then spent some hours persuading a girlfriend that it was her duty to accompany me, and we set off.

The nudist colony was in a sort of manor house hotel, the owners of which had bought a farm with a large lake in the middle. We arrived at eleven o'clock on a cold grey Saturday morning to be met by an attractive, but fully dressed woman, the manageress, who took us up to our rooms. She showed us the bathroom and said that as the whole of the colony would be assembling in the hall to meet us at midday, would we please be down by then, of course without any clothes. My girl, who shall be called Connie, looked glum. It was grey and raining outside, and she thought it absurd to take off her clothes where her instinct would have been to put more on. I pointed out that the hotel was warm and that she would feel very odd in a skirt and blouse when everyone else would be naked. I said I would undress first and then knock on her door and wait for her. In ten minutes she had overcome her nerves and came out smiling. In a few minutes the manageress, still fully dressed, came to fetch us. She led us along a passage to a door which opened on a staircase leading down into the main hall. I noticed the walls were covered with antlers.

The hall was large, rather empty and square. Across it in a large semi-circle were ranged the members of the colony, men and women of all ages and all naked. I admit I had to take a deep breath as I followed the manageress downstairs. Connie had insisted I go first. When we got down the manageress introduced us to everyone in turn. It was a daunting experience. Our fellow nudists were of every shape and size and all white, allowing for the suntan which had turned some brown. At first I did not know where to look, then decided that 'the eyes had it' (to misuse a House of Commons phrase) and moved from one pair to the next with my chin up. Connie was being cheerful and rather flippant behind me. As we trooped into the dining room she whispered to me, 'I could hardly resist ringing the men's bells.'

The weekend was full of surprises. It did not take more than a few minutes to realize that nudity is not an aphrodisiac. The human form has many aspects and almost all are more attractive clothed. Connie had a lovely figure but I began to wish she could cover it. Meals were a hazard. There must have been fifty of us and the chairs with which we were provided had wooden slatted seats so that everyone got up with zebra-like stripes across their bottoms. The manageress insisted that we mix, and would tell me where to sit. Once it was between two very large ladies. We were eating roast beef and the difficulty of cutting it without sticking an elbow into an outsized bosom was such that one inevitably spilt the gravy over oneself or one's neighbour. However, nobody seemed to mind.

The weather cleared and it became a lovely weekend. We spent most of our time on or in the lake, which was equipped with diving boards and dinghies. The young, who dived and swam expertly, looked magnificent. After the first day, one ceased to think about being naked except for at odd moments. I kept feeling automatically for my pockets. Women were allowed bags but no make-up, so I made Connie carry my handkerchief in her bag. Twice a day we did what were called 'gymnastics'. This meant standing in rows with a nude instructor in front of us, doing all the physical exercises one had done at school: arms behind the neck, swinging one's body to right and left, double knee-bend and stretch, press-ups, and bending down with legs apart, swinging first the right hand to the left foot and then vice versa. As one did this last exercise, one's eyes inevitably looked back between one's legs down the row behind, and met an astonishing vista. We returned to New York by boat and Connie admitted she had enjoyed herself.

When I got back to England, friends told me that there were also nudist camps in England and that my article would be much more interesting if I could make a comparison. I went to an address, called Forest Row, which turned out to be in the suburbs of Eastbourne. When I arrived, I found myself in a street of houses, only one of which had a garden with a high wattle fence around it. The first thing I saw when I entered was a lady, naked except for a white mink coat. Somehow Eastbourne did not come off. There was nothing to do, no swimming pool or even ping-pong. If one wanted to swim, one had to dress, get into a car and go down to the beach, where one wore bathing shorts. It was all quite proper, but most people dressed and left the camp for much of the time to go to the movies or the pier. My article duly appeared – illustrated – in the *Sunday Dispatch*. After morning service in church a lady came up to my father, who had preached the sermon, and commiserated with him on having a son who could do a thing like that.

12

A World Tour

It was at Mereworth that Esmond suddenly said to me that he wanted me to go round the world with him. He was not sure how far he would travel himself but when he decided to return home he would like me to continue the journey, writing articles for the *Daily Mail* and *Sunday Dispatch*. We were to start off with his father, who wanted a sea trip, and drop him off either at Alexandria or Port Said. We would then sail through the Suez Canal and the Red Sea to Bombay. After India we were to go on to Burma, Singapore, Hong Kong, China and Japan.

Lord Rothermere had a house at Monte Carlo and it was from there that we set out in the late autumn of 1933, arriving at Genoa and picking up an Italian liner, the *Vittorio*, which made regular trips to the Far East. George Ward-Price, the *Mail*'s roving correspondent, came with Lord Rothermere, and Sir Perceval Phillips, a greying middle-aged, rather portly man who had been a war correspondent and was now head of the foreign affairs staff in Tudor Street, with Esmond.

Harold Harmsworth, the first Lord Rothermere, was not a journalist like his brother Lord Northcliffe, who founded the *Daily Mail*. He was interested mainly in money. His features were coarse and his mind unsubtle, capable of bombast rather than reason. Under him the policy of the *Daily Mail* oscillated between strident advocacy of rearmament and appeasement of the dictators. Ward-Price, who wore a monocle and was an able journalist, echoed his master's voice.

While we cruised through the Mediterranean, Lord Rothermere and Ward-Price played endless games of shuffle-board, interrupted only when the former, who was gambling heavily in currency, sent the latter off to the ship's radio operator to buy or sell francs, marks, lire, drachmas, dollars or pounds sterling by the million. He never dealt in less and when he died in 1940 he left his son huge debts which the latter managed to pay only partly by selling his shares in the *Daily*

Mirror to his cousin, Cecil Harmsworth-King. Esmond and I played deck tennis. Sir Perceval was rather indignant at being made to come on what he called 'a rich man's junket' but was a knowledgeable companion.

I had already seen the Suez Canal from the land and had always thought it rather comic to watch great ships gliding, as it appeared, through the desert; now I was on such a ship myself and I felt the desire to jump from the ship on to the sand which was within a few feet of us on either side. We called at Jeddah in the Red Sea, where Sir Perceval said there was an Englishman who could arrange a day's fishing for swordfish and tuna, but the *Vittorio* did not stay long enough. The passage across the Indian Ocean was smooth and warm and we reached Bombay just after dawn with a rising red sun silhouetting all the city's towers and buildings. On the way we had spent several evenings with the Maharajah of Alwar, a strict Hindu who dressed each day in white, with white gloves. He boasted that he had never shaken hands with an Englishman or any other 'untouchable' without his gloves. He was a fine polo player, but we were told that when one of his ponies played badly it had been burned.

In Bombay we stayed briefly with the Governor, Lord Brabourne, who lived in considerable state in a white house on a hill. While there, we each acquired a 'bearer' who was to stay with us as a personal servant during our tour of India. Mine came from the Punjab, wore a turban and was called Abdul. Before I engaged him he showed me a series of letters written by Englishmen who had employed him previously, from which I gathered that he was a paragon. In many ways he was. He cleaned shoes and boots impeccably, made sweet tea at all hours, stood over the 'dhobi man' (who did the washing) to see that he did not ruin my shirts while slapping them on flat stones, and guarded me and my possessions with a zeal which became exhausting. Wherever we stayed, he took charge of my rooms, often sleeping in the passage outside. He woke me in the morning and was always waiting outside my door when I went to bed. He called me 'master' and made me feel I was the most important man on earth. The bearers belonging to Esmond and Sir Perceval he treated with disdain.

Our bearers joined us on the private train which Esmond had hired for the tour. It was gleaming white and had four coaches, three of them air-conditioned, and a guard's van. It was pulled by a steam engine

94

My father as Canon of Windsor in 1935, in the garden of 4, The Cloisters, Windsor Castle

My mother in the early 1930s

'The Arch' (Cosmo Lang), with me and my elder brother Cosmo, in the garden at Bishopthorpe Palace, 1925

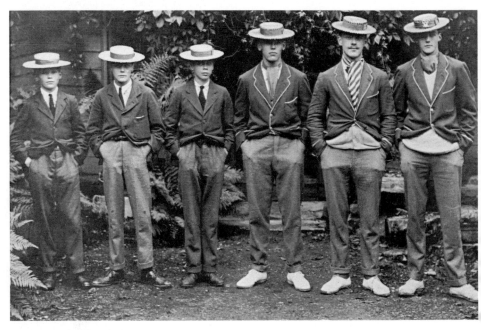

Six Crawleys in 'the Park' at Harrow School, 1922.
Left to right: Charles, myself, David, Eliot, Leonard, Cosmo

With my brothers Cosmo and Kenneth at
Praewood, St Albans, 1929

With John Cowdray at his 21st birthday
party, at Cowdray Park, Midhurst,
Sussex, February 1931

Going out to bat for Oxford against Cambridge at Lord's with
Alan Barber, 1929

with a high funnel; our route had been arranged by Indian Railways, whose head was an English member of the Railway Service. The coaches provided a dining room, sitting room and bedrooms, with an extra coach for baggage and staff. The train did not go very fast and the track was not very smooth, but it was by far the most comfortable way of travelling in India. Our route was to take us to the Central Provinces, the capital of which was Nagpur, then through Rajasthan where we were to visit the princely states of Bhopal and Bikaner. Then we would go up into the Punjab, through Patialia and on to Peshawar from where we would visit both the Khyber Pass and Kohat on the frontiers of Baluchistan, and so back east to Delhi where we were to stay with the Viceroy, Lord Willingdon. Afterwards we were to go to Agra, then down the Ganges to Lucknow, Cawnpore, Benares and Calcutta.

At Nagpur in the Central Provinces we stayed with the Governor, Sir Malcolm Hailey, one of Britain's most distinguished Civil Servants. He was then ruling forty-eight million Indians with forty-eight District Officers, most of them in their twenties, and had only one platoon from the Indian Army upon which to call in an emergency. So far he had only used the platoon on ceremonial occasions. With Sir Malcolm we began to get the feel of India. We had all read the report of the Simon Commission, and were aware of the emergence of elected provincial governments with Indian Ministers. We all knew educated Indians, but what we did not know at first hand was the life of the villages in India and I doubt if we could have found anybody better with whom to begin learning about it. Early each morning, wearing a light grey riding suit and a grey bowler hat with a curled brim, Sir Malcolm took us riding through the villages, telling us the history of the Central Provinces as we went and then dismounting and talking to each of the village headmen and often some others as well, in their own language. We covered a different area each morning. Sir Malcolm knew the name of every headman and often the man's family history. His interest was personal. He trusted his District Officers and would never interfere with them; one felt that at heart he was still a D O himself.

Many years later, after India had become independent, I was able to get to know Indian villagers myself by living among them, if only for weeks rather than years. The welcome that Virginia and I received, and the intimacy we were able to establish with several families, completely belied the impression given by many television series of strained relations between British and Indians. Of course, there were tensions, but in the villages and small towns where the majority of Indians lived, the relationship was generally one of trust and often of affection.

Our journey through Rajasthan was more of a Grand Tour than a journalistic enquiry. At Bhopal the Maharajah, a Moslem ruling a mainly Hindu population, had organized a tiger shoot in Esmond's honour. The camp was deep in the jungle. Large khaki tents had been set up either side of a 'street' of smooth, sandy earth edged by white-washed stones. In front of each tent was a post with a board at its head which bore a printed notice giving the name of the occupant. Inside, the tents were carpeted with Persian and Indian rugs and furnished with a camp bed, arm chairs and a wash stand with tin basins into which one's bearer poured hot water. A separate tent served as a common dining room and sitting room.

For the shoot the guns were spread out across the jungle in a line of 'machans', rough platforms made of branches and built into low trees. Beaters, who had already covered several miles on elephants, on horses or on foot, finally closed in. I was in a machan at the end of the line accompanied by one of the Maharajah's staff. The jungle was very dry; buck and wild pig scampering by made a loud rattle among the dead leaves. Suddenly my companion touched my arm and pointed. About a hundred yards ahead was a tiger moving very slowly and quite noiselessly towards us, turning his head from side to side in suspicion at the sounds the beaters were making behind him. If he continued on his course he would pass about twenty yards to our right. I waited until I received a signal from my companion, then fired when the tiger was about thirty yards away. It dropped instantly. As soon as they heard the shot every beater on foot climbed a tree so that the jungle was festooned with red turbans looking like a forest of giant rhododendrons. My companion looked at the tiger through his binoculars, pronounced it dead, and gave a signal which allowed the beaters to descend.

When we had climbed down I asked him how the tiger had moved so silently over the dead leaves when everything else made such a noise. He explained that when a tiger is frightened or hunting, it opens its claws before putting its foot down and very gently crunches the dead leaves so that there is no sound. As our feet touched the ground I looked back at the machan and noticed it was only about ten feet above the ground. An angry tiger could easily have reached it. Esmond, who had been in the centre of the line, and for whom the tiger was intended, was delighted at my luck. We all took photographs and followed the tiger, which was carried slung upside down on a pole, back to the camp to celebrate. I have its skin to this day and it is now my grandson who plays with its teeth.

From Bhopal we travelled north to Bikaner, ruled by another Rajput. The Maharajah was something of a caricature, with a loud voice, drooping black moustaches and a heartiness which was English rather than Indian. He wore English clothes. But he was a most generous host. Wherever we went in the palace, servants with trays bearing whiskies and sodas would follow us. The food was excellent and the champagne dry. The chief entertainment was a shoot at sand grouse.

A sand grouse is grey rather than red, but it tastes like a grouse. It lives only in hot climates and is hardy enough to withstand considerable variations in temperature. The shoot at Bikaner, which was famous, took place near water holes to which the sand grouse came at dawn. By using a small army of beaters to keep the birds away from the holes for forty-eight hours, the Maharajah ensured that they all came at the same time the following day. Guns were placed in little hides of reeds, scattered at quite wide intervals among the water holes. The birds flew in coveys at a height of about twenty feet and one was warned of their approach by a twittering they made as they neared water. There was no wind so the first shot was comparatively easy, but as soon as a shot was fired the birds scattered and dived like rock pigeon. The number of birds varies each year with the weather and the amount of water. Ours was not considered a good year although ten guns shot nearly two thousand birds in three hours. My gun barrels were too hot to hold with bare hands.

Our next stop was Patiala, further north on the borders of the Punjab. The Maharajah, Bhupinder Singh, and most of his subjects were Sikhs. He was not in good odour with the British because it was alleged that when he coveted a man's wife, which was not infrequently, he contrived to have the husband disappear. There was no evidence of murder but considerable suspicion. When we reached Delhi we even heard talk of suspension of his rule. None of this, however, spoiled our entertainment and for once it was I, and not Esmond, who was the focus of attention. My father had stayed with the Maharajah's father in the 1890s and played cricket on a ground which had recently been made by cutting the top off a hill. The Singh family were all good cricketers, and our host, the heir to the man my father stayed with, ran his own cricket team. His son, a few years younger than me, was nearly good enough to play for India a few years later. My father had written to Bhupinder Singh to remind him of his own visit and after dinner on the first night the Maharajah turned to me and said kindly, 'Mr Crawley, what would you like to do tomorrow?' I had been warned by Colonel Lucas, his English Master of the Horse, that something like this might happen and after slight hesitation I asked if it would be possible to stick a pig.

The Maharajah turned to Colonel Lucas and said, 'Colonel Lucas, Mr Crawley will stick pig tomorrow. You will parade a squadron of elephants, two squadrons of cavalry and a company of infantry and provide him with the horses he needs.' He then turned to Esmond and asked him if he would like to join the party. Esmond said he would prefer to shoot. When that had been arranged, the Maharajah turned back to me and said that as he understood that I had never been pig-sticking before, it might be a good thing if I joined the Patiala Lancers who would be going with me the next morning. After perhaps a quarter of an hour an ADC asked me to accompany him to the Mess, which was in another part of the vast Motibagh Palace. The Lancers were in high spirits. As soon as I entered the room they sat me down, plied me with whisky and sodas and explained the tactics of pig-sticking. The country we were to ride in was not of the reed and sugar-cane variety I had seen in pictures of the Kadir Cup, but dead flat and covered in bushes, the thorns of which were unusually long and strong. The clearings were seldom more than five hundred yards long and when the beaters snuffed out a pig you had to be very quick off the mark. I was told we should ride five at a time in arrow-head formation and I was to take the lead. If the pig jinked when I got close to it, the next man would take it on and I would fall in behind him to the right or the left.

Having made sure I understood the tactics the Lancers then began to enjoy themselves. They were a fine-looking group, all with black beards, moustaches and turbans covering their uncut hair. They looked wonderfully fit. They told me that wild pig could be very nasty, especially when wounded. If by any chance I found myself on the ground, the best thing to do was to lie flat on my stomach, put my hands over the back of my neck and keep still. With luck the pig's tusks would run up my ribs instead of going through them. Then one of them murmured that it was not necessarily pig that we should meet; there were a lot of jaguar around and a jaguar had been known to run alongside a horse and then jump at the rider. If I saw a jaguar, the best thing I could do was to shorten my spear and try and kill it before it killed me. Having worked me into a state of lively anticipation, the Lancers then escorted me to bed. Plenty of whisky had ensured my sleep and we were out soon after dawn.

The weather was glorious and the horses Colonel Lucas provided were handy and fast, but the day did not turn out quite as I expected. What the Lancers had not told me was that a pig is faster than a horse for the first five hundred yards and in that country, where the clearings are so small, the leading rider very seldom makes the kill. It is much more likely to be the second, and more likely still to be the third in the arrowhead. They had also not reminded me that specially schooled horses will stop very suddenly or turn very sharply of their own accord when confronted with several yards of thornbush. So, I started the day in happy ignorance. There were plenty of pig, and riding in line, slapping our saddles and making sharp cries, we would drive them towards a clearing. Once the pig was in the open I rode for it. The Lancers fanned out behind. I had been warned not to lean too far out with my spear, but to hold it close, try and get the horse level with the pig's shoulder, aim for the heart behind the shoulder and let the horse's weight drive the spear in. Several times I got level with the pig, with the point of my spear within two or three inches of its flank, only to find that the pig had plenty of speed in reserve and would draw away with a slow, easy stride. I forgot about the thorn bushes.

A pig jinks almost at right angles. My horse would jump or avoid it with marvellous agility, and only then would I remember the thorn bushes ahead. If we had twenty yards clear, we would probably stay together, but often the pig only jinked at the last moment and my horse turned so sharply that, leaning forward with my spear as I was, I inevitably went over its head. The thorns were savage. When the Lancers returned, their faces were wreathed in grins. Once they had pulled me out of a bush, they would make me bend over and start extracting the thorns from my bottom with their fingers. It took several minutes. By then someone had retrieved my horse and we would start again. Three times during the morning, one of the tailenders speared a pig and there was great rejoicing. It was certainly one of the most exciting and enjoyable days of my life.

*

Peshawar is only a short distance north from Patiala and we spent a few days there visiting the Afghan border at the Khyber Pass and Kohat which overlooks Baluchistan. Kohat was garrisoned by a unit of the Indian Army and the commander, an Englishman, was responsible for law and order in Baluchistan, a country so steep and barren that it was virtually impossible to patrol. Everything depended on his relationship with the chiefs. Some of them were paid or given arms to maintain the peace and, provided the British fulfilled their part, the chiefs confined their aggression to local family feuds.

The Pathans who inhabit most of this part of the world are amongst the most virile of races. The men are dark, swarthy and often very tall and never to be seen without a rifle in their hands and a bandolier over their shoulders. Sometimes as we drove around we heard shots coming from the towers which rise from the mud brick walls of every mountain village. We were told that they were probably aimed at the tower of a neighbouring village, often only a few hundred yards away. Rifles were made locally and we visited a rifle factory where men and women rotated drills by working pulleys with their toes while they used their hands for something else. Looking closely we saw that the drills were converting iron pipes into smooth bore rifle barrels. The finished rifle was reasonably accurate up to a hundred yards and had a lethal range four or five times as long.

My old friend and cricket coach at Harrow, Ronnie Holdsworth, had become deputy headmaster at the school to which most of the sons of the local chiefs were sent, Ismailia College near Peshawar. He was enjoying himself. The college had won a considerable reputation during the Afridi rebellion a few years earlier. The Afridis were an independent Pathan tribe inhabiting a part of Baluchistan and the North West Frontier of India who had risen because the British had failed to stop incursions by Moslem troops. Some thirty thousand Afridis had descended on the Punjab and were only prevented from occupying Peshawar by British soldiers. The school at Ismailia lay in their path and, while the English headmaster was in the middle of a lecture on Greek history, the Afridis had surrounded the school and entered it. All the masters were locked into one room. The tribesmen then assembled the boys in the main hall and conducted a debate on whether the teachers should be killed or not. By a small majority it was decided against, whereupon the teachers were released and returned to their classrooms. From the rostrum in the sixth form the headmaster resumed his lecture with the words: 'After that unforeseen interruption we will continue our study of Alexander the Great.'

Ronnie's current problem was caused by the new Anglican Bishop. As was well known to anyone who lived in the Punjab, the love of Pathans is for males rather than females. Women bear children but otherwise are treated as chattels. The boys in Ronnie's school had passionate affairs and fights; they used knives and daggers and were frequently sent to a hospital which the Bishop used to visit. After each visit he would lecture Ronnie on the evils of homosexuality and tell him that he must do something about it. Having failed to convince the Bishop that the customs of the Pathans were not easily changed, Ronnie had suggested that the Bishop go and visit the boys' parents who lived, sometimes in caves, in distant and inaccessible parts of the mountains. He was now waiting to see what the Bishop would do.

Peshawar was sunny but cold; New Delhi, our next port of call, was hot. Our reception at Viceroy's House was unexpected. I did not know that Esmond's special train was running behind schedule or that he had sent a telegram to the Military Secretary that we would be arriving twenty-four hours late. Outwardly everything appeared to be normal when we arrived. Several of the thousand or so servants of the house, all of them in scarlet and skirted uniforms with sashes and head-dresses, took charge of us and made us comfortable. But before we had met the Viceroy, Lord Willingdon, an ADC came to conduct Esmond and me into the presence of Lady Willingdon. She had a strong face, brown hair, was dressed in purple and sat at a table before which we were made to stand. She then told us that the Viceroy was the King's representative and that when he asked you to stay, you did not send a telegram at the last minute to say that you would be twenty-four hours late. Esmond, she said, was mostly to blame, as he was in charge of the expedition, but then, turning to me, she added that I ought to have known better and prevented Esmond from making such a mistake. After a pause she concluded the interview with the words: 'We shall meet again for dinner.' We apologized meekly and were led away. No further mention of the matter was ever made and we had a delightful visit.

There was a routine at Viceroy's House. Before breakfast we rode out with the ADCs. New Delhi was then so spread out that there was no difficulty in reaching fields without going along a road. Sometimes Lord Chetwode, the Commander in Chief, and his party would join us and we would canter round to some villages on the edge of the city. After breakfast we would see places like Hamayun's Tomb, the Qutb Minar, a fantastic tower begun in the eleventh century and finished in the fourteenth, Jai Singh's Observatory, or Tughlaquabad, a fortress-palace built in the fourteenth century on the site of the second Hindu city of Delhi. There would be Indians and British to lunch, then a siesta, then tennis, which both Lord and Lady Willingdon loved to play, a visit to the inter-racial Willingdon Club[1] or to someone's house in the evening and then a dinner party at which the Viceroy and Vicereine made a royal entry through double doors into the room where everyone was standing. The men bowed and the women curtsied.

One evening after dinner I talked to Zafrulla Khan, formerly a judge of the High Court, and then a member of the Viceroy's Council. He was a Moslem, and although an opponent of the idea of a separate Pakistan, in the end he had to accept it, and became Pakistan's first Foreign Minister. He was a brilliant man and after talking to him one felt the full impertinence of the idea held by many Englishmen that Indians were incapable of governing themselves.

Yet I did not despise the Raj. Indian history had been such a tangle of wars between races and feuds between rulers that without some unifying force it would have disintegrated, like China, and become the prey of every more sophisticated power. The Moguls had imposed order in the seventeenth century but their descendants had deteriorated. One sensed when one was with them that men like Alwar, Patiala and even Bikaner were incapable of bringing their people the full benefits offered by the twentieth century. By giving India order, justice and an uncorrupt administration, the Raj enabled a generation to grow up which made modern India possible. By 1947 the Indianization of the Indian Civil Service had proceeded so far that it was able not only to preserve the unity of the country but to withstand all the stresses created by partition, the abolition of princely rule, the rise of linguistic states and the threat from revolutionary China. The faults of the British were social rather than political. When I returned to India after Independence, I was to hear men like Nehru and Ambdedkar, leader of the untouchables, giving generous praise to us and was able to feel proud of men like Willingdon, Irwin and Linlithgow who had upheld the character and purpose of British rule.

From Delhi our train took us to Agra, Lucknow, Benares and finally to Calcutta. We saw the Taj Mahal by day and by moonlight. From the Fort at Agra, looking across the river Jumna, one tried to imagine what the view would have been like had Jehan been able to achieve his dream and build a twin Taj Mahal, but black, on the other bank. At Benares we went on the river and noticed two clothed and bloated corpses floating by within a few yards of bathing pilgrims, many of whom had brought bottles which they filled with the dirty but holy water of the Ganges.

Calcutta had ceased to be the capital of British India in 1911. The house which Lord Curzon had occupied as Viceroy, the Raj Bhavan, was now inhabited by Sir John Anderson, the Governor. The white marble memorial to Queen Victoria still stood before Government House, and Bengal Lancers, in full uniform with lances and shiny black thigh-boots, sat on their horses at the gates. Another Lancer, on foot, guarded the hall. Calcutta had been stirred by Gandhi's civil disobedience campaign and Sir John had had to deal with serious riots. We talked to some of the young British officers who had patrolled the streets. A lieutenant said that it was entirely up to him whether to give the order to fire or not. More than once his platoon had confronted a crowd several thousand strong and the position had looked ugly. But he added that he would only give such an order if the lives of his troops were in danger and so far it had not been necessary.

*

The flight to Rangoon from Calcutta was interesting because our pilot was correcting his maps on the way. We flew in an Armstrong Whitworth high-wing monoplane. It belonged to Imperial Airways which was developing the trunk route from the United Kingdom to Australia passing through Rangoon, Bangkok and Alor Star. There had been no proper survey of the route and many of the peaks in the Arakan Mountains, along the edge of which we flew, were several thousand feet higher than the map indicated. Over the mountains cumulus clouds rose to a height of 30,000 feet, but the coast was clear.

I remember little of Rangoon except the Golden Pagoda which dominated a city of mainly one-storied houses. The gold leaf on the pagoda shone brilliantly in the sun, but inside it was dark and dirty. Our host was Sir Arthur Page, the Chief Justice of Burma, who had been at Oxford with my father. Thick-set and rubicund with white hair in tufts on the side of his head, Sir Arthur was having some difficulty with taboo. In contrast to the sense in which the word is used in the West, in Burma taboo appeared to mean a sort of general spell. If a man laid a taboo on someone he disliked it could have a near hypnotic effect under which the victim became ill or even died. The Chief Justice told us of a recent case in which the father of a large family was laid under a taboo which made him believe he had supernatural powers and in particular that he could fly. He summoned his family and many friends into his garden, climbed to the roof, dived off it with his arms outstretched and broke his neck. The family charged the author of the taboo with murder. Sir Arthur had tried the case and the man had been acquitted, rightly as he thought. But the verdict had provoked a storm, particularly among those who believed in the efficacy of taboo.

We took to the air again to visit Bangkok, in which city a boat was still more useful than a car. Hardly any of the 'klongs' had been filled in and most of the bridges were only for pedestrians. The markets were all on the water. We flew on to Angkhor Wat in Cambodia, then part of French Indo-China. The aircraft was a French bi-plane, the wires between the wings being fastened by steel safety-pins; the flight was not scheduled but went fairly regularly. The jungle looked impenetrable but after about two hours the pilot found the airstrip and landed close to the ruins. The French Department of Antiquities had only begun excavating the site a few years before and there was a single small hotel in which one could stay. The jungle hid much of the ruins and trees were still growing through the roof-tiles and walls, but nevertheless in scale and magnificence they were the most impressive monuments any of us had ever seen. The vast area covered by the temple courtyards, the size of the towers, the solidity of the great cloisters (for want of the Cambodian word) and the beauty of the sculpture rivalled the best in Europe, India or the Middle East. It is one of the oddities of history that the Khmer civilization, which could achieve such marvels of construction and decoration, had apparently sprung from the jungle in the ninth century and flourished for only four hundred years before disappearing as mysteriously as it came.

As we walked round the cloisters we were aware of a disturbing and persistent noise, as if a wind were blowing gustily through the arches, yet the weather was hot and still. As our eyes became accustomed to the darkness under the stone-tiled cloister roofs, we began to notice shadowy movement: it was the flight of literally billions of bats which had lived there undisturbed for more than five centuries. The noise was the constant whirring of the bats' wings, eerie but not frightening since the animals hardly ever emerged into daylight and the roof of the cloister was at least twenty-five feet above our heads.

We were lucky in the day we had chosen to visit Angkhor. That evening there was a funeral for one of the Buddhist monks who still guarded the temples. We were taken to a great clearing close to the main temple's walls in the middle of which a high tower, a cross between the towers of Angkhor and a pagoda, had been made of wood and paper. On the lowest storey, a little above our heads, was a bier on which lay the body of the monk in his saffron robes. Two wires stretched from the bier to trees on the edge of the clearing, at least fifty yards away, and on each of the wires rode a papier mâché figure of a mounted knight in armour, dressed in silver paper with a spear in his hand. Prayers were intoned, and when they finished, two monks hidden in trees lit the spears (which had phosphorous tips) and then released the knights who flew down the wires towards the bier. As they got within a few feet, they were suddenly pulled back by a string running invisibly just under the wire.

The crowd, which had been streaming in from the jungle for hours and was several thousand strong, screamed with delight and was then silent, waiting for the performance to be repeated. Each time the knights began their descent, the crowd began to applaud on a low note which grew louder and shriller as they neared the bier. Then, when the knights were plucked back, the scream turned into a great sigh which immediately melted into laughter. How many times the knights made the run I did not count, but I have never seen a crowd enjoy itself so much except perhaps at the Bombay Test Match where seventy-five thousand people gave the Indian slow bowler, Chandrasekar, a similar vocal accompaniment as he approached the wicket. Eventually the knights at Angkhor were allowed to plunge their spears into the paper beneath the bier and the whole tower burst into flames. The people gave a final scream of delight, and happily drifted back into the jungle to their villages. Recently, when I have read of the Vietcong or Khmer Rouge fighting among the great temples, I have thought of that day in 1934.

After two days among the ruins we prepared to fly back to Bangkok. The aeroplane had been about half full on our outward journey, but when we rejoined it on the airstrip we noticed that there were many more passengers. The runway was simply a clearing in the jungle, surrounded by trees. Our pilot had pulled the aircraft to the backmost limits of the clearing, but even so apparently had some doubts. As soon as the door was shut he asked those at the rear to leave their seats and crowd up towards the front. We did as we were told, standing over the legs of those sitting near the cockpit. The plane roared off and cleared the trees by a few feet. We resumed our seats with relief.

Subsequent visits to Malaya have obliterated the memories of 1934. I know we went to Kuala Lumpur and Penang and called on the Sultan of Johore, but our stay was short. When we reached Singapore Esmond announced that he and Sir Perceval Phillips were going home; he hoped I would go on round the world and write articles. The 'rich man's junket' had been tremendous fun and we had all become friends, but the prospect of going on through China and Japan, of crossing the Pacific and recrossing America, quicky overcame any regrets at being left alone. I had hardly seen them off on their liner before I was caught up in a new adventure.

13

Treading the Boards

The Long Bar in Raffles Hotel was deserted except for a solitary barman busy polishing glasses. It was around one o'clock in the afternoon and I had just returned from the harbour where I had seen off Esmond Harmsworth and Sir Perceval Phillips. The day was hot. I sat on a bar-stool and ordered a lime juice and soda. After a few minutes a short, rather fat Englishman came in, obviously in a state of some distress, took a stool four or five away from me and ordered a double whisky and soda. The barman knew him and, as he gave him the drink, asked if anything was wrong. The stranger took a long gulp, looked at the barman and said that things could hardly be worse. He was due to open at the Garrison Theatre at seven-thirty that evening, and his 'junior lead' had run away with the harbour-master's daughter. The police were looking for them but were most unlikely to find them in time. Somehow he had to find somebody else. The stranger pushed his empty glass forward, ordered another drink and mopped his brow. Then for the first time he noticed me.

He asked if I was English, apologized for his outburst and introduced himself as James Grant-Anderson. 'My sister and I run a touring repertory company. We have just come from India where we had a marvellous time. Played to the troops up the Khyber Pass, had full houses in Bombay and Calcutta. And now this mess,' he said, spreading his hands. 'We're playing to the troops tonight. I've got to find someone to play the junior lead.'

I asked what the play was.

'*While Parents Sleep*,' he said, 'by Anthony Kimmins. Have you seen it?'

I hadn't, and asked what it was about.

'Oh, it's a love story within a Government House in a colony. Quite funny. The young man is seduced by the Governor's wife.' He finished his drink and rose to leave. 'Well, I must get going. Nice to have met you.' He turned away, but after a few paces stopped, turned back and looked at me.

'Have you ever been on the stage?' he asked.

'No, never.'

'Not in amateur theatricals?'

'Only at school.'

He came towards me. 'It is probably just as well,' he said. 'You're more likely to do what you're told. If you will come on tonight, I will say your lines for you. You won't have to learn a word. You simply do what Lena or I tell you. Lena is my sister and plays the Governor's wife.'

I hesitated. I had nothing particular to do before catching a Japanese boat, the *Taiyo Maru*, to Hong Kong the following day. He pressed me.

'Do come. You might enjoy the experience. As a matter of fact you probably won't be kept very long. We've played here before and never got through our second act. Some of the troops get drunk in the interval and as soon as we are back on the stage pandemonium breaks out. Cat calls, whistles and then everything comes at us, cushions, caps, oranges, apples. It is all good-natured but we have to lower the curtain, and that's it.'

I had made up my mind while he spoke. It would be far more amusing than having dinner by myself.

'All right,' I said. 'Where do we meet and at what time?'

He said he would send someone to fetch me at six-thirty. Meanwhile he would send me a copy of the play which I could read during the afternoon so that I should have a rough idea of what to expect.

I asked what clothes I would need.

'Just what you're wearing,' he replied and left in high spirits.

So began a hilarious fortnight. James was as good as his word. The play arrived and I read it twice with pleasure. It was racy and the dialogue quite crisp. In the second act I had to make love to the Governor's wife on a sofa. I wondered what Lena was like. The Garrison Theatre was a long barrack room with a stage and a curtain. I cannot remember all the details of the play but when I had to make an entry someone would stand by me in the wings and tell me exactly where to go and what to do. When I heard James' voice saying what I thought were my lines, I moved my lips silently. I learned two things quickly: an actor who turns away from the auditorium can say things in a low voice to other members of the cast which the audience does not hear. By the same token, a prompter can speak lines from the wings without being noticed except perhaps by people in the two front rows. When I was on the stage, either Lena or James would tell me quietly where to move. James not only spoke my lines but prompted other members of the cast who had forgotten theirs. I began to enjoy the whole thing.

And James had been right about the audience. The first act went quite smoothly with only a few interjections from the hall, but as soon as we began the second act the atmosphere changed. Hardly a line went by without an interruption and within a few minutes the audience had taken over. Men in uniform climbed on to the stage and started acting themselves. It was useless to say our lines because no one could hear. Then things began to be thrown, particularly the cushions which were on every chair in the auditorium. James kept his temper, told each of us to leave the stage quietly, persuaded the soldiers on the stage to return to their seats and lowered the curtain. The performance was over. When some officers came to apologize for the men's behaviour, James gave them drinks, told them he had known it would happen and sent them away with the impression that he had thoroughly enjoyed himself. In a way he had. There had been a long tradition of touring companies roaming the Empire; the Grant-Andersons' predecessor had been a man called Salusbury and the cast had included Noel Coward. Success depended upon improvisation and good nature. Sometimes after a long journey the company would find that although the cast had arrived at its destination, the scenery or clothes (or both) had been lost on the way. The producer would then have to create an illusion of furniture with empty packing cases and upright chairs. Each tour was an adventure and to bring one to a conclusion constituted a triumph.

As we sat and talked after the show was over, James and Lena regaled me with their experiences. Lena was small and vivacious with large grey eyes and an attractive voice. On the stage she was totally professional, prepared for every mistake, determined only to get through the performance. As they relied for perhaps a quarter of the cast on actors and actresses picked up locally, they often had to adapt parts to suit the performance. Before the night was through they had persuaded me to accompany them to Hong Kong and Shanghai, in each of which cities they were to play for a week. Their company was also travelling on the *Taiyo Maru* and they would rehearse me during the voyage. There were two plays to be learned, each of which was to be performed for three nights. I cannot remember the name of the second play, partly because we never performed it, but I did not like it as much as *While Parents Sleep*.

The journey from Singapore to Hong Kong took four days and four nights. James had scoured the ship for a place to rehearse and had decided on the upper deck, which, except for air vents, was clear. He persuaded the purser to provide a garden seat and one or two deck-chairs, and for several hours a day he and Lena took me through the play. I could remember the lines but I was wooden and self-conscious. One morning Lena got quite annoyed during the love scene and pulled me down on top of her by my hair. 'I know I'm not as unattractive as you make me feel,' she said. 'You have got to *want* to kiss me.' That evening the purser approached James and asked if everything was all right. A member of his crew had reported that Lena needed protection.

There was a proper theatre in Hong Kong and our first day was spent in full rehearsals. James had managed to recruit members of the local dramatic society to fill minor parts and we opened on schedule next day. There was a full house and the Governor and his house party occupied the front row of the dress circle. We had a good reception. I learned how important it was to keep up the pace during the perform-ance. When someone forgot their lines, James or Lena would ad lib until they remembered or heard the prompter. Once James asked me a question which was not in the script to give me my cue. On the third night one of the girls from the Hong Kong Dramatic Society had an argument with another member of the cast half an hour before the performance was due to begin and ran away down the street. I was just entering the theatre when James came panting up, pointed her out as she disappeared into the crowd, and told me to go and fetch her back. I caught her up and persuaded her to return. She was essential to one scene in which the Governor's wife played the piano. Lena couldn't play a note and simply sat and pretended while this girl played off-stage.

On the fourth night we were due to change plays but James had been unable to recruit people to play two vital parts, so when we got to the theatre he announced that it would be *While Parents Sleep* again. We had not let anyone else know except the stage manager. The Governor and his party again occupied the front row of the dress circle and, when the curtain went up and they saw they were in for a repeat performance, they all rose and left. James had warned us that it might happen so we took no notice and hardly anyone else moved. Afterwards he remarked that he would have to return the Governor his money but he thought the old so-and-so might have waited for the end of a scene.

I had never been to Hong Kong and I remember it as being almost rural. There were no sky-scrapers and the only crowded streets were down by the shore line. Government House stood on a hill outside the town and the road beyond it up to the Peak was bounded by grass and trees. The view from the top looking towards the mainland was beautiful. At night it became a fairyland of lights, the ferries moving like fireflies across the water. Lena and James took me up to the Chinese frontier on the mainland and I watched the constant traffic of pedestrians, many carrying huge bundles across the bridge. In the outskirts of Kowloon, two million people lived in shanty towns made of petrol drums and corrugated iron which were as stinking and filthy as the slums of Calcutta. The flow of refugees from China proper was constant and if the police, very smart in their shorts, shirts and blue-peaked caps, caught any, they used to send them back. But as soon as a refugee got into a shanty town there was no hope of finding him.

I had agreed to remain with the company while they played *While Parents Sleep* in Shanghai, which meant three evening performances and a matinée. Again we had a proper theatre and a good reception. But in spite of the fun we had all had together, I was glad to leave and begin to travel through China. No doubt to a professional actor the subtle differences between performances of the same play are interesting; I had noticed how on some nights a scene would drag and on others go like a bomb, and it was also true that audiences differed enormously, some seizing every point and laughing instantly and others seeming sunk in torpor. Yet for me, even if the timing was good and the audience appreciative, the repetition of the same lines night after night began to pall. At the end of the week I saw the Grant-Anderson Company off to Tokyo. I was not to meet James and Lena again until more than forty years later, when they suddenly came to see me in London. Both were as full of vitality as ever and were still working in the theatre.

In four days I did not see much of Shanghai. I remember the great

Bund, an elevated embankment which ran the length of the sea shore, on which stood all the great trading houses, banks and department stores. I can see in my mind's eye literally thousands of rickshaws, parked in groups of a hundred or more, or being pulled by hungry-looking coolies in ragged shorts and shirts who ran until exhausted. Ships were anchored outside the harbour as well as in it. In the night clubs girls in beautiful brocade dresses with skirts slit almost to the thigh danced so lightly that you scarcely noticed them on your arm. It was, I knew, and had been for a hundred years the largest commercial city in China, where families like the Sassoons and Kadooris acted as negotiators between Europeans and rich Chinese and made great fortunes. There cannot have been more than a few thousand Europeans in the city even in 1934, yet they dominated life from behind the Chinese façade.

I stayed with John Keswick, a contemporary who had been at Cambridge and was then in charge of the Shanghai office of the family firm of Jardine Mathieson, about which the book *Taipan* was later written. He brought a party to see the play and gave me a glimpse of the international life he led in which French was the lingua franca of the Europeans and English was used when talking to Chinese. Few Europeans spoke any Chinese dialect. John also gave me introductions to people living in other parts of China and determined the next stage of my journey. He had an American friend who flew an amphibian courier service up the Yangtze River and sometimes took a passenger. John had flown with him and said that the journey through the gorges in an aircraft was thrilling. His friend agreed to take me and I left Shanghai next day.

14

War Lords

Nanking was as impressive as I had been led to expect; the walls were vast and the main streets wide and tree-lined. One could easily have spent several days there. But I had my amphibian to catch and had to reach Wuhu, about twenty-five miles away, as quickly as possible. I was told I should go by bus. When I boarded the bus it was full of Chinese passengers, many of whom were already standing in the aisle with their heads bent at an acute angle against the low ceiling. I was wondering where and how to jam myself in when, to my surprise, I saw an empty seat at the very back next to an open window. It seemed too good to be true. I assumed that the Chinese did not like draughts, plumped myself down and put my rucksack under the seat. At first I marvelled at my luck, but after twenty minutes or so I began to understand.

There was apparently a notice on the door in Chinese, forbidding spitting in the bus. Until then I had not realized that spitting in China was not merely considered healthy and more polite than blowing the nose, but had become almost a national pastime. In cafés, where there was a spittoon on the floor, Chinese would bet against each other as to who could hit it from farthest away. After spittle had landed on my face and clothes a dozen times, I realized that my open window was the spittoon for my side of the bus. There was little I could do. The journey was going to last more than two hours, but the bus was too full for me to move and in any case there were no empty seats except the one by the open window on the other side. I was too tall to stand with my head jammed against the roof. Somehow I had to defend myself.

I took a large notebook out of my rucksack and by holding it open in front of my face, tried to mitigate the worst effects. This worked for a time. The trouble was that the Chinese saw what was happening and began to laugh. They then turned what had been a natural hazard into a game. Each time the bus stopped and people got off, the newcomers were quickly inducted into the game and it began with renewed vigour. Occasionally, when a shot hit the notebook with a particularly sharp crack, I would shout applause, but this only encouraged them. As the bus emptied at Wuhu, several Chinese, laughing uncontrollably, lifted me out of my seat and led me to a water pump which was near the bus-stop. There they made me take off my coat while they sponged it down and helped me put it on again, all the time laughing and bowing. I threw away the notebook. I had learned one lesson. In those days, the Chinese loved above all to laugh. If you could make them laugh you were their friend.

*

The amphibian lay out in the river. There was only one passenger seat, in front of the pilot. The first stop was Hankow (Wuhan today), a little more than two hundred miles away across land and lakes. The river was at least half a mile wide. We came down in mid-stream and taxied to a jetty. While the pilot delivered his packages, I went into the town and soon got lost. I did not know the Chinese for 'river' and so I borrowed a stick and began drawing what I thought looked like one in the dusty street. A little crowd gathered and tried to guess what I wanted. Then I drew an aeroplane and they all laughed and clapped and led me down to the river. I gathered they had seen the amphibian alight.

A slighter shorter flight took us to Ichang at the exit of the gorges which begin where the river passes between the mountains Fangdon Shan and Guanmian Shan about a hundred and fifty miles to the west. When we took off from Ichang we flew low, just above the water, and soon the mountains closed in on either side, in places rising vertically to a height of between three and four thousand feet. Every now and then we would rise a few feet to clear the sails of a junk or the funnel of a steamer coming downstream.

The Yangtze Gorges are listed as one of the wonders of the world because, when the river is in spate, they compress a greater volume of water into narrower confines than occurs anywhere else. In Wind Box, for instance, the steepest and narrowest gorge, the water rises 275 feet. It was almost at its lowest when we passed through and the noise of our engine echoed between the cliffs which towered above us. As the river twisted it would often seem as though we were flying into a solid rock-face, but the pilot had flown through many times and was thoroughly enjoying himself. We landed finally at Chungking, more than a thousand miles as the crow flies from the Yangtze's mouth and nearly double that distance on the water.

At Chungking I became aware of the chaos which then characterized the administration of China. A friend of John Keswick met me, and as we made our way by bicycle rickshaw to a hotel, I noticed that many houses were cut in half, as if a giant knife had sliced through them. People still lived in them and one could look straight into rooms where the beds were in position against the wall and clothes were hanging on pegs, all open to view from the street or from the houses opposite. My friend explained that the Provincial Governor, who was really an independent War Lord but ostensibly a supporter of Chiang Kai-shek, had decided that he needed a military road through the city and, without consulting anyone, had simply gone ahead and cut a great swathe through the houses. The inhabitants had nowhere else to go and clung precariously to what was left to them.

The city of Chungking rises on the banks either side of the river and our route soon became too steep for rickshaws. We took to our feet and hired coolies to carry our suitcases. In a steep, narrow street jammed with porters and pedestrians, I saw a Chinese gentleman being carried in a chair coming round a corner and descending towards us. He was dressed in silk robes of a greyish colour and wore a little black hat shaped like a cupola. His thin, black moustache drooped down on either side of his mouth to below his chin. As he approached, everyone pressed back against the walls. With an air of great disdain he looked straight ahead, every now and again spitting to one side. The men carrying the poles on which his chair rested were bare-footed, wore black shorts and were naked from the waist up. They kept shouting, warning people to get out of the way. I asked who the man was and was told that he was a high official of the city.

For the first time I began to feel I was in the 'real' China. Such roads as there were in Chungking were confined to the water's edge. On the steps and in the streets and alleys which climbed the great banks there was no wheeled traffic and I remember few pack animals. Everything was carried by people who swarmed around, talking little, grunting and sweating under the weight of their loads. Their clothes were drab and often ragged; blue and black predominated among both men and women. The women wore tightly buttoned tunics and skirts, and the men wore shorts, occasionally trousers of a kind or dungarees. Quite often an elderly woman hobbled by with feet too tightly bound to allow her to walk properly.

When we reached our hotel, which stood high above the city, John Keswick's friend took charge. He told us that because all the pilots (I suppose they were the skippers, but everybody called them pilots) of the Yangtze steamers smoked opium, Chungking had some of the most picturesque opium dens in China. He seldom smoked, but thought it might be an interesting experience for me so we went down to a den before dinner. I do not remember the outside of the building, but as soon as we were inside the dimly lit den, I saw men lying on elegant, polished, bare wooden couches, smoking through dark wooden stems which looked more like small musical instruments than pipes. Next to each man sat an attendant. There were some silver gadgets on a small table by each couch, and as soon as I was comfortably settled, my attendant took what I assumed to be opium from a bowl, rolled it into a little bullet-shaped pod, put the end of the pod into the hole in the end of the wooden stem, handed it to me and then lit the pod. It all seemed simple.

I drew on the pipe and smoke came quite gently. Hoping for a delicious sense of well-being, I lay back. Much sooner than I expected, perhaps after five minutes, the pod had dwindled and the attendant took back the pipe, rolled another pod and handed them back again. I repeated the performance, taking my time and waiting for a sensation. When the second pod had nearly vanished, I did experience a sensation but it was one of faint nausea. I persevered, but towards the end of the third pod I had to leave the room suddenly so as to be sick. My friend meanwhile was enjoying himself and I waited until he felt he had had enough. I knew that millions of Chinese smoked opium in moderation and that people like the Yangtze pilots smoked it because they found it quickened their perception. I had not met anyone who was an addict or who disliked it, but although I visited several more dens in Chungking during the four or five days I was there, I never got further than the third pipe and never left without being sick. I gathered that this was not a common effect and sadly concluded that there was something in me that rejected the drug.

The return journey to Hankow was by steamer. The river was so low that two Chinese members of the crew with long poles stood either side in the bows sounding the depth of the water. The pilot at the wheel occasionally smoked opium; I found a Chinese who could interpret. The pilot said that there were two periods when the river was dangerous. When it was at its lowest – as now – there was a constant danger of running aground; when in spate, the volume of water going through the gorges was so great that it caused whirlpools which went to a great depth. On average, each year three junks and a steamer were lost, sucked down by whirlpools. The pilot said that he would never take a steamer through when the river was in full spate.

At Ichang, while we were still alongside the quay and most of the passengers were on deck, a middle-aged couple, dressed like peasants and holding the hands of a little girl between them, approached the group with which I was standing. My Chinese friend asked them what they wanted, then turned to me, saying, 'They want you to buy their daughter.' She was a sweet-looking child of thirteen with her hair in plaits. The parents literally begged me to take her. They were asking a pittance – ten pounds, I think – but that was not the point. They said they knew I would give her a home. She would do anything for me and would always be loyal. They seemed to me to love her.

I took my interpreter aside and asked him for his opinion. He replied that such incidents were quite common. Chinese peasant families regarded boys as an asset and girls as a liability. Often girl babies were put out on a hill-side to die. He had no doubt that this couple were genuine and that if I could possibly take her with me I would be doing a good deed. I was moved, and considered the question seriously, but the difficulties seemed insurmountable. I was not worried about arriving back at 4 The Cloisters with a little Chinese girl; my parents would have understood. But what then? Would she be allowed to settle in England and work? Who would look after her; how would I educate her? More immediately, how was I to cope with her on the rest of my journey – in Peking, in Japan, crossing the Pacific, crossing the United States? It was plainly impossible. After I had said goodbye to the couple, who looked sad and wandered around the ship, I asked my friend what would happen to the girl.

'Somehow they will get rid of her,' he said. 'They have too many children and are very poor.'

Outside the big, modern cities, one was surrounded by poverty in China. There were no fat people in the streets of Hankow or

Chungking. Faces were pinched. The expectation of life among labourers was only around forty-five years. Although coolies and rickshaw drivers had to work long hours, they had little real stamina because they were under-nourished. The train from Hankow to Peking crossed miles of open country in which villages of squalid shacks of mud and corrugated iron, or even thatched straw, were scattered on the hillsides. There were no roads, drains or sanitation, and very rarely any light other than candles or primitive oil lamps. Electricity was confined to the railway and the few towns. Every now and then I would see from the train a figure lying at the edge of a village on a pile of straw. When I asked why it was there, I was told: 'He has been put out to die.' (It was always 'he'.) The village hovels were too crowded to accommodate a dying man; so long as the weather was fine he was better off outside. Children played around him, and his family took him what he needed to eat or drink but then could get on with the arduous business of living.

15

From Peking to Hollywood

At a railway junction called Shanhaikwan, I came across the Japanese army. The Japanese had built the railway from there to Peking as well as other railways in Manchuria and, under a formal convention, were responsible for their maintenance. Just as the concession the Europeans had won for their trade along the Yangtze allowed them to station gun-boats on the river, so the Japanese had gained the right to patrol the railways in Manchuria and see the track was properly maintained. When we pulled into the station, a Japanese army colonel was on the platform and I was introduced. He was formal and polite, but I noticed that the Chinese were obsequious and clearly afraid of him. The Japanese presence was legal and necessary but there was no doubt that they were using their concession as the means of gaining control of the whole of north-eastern China.

In many attempts promoted by the League of Nations to arrange a ceasefire, the Japanese constantly demanded that Chinese troops withdraw behind the Great Wall to reduce 'incidents'. To the Chinese assertions that the incidents were the work of bandits, the Japanese Prime Minister replied, with justification, that there was little difference between Chinese troops and bandits.

As always, the Chinese Government was too weak to take any action. In the early 1930s Chiang Kai-shek had lost control of most of his Provincial Governors and they in turn had largely lost control of their troops. The situation had reached stalemate. The Japanese did not dare declare war on China for fear of antagonizing first the Americans, who were supporting Chiang Kai-shek, and second the Russians, who had rights in stretches of the Manchurian Railway and whose army was only a few days' march from Changchun, the new capital of Manchukuo. The Japanese, therefore, paid lip-service to all attempts to arrange a ceasefire, politely received commissions of enquiry from the impotent League of Nations and continued to strengthen their hold on the north-east of China. Chinese students and some Chinese leaders frequently demanded a declaration of war on Japan, but Chiang Kai-shek knew that that was just what the Japanese wanted. He also knew that he could not win such a war and had to content himself with protests. At one point he had asked the United States to intervene, but they refused.

In Peking all this was well understood, particularly at the British Embassy, where the Third Secretary was Harold Caccia, who had been in his last year at Trinity when I went up to Oxford in 1926. He must be one of the most versatile men ever to have joined the Foreign Service, as readers of Harold Macmillan's *War Diaries* will have gathered. Harold and his wife Nancy, whose brother had also been at Trinity, had rented a half-ruined temple on a hill outside Peking for use at weekends. I went to stay with them.

Harold's life touched mine most closely at the extremes. In the Eton v. Harrow Match at Lords in 1924, he had been the opening fast bowler for Eton. Fifty years later, almost to the month, when the time came for me to nominate my successor as President of the MCC, I chose Harold. He was in America at the time and I had to telephone across the Atlantic to find out if he would accept. He did so at once. It was at a time when the position of South Africa, one of the first countries to play Test cricket, was being hotly debated because of apartheid. No one could have handled the international cricket conference with more tact, but Harold was unable to persuade the coloured members of the world's cricketing community that reincluding South Africa in the Test series would do more to modify apartheid than continuing a boycott.

The Forbidden City in Peking, the palace of the former Emperors which had been opened to the public since Sun Yat Sen's revolution in 1911, is another wonder of the world. It is not compact and easy to photograph, like the Taj Mahal, but spreads across many acres. Little canals between white marble terraces with white marble balustrades are spanned by beautiful arched bridges; there are temples, in particular the blue-tiled, multi-tiered Temple of Heaven, floating pavilions and delicate trees. It has mystery and magic, and no one who has any appreciation of beautiful surroundings can fail to be entranced.

The next most striking buildings in Peking were the city's ancient gates. All except one, I believe, were still standing in 1934; massive structures with what might have been described as rectangular barracks or hotels, surmounting great arches. The walls had been breached by builders in many places over the years but still flanked each gate for a considerable distance, so that Peking had the character of a walled city. In the 1980s I am told that only one gate and practically nothing of the walls are left.

From Peking I went by train to Mukden (now Shenyang) which had just yielded to Changchun the dubious honour of being the capital of the new state of Manchukuo. Disappointingly, I can remember practically nothing of the visit except that the Japanese presence was very obvious in the railway station, less so in the town. There was a British Consul who strongly advised me against going on to Harbin, where large numbers of Russian refugees from the Revolution of 1917 were still living and where the night clubs were said to be some of the best in the world. The Consul said that unofficial fighting had broken out, not only between Chinese and Japanese, but between Japanese and some Russians in the area. He thought it quite likely I would not even get there. I took the train instead to Pusan, the port in what is now South Korea from which one embarks for Japan.

*

Nobody had told me about Korea. It was not until I had crossed the frontier in the train and noticed people in the fields wearing different straw hats – a narrower brim with a white veil that passed under the chin – that I learned I was no longer in China. My informants were Japanese travellers who said that the Koreans had always hated the Chinese in the way the Irish hated the English. I looked at the countryside with renewed interest but saw nothing that foreshadowed the great conflict which was to break out twenty years later, or the economic boom in South Korea which followed it.

From Pusan I took the ferry to Shimonoseki, the port and railway terminal on the south-west corner of Honshu, the main island of Japan. The train ran exactly on time and during the journey, which lasted through the night, I experienced the gentler side of the Japanese nature. The coach had a gangway down the middle with seats on either side but was narrower than American or even European coaches. I had a seat to myself, but when I stretched out to try to sleep I found it too short to curl up or get comfortable, so I stuck my legs out and rested my feet on the arm of the seat across the gangway. For some time nobody tried to pass and it must have been well into the night when, half asleep, I noticed a railway attendant approaching. He stopped when he came to the legs which barred his way, but instead of disturbing me or even lifting my legs, he went back down the coach and returned with some low steps. These he put close to my legs, climbed up, stepped down over my legs without touching them and went on his way, leaving the steps where they were. I was already conscious of how short the Japanese were but had not thought of the problems this created for them. The availability of the steps showed that they catered for foreigners in a most practical way. On two or three more occasions during the night Japanese wanted to pass and each time they used the steps, lifting them over my legs if they were on the wrong side, but never touching or waking me. In the early morning I walked down the coach myself and noticed that Japanese men and women had no difficulty in curling up on their seats; they were sleeping quite comfortably.

I left the train at Kyoto and went into the countryside to look at the cherry blossom, for which the area is famous. There was a park in the town which was thronged with Japanese, mostly wearing kimonos, the women in bright colours with broad sashes and their hair dressed with combs in classical Japanese style. Whole families were out together, pausing frequently, smiling and exclaiming at the beauty of the blossom. The scene was picturesque. I often used to think of it a few years later when, as a prisoner of war, I heard of the horrible things the Japanese did to the airmen and soldiers they captured.

I was walking by myself in Kyoto park when two young Japanese joined me. They both spoke more than a little English and told me they were students. They wore a sort of uniform and it occurred to me that they might be agents of the police, but they were friendly. I said I wanted to walk in the fields. We went through the park and out into the countryside where the fields were mainly rice paddies. Often we had to walk along the raised edges of a paddy because the rice had been flooded. It was slow going. The young men were inquisitive about England. I tried to describe our fields and hedges, what we grew and how we harvested.

We went into three or four little farmhouses. In the last house the farmer and his family were having their midday meal, and insisted that we join them. We all sat on the floor, which was covered with finely plaited split-bamboo matting, round a very low table on which stood an iron cauldron over a charcoal fire: they were cooking and eating sukiyaki. While the farmer's wife added little cubes of pork, beans of different colours and sizes and other vegetables to the cauldron, the students plied our host with questions, every now and then translating for me. I gathered that the family income was less than the equivalent of two hundred pounds a year, but that they enjoyed their life. As soon as children could be useful they worked in the house or on the farm; the two eldest went to school. The family made most of their own clothes, but the parents had bought one kimono each for special occasions. They all went barefoot in the fields, and otherwise wore those wooden-soled sandals which are held on by a thong between the toes.

In the afternoon we visited more farmhouses and were eventually invited to stay the night. This house, like all those we entered, had practically no furniture and the floors were covered in bamboo matting. From the ceiling hung more bamboo matting, sections of which were rolled up when a room needed enlarging or rolled down to make a partition or cover a window. The matting was wonderfully clean and of a natural beige-yellow colour. If dirt was brought in from the farm, the mat was simply rolled up, taken outside and washed at the hand pump, which was the only water supply. There were no pictures, perhaps because there were so few solid walls. The partitions were so mobile that one could hardly talk of a room, but the parents did sleep behind one partition and the children all together behind another. The students and I slept in the room in which we had eaten. Everyone lay on the floor, their heads on hard, cylindrical blocks of wood or on rolled-up matting. They used candles for light, but went to bed early and got up at dawn. I did not go into a house in a town, but the students told me that their general character was very similar; nearly all were bungalows and used bamboo matting on walls and floor.

In England at that time it was generally assumed that Japanese competition was 'unfair' because their goods were produced by 'sweated labour'. I did not get that impression. I was only ten days in Japan on that visit, but whether in cotton mills in Osaka or the countryside around Kyoto, the people looked fit, cheerful and neat. There were no ragged children, no beggars and very little dirt. On the other hand, it was clear that the Japanese demanded fewer aids to life than Westerners. There was an absence, not only of furniture, but of gadgets. When a single bowl suffices for a meal, you do not need a dish-washing machine, nor do you need partitioned drawers in which to put away chop-sticks. Bamboo matting is not cleaned with brooms or dusters. Where there are no mantelpieces, you want fewer ornaments. I saw few signs of recreation. There was no mechanical music blaring out in Kyoto park and no radios in the farmhouses. In Tokyo the cinemas were crowded, and the cafés and bars where people drank sake provided music, but my main impression was of a disciplined society, dominated by the family, for whom the main purpose in life was to find satisfaction in an occupation.

*

I had caught amoebic dysentery in China and was told to rest so, after leaving Japan, I stopped at the island of Hawaii and lived with a Hawaiian family for three weeks in a little village whose houses were lapped by the Pacific Ocean. An old lady I had met in China, herself a Hawaiian and a friend of Jack London, who had written stories about the Polynesians, had given me the family's name and the name of their village. It was an idyllic visit. I was weak, slept inordinately and listened to the guitars which accompanied the songs all down the village street.

When I got stronger, I caught a boat that was loading cattle at all the islands on the way to Oahu. It was a fairy-story. The only other passenger on the boat was a very pretty American girl of about my age. We fell in love and had a blissful four or five days. The boat would anchor off each island and the cowboys would drive the cattle out to sea. We would then watch them being winched up in slings and dropped into the hold of the ship. Off Mauai we smelled pineapples, off Molokai gardenias. We were both sad when we reached Honolulu in the island of Oahu and she promised to come and see me off next day. I left by boat for Los Angeles with garlands of gardenias around my neck to the tune of 'Aloa'. What I did not know for another forty years was that after leaving me she went back to Honolulu and persuaded her boyfriend to take her up in an aeroplane to buzz the ship goodbye. I was not even on deck to see her aeroplane. In a letter she wrote me in the late 1970s (she had read my address in *Who's Who*) she said she thought she might now tell me what had happened: the aeroplane had crashed on landing and she had been severely injured.

In Hollywood I had introductions from Esmond Harmsworth to the Fox–Movietone Corporation, of which he was a large shareholder. Those were the great days of Hollywood. I watched Jean Harlow and Franchot Tone creating havoc in their studio through the jokes they played on each other while riding bicycles. A special allowance in the budget had to be made for Wallace Beery to go home and see his mother every other month. I met Spencer Tracey and Myrna Loy, who were just emerging as stars; Danielle Darieux was the favourite of the fans. At night the stars made a gala entry down the avenue of palm trees leading to the Coconut Grove restaurant, and starlets waited at the end of the telephone.

I had been told that the only way to find out the truth about any film company was to talk to their accountants. The task was made easier because they were all Scotsmen. They deplored the extravagance of the film-makers, but there was no television and so long as one film in three was a winner, they thought the industry would survive. It was not the money-making machine it appeared on the surface, but Hollywood then had a style it never recaptured.

After a dazzling three weeks I flew to New York to catch a boat home. Bill Astor had told me I could use his flat in New York, but that I must not be surprised if I found someone else in it as well. I found a good-looking young man in the depths of depression. He wanted to stay in America but had been looking in vain for a job for many weeks. As a last resort he had decided to go to Hollywood and see if he could get taken on as a film extra. He left the day after I arrived. His name was David Niven.

16

The Fertile Crescent

For most of the next two years I sat at the sub-editors' table of the *Daily Mail*. There were two shifts, one beginning at six p.m. and ending around two a.m., the other starting at eight p.m. and lasting until four a.m., by which time most of the news from abroad was drying up and the rest could be left to the day shift which came on later in the morning. In the summer, instead of going back to Reeves Mews, I would often drive down to my parents' house at Windsor in the middle of the night so that I could spend the day in the country, going for long walks in the Home and Great Parks, occasionally playing a game of golf or cricket. It was an orderly life which made one see the newspaper as a whole.

The sub-editors themselves were often interesting individuals. Some had been on the paper for twenty or more years; one had begun as a messenger boy. Another was the author of many detective novels. Several worked in other jobs in other newspapers by day, but regarded 'subbing' as their bread and butter. They were almost all friendly and all had developed a capacity for drinking endless cups of tea.

But there was another, and less satisfactory, side to the work. I began to find the politics of the *Daily Mail* insupportable. Lord Rothermere was becoming positively sycophantic towards the dictators and had recently sent George Ward-Price to Germany, Italy and Japan to interview Hitler, Mussolini and even the Japanese Emperor, always portraying them in a favourable light.

The year 1935 saw the launching of Mussolini's attack on Abyssinia, and 1936 Hitler's occupation of the Rhineland and the beginning of the Spanish Civil War, in which fascist troops and airmen gave open support to Franco. Many people in England had by now begun to feel that appeasement had gone too far and that a stand against the dictators should be made sooner rather than later. I was among them.

Although I did not favour military intervention in the Spanish Civil War, I did support sanctions against Mussolini's Italy and hoped for action in the Rhineland. When a verbal instruction was passed round the office that nothing unfavourable to Hitler, Mussolini or the Emperor of Japan was to appear in the paper, I knew the time had come for me to resign.

The verbal instruction was not the only reason for my wanting to leave. During the past five years the editor of the *Daily Mail* had been changed almost annually and the present one was alleged to have got the job because he knew Paris and was adept at finding the sort of women Lord Rothermere liked. The quality of the paper was rapidly declining. I did not imagine that Lord Rothermere would live long, and knew that Esmond Harmsworth would then succeed to the proprietorship.[1] But although Esmond was and remained a friend, I had come to realize that his chief talents were financial and that his interest in the contents and policy of the newspaper was only spasmodic. He was liable to be influenced by the last persuasive man or woman he had seen. Esmond had made it quite plain that he hoped I would stay with him and play a leading part in the newspapers the family owned, but I realized that the newspapers were very much a family concern and that any influence I might eventually have could only be exercised by humouring Esmond; much of my time and energy would have to be spent doing just that. In other words, success or failure would depend more upon anticipating another man's whims than upon the merit of one's work, and I did not want that sort of life.

I had no capital and was dependent upon what I earned so I did not act precipitately. My main aim was to start work on my own and I was already in search of backing to make documentary and educational films. It was only when that plan was complete that I went to see Esmond in his office and told him my decision. I thanked him for all the fun and experience I had had with him but went on to say that I knew I had to be on my own. I explained about the films; he asked several questions to make sure I knew what I was doing and then said that if that was how I felt, of course I must go. I then told him how working in South Wales had given me an interest in politics, and that I was about to join the Labour Party and hoped one day to stand for Parliament. He was pleased at that, said he had always felt I should do well in the House of Commons and that it did not much matter which side I was on. I was surprised, because only a few days before, an uncle by marriage, Cuthbert Headlam, who had begun life as a clerk in Parliament and later been a Conservative Member and Junior Minister, had said exactly the same thing. In my new-found enthusiasm, I felt that both men had become cynical. Esmond ended by saying that I would always be welcome in his house and he hoped I would come and see him.

*

Documentary films were a new adventure. The idea that slices of real life could make a film which the cinema public would accept as an addition or even an alternative to fiction, had originated with Stephen Tallents, secretary of the Empire Marketing Board, who was beginning to use film to explain and popularize the British Empire. Tallents had picked John Grierson to launch the idea, a man whose attitude to film as an educative medium was one of almost religious fervour. *Drifters*, a film about Scottish herring fleets, was shown first with Eisenstein's *Potemkin* at the Film Society in November 1929. It was a beautiful film, vivid and dramatic; watching it, one felt part of the crew. The reception was rapturous. 'Unquestionably the best British film that has been made,' said the *Spectator*, and the dailies and weeklies echoed the praise. *Drifters* went straight into the huge Stoll Cinema on Kingsway and was then shown throughout the country.

Working first for the Empire Marketing Board and then for the General Post Office Film Unit, Grierson set about training a group of producers who, in the next decade, achieved the great age of the documentary film. Several films were shown in a thousand or more cinemas. Eventually, however, the film industry turned against them, largely because they were made with public money and were therefore a form of subsidized competition undermining the privately financed fictional film. It was not until the arrival of television that the documentary came back into its own.

Meanwhile I had consulted Cosmo Lang, now Archbishop of Canterbury. I had talked to him about documentary films and particularly about Arabia and Palestine, where the life of the Bedouin seemed hardly to have changed for several thousand years. It must, I thought, be possible to bring to life the books of the Old Testament from the time of Abraham onwards. The Archbishop said that if I was serious he thought he might be able to persuade someone to put up the money. I worked on the idea through the summer of 1936 and concocted a plan which called for an initial outlay of ten thousand pounds. The Archbishop then sent me to see Lord Wakefield, the industrialist with a passionate interest in aviation. I did see him and propounded my plan. My main point was that although people had dramatized history and the Bible since films were first invented, no one had used archaeology, the life of the desert or of Palestine, to show the setting in which the events took place. When Lord Wakefield asked me how I would distribute the films, I said that distribution on any commercial scale depended upon getting the support of one or more of the major education authorities. I did not pretend it would be easy, but if the films were as graphic as I hoped, they would sell themselves as an aid to teaching, just as the magic lantern had once done.

Whether Lord Wakefield liked the idea I could not tell, but at the end he said, 'I must tell you that you have a most persuasive sponsor. I will give you ten thousand pounds for your project. But although I shall be interested to hear what happens, I want it clearly understood that I do not ever expect to see any of my money again.'[2]

An expedition was quickly organized. Through the good offices of the Religious Film Society I recruited Norman Spurr, whose father was a well-known Nonconformist scholar, as my chief technician. Norman had already made educational films in both black and white and Kodachrome, the only existing 16mm colour film, and was his own cameraman and film editor. We decided to film in both 16 and 35mm film in case we felt able to include a documentary for the cinema on the current situation in Palestine, which was steadily deteriorating as Hitler stepped up his persecution of the Jews and the United States increased its pressure on the British Government to relax the terms of the Mandate under which we ruled the territory and to allow more Jews into the country.

Norman Spurr brought in a Canadian freelance cameraman named George Rutherford, who had his own 35mm camera. I recruited my younger sister, Anstice, and two of her friends, Diana Carroll and Margaret Vane, to act as camp organizers and general helpers. The company we formed was called School Films Limited.

We bought an estate car and had an engine put where the back seat should have been, to generate power for lights to be used in the desert.

Photo-floodlights were even then easily portable and very good. We stayed a night at Lambeth Palace and were waved away next morning not only by the Archbishop of Canterbury but by William Temple, who had succeeded him as Archbishop of York. It was February 5th, 1937. After a night in Paris we motored to Bari and took a boat to Haifa. Through the recommendation of the Archbishop, we were allowed to camp in the garden of Bishop Graham-Brown's house in Jerusalem.

We were to stay in Palestine for nearly six months. Our guidebook for the biblical scenes was George Adam Smith's *Historical Geography of the Holy Land*, and I still think of Palestine in terms of Mount Carmel, the Plain of Esdraelon, Megiddo, Mount Tabor, Capernaum, Jericho and the Mountains of Moab – those mysterious blue mountains the other side of the Dead Sea. Broadly, our filming fell into two parts: present-day Palestine and the background to the Old and New Testaments. For the modern film we covered new Jewish settlements and kibbutzes like Nahalal and Rehovoth, Arab and Jewish olive groves, the ports of Jaffa, Acre, Haifa and the Jordanian frontier force commanded by Colonel Glubb on behalf of the Emir Abdullah, ruler of Trans-Jordan, whose capital was Amman. The frontier force was a part of the army at the disposal of the High Commissioner, Sir Arthur Wauchope, who was also Commander-in-Chief. General Dill was in command of all British troops.

We spent a lot of time in Jerusalem, a city holy to Jews, Christians and Moslems. I remember interviewing Haj Amin Husseini, the Grand Mufti of Jerusalem, known as 'the Fox' and very suspect to the British administration. I also interviewed Dr Magnus, head of the Hebrew University on Mount Scopus, Dr Richmond, the head of the Jerusalem Museum, and the Emir Abdullah in Amman. Although the Bishop's garden was our base, we camped whenever and wherever we thought it necessary, or stayed in hostels.

After filming the fishermen on Lake Galilee who used those three-cornered nets sprung on bamboos which are common to the whole of the Orient, we stayed with Father Tapper, a German who kept an inn on the northern shore and made his own wine. He was a great local figure and an indiscriminate host; he would receive at his inn anyone who lived in Palestine of any race or colour. Fortunately our mosquito nets were still new – none of us had ever experienced such a sustained bombardment from such enormous mosquitoes.

After weeks of negotiation with the authorities of the Church of the Holy Sepulchre and much help from Sir Arthur Wauchope's office and from Bishop Graham-Brown, we were given permission to film the Ceremony of the Holy Fire, which takes place in Easter Week. It had never been filmed before and Norman and George spent many days fixing the lights on the cornice of the rotunda under the dome. We all camped in the Church for three nights in the company of about two thousand pilgrims who had come from throughout the Middle East and slept on every altar, altar step and any other available flat space. We had been warned to keep a close watch on all our equipment.

The ceremony has often been described. A monk enters the Holy Sepulchre (whose authenticity is doubtful) with an unlit taper. He emerges with the taper 'miraculously' alight; hundreds of pilgrims, monks and visitors then light their tapers from it until the floor of the rotunda, which is always in a dim light, looks from above like a galaxy of swaying stars. There is tremendous clamour. The members of the three religious denominations which govern the Church of the Holy Sepulchre – Orthodox, Armenian and Latin – then process around the rotunda in turn, all the priests wearing full robes and singing their liturgies one after another. The singing, particularly of the Orthodox and Armenians, many of whom were of Russian origin, is magnificent. The ceremony lasts several hours. We filmed it in both black and white and Kodachrome and managed to get gramophone records of all the liturgies. The film was used by the Religious Film Society for many years.

Another bonus came as a result of my joining the 601 Auxiliary Air Force Squadron in England. The Honorary Air Commodore, Sir Philip Sassoon, was also Under-Secretary of State for Air. He had heard of our expedition and asked me if we wanted to do any photography from the air. When I said yes he arranged that the RAF squadron stationed at Ramleh should fly us whenever we wanted. Their aircraft were Gordons, medium bombers not unlike our own Demons, with a mounting for a rear-gunner at the back. Instead of a machine gun we mounted the 35mm film camera in the gunner's cockpit and, as a result, got some first-rate air film, particularly of the Wall of the Temple and the Dome of the Rock which stood above it. We used to fly up from the plain in the west, come as low as possible over the brook Kedron, and film the Great Wall almost from below, carrying on over the city to the Jaffa Gate. We also flew to Huleh, the most northerly part of Palestine, filmed Mount Hermon (which was in Syria) and the swamps below Lake Huleh, which were really the source of the River Jordan and have since been drained by the Israelis.

But most of our work was done in the desert in Syria. Our rough plan was to follow 'the Fertile Crescent' which stretches from the Euphrates to the Jordan and was the northern route of the mainly Semitic tribes which, over the centuries, came out of Arabia. Many of these were and remained nomadic, like the tribe of Israel to which Abraham belonged. We followed the crescent from west to east, the opposite direction to that taken by Abraham.

In order to get an impression of the land of the Philistines (from which the name Palestine derives), as shown on Adam Smith's map, we set out for the coast of Palestine towards Lebanon and Syria. Our estate car had desert tyres, that is, of low pressure and large circumference, and we had little fear of sand, so we followed the coast. Having surveyed the ruins of Tyre and Sidon, we drove along the beach towards Tripoli. We were hot and dusty and the sea was inviting, so we decided to camp on a broad and flat stretch of sand which seemed totally empty. We swam, ate supper and pitched our beds in a cluster, not bothering about tents. It was just daylight when we were woken by a loud hooting which seemed to come from only a few yards away. Indeed it did. We opened our eyes to see a steam engine with a high funnel pulling a passenger train, halted within ten yards of where we were sleeping. There had been no sign of railway lines the evening before and there was none now; but there was the train. We leapt up, folded our beds, pulled our equipment to one side and waved the train on. It took some time to get going again because most of the passengers had got off to examine the cause of the delay. Amid much laughter and good wishes we watched the passengers re-embark and go on their way. The railway lines were still covered in sand.

Soon afterwards we turned inland towards the River Orontes and took the road – it was really only a dirt track – through Homs and Hama towards Aleppo. We filmed the giant water wheels which had irrigated the plain for more than two thousand years and, in Hama, following a local custom, we had tea with the owner of an Arab stallion in the stallion's box so that we might admire it at our leisure. Whether it was in Aleppo that we met Jacques Edinger, a young French journalist who was also touring the Middle East, I am not sure. But wherever it was, he took us in tow. If we wanted to film Bedouin life, he said, we had to get in touch with a Lieutenant Cazenave, of the French Foreign Legion, who was the real head of the Controle Beduin in Syria. Jacques said that if we could find room for him, he would accompany us to Damascus and put us in touch with the authorities. In Damascus we found out that Lieutenant Cazenave was stationed at Palmyra, about a hundred and fifty miles to the east. We reached it by taking a stretch of the Nairn Highway, a track in the desert marked out by white-painted stones, which eventually reached Baghdad in Iraq. Along this route the Nairn Transport Company ran a bi-weekly service in Pullman coaches complete with lavatories and buffet, which covered the distance of five hundred and thirty miles from Damascus to Baghdad in twenty-six hours (as my 1934 guidebook records). The desert was flat and treeless and mostly had a hard gravelled surface over which motor cars could travel at speed.

The barracks of the Foreign Legion, spick and span with white-painted gateposts and a swimming pool, were just outside the ruined city of Palmyra. There was no difficulty in locating Lieutenant Cazenave, who was famous for more things than control of the Bedouin. As we approached his tent we were asked by the orderly who accompanied us to wait. The orderly pointed to a sort of pyramid of shiny three-gallon petrol cans which rose behind a tent and said, 'When the water cascades the lieutenant will soon be with you.' In a moment a pulley released the topmost tin which poured its water into the tin below it, which did the same to the one below that. We could not see the bottom tins but we were assured that this was the only water closet in the Arabian desert and was wholly efficient. Its inventor was soon shaking our hands.

Cazenave was an enthusiast. He liked the Bedouin and knew all the sheikhs by name. When we explained that we wanted to film nomadic life as it had been lived by Abraham, he said at once that we must visit the Sbaa, a tribe which at that moment was further east, towards Mozul, but was moving this way. He would guide us to them. He warned us not to try and film until we had been with them at least two days, as they adhered strictly to desert rules of hospitality. At some point, either at the end of the second day or on the morning of the third, the Sheikh would ask us in what way he could be of help. We knew the rules of desert hospitality from reading Doughty's *Travels in Arabia Deserta* but it was important and interesting to know that they were still so strictly preserved.

When I said that I also hoped to persuade one of the tribes to cross the Jordan as Joshua had done, Cazenave laughed and said that the crossing today would probably not be very different. But the only tribe which would do that for us, he added, would be the Rualla, who had sub-tribes near the Jordan and plenty of horses. 'I know old Nuri well,' he added, 'and his son Naif, who was educated in France. I will take you to them myself and Monsieur Edinger and I will help you to persuade them to co-operate.' As an afterthought he added, 'I do not believe it will create difficulty for you, but I should warn you that the Sbaa and the Rualla are at the moment engaged in a feud. Each has some powerful cars on which they mount machine guns and they carry out raids on each other's camps. There have not been heavy casualties but you must not get involved. It is probably best that you pretend to know nothing about it. You should not travel directly from one tribe to the other.'

We found the Sbaa after driving for many hours across the desert. Their black tents (there were about a dozen) were stretched in a line underneath a sand bank. It must have been about five o'clock in the evening when we drove up to the largest tent. There was no sign of life. I noticed an open sand-coloured truck parked in an end bay of the tent but the main floor area, covered with what looked like a large Persian carpet, was empty. Cazenave disappeared behind a screen at the far end and in a minute we heard women's voices joined with his. When he reappeared he said that the men would soon be back. Apparently the tribe was having a hard time because so many of their wells were dry, so the Sheikh had taken one of the cars and was making a tour of the wells which lay ahead. All the young men and girls were with the flocks. The lieutenant said that we would wait and proceeded to squat cross-legged on the carpet.

After about half an hour there was the sound of an engine, and a second truck, with a machine gun mounted in the front, drove into the end bay of the tent. The Sheikh was a surprising young man wearing, not the aquel and the keffiyeh common to most Bedouin, but a dark cloth wound into a loose turban round his head. He greeted Cazenave as an old friend with a salaam and then an embrace and they sat down together on the carpet in a vigorous conversation which lasted perhaps a quarter of an hour. The rest of us squatted in a semi-circle a little apart but facing the Sheikh and Cazenave. There was much laughter between the two and towards the end I could tell from their gestures that the lieutenant was explaining our presence to the Sheikh. Eventually the Sheikh rose and Cazenave introduced us. After the Sheikh had greeted us all he made a little speech in Arabic which Cazenave translated. He told us he was honoured by our visit and apologized for not having been there to receive us. He also apologized for not killing a goat and offering us a feast that night, but as the well he had been counting on was dry, they had to move on very early the next morning to where he knew there was water. He hoped we would accompany them. A woman in black, sitting in a far corner of the tent, was rocking a goatskin. Cazenave said she was making cheese for the morrow.

We slept where we were, wrapped in blankets, and were woken well before dawn by the Arab women who were beginning to strike the tents. For the next hour or so, while the Arab men sat in the sand with blankets over their shoulders, playing with the children and some of them plucking single-stringed lutes, the women lowered, folded and packed the tents on to kneeling camels, tying on all the pots and pans with cords so that when the camels rose there was a tremendous clatter. The women wore no veils, but sometimes, when one of us was looking at them, they would draw a fold of their black dresses across their faces. The young men and women had already gone ahead with the sheep and goats. The young camels followed their mothers. During all the many days we spent with the Bedouin I never saw a man do what would be called manual labour in the camp. Men were the warriors, hunters (with seldom anything to hunt), goat and camel herdsmen, and they exercised family authority under the Sheikh. This often took the form of endless discussion – the Majlis – which took place informally on the carpet in the Sheikh's tent.

The pace of our caravan was the pace of the slowest camel so that it took us two days to reach the well which the Sheikh had reconnoitred. Each day, as soon as the sun was high, we pitched camp and slept or read in the shade of a tent through the afternoon. After sunset we had the same meal: dates, unleavened bread and goat's cheese. Because of the shortage of water we only had tea twice in the day. We became thirsty. But the first two days of movement were invaluable because they enabled us to get the rhythm of Bedouin life and to see exactly what we wanted to film. On the third evening, when we had at last reached the well which had water, the Sheikh killed a sheep and gave us his feast. The sheep was roasted and served whole and eaten with rice. We copied our hosts: we took a small handful of rice, kneaded it in our fingers and put it in our mouths and then, still with our fingers, chose a piece of meat off the carcass and ate rice and meat together. Every now and then the Sheikh would choose a morsel he thought particularly succulent and present it to one of us. He gave me one of the sheep's eyes – as I had been warned he might – and I managed to swallow it whole. But when he gave me the ear, which was solid gristle, I found it impossible to chew and managed to slip it under the carpet when no one was looking.

There was a full moon and Lieutenant Cazenave left for Palmyra when the feast was over. He said the Sheikh liked us and had already agreed to let us film whatever we wanted during the next few days. He would raise the matter with us in the morning. The lieutenant said that if we offered to pay for the sheep, and gave another twenty pounds for the privilege of filming, the tribe would be delighted. He added that we would soon be approaching the line of pumping stations belonging to the Mozul Oil Company and that there we might be able to get water for our car and perhaps petrol if we needed it. He suggested that we leave the Sbaa when we reached the pipeline and follow it at least to Station 3 (the stations on the pipeline were numbered T_1, T_2, T_3, and so on), where we would certainly get news of the whereabouts of the Rualla. He himself would keep informed of our movements and would be with 'Old Nuri' before we arrived. 'I shall be very glad to see the old man again,' he said. 'It is some time since we met.'

With the departure of Cazenave we had lost our mentor and interpreter, but during the last six months in England I had learnt elementary Arabic at the School of Oriental Languages and with that and the Sheikh's smattering of French we managed quite well. The Bedouin loved the filming. By day it was easy and at night we set up our photo-floods all round the tent and filmed what must have been very like a real Majlis. Luckily we had brought the still camera and we were able to promise our host that Cazenave would bring the tribe pictures of themselves. The engine to generate the power for the lights worked perfectly and for three or four days we filmed every detail of nomadic life. The Old Testament came to life before our eyes. We were able to film not only the constant movement of the tribe but also the work done by the women, the making of cheese and rancid butter, the herding of the sheep and goats. We were woken at dawn each morning by the voice of the mullah who had gone a few yards into the desert, spread his mat and, looking towards Mecca and bowing until his forehead touched the ground, called us all to prayer. If the Arabs in the tent were still asleep, as was usually the case, they did not move, but I noticed, when I went out to the mullah, that some of the young men with the goats and camels would also turn towards Mecca, kneel and touch the sand with their foreheads.

Although two wells we passed had water, the tribe was moving slowly and with difficulty. Jacques Edinger, who also had a smattering of Arabic, said that the Sheikh had told him that because of the drought, the Rualla had agreed to a truce in their feud with the Sbaa. The Sheikh had also said that the following morning we should reach one of the pumping stations of the pipeline where there would certainly be water for us; if we could get any for the tribe he would be grateful, but he was not hopeful as he had often tried before and had always been refused. We were so thirsty that, on receipt of this information, we drained a little water from our car radiator and made tea with it. It had boiled so often we were sure it could not contain any impurities.

Perhaps an hour after dawn next morning, as we moved with the caravan, we saw in the distance a compound surrounded by high wire mesh. We drove up to the gate. The rows of bungalows within the compound had flowers in their gardens and their green lawns were already being watered by sprinklers. After a few minutes the gate opened and a man on horseback, smartly dressed in brown riding boots, beige breeches and – of all things – a bowler hat, emerged and asked in English if he could do anything for us. I said we would be grateful for some water and he showed us where to go and get it. When I said that the Arabs with whom we were travelling were also short of water he politely replied that he was sorry but he was sure I would understand that if they ever started supplying the Bedouin the demands would never cease. I expostulated, but as he was adamant I thought it was better to get what we could. We took some spare 'bidons' back to the Sheikh and then sadly said goodbye.

We were in sight of Mount Hermon when we reached the Rualla. As we drove up I saw two open Rolls Royces with machine gun mountings in front parked in the end bay of Sheikh Nuri's tent, which was much larger than the tent which had recently been our home. Nuri, who had turned eighty, was small and thin, with a hawk-like face and bright eyes. Naif, the one of his many sons who we were told would succeed him, was also small but thicker in his features. According to Lieutenant Cazenave theirs was one of the most important Bedouin families and Nuri had influence in Damascus as well as in the desert.

Our business was quickly settled. By the time Cazenave left, on the day after we had arrived, we had Nuri's blessing and Naif's enthusiastic co-operation for the crossing of the Jordan. He promised to tell the groups of his tribe who lived near the river. Jacques Edinger had been particularly helpful with Naif and had sat up half the night talking Arab politics. Naif, whose French was flawless, promised that they would supply around a hundred horsemen, the same number of camel riders and a group which would carry baggage, women and children across the river on rafts made of poles attached to inflated goat skins. This was the traditional method of crossing the few rivers the Bedouin ever encountered.

The only section of the River Jordan which would have enough water to make the scene realistic, lay at the mouth of the Wadi Faria. Saud, our guide, was a relation of the Sheikh of the Wadi Faria and we were soon on excellent terms, sleeping in the Sheikh's tent and making all the arrangements for crossing the Jordan. Our friendship was sealed by a comic accident. In the middle of one night, during a sudden squall, the Sheikh's tent collapsed on all of us as we slept. Apart from the roughness of the goat's hair cloth, the first sensation of which I became aware was the passage of feet on top of us. At first the feet were small, but when something large, soft and heavy landed on my legs I realized that not only sheep and goats but camels were walking over us. With difficulty I communicated with Norman, who had been sleeping next to me, but our exchanges were interrupted by such a gale of laughter from our hosts that it was impossible to hear what was said. After a few moments we realized that if we wished for release and fresh air we would have to obtain it ourselves. One by one we groped our way on all fours to the edge of the fallen tent. The Arabs were laughing so much that it was several minutes before they joined us.

When it came to filming, everything went perfectly. The horsemen threw themselves into the spirit of the thing, galloping into the water, waving their swords and yelling. The more decorous camel riders continued along the bank until they found a section of the river where the water was only a trickle. The goat-skin rafts, carrying women, children and baggage, were pushed across pools by men who thoroughly enjoyed their bathe. How much it resembled Joshua's crossing can only be guessed at, but the scenes were to be described only as a reconstruction and were arguably as close to the original as it was possible to get.

*

Back in London we cut and edited the film. There were three productions. First, a series of six 15-minute, 16mm films on the Old Testament (in black and white), with a commentary and accompanying notebooks for the use of teachers in schools. We had worked out that, if only two education authorities ordered enough copies for regular use in their classrooms, we would recover our money in two or three years. Second, a full-length 16mm film called *From Abraham to Allenby*, which included everything we had shot and of which some sections were in colour. Money was running short so for this film I actually spoke the commentary to the pictures. Third, a 35mm 30-minute black and white film called *Between Two Worlds* which dealt with the situation in Palestine as we saw it at that moment.

Although only one education authority showed interest – it only ordered one copy of the series of six – we were not wholly without success. As a result of one of the private showings of *From Abraham to Allenby*, the Canadian Pacific Railway invited me to tour Canada with the film, which I did in 1938, and *Between Two Worlds* was accepted by one of the smaller cinema chains and shown during the next year or two. But Lord Wakefield's forebodings were justified. We were never able to repay him a penny and the little we earned was only just enough to cover our bills from the laboratories. A few years later, when I was a prisoner of war, my father found all the tins of film and accompanying notes in my room at the top of 4 The Cloisters, at Windsor Castle. He gave them all to the Religious Film Society who told me, years later, that they had made very good use of them.

But although School Films was not a successful commercial venture, it formed an important landmark in my life. I had learned that documentary films were an effective method of reporting, and that my ideas about the use of film were acceptable. I had learned how to use 35mm and 16mm cameras and how to cut and edit film physically as well as conceptually. I had also learned that to work for oneself is infinitely more rewarding than to work in an office, and that it was worth taking considerable risks to preserve one's independence.

Auxiliary Air Force

In between editing the film and taking it across Canada, I had joined the Labour Party. This gave me an extraordinary sense of freedom. For too long I had allowed the need to earn a living to dictate my way of life. Ideas mattered. All the crises which had been the background of my existence – the coal strike of 1922, the General Strike of 1926, galloping inflation, the collapses of the New York Stock Market, the failure of banks in Europe and America, chronic unemployment – suddenly seemed soluble. Socialism was the answer. If one could eliminate individual greed generated by the profit motive and substitute the ideals of service and common ownership, the root causes of all these problems would disappear. I met a lawyer who was a friend of Stafford Cripps and unburdened myself to him. He confirmed my belief by explaining that socialism was a way of life. One had not just to preach it, but live it. I felt born again. At once I decided to try and get my name on the list of candidates for Parliament.

The only Labour Member of Parliament with whom I had even a tenuous link was Hugh Dalton, whose father had been Canon of Windsor and had lived in 4 The Cloisters, which my father now inhabited.[1] I had never met Dalton but I wrote and told him of the double coincidence, our fathers living in the same house and a son of each joining the Labour Party. I was at once asked to visit him in the House of Commons.

Hugh, as he at once invited me to call him, was tall, spoke in an embarrassingly loud voice, and had the curious habit of dipping his forehead when he talked so that his eyes always seemed to be looking up at one from under his brows. At that moment he was Chairman of the Labour Party, carrying on a vigorous campaign to try and force it to recognize the necessity for rearmament and to defeat Sir Stafford Cripps and the Socialist League as well as James Maxton's

Independent Labour Party who were advocating a united front with the Communists to defeat the Government's rearmament plans. When I told him I had just joined the Auxiliary Air Force he said he would not only see that I was put on the Candidates' List but do his best to ensure that I was adopted for a winnable seat. Within a year, in the autumn of 1937, I was invited to go before the Labour Party Committee of the constituency of North Buckinghamshire, which included not only Buckingham but the railway towns of Bletchley and Wolverton, and was adopted as prospective candidate for the next general election, due in 1940. The seat was held by a Conservative with a majority of 6,588 and I did not rate my chances very highly.

The part-time agent for the Party was a young man called Ray Bellchambers who had been to Ruskin College in Oxford and was a pragmatic socialist, more interested in better housing, mains water supply and electricity in cottages than in nationalization, which he supported only as part of the Labour creed. He found me a friendly railwayman called Reg Butler who, with the consent of his wife, Nancy, would give me bed and breakfast in Bletchley whenever I needed it. I forget what I paid, but it was very little, and I went down as often as I could find the time. I soon realized that except for local committees in Bletchley and Wolverton, which consisted almost entirely of railwaymen, there was virtually no organization. To have any chance in a general election, we had to create a system of wards in every sizeable town and have a representative in every village. The constituency stretched from Olney in the north to Brill some sixty miles south, and was in places about fifty miles wide. My time was filled with film work and I was also flying most weekends.

However, on my return from Canada in the autumn I arranged to go and live with the Butlers for six months so I could get down to organizing the constituency. Money was a problem. The funds for the Palestine films had been exhausted and little was coming in. However, British Movietone, whose editor, Gerald Sanger, had been on the *Daily Mail*, came to the rescue by inviting me to act as an understudy for Leslie Mitchell, the well-known reader of Movietone News. It meant reading the news whenever he was away or wanted a day off, and was quite well paid. I also did occasional work for the BBC, particularly for the newly founded television department.

I had given up my flat when I went to Palestine in 1937 and gratefully accepted my parents' offer to make Windsor my base when I was not in Bletchley. They had always kept my room overlooking Eton available for me. This was particularly generous as neither had any sympathy with the Labour Party. My mother had been embarrassed when I joined it, and although my father understood the reasons and would discuss them, he never accepted my views.

By then, however, the prospect of fighting anything as peaceable as an election was becoming unreal. Ever since Hitler's reoccupation of the Rhineland in 1936, I had been convinced that war had become inevitable. That was the one occasion when the movement of a single French division would have forced Hitler to abandon the enterprise and might well have caused his downfall. France, which had occupied the Rhineland in 1923 only to find that it cost her more than any reparations she was likely to receive, was not going to move without the British, and the British were more interested in signing Lord Robert Cecil's peace pledge than in facing reality. Hitler was able to ignore Eden's suggestion that the Rhineland should not be militarized and proceed with his plans to annexe Czechoslovakia and Austria.

It was in 1936, therefore, that I revived an ambition to join the Auxiliary Air Force. I had always wanted to fly. Several years before, while still at Oxford, I had been invited by the then Commander of the 601 (County of London) Squadron, based at Hendon, to apply for membership and was given a trial by the adjutant, Sir Dermot Boyle (later Marshal of the R A F.) He had pronounced that I was suitable material but war did not then seem imminent and I had allowed other preoccupations to take precedence. This time I applied in earnest and was accepted. That many leaders of the Labour Party were still preaching disarmament only strengthened my resolve. Like Dalton I knew that war had to come and I wanted to be ready for it.

The Auxiliary Air Force, of which 601 was one of the original Squadrons, had been founded in 1925 by enthusiasts who had flown at the end of the First World War and believed that pilots could be trained to fly military aircraft while doing an ordinary civilian job. It was organized in County Squadrons by the Air Ministry, which also supplied instructors; but all the pilots and other ranks – fitters, riggers, armourers – were volunteer civilians who gave one or more evenings a week at a headquarters where they received technical instruction, and many weekends at the aerodrome where the Squadron flew. Most important of all were the annual 'camps' which lasted a fortnight and were held at different RAF stations around the country. Every member of the Squadron was expected to attend. It was the only occasion when the pilots could practise with live ammunition at targets on the ground and familiarize themselves with the Vickers machine gun.

A book has been written about 601 Squadron by one of its post-war pilots, Tom Moulson,[2] which captures much of the spirit in which it operated. Perhaps because flying was still something of an adventure, even in the 1930s, the pilots were a group of independent young men, several of whom were rich enough to own their own aeroplanes. Loel Guinness, Max Aitken, Whitney Straight, Willie Rhodes-Moorhouse and Archie Hope had all done many hundreds of hours flying privately and would often bring their aeroplanes to land in fields close to any pub in which the Squadron was relaxing. Roger Bushell, a barrister who was later shot on Hitler's direct orders after escaping from a prison camp in Germany, once overshot such a field in the Romney Marshes when flying an Aeronca belonging to Max Aitken. Bursting through a hedge on to the road, the little aeroplane decapitated a signpost and disintegrated. The signpost, bearing the words 'To Dymchurch', became a regular ornament on the dinner table of the Squadron's town headquarters near Notting Hill Gate. Max soon had another Aeronca in which he used to take me hedge-hopping. Philip Sassoon, the Honorary Air Commodore of the Squadron, also had his own aeroplane, a de Havilland Dragon Fly in which he used to ferry members of the Squadron down to his house, Port Lympne, in Kent.

I learned to fly at Hendon Aerodrome with Squadron Leader (later Air Vice-Marshal) John Hawtrey, who had been seconded from the Royal Air Force to be both adjutant and senior instructor to 601 Squadron. The aeroplane was an Avro 504, surely one of the most indestructible elementary training aircraft ever built. It was a bi-plane with large wings and a fixed undercarriage which contained a certain amount of rubber. Many times I would flatten out to land, imagining I was a foot or so above the runway, when in fact my height was ten feet or more, and drop the aircraft like a stone. The wheels seemed to splay out beneath us and then gradually come together again so that we never even felt a jolt. After the first few 'circuits and bumps', John hardly ever touched the controls. It was a grass airfield and the aircraft would often swing sideways in the wind so that I took off almost at right angles to the direction I intended. John sat impassively behind me, every now and then making a comment and always encouraging me whenever I did anything right. One gradually came to understand that an aeroplane has to fly unless the pilot does something which prevents it from doing so.

One day after quite a short lesson, John got out of the back seat when we landed, came up close to me as I sat in the cockpit and said, 'She's all yours, do half a dozen circuits and landings and when you've finished taxi over to the hangar.' He then walked away to his office. He had given me no warning that I was to go solo and although I had had many lessons, my total flying time was less than four hours. It was a great moment. When I had carried out his instructions, he came across the airfield grinning and congratulated me.

As my confidence increased, John took me through all the elementary aerobatics, tight turns, loops, rolls off the top, slow rolls, stalls and so on. Camp in 1938 was at Shoreham in the south of England, and after our guest night John Hawtrey, thinking perhaps that I was suffering from a hangover, put me through a testing half-hour. We took off at five a.m. and as soon as we had gained enough height, he told me to tighten my seat straps because we were going to do 'some inverted flying'. I remember him saying that the aircraft could fly upside down for several minutes without the engine giving any trouble and that as soon as I felt comfortable hanging in the straps, he would hand the machine over to me. Although we were both wearing parachutes, there was a momentary sense of alarm as he turned the aircraft over, but after a few seconds I felt quite comfortable hanging in the straps. He began to make me turn and get used to the controls working in the opposite to normal direction – for example, when one pulled the stick back, the nose of the aircraft went down instead of up – and we ended with a loop which began from the inverted position and from the top of which I rolled out into normal flight.

The aeroplane with which 601 Squadron was equipped in 1937 was the Demon, a two-seater Hawker bi-plane, powered by Rolls-Royce engines with a metal ring for an air-gunner behind the pilot. Sometimes we flew alone, sometimes with a gunner. The top speed was 160 mph but it was a wonderfully manoeuvrable aeroplane. One of our standard exercises was to practise 'forced landings', which meant side-slipping into a pre-selected field, touching down and then flying on again without stopping. By side-slipping steeply over the hedge we could get into almost any field, but one needed at least two hundred yards clear run to get out. I often used the field next to Edward Paget's house, below Ivinghoe Beacon, and sometimes stayed to lunch with him. Edward, our neighbour during the early years at Bishopthorpe and the only one of my old friends to share my interest in flying, worked in the Stock Exchange, but was still riding in steeplechases and flew his own aeroplane to race meetings. Once I got stuck in his field. It had rained heavily during lunch and the wheels sank into the ground. Edward and I were having difficulty in swinging the aeroplane around when a third man appeared and by lifting the tail managed to get the wheels out of their rut. I never discovered his name, but Edward told me later that he was an Air Vice-Marshal who lived just the other side of the field.

Another expedition almost ended fatally. It must have been in the autumn of 1937 when I was still editing the films shot in Palestine. I wanted shots of cumulus clouds and so, having consulted the weather maps, set off for South Wales with another pilot who knew how to use a film camera in the air-gunner's seat. His name was Guy Branch. We found lovely white, woolly clouds rising to twenty thousand feet over the Brecon Beacons and wove in and out of them for half an hour until Guy had exhausted his film. By then the clouds had thickened, and as we were low on petrol we had to come down through them. It was the first experience for both of us of cloud flying and I discovered at once how easy it is to lose one's sense not only of direction but of stability when one has no horizon. We started turning and side-slipping unintentionally. The only instruments to help us were a compass for direction and a glass tube rather like a thermometer containing an air bubble which indicated whether one was climbing or descending. So long as most of the bubble was above the line across the centre of the tube, then we were descending. As there was a good deal of turbulence one had to concentrate to keep it that way. Guy, looking over my shoulder, kept his eye on our air speed to make sure we did not stall.

After a few miles in dense cloud, the engine began to splutter and I turned on the reserve tank, pulling a lever above my head. This meant we had half an hour's petrol left. Coming through the cloud at a thousand feet we saw water below us. Guessing rightly that it was the

Bristol Channel we flew due east, followed a railway and when we saw a station ahead, came down so as to read the station's name. It was Tidworth. The map told us that Netheravon was not far away, and as we knew that the Central Flying School of the RAF was there, we landed and asked for petrol. We were given not only petrol but an excellent lunch and consulted our hosts about reaching Hendon. They got a weather report which told them it was clear over London with a cloud base of three thousand feet. There was low cloud drifting across the aerodrome, but we felt that we could follow the railway and should have no difficulty.

After taking off, a drift of low cloud blotted out the hangars in front of us and, when I suddenly saw them looming up quite close, I went hurriedly for the throttle with my left hand to make sure of clearing them. But instead of accelerating, the engine began to splutter and I had to turn back towards the airfield to avoid hitting the hangar roof. I just had enough speed to complete the turn but not enough to straighten out the aircraft and we landed crabwise on the grass. The undercarriage collapsed and the wings half folded. Guy jumped out of the air-gunner's seat, but the centre section of the fuselage had buckled over my head and I could not move it. The aircraft had caught fire and flames began licking my face. I shouted to Guy, who came back at once, stood on the bottom wing and, ignoring the flames, bent back the centre section and lifted me out. Fortunately, although of slight build, he was an exceptionally strong man. If the petrol tanks had exploded, he would have been killed with me.

When the flames had been put out, the Netheravon instructors examined the cockpit and told me that in going too hurriedly for the throttle I had also pushed forward the choke lever which lay alongside it and had flooded the engine. Guy was unhurt and I only had a few blisters on my cheeks. We went back to London by train. A few weeks later, after I had written a full report, Guy was awarded the Empire Gallantry Medal, shortly to be superceded by the George Cross to which all holders of the Empire Gallantry Medal became entitled. But by then he had been killed, shot down over the English Channel in 1940.

A Declaration of War

In the event of war the Auxiliary Squadrons became part of the front line of Fighter Command. When 601 Squadron was called up during the Munich Crisis in 1938, I was in Canada showing my films and was not called home.

On the morning of September 3rd, 1939, I was sitting with my mother in the Lansdowne Club in Berkeley Square listening to Mr Chamberlain on the radio. The air raid warning sirens began as soon as he had finished speaking, and my first thought was to get my mother out of London as quickly as possible. I had already been called up and was in uniform. We went straight out to the car and I drove through the rapidly emptying streets, waving imperiously at air raid wardens who lowered their hands when they saw my Air Force cap. We reached Windsor in less than half an hour along the old Great West Road.

We had been expecting war for so long that its declaration was something of an anti-climax. The members of our Squadron had been sitting in deck-chairs outside our mess at Hendon for several days awaiting instructions which never came. It was a relief to know that at last we would be told where we were to go. I do not remember philosophizing or having sad or profound thoughts; the prospect of action was exciting. Had one had doubts about the necessity to fight, it would have been different, but no one I knew had any doubt at all. One realized that the chances of survival were small but that was not a thought to dwell on. One hoped that one would not be too afraid and longed to get cracking.

We already knew that the squadron was to be re-equipped with twin-engined short-nosed Blenheims and to have the role of night fighting. I had my 'wings' but was not fully operational; as all our instructors were to leave us as soon as war was declared, I had been told I would have to go on a conversion course to learn to fly twin-engines.

Before the end of the month the Squadron went to Biggin Hill in Kent to train for night fighting and I went to South Cerney in Gloucestershire. The catering for the mess of four hundred officers was run by a young Canadian pilot who had been working for the Canadian Pacific Railway. For three shillings and sixpence a day he provided us with better food than you could get in most hotels. I thought sadly of the food at Harrow and wondered why nobody had learned how to feed five hundred boys equally well.

One day I had to make a belly landing. I had been on a cross-country in an Oxford trainer and when I came into land and put the wheels down, the indicator light which signified they were locked did not come on. I reported this to the control tower and flew round for nearly two hours doing everything they told me including using the hand pump but to no avail. The wheels went down each time I pressed the knob, but the light never came on. I suspected it was only an electrical fault and, knowing that aeroplanes were in short supply, I told control that I was quite ready to make a landing without the indicator light if they would allow me to. They refused. Finally, when I was low on petrol, they told me to land on the grass beside the runway with my wheels up. I did this successfully, but of course the propellors were bent and the engines needed a complete overhaul. I never heard whether the fault was electrical or in the locking gear, but the experience was to prove valuable later on.

I came out equal top in the conversion course and rejoined the Squadron which had moved to Tangmere in Sussex, still flying short-nosed Blenheims. No less suitable aircraft for night flying could be imagined. The Blenheims were too slow to catch a German bomber and, when the four machine guns lodged under the fuselage were fired, the aeroplane seemed almost to stop. The cockpit was covered in glass like a greenhouse so that when one was caught in a searchlight the light was so dazzling it was almost impossible to see the instruments. On my first night back at Tangmere I went up as an observer with Jack Riddle, one of two brothers in the Squadron, on a patrol over London. The searchlights not only found us, but held us for minutes at a time. Whether the anti-aircraft guns whose flashes we could see below were firing at us, we never knew; nothing burst close enough to matter.

We did learn, however, that our anti-aircraft gunners were incapable of identifying an aeroplane by its silhouette. Sometimes we were sent on patrols along the English Channel and told to come back down the Thames estuary. We never flew very high, but even if it was a clear night, our own anti-aircraft batteries opened up at us from both banks of the river. We knew several people in the batteries and when we got back we would ring them up and tease them about aircraft recognition and tell them what bad shots they were.

The arrival of Hurricanes in the New Year changed everything. We were given three weeks to familiarize ourselves with the new machines and then became part of the daylight defence of London. During the period of familiarization I made a bad mistake. We were flying in formation and I was on the wing. One had to keep within a foot or two of one's neighbour or one could easily be left behind on a turn. I was concentrating and enjoying it. Brian Thynne, our Commanding Officer, was leading but when we came in to land, as I thought, he went on round the circuit again. This happened a second time and I realized that something must be wrong. I turned on my inter-communication radio to hear Brian's voice saying quietly, 'Aidan, you bloody fool, put your wheels down.' We landed next time round and I was mercilessly teased.

Shortly after this Brian left to take command of a station, and Loel Guinness, a member of the well-known brewing family, who had owned his own aircraft for years and was a former member of the Squadron, took command. We did high-level patrols over the Channel and I remember thinking that if my engine cut out I could easily glide down and land in either France or England. Occasionally we were scrambled, but it was always a false alarm. We saw no Germans. Several Squadron wives came and stayed in the area, and one day Virginia Cowles, the American war correspondent who had become a friend during the past two years, came down to visit us. Years later, when we were married, she told me that she was standing next to Loel when our formation flew over the airfield and he remarked how well I was flying.[1]

There seemed to be no end to the 'phoney war' and life at Tangmere became monotonous. Then one day, at the end of February 1940, the adjutant, John Peel, came up to me and said that the Squadron had been asked to suggest someone to join the Balkan Intelligence Service. Would I like to go? It would mean being based at Istanbul to start with and he thought I would find it interesting. 'If the war really develops you can always return to flying later,' he added. I discussed it with friends and decided to accept. It meant becoming an Assistant Air Attaché with the rank of Squadron Leader on the staff of the Ambassador in Ankara, with the right to report directly to the Air Ministry. Within a week I was on the Simplon–Orient Express bound for Istanbul.

The Embassy had been most efficient in preparing for my arrival. The Ambassador, Sir Hughe Knatchbull-Hugessen and Air Commodore Robert George, my immediate boss, were both in Ankara, but the Consul-General, Mr Campbell, the Assistant Military and Naval Attachés and the Passport Control Officer who ran the local branch of the secret service – a Mr Whittall – all inhabited the great Embassy in Pera, built in the eighteenth century for Sir Stratford Canning, probably the most respected representative the British have ever had in the Middle East. Between them, they had rented me a large penthouse flat at the top of a high-rise building overlooking the Bosphorus, found a Greek couple to look after me, provided an Embassy car and driver and engaged a clerk named Embery, a South African, who had already furnished my office. I had met Bobby George and his pretty wife Betty when he was an Honorary Commodore of an Auxiliary Squadron in England. He rang up that night and suggested I come to Ankara as soon as possible so that we could have a talk.

Ankara, a night's train journey from Istanbul, is set in a huge but barren bowl of the Anatolian mountains, an ugly modern city without any striking buildings. I stayed with Bobby and Betty and was taken to see the Ambassador. Sir Hughe said that his chief headache at that moment was the pressure being put upon him by the British Government to induce Turkey to enter the war on the side of the Allies. It was a futile effort. The Turks were determined to avoid being drawn into the war for fear of being attacked by the Germans. Whenever he tried to persuade them otherwise, they always asked the same question: what could Britain do to help them prevent or withstand such an attack? The answer was always so plainly inadequate that it was greeted with polite smiles. There was plenty of goodwill towards Britain, partly inherited from the days of Sir Percy Lorraine, the British Ambassador in the 1920s who had become Kemal's poker-playing adviser and confidant. But there was also a pro-German faction in Ankara and the army which Franz von Papen, German Chancellor before the rise of Hitler and now German Ambassador to Turkey, was careful to cultivate. Sir Hughe's fear was that if we pushed the Turkish Government too hard it would become more and more inclined to listen to von Papen, who outwardly championed Turkish neutrality and was able to offer considerable inducements in the way of arms to maintain it.

We talked in a sunny sitting room, the chairs and sofas of which were covered not only with bright chintzes but with innumerable papers many of which I noticed were marked 'top secret'. I remarked on this to Bobby and he replied that he didn't think the Ambassador was very security minded, but of course everything would be put in a safe at the end of the day. Three years later, when as a prisoner of war I read a book about 'Operation Cicero' in the German press, I wondered whether this laxness had prompted 'Cicero', the code-name given by the Germans to Sir Hughe's valet, to embark on his career as one of the most successful of all spies. There could be another explanation. The book, written by L.C. Moyzisch, the attaché from the Reich Security Department at the German Embassy in Ankara who was made responsible for 'Cicero', makes it plain that at some point the British became aware of 'Cicero' and from that moment onwards his contribution was virtually useless to the Germans.[2] It is possible, therefore, that the British knew about 'Cicero' from the beginning and that the top secret papers which he so successfully photographed were all planted by the British secret service. Ribbentrop, the German Foreign Minister, always suspected this and for once he may have been right.

But the impossibility of involving Turkey in the war did not mean there was nothing we could do to help it maintain its neutrality. Bobby George introduced me to one of the 'infiltrated' airmen, Wing Commander Teddy Huddleston,[3] who had been part of a team of flying instructors sent to Turkey in 1939 and who had volunteered to stay on as an adviser when the team was sent home at the outbreak of war. I was to accompany Teddy, whom I had already met playing cricket in England, on a tour of Turkey to select sites for the storage of a large number of 500-lb bombs with which we had agreed to supply her. We would be flown around in Turkish military aircraft and later, when the bombs arrived, we would be asked to supervise the unloading and siting of bomb dumps in different parts of the country.

The tour took us to many of the Turkish Air Force bases, including one on the north coast near Samsun, and out to Erzerum in the east.

There we were introduced to an old lady in Turkish peasant dress who in 1916 had borne arms when the Turks repelled the Russian advance. We also attended a great party in the mess after the circumcision of one of the officers' sons.

The proposed sites for bomb dumps were mainly ruined or old and disused mosques, some of which had originally been built as churches by the Armenians. Quite often they were in isolated positions, the villages which they once served having been totally destroyed during the Armenian massacres of the 1920s. We refrained from asking questions. Our tour included the Gallipoli Peninsula whose scrub land was easily accessible from the sea and provided excellent cover for dumps of bombs. One of the Turkish officers was a historian who explained the 1915–16 campaign to us. Rusty barbed wire, water bottles and trenching tools were still lying in the sand dunes behind Anzac Cove; the dunes were so steep and the sand so soft one could well understand how difficult it would have been for our troops to advance under fire. Nevertheless, our guide reminded us, when General Hamilton's troops landed, there were no Turkish troops on that part of the peninsula. Had he persevered immediately instead of giving his troops forty-eight hours' rest, they could have reached the Sea of Marmara in a few hours and almost certainly have secured a bridgehead. In the event, only one Turkish reserve division reached the dunes during those forty-eight hours, but that was sufficient to prevent our troops making headway when the order to advance was given. It is one of the quirks of history that the leader of that division was Lieutenant-Colonel Mustapha Kemal, later known as Kemal Atatürk, founder of modern Turkey.

It is alway exciting to go through the Dardanelles. The width at its narrowest is only eight hundred yards, and the old Turkish gun emplacements on the steep banks at Chanak and Kilid Bahr are not only plainly visible but have 'March 1915' picked out in white chalk to remind one of the date of the British attack. We steamed close under one of them while our self-appointed guide pointed out that although the range was point-blank it would have been impossible for the Turkish 16-inch gun barrels to be depressed sufficiently to hit us.

19

Bombs and Belly-Dancers

The bombs were unlikely to arrive before June, so I returned to Istanbul. Although it has been my dream city ever since that first visit, it is only fair to say that it does not appear in that light to everyone. Most of the streets are narrow and dirty, the roads tortuous. Except along the shore of the Bosphorus where some picturesque old wooden Turkish houses remain, the domestic architecture is ugly and without character. In spite of the attempt by Kemal Atatürk to exterminate stray dogs, they still abound. The traffic, even in 1940, was appalling. Sometimes during the rush hours it could take an hour to cross Galata Bridge. The waters of the Golden Horn which pass beneath the bridge were slimy and smelly. I was never able to discover the features that gave it such a romantic name; now it was just a disused inlet of the sea.

We were living a curious half-life. Western Europe was being torn apart by a war which might at any moment engulf us, but meanwhile, on the surface, we were at peace. Every day in the streets and cafés we would rub shoulders with Germans and Italians, Russians, French and Greeks and give no sign that our friends and relations were busy trying to kill each other. One would find oneself politely giving way in a bookshop queue to a lady who gave her order in German and in the Istanbul Club would sit at tables between groups of Italians and Germans. At dances at the Moda Yacht Club we had to be careful that our Turkish friends did not invite us to join parties which included our enemies.

My two fellow assistant military attachés, also part of Balkan Intelligence Services, were Major Guy Sitwell, whose long, narrow face, high-bridged nose and receding forehead made him look rather like his cousin Edith, and Commander Vova Wolfson, RN, part-Russian, part-Jewish, clever and friendly, who had known Istanbul before the war. The Consul-General was informed of the movement of

154

all ships passing through the Bosphorus or Dardanelles or entering Turkish ports and would consult Vova as to their bona fides if any were suspicious. Guy kept in touch with the officers of the Turkish garrison and I with the handful of Air Force officers who controlled the International Airport at Yesilköy. But there was little to do. We read a host of cables, received a few visitors passing through on their way to or from Ankara, and in the evenings watched a glamorous belly-dancer in Taxim Square's main café, or went to the best restaurant in the city which was sited in a sort of cave and run by two Polish ladies. Polish refugees came through Istanbul all the time trying to join General Anders' army or get to England. I saw those who had been in the Polish Air Force and would try to arrange for them to go to London where the Air Ministry had a high opinion of their fighting qualities.

By mid-May, Hitler's attack on France was absorbing all our interest. I knew 601 Squadron would be involved, and longed for news, but not even Bobby George could supply it. I would walk past the German Embassy in Pera, which was almost as grand as ours but had the advantage of looking over the Bosphorus, and entertain wild schemes of blowing it up. Major Hulme, one of the regular military attachés, sent round a minute reminding us how close the enemy were and insisting that we all have loaded revolvers on our desks in case a German commando tried to raid us. Once, a splendid figure, Admiral Kelly (retired), descended on us from London via Ankara and took several of us to visit a gun-runner who had a large house on the banks of the Bosphorus, guarded by several Dobermann Pinschers. Ignoring the dogs sniffing at his heels, the Admiral strode into the house and, over drinks, conveyed to our host, a man of undisclosed nationality who looked far too rich and polished, that we knew of his gun-running activities and that it would be most unfortunate for him if any of his weapons were found to be in the hands of our enemies. The Admiral was met with a charming smile and a disclaimer that any such weapons existed.

In the summer the bombs began to arrive and I was ordered to Izmir (formerly Smyrna) to await a ship which was on its way through the Aegean Sea. Rooms had been booked for me in an hotel at the north end of Izmir's great bay and I spent the days of waiting visiting people to whom I had been given introductions, particularly a well-known carpet dealer who displayed his wares on the sea front about half a mile south of the hotel and was happy to give one the names of Germans or Italians who did business with him. The weather was glorious and quite hot by midday. Every morning at seven o'clock I paid a fisherman to come to the hotel jetty and row me out into the bay to swim among the shoals of sardines which glinted in the water. When the ship arrived it anchored in the middle of the bay. I was taken aboard by Turkish officers and introduced to the captain and to a British naval artificer who had been responsible for loading the bombs. He showed them to me, lying in the hold in the centre of the ship; the main hatch was open in preparation for the unloading. But the Turkish dock workers refused to handle the bombs, saying they had no guarantee they would not explode. The artificer explained to them and to me that the bombs had no fuses and were therefore in no danger of exploding. The men still refused to lift them so I asked the captain to lower me on to the bombs so that I could jump about on them while the dockers watched. Eventually this did the trick. Slings were lowered and the bombs were winched up one by one and lowered over the side into a barge which took them ashore. They were then loaded into lorries and taken to pre-selected sites in the hills outside Izmir, where they were stacked among gorse bushes. There was an airfield only a few miles away to which they could easily be transported if the need arose.

With the fall of France the Balkans suddenly became important. It seemed inevitable that whether or not the Germans invaded England, the Rome–Berlin Axis would occupy the Balkans so as to make sure of Rumanian oil and probably would attack Greece and even Russia. I received a telegram from the Air Ministry warning me that I was to be posted to Sofia, the capital of Bulgaria. Bobby George rang up the same day and asked me to go to Ankara at once to say goodbye. I caught the night train and spent the next day being briefed.

That evening we dined at a restaurant much frequented by diplomats, to find the French Ambassador, René Massigli, and his wife Odette at the next table. The Georges had been on intimate terms with the Massiglis and were incensed that since Pétain had signed the armistice they would not even speak to their English friends. When the Massiglis came to London as de Gaulle's emissaries, I asked René if he did not feel he had carried his loyalty to Pétain too far in boycotting the British in Ankara in 1940. He replied that he still did not see what else he could have done. If he had maintained his former intimacy he would have been recalled to France. At that time he did not support de Gaulle and his duty was to be loyal to Pétain. It was only in 1942, after the Allies had invaded North Africa, that he changed his mind. He had an interview with Pétain during which the old man actually said to him that he hoped the Germans would win the war. On that he made plans to escape from France and go to London.

20

Posted to Sofia

In Sofia one felt closer to the war. Our Ambassador, George Rendel, had tried to prevent King Boris, himself of German descent, from joining the Axis and had had some success through 1939. King Boris was shrewd enough to see that once Bulgaria got drawn in to the war his days as a monarch would be numbered. But when Hitler lost the Battle of Britain, German pressure on the Balkan countries became irresistible. In November 1940 one East European leader after another was summoned to Berlin and ordered to join the 'New Order in Europe'. It was made quite plain that if they refused they would either be deposed or attacked. The first to succumb was General Antonescu of Rumania, who had forced King Carol to abdicate in September. He welcomed the German troops which occupied Ploeşti oilfields and strategic points in his country in November 1940 and joined the Axis pact which included Japan. Dr Tuka, the ruler of Slovakia, followed. King Boris avoided joining the pact for the moment so that the British and other Western missions were able to remain in Sofia through the winter, but the indications were clear.

The Embassy was small but active. The Press Attaché, Stephen Runciman,[1] tall, thin and scholarly, was not only expert in Bulgarian history but spoke the language fluently and made himself extremely popular. Our Military Attaché, Colonel Alec Ross, dark and swarthy with a black moustache, who had married a Pole, spoke Russian and a little Bulgarian as well. His assistant, Cavan Elliot, a member of the Balkan Intelligence Service, was organizing a resistance movement to operate when the German occupation began. We also housed the first representatives of SOE (Special Operations Executive) who arrived flush with money, in the distribution of which, as we thought, they were not always wise, and a Passport Control Officer who employed many Bulgarian agents and reported directly to 'M' in Whitehall.

My clerk, Embery, who came with me from Istanbul, had found an office alongside Cavan Elliot's on the top floor of an office block which the Embassy rented. We were kept busy verifying and usually denying rumours about which the Air Ministry in London asked endless questions. German troops were reported to have crossed the Danube from Rumania in large numbers; German military aircraft were assembling on Sofia airfield. We still had freedom of movement and I took photographs of the whole Sofia airfield with a telescopic lens, showing that the few aircraft using it all had Bulgarian markings. We soon realized that the rumours were originated by the Passport Control Officer's agents who were anxious to earn their money. At one point Cavan and I got so irritated with repeated reports of German crossings of the Danube that we took my car, an old-fashioned Buick, motored up to Lom and turned east along the south bank of the river where the crossings were supposed to be taking place. There was no sign of any troops, German or otherwise, and the interpreter we took with us said he was sure the people were telling the truth when they said they had neither seen nor heard of any crossings. There were no bridges.

We had booked in at an hotel in a small town and were having supper when some policemen walked in and said they had received instructions to accompany us back to Sofia by train. Our car would be driven down for us. We had been away three days, seen all we wanted, so made no objection. The train journey was comic. The young policemen, who were armed but very nervous, occupied the compartments on either side of us. To tease them a little we would every now and then open our window and lean out. Immediately heads appeared on either side of us. We would smile at them and shut the window again. They were greatly relieved when we reached Sofia and they could drive us back to the Embassy.

Cavan Elliot's main work consisted of distributing small bombs and radios to Bulgarians who were forming resistance cells. There were more of these than might have been expected. In spite of the fact that their King was a German, the Bulgarians maintained that it was the Russians who had liberated them from the Turkish Empire, and Russians have always been their friends. As soon as the whisper went round (in February 1941) that the Germans were planning an attack on the Soviet Union, a large number of Bulgarians joined the resistance.

Cavan, who was an explosives expert, received his supplies in suitcases sent by diplomatic bag. He would store them in a room between our two offices and do his tests quite openly in his own room or in the passage. We were well protected from interruption. When a large batch of bombs arrived, the suitcases would reach the ceiling and overflow into my room. I would often lend him a hand and he would explain the fundamental characteristics of the bombs. One day he received a new type of fire bomb which he had been told was suitable for destroying archives: quite a difficult thing to do without attracting attention because closely packed reams of paper do not burn easily. The Ambassador had asked for such a bomb but Cavan thought it best to wait until he was away for a few days before carrying out the test. He needed a safe packed with sheets of paper and the only suitable one was on an upper floor of the Embassy proper. Cavan had a key and when the Ambassador departed he asked me to help him. We had to work at night.

The fire bomb was shaped like one of those small tubes which carried messages through pipes in a newspaper office: a cylinder about a foot long. Cavan had drilled a tiny hole in the side of the safe through which he could pass a wire connected to the bomb. He had already filled the safe with old files and after laying the bomb in the middle of them he threaded the wire through the hole and locked the safe. To a layman's eye the door of the safe fitted so tightly that it seemed impossible even to pass a hair through it, yet when Cavan pulled the wire and ignited the bomb, sheets of flame came through the sides and top of the door and started blackening the ceiling. He had not expected this but said that when the initial explosion of the fire bomb had spent itself the flames would die down. We armed ourselves with the equivalent of two minimaxes and waited. After what seemed an age, during which I thought the whole embassy might catch fire, the flames died down. Then we had to wait for the safe to cool. When we finally opened it the files had been reduced to a heap of paper ash. Cavan was gratified and with his clerk spent the next morning repainting the walls and ceiling of the room where the safe stood. When the Ambassador returned he was delighted to learn that he need worry no longer about how to destroy his files in secret.

Christmas came and went and snow descended on Mount Vitosha, which rises for several thousand feet just outside the city of Sofia. One morning, Alec Ross, the Military Attaché, rang and asked me to go to his room. He had received an extraordinary communication. A Bulgarian peasant farmer named Kiroff had been to see him and told him that his daughter was married to a German called Baur who was Hitler's personal pilot. Kiroff said that his son-in-law wanted to stop the war and had offered to fly Hitler to England on the next suitable occasion if we would give him the necessary instructions – how to approach the English coast, what signals to flash, and so on. Later I saw Kiroff twice with Alec Ross. He had brought photographs of Baur with his wife and children so that we could test his veracity. Alec asked me to send the photographs to the Air Ministry and get a report from them. The Air Ministry confirmed that Hitler's pilot *was* called Baur and that he had a wife and two children, but told us that so far they had not found anyone who could definitely verify whether the people in the photograph were the Baurs or not. They added that just in case anything came of the idea, Baur should approach the English coast at Manston in Kent with his wheels down and at a height of not more than three hundred feet, flashing a signal which they set out. Alec saw Kiroff again, gave him the message and arranged to meet him at an address in Belgrade on a day in the following week. Kiroff would then give us a definite answer. At no time did he ask for money.

At this point Alec brought in the Ambassador. George Rendel was as sceptical as we were but the whole episode was so curious that he sent a telegram to Sir Alec Cadogan, the head of the Foreign Office, setting out the facts and asking whether we should go ahead. A telegraph came back saying: 'Anything is worth a try,' signed Cadogan, so Alec Ross and I went to Belgrade. Hugh Macdonald, the Air Attaché in Belgrade, was amused and encouraging. After all, we had nothing to lose. Alec and I went to the address we had been given a little before time and waited. Nobody came. We went the next evening with the same result. Then, not surprised but a little deflated, we returned to Sofia. We never heard nor saw Kiroff again. I read a year or so later that Baur had retired but there was no suggestion that he was in any sort of trouble.[2]

In early February we had two unusual visitors. A beautiful young Polish woman called Christine Gyjiska and a round-faced, jolly ex-Polish officer called Andrew Kowerski walked into my office and said they had just driven from Budapest. Both had been working for the Polish underground but had been arrested in Budapest and interrogated under the muzzles of sub-machine guns. Fortunately the interrogators, Magyar officers who hated the Germans, had let them go. They had brought with them several rolls of microfilm which showed that large-scale preparations were being made by the Germans in Poland for a campaign against the Russians. Ths was the first positive evidence of its kind, and having sent a report both to Cairo and London, I arranged for Christine and Andrew to take their films via Istanbul to Egypt. I was soon to learn that Christine was already a legendary Polish heroine.

As February wore on, life became a little more tense. Both Cavan and I were obliged to change our apartments as the Ministry of Foreign Affairs needed them. Embery found me a new one which was immediately below that occupied by the Chief of Staff of the Bulgarian Army. I had warned the Air Ministry that I thought a German occupation imminent and on March 1st I heard that German troops had crossed the frontier from Yugoslavia. Next morning I drove immediately to the Sofia airfield, parked behind some bushes and watched. Several transport aircraft landed, carrying high-ranking German officers who were warmly welcomed by their Bulgarian counterparts. I took some photographs and returned to Sofia. Climbing the stairs to my flat, I saw jackboots above me. From the voices I overheard, I judged that they belonged to German officers. But luckily I was not seen or discovered and was able to tune in to the BBC on the wireless. I heard first that the Bulgarians had invited the German Army and Air Force into their country, and second that King Boris was on his way to Berlin to sign the Axis pact. That meant that we should have to leave Sofia, probably within forty-eight hours.

Next morning I went out into the streets and saw small groups of people standing about, waiting quietly. At about eleven o'clock German tanks and armoured cars rolled down the main street and fanned out into the city. I stood and watched them. When I got back to the Embassy I was told that the Ambassador had heard that Cavan and I were to be arrested. We were not to go back to our flats but take the next train to Belgrade; Yugoslavia had not yet been attacked by the Germans and still had communications with the free world. Our clerks would collect all our things and bring them on the special train which was to take Rendel, his daughter Anne and the rest of the Embassy staff to Istanbul as soon as they were ready to leave. Cavan and I reached Belgrade without incident and within forty-eight hours were on a train to Salonika. We arrived at Istanbul thirty-six hours later.

I took Cavan straight to the British Embassy. There we met our clerks and Embery told me the news. Cavan's clerk and he had left Sofia with the Embassy party the day before, having packed all our things in suitcases. Before getting into the train they had counted the suitcases on the platform and found that there were two more than they expected. They opened the ones they did not recognize and saw what they took to be radio batteries inside. Knowing the work that Cavan had been doing, they assumed that these were for sets he had not had time to distribute and put them in the luggage racks with the others. The party reached Istanbul safely, was met by a team from the Embassy, and taken to the Pera Palace Hotel. Embery's wife and father-in-law lived in Istanbul so he went straight to their home and dumped his luggage, including one of the extra suitcases, in the hall. He then set out on foot for the Pera Palace. As he came up the hill towards it he heard a loud explosion and saw the whole front of the hotel come out into the street. He had been worried throughout the journey by the extra suitcases and the explosion confirmed his fears. He immediately rushed back to his father-in-law's house, grabbed the suspect suitcase and ran through the streets to a quarry where he dumped it and alerted the police. Luckily the time-fuse in that suitcase had been even more faulty than the one which had exploded the bombs in the hall of the hotel, so the police were able to defuse it before the bombs went off. It transpired that the bombs had been placed among the Embassy luggage by a Bulgarian terrorist organization who had intended them to go off in the train, killing the entire staff. But it was not until the party were registering in the hotel foyer with their suitcases on the floor a few yards away, that the bombs had exploded. Eleven people were killed and many more injured. George Rendel was upstairs in his room; his daughter Anne was saved by a marble pillar which stood between her and the explosion. Embery's presence of mind had not only saved the lives of his wife and father-in-law, but probably of several others in neighbouring houses or in the street. He was later awarded a medal for gallantry.

When Cavan and I arrived next day, Bobby George came down from Ankara to see us. He asked me what I would like to do now that the

Balkan Intelligence Service was being wound up. Within a week he had arranged a passage for me on a ship leaving Mersin, in southern Turkey, bound for Alexandria. I was to report to RAF headquarters in Cairo.

21

Desert Action

We left Mersin at night, heading for Haifa in Palestine. Our ship was pitch dark but there was a moon and our wake must have been clearly visible from the air. We had two naval gunners on board, one in the stern and one in the bows, armed with light anti-aircraft cannons. I went on deck with Lord Carlisle, who was also on his way to Cairo from Ankara, and talked to the gunners. They said that the nearest German aircraft must be based in Greece, which the British were in the process of evacuating. Only a long-ranged aeroplane could reach us and they did not expect to see one. Nevertheless, after half an hour at sea, while we were still on deck, we heard the sound of an aeroplane and soon a twin-engined aircraft started circling the ship, quite low down. It never came over us and it was difficult to get a clear silhouette, but one of the gunners said he thought it might be a Heinkel. Both of them swivelled their guns and followed it, but neither fired. After circling us three times, the aircraft finally flew away to the west.

We kept close to the Palestine coast and reached Haifa the following evening. I had been told to report at Lydda where there was a Royal Air Force training school. I was hoping for a few hours' flying practice before going on to Egypt. The Commanding Officer there was Wing Commander Paddy Dunn (later Air Marshal Sir Patrick Dunn) whom I had known before the war. He was smart, cheerful and efficient but said that he had so many pupils he could not give me more than an hour's flying. He had no Hurricanes or Spitfires, but I could take a Kittihawk which had recently been delivered. Gratefully I climbed into the cockpit. It was heavier and slower than a Hurricane, but at least I got the feel of an aircraft again. Paddy arranged for me to get a lift down to Cairo.

When I reported at Royal Air Force headquarters in Cairo, I was told I would probably be posted to Syria where we were about to engage the

Vichy French. This pleased me, as I knew that my younger brother, Kenneth, was going there with the Somerset Yeomanry. I then ran into Peter Oldfield, with whom I had played cricket for Oxford, who asked me to stay at his home. He told me that Elizabeth, his wife, had turned their flat into a sort of lodging house for friends. The flat was at the end of a passage in an apartment block. When I rang the bell the door was half opened by a figure in a tarbush who stared fixedly at me before letting me in. This was 'Mo', an Arab servant later made famous by Sir Charles Johnston in his book *Mo and Other Eccentrics*. Fortunately, Peter and Elizabeth had only 'borrowed' him for the night; Mo was famous for appraising those who came to the door, taking an instant like or dislike, and if the latter, shutting the door on them immediately. Had he been at his own master's flat he might well have refused to let me in. Elizabeth deserved a medal for her hospitality. Peter was later shot through the neck when serving with the SAS; it is a miracle that he is still alive.

To my amazement I had found that my brother Kenneth was also staying at Peter's flat, on a week's leave from Palestine. Neither of us had more than a few days in Cairo but we managed a game of golf at the Gezira Club and I played a game of cricket in which, he reminds me, I was bowled out for nought by the 'pro', a Mr Hammond. We went to a night club which compared unfavourably with those I had recently seen in Sofia, Belgrade and Istanbul: there were no belly dancers and no one with whom to do the Slav 'teapot' dance. Then suddenly Kenneth was recalled to Palestine and I saw him off at Cairo station. As he leaned out of the window waving goodbye I remember thinking how absurdly young and handsome he looked. He was twenty-six and neither of us expected to see the other again.

Within a few days of Kenneth's departure, I was posted, not to Syria, but to 73 Fighter Squadron at Sidi Hanish in the Western Desert. As Commander of 'A' Flight, I was told that I should be in active command of the squadron. I confess I had misgivings. I knew from my experience at South Cerney that I was at least average as a pilot, but I had never commanded a flight or fired a shot in anger. On the other hand, from what Paddy Dunn had told me at Lydda, I realized that the Middle East Air Force must be hard pressed at that moment to find pilots, even with my limited experience. The squadrons which had been longest in the desert had recently been sent to Greece and Syria and those left were being reorganized and re-equipped with Hurricanes. I decided therefore to say nothing and do my best.

My farewell to Cairo was dramatic. I was asked if I would mind ferrying to a neighbouring squadron a Hurricane which had been adapted to carry 20mm cannons, one on either wing. Thinking that this was further proof of the versatility of the Hurricane, I said yes, and duly arrived at Heliopolis where the aeroplane was waiting in a hangar.

I could tell that the flight-sergeant who took me to the aircraft was slightly apprehensive. 'You won't have any difficulty,' he said. 'Another officer took one of these aircraft out last week. But we haven't much room on this airfield and so we've moved the aeroplane as far back as we can get it in the hangar. We'll hold her down while you rev up to full throttle and I'll signal to you when you are to let go the brakes.'

We were now entering the hangar and I saw the Hurricane parked with its tail almost touching the back wall. Some aircraftmen were standing by the wings. On top of each wing was a 20mm cannon with an oblong bubble about twice the size of a rugby football sticking out behind it. I then looked out in front and saw a line of palm trees about twenty-five feet high at the other end of the field. These I should have to clear. But for the cannon I should never have given it a thought, but I believed the flight-sergeant when he said that a take-off had already been successfully achieved, and got into the cockpit. Two men stood holding the end of each wing and two more were on the tail plane. I revved up to full throttle and saw the flight-sergeant at the front edge of the hangar drop his hand. I released the brakes and we shot forward. The take-off was quite normal but I noticed that the aircraft seemed heavy; at our angle of climb I thought we could just clear the trees. We did, with three or four feet to spare, and I set out due west. When I landed at the desert airfield the squadron leader came to greet me as I got out of the aeroplane. He looked rather grim. 'You must forgive me if we don't give you a very warm welcome,' he said. 'We had hoped never to see another of these bloody things,' indicating the aeroplane I had just brought in. 'They are death traps and I have already lost two of my pilots because of them.' I knew just what he meant, having flown the aeroplane, but I said nothing. 'Of course it's not your fault,' he went on. 'It's just a bloody silly idea of someone at headquarters.' I got into his jeep and he drove me the few miles to Sidi Hanish.

At Sidi Hanish I found that almost all the pilots had recently come from flying schools in Rhodesia and South Africa and that although they seemed to be of high calibre, they were very young, some still only eighteen or nineteen years old. They had been operational only in the last two or three weeks and their flying had been limited to patrols over the sea. The exceptions were Oliver Green, the Commander of 'B' Flight, who had been with the squadron for some time, and two Free French Pilots, Lieutenant Litov and Sergeant Lejeune, who had fought in France in 1940.

Since Rommel's first offensive had ended at Halfaya at the end of May, nothing much had been happening on the ground. The front line was along the Egyptian frontier with Cyrenaica, the British right on the Mediterranean coast a little east of Sollum. Rommel, who had advanced four hundred and fifty miles in two months from El Agheila, was reorganizing his lines of supply. The British Army was building positions from which to resist his next thrust.

But Rommel had bypassed Tobruk, which was garrisoned by the 9th Australian Division, and the main task of 73 Squadron at the end of May was to provide air cover for the barges which were taking supplies to the beleaguered garrison. This meant flying about ninety miles out to sea, finding the barges which kept well away from the coast, circling above them at heights varying from nineteen to ten thousand feet for an hour, and then being relieved by another squadron. The Germans and Italians had fighters at Gambut, about eighty miles west of Sollum, El Adem, further west and near Tobruk itself. We were told that the nearer the barges got to Tobruk the more likely the enemy were to attack us. If they came we would only have from ten to fifteen minutes' petrol for a fight if we were to have any chance of reaching our base again, but that was probably sufficient. We started the patrols when the barges were opposite Fuka Point on the coast to our north and continued them for the two days and nights it took them to reach Tobruk. While I was at Sidi Hanish we never actually saw the enemy but the patrols were good training exercise and Tobruk survived for another year.

In between the barge patrols, Ollie Green and I would lead our flights in practice fighter attacks: one flight simulating bombers and flying in from east or west, the other scrambling and then climbing for the attack with the sun behind it. In the evenings, when there were no patrols or practices, we would crowd into the squadron command car and drive north to the coast at Fuka Point for a bathe off the rocks. Because of night attacks by German bombers, we turned in early and I would walk round the tents to see that the blackout was being properly observed. Once or twice sticks of bombs fell quite close to our lines but there were no direct hits.

At the end of June, when Tobruk had sufficient supplies for the moment, we received a signal that in July we were to begin a series of offensive sweeps across the Egyptian frontier, the object of which was to destroy enemy aircraft on the ground and any convoys of lorries we might see. We guessed that the idea came from the sweeps which the Royal Air Force in England had been carrying out with mixed results over Belgium and France. However, conditions in the two theatres of war were very different. The fighters leaving Britain came in from the sea and often had at least partial cloud cover. The time between their first appearance on the German radar screens (all of which had been captured from Allied supplies after the collapse of France) and reaching the outer limits of their range could only be a few minutes, and unless all enemy aircraft were scrambled over a wide area there was a good chance of our fighters finding some on the ground or of catching them as they took off. Conditions in the Western Desert were almost the opposite. Neither side had radar but there was seldom any cloud, and visibility was at least twenty miles from any ridge or escarpment. Germans manning the front line would have time to give warning of approaching British aircraft and make sure that all their own aircraft were evacuated from the forward aerodromes in Cyrenaica, while those further west would be scrambled and reach a height from which they could attack us once we crossed the frontier.

The signal stated that 73 Squadron was to lead the first sweep consisting of eight squadrons which would assemble over Sidi Hanish, the top squadron flying at twenty thousand feet and the others at intervals downwards. We were still discussing our tactics among ourselves during the morning when a Lysander bearing South African markings landed and a Colonel Wilmot came to see me. He too had received the signal and shared our anxieties. He asked me whether I would fly with him that afternoon to see the Air Officer Commanding, Western Desert. We sent a signal announcing our arrival and set off together.

Air Commodore R. Collishaw, a Canadian who had become a

fighter ace in 1918 and had wide experience in such diverse places as Russia, Persia, the Sudan and Britain in the inter-war years, had recently won new laurels for his handling of the Gladiators in No. 202 Group during Wavell's successful campaign against the Italians in 1940. He had his operations room underground near Ma'aten Bagush in the desert west of Cairo. He received us, listened to what Colonel Wilmot had to say, which included alternative tactics for a sweep, but made it plain that he did not agree with our objections. He told us before we left that the operation would take place at the end of the first week in July.

When zero hour came for the sweep, both flights of 73 Squadron were waiting on the ground with their engines running, ready to take off in formation. Within a few minutes of departure, six squadrons were orbiting above us at different heights. The eighth squadron, (we were the seventh) who were to provide top cover, did not appear so I said over the intercom that we could not wait. At that moment, Robin Johnston, a member of my flight, called me to say that his engine had stopped and he could not restart it. I replied that I was sorry, but we would have to leave him behind.

As the leading squadron, we flew at a height of eight thousand feet while the others stepped up behind us. Our target was Gambut airfield, about eighty miles west of the frontier which we crossed south of Sollum. As we flew over eastern Cyrenaica we saw more than one airfield where Gambut was supposed to be and Ollie Green, who had been across the frontier before, broke radio silence to tell me which strip our target was. As we descended, I could see that there were only a few aircraft on the field but we came down to a height of about twenty feet and then swept over it firing at whatever was there. I noticed that two of the aircraft which I was strafing were dummies and, as I crossed the northern perimeter of the airfield, heard a thud in front of me. I realized that my machine had been hit by a bullet, but my dials showed nothing unusual so I turned east towards home and looked for targets on the coast road. I glanced behind me and was surprised to find I was alone.

I had climbed to about a hundred feet when I saw some lorries on the road in front. As I came down and fired at them, men dived out of the back and rolled to the side of the road. One of the lorries lurched sideways. As I flew on, some black puffs began to appear in the air around the aircraft and I realized that anti-aircraft guns were shooting at me. None of the puffs was very close. I also saw two columns of smoke rising from the ground away to the south as if aircraft had crashed and exploded. I glanced at my gauges and saw that the engine temperature was off the dial. I shot up some more lorries, then noticed steam coming through the cowling. I could see the sea in front of me so turned a few degrees south, hoping to cross the frontier and land in the desert behind our lines. But in what was probably seconds rather than minutes the steam, now mixed with black smoke, had become so thick that I could not see ahead. I undid my harness and stood up in the cockpit, looking for a place to land. The black puffs came closer as my speed dropped. Within half a mile or so I spotted what looked like a flat stretch of desert, sat down in the cockpit, cut the throttle and, looking over the side of the aircraft, levelled out. With a juddering that reminded me of my belly landing at South Cerney, we ploughed through the desert and came to a stop.

I sat still for a moment, registering that this was the end of a brief and inglorious action, then picked up my revolver and climbed out, hoping to be able to make off into the desert. But at once I saw khaki-clad and armed figures running towards me from all sides, the closest only about thirty yards away. I stood and waited, feeling rather foolish, until a German officer holding a revolver came up to me. He pointed to mine and I gave it to him. He then led me away, ordering two men with sub-machine guns to come with us. As we walked, I suddenly heard a burst of machine gun fire. One of the German soldiers had climbed into the cockpit of the Hurricane and pressed the firing buttons. The nose of the aircraft was in the sand and the bullets ricochetted off the hard desert and whined away over our heads. The officer yelled at an NCO to get the man out of the aeroplane.

Captivity

I was taken to the Transport Section of the Afrika Korps Unit and waited several hours under guard until a lorry took me to a guard house at Bardiyah, where I was to spend the night. It was on the edge of the cliff overlooking the Bay of Sollum and I thought that if I could escape I might climb down the cliff and make my way along the shore in the night. But the guards were wary and kept me at the back of the hut away from the door. I had to struggle to banish all the depressing thoughts that crowded in on me, but kept telling myself to keep alert for any opportunity that might present itself. Next day, another officer came and said he was taking me to Rommel's headquarters for interrogation. I was given shaving things, put into a lorry and driven for about an hour through the desert.

Rommel's headquarters consisted of a command car and perhaps a dozen small tents pitched in a circle. The atmosphere was alert and I had the impression that the whole outfit could be moved within a few minutes. I shared my captors' meal and waited under an awning by the command car through the afternoon and evening, but Rommel never came. Next day I was taken by lorry to Derna, a journey which took several hours. We travelled mainly across country, from army unit to army unit. The dust we threw up was often so thick that if I could have dropped off the back I might have escaped; but I was kept in a corner just behind the driver with an armed NCO next to me and several other soldiers between me and the back.

At Derna I was put in the guard house of the officers' mess. At about seven in the evening an orderly came to take me to the mess itself. I was shown into the hall where the officers were dining and put behind a screen a few yards from their table, where I was served the same meal. It had come entirely out of tins but was well cooked. There was a buzz of conversation but the meal was very formal. I could see some of the officers through a chink in the screen. When the Commanding Officer rose, the others rose too and there was much clicking of heels. Then an officer who spoke a little English came round the screen, asked if everything had been all right and then said that I would spend the night in the guard room and be flown early next morning to Greece.

I slept on the floor of the guard room and next morning, just before dawn, was escorted to a three-engined JU 53 which was waiting at one end of the airfield. The aircraft was full of Germans in uniform. I sat at the back with a guard beside me and, knowing that thirteen of these troop carriers had been shot down by our fighters during the past fortnight, I thought it quite possible that we should never arrive; however, we passed over Crete without incident and reached Greece in about three hours. Apparently the pilot, who was very young, landed down-wind for after taxiing rather fast, we suddenly swung round violently and stopped near the edge of the field. I was put in a white-washed cell next to the guard room. I had no idea where I was but managed, with my smattering of German, to ask the guard who brought me soup with lumps of meat in it. He said that we were at Tatoi. I spent three days in that cell, during one of which I was interrogated by an officer who spoke perfect English and before the war had lived in Mahdi, a smart suburb of Cairo. It was at Tatoi that I first experienced the real pangs of being a prisoner. There was a barred window in the cell which was low enough for me to look out. I could see aircraft landing and watch people walking home at dusk. Sometimes little family groups of Greeks would pass quite close, keeping to the perimeter of the airfield. I remember a yearning to join them which became so acute it caused physical pain. However poor they were and in whatever hovel they lived, they were free to walk where they would, and to laugh and play together, while I was cooped up like a dog in a kennel.

On the fourth day I was taken by train to Salonika, in northern Greece. There the Germans had set up a transit camp to hold British prisoners still trickling in from Crete and even occasionally from the Greek mainland itself. The camp was not far from the station and when I arrived I found about a hundred army officers, the senior of whom was a Major MacNab (whom I was to meet again after the war when he was in charge of Government hospitality at Lancaster House). There was one welcome familiar face, my fellow flight commander from 73

Squadron, Oliver Green. He answered at least some of the questions which were still troubling me.

He had followed me down to strafe Gambut, but when he saw that the aircraft on the ground were either dummies or wrecks, he had turned back to the south-east with his flight to try and get across the frontier south of Sollum and reach Sidi Hanish. He thought one or two of my flight had joined him, which explained why I had found myself alone. Ollie had kept low but his flight were soon 'jumped' by an Italian squadron which had been waiting for them a little further west. He thought our own cover squadrons must have gone home when they saw us turn east, because the Italians were not interfered with. He saw three of our aircraft shot down and was then attacked himself from above. His engine caught fire and as he just had enough height to use his parachute, he bailed out. Thereafter his experience had been much like mine although he had not seen Rommel's headquarters and had arrived at Salonika two days before me. We talked long and earnestly about what else we might have done but agreed in the end that it had been an ill-conceived operation.

Salonika was a bad camp. The Germans guarding it were reservists, trigger-happy and nervous. The night after my arrival was disturbed by a long burst of machine gun fire and when we woke in the morning we saw sixteen bodies draped at different heights and angles on the barbed wire of the perimeter fence the other side of the field. They turned out to be Israeli soldiers who had been with our army in Crete and, suspecting their fate, had tried to escape rather than be sent to concentration camps. A Canadian warrant officer was so affected by the sight that he set out alone across the football field, presumably to see if any of them were alive. The guards shot him down too, as we watched. For the first time I understood what was meant by one's stomach turning. I was so angry that I was almost sick. We called the Germans every name we could think of, but Major MacNab said quietly that he thought it would be a good thing if we all went indoors.

It was the end of July and very hot. Our huts were verminous. We took to sleeping outside in the space between the barracks, close to the buildings. One night, without any warning, a patrol of German guards opened fire with automatic weapons down the path alongside which we were lying. Luckily no one was hurt. Ollie and I were much relieved when, during our third week, we were summoned to the guard room and told we were leaving for Germany that afternoon.

The train journey to Germany was surprisingly exciting. Soon after we left Salonika the engine slowed down to a crawl as we passed a line of railway oil tankers, derailed and lying on their sides. It was the first of fourteen derailed trains, mainly oil tankers, which we passed before we reached the Austrian frontier. How many of the derailments were due to the recent fighting in Greece and Yugoslavia it was impossible to tell, but I liked to think that most were due to the bombs Cavan Elliot[1] had distributed to the underground forces from Sofia.

At Belgrade our guards bought some German newspapers and magazines and passed them to us when they had finished reading. As we went slowly through the lovely valley of the River Sava, where the railway often ran along the river bank, Ollie, who was sitting opposite me next to the window of our compartment, leaned forward and handed me a copy of the *Berlin Illustrierte* magazine saying, 'I think you might be interested in this.' On the cover was a full-faced picture of me, described as 'Squadron Leader Crawley, the explosives expert of the late British Embassy in Sofia, and a dangerous member of the British Secret Service'. A long article, for which my German was just good enough to give me the sense, then described how I had misused the diplomatic bags to import all kinds of bombs and had then distributed them to anti-German resistance fighters throughout the Balkans. Except that it had substituted me for Cavan Elliot, the article was quite well informed. I thought that perhaps some member of our Embassy staff had been interrogated by the Germans and had made the substitution deliberately or through ignorance. When I had finished reading I waited until no one was looking and dropped the magazine through the open window. Since I had two days' growth of stubble on my face and was still dressed in the dirty khaki shirt and shorts in which I had been shot down, I looked nothing like the neatly dressed head and shoulders which appeared on the magazine, but it was this experience which caused me to give a false Christian name when the time came for me to register formally as a prisoner of war in Germany. To have taken a false surname would have created difficulties, since I had already said it was Crawley, but the choice of Stafford as my Christian name (it was my father's second Christian name) and the fact that I now had the lower rank of flight lieutenant, might put the Germans off the scent if they ever came to suspect that I was connected with the 'explosives expert'. So far as I know they never did. Certainly, when two years later I was in the hands of the Gestapo, there was no hint that they knew I had been in the Balkan Intelligence Service.

In Vienna we not only had to change trains but also wait some days for the one that was to take us to Frankfurt am Main. At the time, we had no idea where we were going or how long we should remain in the city gaol to which we were taken. We were put in single cells, each with a lavatory, a 'bed' which folded up into the wall, and a blanket. There was a little trap in each door through which the warders passed us food. Our only way of communicating with other prisoners was in the washroom, to which we went under guard. The guards had abandoned any effort to prevent people talking since they could never tell who had opened their mouth. My little stock of German was increasing daily and I managed to discover that although perhaps half of the inmates were common criminals, the rest were there for political reasons.

In the morning a warder opened the door of the cell and put a mop and pail of water inside, indicating that I should clean it out. I knew enough about the Geneva Convention to be sure this was not how officer prisoners of war should be treated, so I shook my head and said firmly that I was a '*Kriegsgefangene*' and an officer and that officers '*nicht waschen grund*', which was the best word I could think of for 'floor'. A little later an NCO warder came along and I repeated my protest, more heatedly. I ended by demanding to see the Kommandant. At the end of perhaps another hour I heard marching footsteps and an officer of the *Wehrmacht* and two armed soldiers appeared at the door with the NCO. He said that the NCO had reported that I refused to obey his order to wash my floor. This time I was really indignant and spluttered in a mixture of English and German about the Geneva Convention and the treatment of officers of which he, as an army officer, must know. I again asked to see the Kommandant, which he refused; but something must have got home to him for in a little while a warder came in and quietly removed the bucket and mop.

For the next two days I was left alone. On the morning of the third day, I was taken out of the cell and put into a lorry, where I found Ollie. We were then transferred on to an ordinary passenger train bound for Frankfurt. In the train Ollie told me that on his way to the washroom he had heard me shouting at the warders and was afraid that we both might be beaten up or shot. I replied that he could have been right, but as it turned out I thought my protests had made them want to get rid of us as quickly as possible and that was why we were now leaving.

From Frankfurt we were taken to Dulag Luft (Durchganglager Luft) near Oberursel, a transit camp which was also an interrogation centre. There we found perhaps a hundred British Air Force prisoners, some of whom had become a sort of permanent staff to the camp. The senior officer was Wing Commander H.M.A. ('Wings') Day[2] who had been shot down in a Battle aircraft while doing a reconnaissance over Germany in 1939. He was to become the most celebrated senior British officer in Royal Air Force prisoner of war camps and was not finally released until the middle of May 1945. Also there was Roger Bushell, a Flight Commander in 601 Squadron, and Commander Jimmy Buckley, an intrepid sailor who later drowned in the Baltic while trying to escape from another camp. The Kommandant of Dulag Luft was Major Theo Rumpel, who had been wounded while in Hermann Goering's Squadron in 1918, gone into business after the war and had come back in 1937 to join the German Air Force Intelligence Service. He was an honourable man and a clever intelligence officer. Several years after the war, when he was once again in business, he came to visit 'Wings' Day in England. I gave them both lunch at the House of Commons.

I stayed at Dulag Luft for about three months and was then moved with several other prisoners to the castle of Spangenberg, near Kassel, where we joined General Fortune and other members of the 51st Division who had been surrounded in France in 1940 and forced to surrender. In the spring of 1942, the Royal Air Force contingent was transferred to Stalag Luft III, near Sagan in eastern Silesia. After six months we were moved again, this time to Schubin in Poland.

A Sudeten Schoolteacher

Schubin is a small town lying about a hundred and fifty miles due west of Warsaw. From 1939 to 1945 it lay in the newly created German province of Warthegau. The main buildings of our camp had formerly been a large private house, then an infirmary and most recently a Polish girls' school which, with all other Polish secondary schools, had been closed by the Germans. The main buildings were attractive and the grounds included a playing field and two large vegetable gardens. Twelve red-brick barracks had been built to house prisoners and round the whole estate the usual barbed wire fences and guard towers had been erected.

'Wings' Day was once more our Senior British Officer. The Luftwaffe Kommandants to whom Day had been accustomed were reasonably relaxed in their dealings with prisoners, but the Kommandant at Schubin, a Lieutenant-Colonel of the Wehrmacht who had lost a leg on the Western Front in the First World War and wore a monocle, tried to make Day stand at attention while in his presence, barked at him in German and told him not to speak unless he was spoken to. Finally, during one such encounter, Day, without losing his temper, told the Kommandant that they were of the same rank in their respective forces, that he had served his King and Country for twenty-five years and was only doing his duty by making complaints about the camp, which was no better than a pigsty. He then saluted and went out.

Day arrived back in the compound still shaking with rage while the rest of us were being dismissed from a roll call. He stood on a bank, told those of us who were beginning to move to stay where we were, and in front of the German guards, who might or might not have understood, said that the Kommandant had just been very rude to him. 'He hopes to retire as a General,' he added, 'but he won't. We'll break him. We have already broken one Kommandant by escapes, so now we are going to escape in a big way. I want to see him court martialled within six months. Get cracking.'

Day fulfilled his threat with a month to spare. Several tunnels had already been started from different 'blind spots' and Day decided that although they were of varying lengths and therefore would be finished at different times, all should be broken on the same day. This would add to German confusion and doubly embarrass the Kommandant. Because of the seismographs sunk into the ground at different depths around the perimeter of the camp, the tunnels were dug with ordinary table knives and similar implements, to avoid vibration and noise. At Stalag Luft III the earth had been so sandy that a knife was an excellent tool; at Schubin the earth was more solid and digging took longer. On the other hand, tunnels did not cave in so easily and needed less wooden shoring.

With so many tunnels being dug, disposal of earth was a problem. In the tunnel itself it was simply pushed back by the chain of diggers, using their hands and feet, as far as the entry shaft, where it was put into sausage-shaped bags which could easily be hung on a belt and carried under an overcoat. But the tailors' department had come up with an admirable refinement: the sacks were narrowed and lengthened so that they could hang down inside a trouser leg. A form of zip was sewn on to the bottom of the sack, from which a string led through a hole in the trouser pocket to the wearer's hand. When the man wearing the sack pulled the string, the earth trickled out onto the ground through the bottom of his trouser leg. By walking several men deep, it was possible for those behind to tread the earth into the ground. It was a cold winter and there was often snow on the ground, and the muddy mess of the playing field or paths made it impossible to detect the earth from underground. The sacks affected the walker's gait a bit, so that those carrying them were called 'penguins'.

In February we received bad news. The whole camp was to be moved again, sometime in March. Day at once changed his tactics. The only tunnel nearing completion had its entrance in the main latrine which was housed in a red-brick building a little more than thirty yards from the wire. German guards seldom bothered to enter the building and Day decided that it should be finished and used at once. Wooden lavatory seats lined the walls, and the entrance to the tunnel was underneath the seat farthest from the door.

Complaints about the amount of earth in the ordure were received from the Polish driver of the cylindrical tank which emptied the pit, but these never reached German ears. The driver was nervous only that his pumps might get blocked and so spoil the whole effort. He did more and offered to take two prisoners out in a section of the urine tank, specially cleaned for the purpose. The offer was accepted and that escape took place successfully the evening before the tunnel was broken so the Germans might think that the two prisoners who had really escaped in the tank had gone out of the tunnel with the others. In this way no suspicion could possibly attach to the Polish 'honeycart' driver.

The tunnel had been begun in early January and when it was finished at the end of February it had travelled a distance of forty-three yards, descending at some points to a depth of seventeen feet to avoid the buried seismographs. It came out exactly as planned in one of the runnels of a potato patch which led away from the wire fence. The last three feet of earth in the exit shaft were left to be dug out by the escapers themselves and room for this earth had been left at the base of the shaft and on the floor of the tunnel itself, the sides and roof of which were shored with wooden slats taken from beds.

Thirty-three prisoners who had either dug the tunnel or earned a place by other work were selected to go out, the last man being 'Wings' Day himself. The night chosen was March 5th, 1943, and all the escapers had to be filtered into the latrines in ones and twos before lock-up, which was at seven p.m. Once underground, seventeen were to lie head-to-toe in the tunnel itself and sixteen to be crammed into the specially excavated chamber from which the tunnel started. By six-thirty that evening the last man had been pushed into the chamber, the brick trap door was replaced and the latrine deserted. I was among those lying head-to-toe in the tunnel.

The tunnel was not to be broken until ten p.m., which meant we had a wait of three and a half hours. No one spoke. Water dripped ceaselessly from the ceiling of the chamber where the sixteen men were tightly packed together. The stench of the ordure coming through the hole in the wall by the cess pit was almost overpowering; in the tunnel itself the air became increasingly foul through lack of oxygen. The wait seemed interminable. I was conscious of the different noises men make when breathing heavily in a confined space. My thoughts were of what lay ahead. A Polish officer in the camp, who heard I was going to be among the escapers, had given me the name of some relations of his who lived in a village about twenty-five miles north of the town. His name was Alexis Kowalski. He spoke good German and had worked for me as Intelligence Officer, making contact with several German guards and supplying a lot of useful information.

He had described his relations as a very close-knit family. Pete Kowalski, the father, had been an officer in the cavalry and then a prominent resistance leader; his wife, Tania, was a loyal and delightful woman who kept their farm going while Pete was away; and their daughter, Kate, was only eighteen, rather a flirt and a special favourite of his. Alexis had said that until the Germans had occupied the Balkans, Pete had been very useful to the Allies. Thousands of Polish soldiers had been passed through Rumania to Greece and Istanbul (which I knew to be true) and a regular courier service had been run across the Carpathians carrying information and photographs of identifiable German troop units.

I had promised him faithfully that I would never divulge the name of his village and I am keeping the promise now, but he gave me exact instructions how to get there from Schubin. Alexis himself had refused to escape from Stalag Luft III because his squadron had been disbanded in England owing to heavy losses and he thought he might be more use helping all of us. He was a charming and intelligent man and I thought how lucky I was that he had given me a definite goal for the first two days of my escape.

Then suddenly a welcome blast of cold air coming down the tunnel told us that Asselin, the Canadian who had designed and supervised the whole operation and gone down the tunnel first, had cleared the last three feet of earth and broken through to the surface. When the feet on which I was breathing moved, I wormed my way forward a few inches at a time.

As we lay in the tunnel, news of the progress up in front was passed back down the tunnel in whispers. Some of the escapers kicked down more earth than was necessary and the tunnel became partially blocked where it curved upwards towards the shaft. This earth had to be pushed back by each man to the one behind him. One or two got stuck when their heads were only two or three feet from the open air and had to clear a way out of the exit shaft with their hands. One rather fat officer took forty minutes to free himself and was so exhausted that he failed to get far. But at least he had enlarged the hole and those coming after him had less trouble.

As I pushed the last of the earth to the man behind me, I remember worrying that my clothes would become muddy and wondered how to get them clean. The tailors had done me proud. My blanket 'plus-four' suit had been dyed brown, the knickerbockers fastening just below the knee. My Air Force overcoat was its true colour but was transformed by large black civilian buttons. A friend had lent me suitable stockings. I was pushing in front of me a small suitcase and a trilby hat which had been bought with chocolate from a Polish worker. As I emerged from the exit shaft, I put on the hat and then lay for a few seconds looking back into the brightly lit camp. My watch showed that it was just after eleven-thirty p.m. It was a wonderful moment. At first I could scarcely believe that the guard who was patrolling with his back to me ten yards away would not see or hear me; then I remembered that looking away from the bright lights into the darkness he would see nothing at all and it was up to me to ensure that he should hear nothing either. I wriggled my way along the potato furrow and only stood up when I came to the end, about twenty yards further on. I wiped the mud off my coat as best as I could and started along a track towards the trees which began after about fifty yards. Thus far the light from the camp made it possible to see.

Once in the forest, which consisted mainly of fir trees, I chose a 'ride' which pointed north and began walking. The phosphorus on my button compass showed up quite clearly. I had only been going a few minutes when a dog started barking. I realized it was loose and was coming my way, and suspected from the bark it was an Alsatian. I turned off the ride into the wood and was relieved to see a pond in front of me. As the dog was getting closer than I liked, I walked into the pond nearly up to my knees and stood still. There must have been a moon because there was some reflection on the water on the far side, but I myself was in black shadow. I must have waited about ten minutes, listening to the dog going round the edge of the pond; then I heard a man call and the dog stopped barking. I made my way out of the pond and found the ride again. I was glad I had not worn trousers, because only my shoes and stockings were wet. I walked for several hours and then lay down in a little plantation of what looked like Christmas trees planted close together. The grass was long and tufted and I was completely hidden. I went to sleep.

It was getting light when I awoke and I felt cold. Then I heard a man moving about with a horse and cart, so I crept along until I could see him. He was collecting wood and going away from me in a westerly direction. I stood up, did what I could to clean my coat and continued northwards. Quite soon I could see through the trees to open country. A path led between fields of green corn to a village, perhaps a mile away. I knew that I had to go through this village and take a track at the far end which headed north-west, towards another village several miles further on. There were few people about, but as I walked along the raised mud path that ran past whitewashed houses, a man who I felt sure was a Pole came towards me. I think he took me for a German because he said nothing as he passed. Then he stopped and called to me. I turned and he came up to me, saying in French, 'When next you spend a night in the forest, you must wipe the mud off your coat.' He then proceeded to brush the back of my coat with his hand, wished me luck and walked on. I had been right to be worried about the mud.

The track running north-west was really an earth road. I walked for at least an hour and then, coming over a low rise, saw a village ahead. My instructions from Alexis were to skirt the village to the left and make for a farmhouse which I would see about a mile further on. It was now about seven-thirty and there were more people about, some of them taking horses and carts into the fields. There were no hedges, so I could already see the farmhouse Alexis had spoken of. No one took any notice of me.

When I reached the house I knocked on the door and a woman opened it. I said Alexis's name and her face broke into a smile. I knew this must be Tania Kowalski and she had obviously been expecting me. Grey-haired, short, rather plump, but warm and friendly, she took me into the kitchen, looked me over and by sign language indicated that I must take off my clothes. She gave me a blanket to put over my shoulders as she took each garment from me and at once started brushing the coat and knickerbockers. She then called to someone next door and her daughter Kate came in. She also must have been expecting me because with a broad smile she took my stockings and shirt and began to wash them.

I draped the blanket around me and sat on a chair at the table. Mrs

Kowalski stoked the wood-fired stove, gave me bread, jam and some ersatz coffee and then laid my clean clothes on the backs of chairs in front of the stove. She and her daughter talked and laughed as they worked and I began to feel sleepy. Seeing this, Mrs Kowalski took my hand and led me through into the sitting room where there was a sofa. She brought me another blanket and I was soon fast asleep. It was midday when I woke and I knew that Pete Kowalski had come in because I could hear his voice. By now most of my clothes were dry and they brought them to me. When I was decent they called me into the kitchen where there was a basin of hot water for me to wash and shave. My razor was in my suitcase which was filled mainly with food. I gave them chocolate and Nescafé, which they had obviously not seen for some time. For lunch we had bean soup and a hot-pot of vegetables with lumps of pork in it. I was afraid they were giving much more than they could really spare.

After lunch Mr Kowalski, a small, thin man with an air of authority, took paper and pencil and began to show me, by signs and noises, where I must go next day. It was to a town called Nakel, about twenty kilometres away, from where I could catch a bus to Posen. In Posen, I already knew, I could take a train. I had to walk to Nakel, partly by track and partly by road. He drew a plan of the town and showed me the park and the bus-stop. I slept again all the afternoon and was given more soup and hot-pot in the evening. At about nine o'clock Mrs Kowalski took me out to the barn at the back of the house, showed me a half-demolished haystack and indicated that she would wake me at five in the morning.

The next day was fine and I reached Nakel before ten o'clock. I found the park and sat on a bench in the sun. The bus for Posen went at noon and after an hour's drive, dropped its passengers at the railway station. I had time to kill, so decided to have lunch. My papers, all beautifully forged, described me as a Sudeten German schoolteacher travelling from Breslau to Berlin, to which city I was being transferred. I had therefore to use the restaurant marked 'For Germans Only'. It was full of officers in uniform giving lunch to their families. I saw an empty chair at a table occupied by an officer, his wife and two children, asked if it was taken, and sat down. The officer's wife asked me politely what I did and where I was going and I told her, but there was no need to join in the general conversation. I was glad to notice that my accent caused no comment. I had studied German quite hard for the past two years and having heard it spoken so often could now pronounce it well. So long as I did not enter into a long discussion, I felt I could pass for what I was pretending to be.

When I walked into the station to catch the train, I saw a queue of men in uniform going through some kind of police security check on the platform. I showed my ticket at the barrier and walked slowly past the queue. Then one of the policemen called me back. I apologized and said I thought the check was only for the military. He said, 'No, for everybody.' I gave him my papers: a travel document, identity card and a letter on embossed notepaper from the Ministry of Education in Breslau saying that I was a teacher being transferred to Berlin. He examined them carefully. As he handed them back to me he said, 'If only all papers were as clear as yours, what a much easier task we should have!' I thanked him and boarded the train.

I sat by the left-hand window of a compartment which was occupied by two officers and their wives and two single men, both in uniform. I had bought a *Völkischer Beobachter* and sat reading it. There was no need to talk. Soon after leaving Posen, I looked out and saw lines of soldiers combing the fields as if beating for partridges ... then I realized they were looking for us. At a town called Schneidemühl we were all turned out and told that the train for Küstrin and Berlin would leave in two hours' time. I followed some other passengers and strolled through a large park on the edge of the town. It was again a lovely day. On my way back to the station a young couple came towards me walking arm in arm. As they passed I heard the woman say, 'What a smart overcoat.' 'Yes, but what a rotten suitcase,' replied her companion. I had forgotten how bedraggled the suitcase had become and made up my mind to buy a new one. I had plenty of Deutschmarks which had been sent out to us in books and other parcels, from the Air Ministry.

It was dark when the train left Schneidemühl for Küstrin and Berlin. We were the same party in the carriage and all slept fitfully until we reached Berlin at six-thirty in the morning. I made my way to the washroom on the platform, and the first person I saw in the entrance was Robert Kee (later known to millions in Britain as a television interviewer). We gave no sign of recognition, but it was good to know he had got that far. After shaving and washing, I went into the canteen and had the *Stammtisch*, the dish of the day. Then I caught the underground to the Sudbahnhof where I hoped to catch a train to the south. On the underground I sat between two rather fat Germans in civilian clothes, both of whom were smoking cigars even at that hour. For safety I had discarded the papers in which I was described as a Sudeten German schoolteacher and assumed the second batch, which identified me as a French electrician (I had chosen the name Carpentier, after the great French boxer) being transferred by my company from Berlin to Landek, a city south of Innsbruck. In the prison camp I had taken lessons in handling fuses, plugs and other elementary electrical appliances in case of emergency.

The Sudbahnhof was crowded and frustrating. The railway lines to the south had been disrupted by British bombing and the notice board said that an announcement would be made when the next southbound train would leave. I enquired at the information desk and was told that the delay would last at least forty-eight hours. Knowing that it was possible to stay two nights in any hotel without being reported to the police, I walked away from the station and booked in at a little hotel in a side street, called Der Adler. But the delay was a setback. My object was to get close to the Swiss frontier as soon as possible and it seemed to me that with every hour the risk of chance exposure must increase.[1]

I treated myself to lunch at a restaurant recommended by the hotel porter, found a shop where I could buy a new suitcase, visited a cinema which was almost empty, returned to the station to find that no trains were expected to run that night and went early to bed. Next morning I checked out, determined to spend the day in or near the station in the hope of catching the first train south. It was a rule that no one could spend the night in a station unless they had a ticket, so I bought one to Munich and waited. Twice police came round and examined all tickets. I sat dozing on the floor with my back to the wall, flanked by other would-be passengers. Some time before midnight the departure of our train was announced.

The journey was slow, punctuated by delays due, so my companions said, to repairs to the track. In my compartment were three women, two wearing fur coats, and two men in uniform. In the morning we reached Nuremberg where we all had to change trains. Once again there was a delay of several hours. I went for a walk in the town and was struck by the absence of bomb damage. The schloss and the old walls with their great gateways were intact and life seemed normal. The sun was shining and I went and sat on a seat in a park where I was joined by two nurses pushing perambulators. They chatted amiably and I walked a little way with them. I lunched near the station and then waited once more for the train.

We reached Munich before midnight and again I had to change trains. No sooner had I bought a ticket for Landek than the air raid sirens sounded and everyone was herded by police down into the shelter. It was a large white-washed cellar-like room lined with benches on which we sat huddled together. Several people had brought bottles of wine which were passed round, and someone began a song which was quickly taken up by those who knew the words. Then the bombs began to fall and there was silence while we listened to the thuds. The thuds got closer and then gradually receded. A discussion on air raids began. It was at once agreed that the raiders must be British because the Americans never came at night. A woman in front of me expatiated on the bombing of the Ruhr, telling us all that the 'Müncheners' did not know what air raids were like. She had been trapped in shelters by fallen buildings in Essen and had not been rescued for hours. Several others who were refugees from West Germany backed her up. After about an hour the all clear sounded and we trooped back into the station which had not been hit. Although I had never experienced an air raid in England, I could not help feeling that the behaviour of German civilians must be very like that of Londoners: resigned but good-natured. I did not believe that bombing alone would crack German morale.

The train from Innsbruck ran on a single line through the mountains which were covered in deep snow. My plan was to get out at Landek, wait in the town until dark and then make my way down to the banks of the River Inn and walk by night along its western bank until I came to Switzerland. I had a map from Stalag Luft III which had been drawn by an army officer who had successfully used the route. It showed the Swiss frontier and the point at which I must leave the river. On the train, which was chugging slowly through the mountains, my papers were examined by a man in civilian clothes accompanied by police. The examination proceeded like all the others, and my papers were politely handed back to me. I was sure these were the frontier police and felt a surge of relief; with luck this should be my last hurdle before taking to my feet for the last lap. Perhaps a quarter of an hour later I saw to my surprise another posse of frontier police enter the carriage and begin examining papers once more. They were as polite as their predecessors but, for the first time since I had started my train journey, they kept my papers and said they would return them to me later.

This was a critical moment and I considered the possibility of jumping off the train, which was still moving at only a few miles an hour. But the railway line was cut into the side of a steep hill, the snow was several feet deep, and I realized I was unlikely to get very far. Since my papers had passed so many tests, I clung to the hope that they would be returned to me. However, when we reached the next station the same frontier police came back into the carriage and asked me to accompany them. At the village police station I feigned great indignation and demanded my papers back. The police left the room and, when they returned, their tone was sharper. They had telephoned Landek and discovered that the firm for which I was supposed to be going to work as an electrician did not exist. Would I now tell them the truth? I realized the game was up, told them I was an escaped prisoner of war and gave them the number on the metal disc I was wearing next to my skin.

They seemed greatly relieved. They told me they had been warned that one prisoner from Schubin was still at large and that the frontier guards on the train had been doubled. But my papers had been so convincing they could not be sure until they checked. I asked why, if that was so, they had suspected me, and they said it was because I looked so exhausted. I had not been aware of exhaustion but when I thought about it, I realized I had not slept properly since I left the hotel in Berlin.

I was taken in stages back to Innsbruck. I felt completely numb. I had always known that the odds were against me but as the journey had progressed and one danger after another was overcome, I had begun to believe I would get out of the country. Had my accent given me away or had I been caught in the railway station for breaking a rule I did not know, I would have accepted defeat more easily. But to be suspect because I looked exhausted was humiliating. I felt as depressed as I had when waiting for the German officer to take me prisoner as I stood by my Hurricane in the Libyan desert.

From Innsbruck I was motored to the mess of an Austrian Alpine regiment where I was fed and put in the guard room. A captain came and told me that next day I was to be returned to my camp. But I was taken instead by car to an interrogation centre about two hours away, the exact location of which I never discovered. I could only tell from the sun that it was in a northerly direction. There I was put in a white-washed room in the attic of a many-storeyed building, the walls of which were covered in graffiti: 'Kept ten days without water', read one, and another: 'Beware of these S S bastards'. Some were in what I took to be Polish and others in Greek or Hungarian, but the fact that they were still on the wall made me suspect they were fakes intended to intimidate.

At intervals during the next few days and nights I was taken to a room on the ground floor where I was interrogated by English-speaking officers of the Gestapo under very bright lights. It soon became clear that they thought our escape from Schubin had been planned in collaboration with an underground organization in Czechoslovakia. I was plied with questions about visits to Prague, people I knew there and our links in the camp with Czech nationals. Fortunately Czechoslovakia was one of the few countries in Eastern Europe I had never visited and although there had been a Czech in our camp I did not know him. I simply had to stick to the truth. It was an unpleasant experience because the lights in my attic room were never turned out, and I was kept awake by constant visits. Every now and then threats were made that, if I remained unco-operative, my interrogators would reluctantly be obliged to hand me over to colleagues who would use other methods to make me talk. I would then refer to the Geneva Convention and say that, having acknowledged that I was a prisoner of war, I was sure they would not wish to act in breach of it.

After a few days (I found it hard to distinguish between day and night for the only window was blackened) they gave up. I was put on a train and eventually arrived back at Schubin, where I was made to share a small single room with our Senior British Officer, 'Wings' Day, who had been under arrest since the S S had taken over the camp. He had got out of the tunnel successfully but after two days' walking was given away by a member of the Hitler Youth who led him to a farmyard and then alerted the police. He was enjoying the frustration of the S S who had found nothing during their searches of the camp, partly because all forged papers, maps and wireless parts were hidden in a false bottom to the empty beer cask which S S members themselves often used as a stool. He also told me that the tunnel had remained undiscovered throughout that first night and that Wing Commander Hull had gone to the latrine at seven in the morning and used the tunnel in broad daylight without any German guard seeing him. What pleased 'Wings' more than anything was that the Kommandant who had been rude to him was under arrest and facing a court martial. Eventually the camp was returned to the care of the army, a new Kommandant was installed and prison life returned to its normal routine.

24

Prisoners of War

Although the organization of escapes was by far the most important activity in every camp inhabited by Royal Air Force prisoners, some other experiences preoccupied us. For example, real hunger was new to all of us. It was not a permanent state, yet had we been dependent on the rations provided by the Germans, many of us would not have survived. Those rations, as we soon learned, were not the equivalent of those issued to German depot troops, as laid down in the Geneva Convention, but of the lowest civilian grade, designed for people who were too old to work. They had been calculated upon the assumption that prisoners would receive Red Cross parcels. Most of the time we did receive them and we had no evidence that any parcels were stolen. But because of Allied air raids which concentrated upon ports, marshalling yards and railways, the arrival of the parcels was often interrupted. There were periods when no parcels arrived for three months or even more.

I was in charge of the kitchens in the East Compounds of Stalag Luft III, an appointment owed not to any culinary skill but to the facts that I was head of the camp intelligence organization, spoke German and that it was to the kitchens that most Germans came. I therefore knew pretty accurately the nature and quantity of the food we received. The basis of our ration was swedes, alternating occasionally with pumpkins, both of which we boiled in large vats. These roots were supplemented by an always inadequate quantity of potatoes and bread. Perhaps once a quarter the carcase of an old horse or cow was delivered. Since one carcase divided among two thousand mouths was so little, we distributed the meat in rotation among barracks. The offal was considered by the cooks to be their own perk; the tongue, heart, brains, liver and kidneys went to the messes of the cooks themselves or their friends.

In Stalag Luft III we were fortunate in having an officer who was an expert in nutrition. David Lubbock, who came of a family of scientists, had married a daughter of Sir John Boyd Orr (later Lord Boyd Orr), and with his father-in-law had written a small book in 1939, *How to Feed the People in War Time*, which was to become the basis of the British Government's rationing scheme. In 1940, David, feeling that he must do something more active, joined the Royal Navy. In late July 1941, as a sub-lieutenant observer in an Albacore aircraft operating from an aircraft carrier, he was shot down while engaged on a raid on Kirkenes in northern Norway. An attempt to walk to Russia through the tundra failed and in due course he reached Germany. In prison he applied himself to the problem of food.

David told us that an average-sized man leading the sort of life that is possible for a prisoner of war needs 3,000 calories a day for full health. Had prisoners been able to sleep for the greater part of each twenty-four hours, they could have survived on the 1,600 calories a day which the Germans provided. (Sometimes it fell as low as 1,100 calories.) But young men do not want to sleep most of any day and prisoners were unusually active. The result was that we were often hungry. In my own mess, one officer each week was responsible for distributing the rations for the day. When my turn came and no Red Cross parcels were available, I remember cutting a small potato (or half a larger one) into thin slices, cutting one very thin slice of bread and setting these beside a bowl of boiled swedes as the main meal. If we had saved some sort of paste from the last batch of parcels to go on the bread or potatoes, we were lucky. We made up for the shortages by competing to see who could imagine the most delectable meal to be ordered as soon as we got home, an exercise enhanced by the fact that it was subject to no financial constraints. David calculated that if the Red Cross parcels ceased altogether, we would all be incapable of more than a minimum of exercise within eighteen months, and many would die within two years.

Even in a prisoner of war camp there were some moments of pure pleasure. On summer evenings between eight and nine o'clock, the lone figure of a German guard carrying a trumpet would often be seen walking along the outside of the wire and disappearing into the forest. He was the chief trumpeter of the Munich Symphony Orchestra. Alone, hidden among the trees, he would play the arias from well-known operas for perhaps an hour. Surprisingly the pine forest seemed to act as a sounding board, for the notes came to us with astonishing clarity. The camp fell silent. When he returned many prisoners went to the warning wire to thank him.

Occasionally we had a different sort of concert. A compound containing several hundred Russian prisoners stood only three hundred yards from our own and could easily be seen by anyone walking round our perimeter track. On fine summer evenings, if we saw the Russians beginning to congregate, we would again fall silent and gather in one corner of the camp to watch. Soon a massed choir would begin to sing Russian folk songs while others danced. Although they were underfed, the volume of sound the Russians produced was astonishing; they seemed to us to dance as brilliantly as those army and navy teams which between the wars had sometimes come to London from Moscow. When we left Stalag Luft III in January to begin our westward march, we had to pass the Russian compound. From every home-made sledge we were pulling, tins of food were thrown over the wire; we liked to think that for a few days our Russian allies ate better even than when they were free.

Some of the by-products of escape were interesting. Solitary confinement is a case in point. A period in the 'cooler', as the punishment block in prisoner of war camps was called, was really a rest cure. Prisoners were in a cell by themselves but could read and write and during meals or in the washroom, talk to their neighbours or to the guards. During one such period I remember reading *Gone with the Wind* straight through twice.

Real solitary confinement meant something different. I never experienced it for more than six days, but because one never knew how long it would last, one had to attune oneself immediately. Alone within four white walls in a space ten or twelve feet long and five feet wide, with a small window too high to see out of, unable to read or write or even to communicate with a guard – meals were pushed through a trap in the door on to a shelf which was hinged to receive them – one's first care was to keep control of one's mind.

Memory improves with use and most people developed a system of recollection: lines of poetry, the content of books, people's names and faces, conversations and details of rooms and places one had known. Inevitably one became drowsy and then could begin all over again. But there came a point when memory ran out or became repetitive and one began to wonder about one's self. Was the mind really only a sensitized plate, receiving impressions from without? When there were no such impressions, no sounds or sights to stimulate thought, no exchange of words or facial expression, did one generate thought from within? Or did one's mind only provide muddled and meaningless recollection? Had one, in other words, a *real* self or was self an amalgam of external sounds and images? I remembered once reading in a book about St John of the Cross that his most severe discipline was to attempt to make his mind a blank so that it could receive whatever imprint God desired to make upon it. Lacking that degree of faith or discipline, I came to the conclusion that because my mind persisted in asking these questions, that itself provided the answer. I was not just a passive recipient of external impulses but a person capable of generating an idea, possessing a distinct personality and a soul.

After the war, when I read books by or met people who had spent weeks or even years in such conditions, I found that they had begun with much the same experience. One – sadly I forget his name – had so systematized his thought that when finally released and put on a bus with other men, he begged to be taken back to prison at the end of the journey. Pierre d'Harcourt,[1] who became a friend in the 1970s, told me that at the end of two years' solitary in Fresnes prison (which included torture), he had remembered two thousand lines of poetry.

In Stalag Luft III I used to discuss the nature of 'self' with Humphrey Whistler, who was to become Head of an Anglican Order, the Muirfield Fathers, after the war. Under his influence I almost came to the point where I could believe in a God who could communicate with individuals; but when he told me that to become a real Christian I had to surrender my will to the Church, I found myself resisting.

If you believe the teaching of the Church to be divinely inspired, then there is good reason to submit your will to those who import its instruction. If you do not, then the Church is a human institution and by obeying it unconditionally you are submitting yourself to one of many groups of people who claim to have a monopoly of absolute truth, like the Mullahs or the Communist Party. The more I see and read about the universe, the less possible for me becomes acceptance of the Church's claim. I have a deep respect for it and for many of those who serve it, but my respect is sentimental, not rational. Julian Huxley's book on evolution had reached our prison camp in 1943 and although he suggests at one point the possibility of a guiding force in the universe, I could never bring myself to accept this view.

Why should not accident be the answer? Because our minds are finite we inevitably search for a beginning and an end. It is almost impossible to conceive of infinity. Yet what beginning or end is there for the universe? Is a 'Big Bang' theory really tenable? What existed before the bang? Would there not be endless space out of its range? And what possible beginning or end can there be for time? The intricacy of the molecular system, the separation of the species are the products of time. Even if they develop what seem to be laws of nature, there are always exceptions. In a sense, accident is what makes life bearable.

Humphrey was a saintly man who had a strong influence on many people's lives. Partly because of him I found that being a prisoner increased my respect for human nature. When men from so many different backgrounds are forced to live together at such close quarters, one might have expected constant bickering. The opposite was the case. Most prisoners showed astonishing tolerance and restraint. When food was short, they accepted their meagre rations with a laugh; when a mass escape demanded that everyone, however small their interest, should take a share of keeping watch or dispersing the sand from a tunnel, they did it uncomplainingly and conscientiously. I suspect that we laughed more in twenty-four hours than we ever did before or since.

Of course, there were exceptions to the general rule. One was a young Texan who had joined the Eagle Squadron, which consisted of Americans who volunteered to fight with the Royal Air Force before their country had entered the war. He stood about six feet four and provided a moving example of a Texan's individualistic spirit. When he came into our mess he accepted perforce the disciplines we had imposed upon ourselves and when, after a few weeks, food parcels began to arrive for him from his home, he threw them on to the table for us all to share.[2] But although he entered into every phase of our life with enthusiasm, the strain of rationing became too much. One morning he said he was sorry but he could not go on sharing his parcels. He had been brought up in a world where everyone was taught to look after themselves and if he had the luck to be receiving private parcels and we didn't, then it was just too bad for us. His parcels continued to arrive, but he went to collect them himself at the food store and we wondered where he would eat them. It did not take long to discover. The latrines were open trenches above which one sat on a long pole. At one end of the pole I saw our Texan with his parcel on his knees, munching away. But he had forgotten the wasps which descended on him in swarms. I never saw him there again and soon after he was transferred to an American compound which was formed as the daylight bombing raids got into their stride.

An Englishman known as 'the Chemist' was less attractive. For two or three years he ran a poker school and collected large sums from young men who had never played before. (Until 1942 cheques sent home through the Red Cross or the Protecting Powers were honoured by British banks.) He also built a home-made still in which he produced alcohol for every festive occasion and sold it for outrageous prices, paid in kind when cheques were forbidden. The rule for a still was that if the liquid which dripped into a jug burned blue, it was pure, but if it turned yellow it was poison. The intervening stages were crucial. The headaches the Chemist's alcohol produced were eloquent testimony of the category to which it belonged. My last memory of him is during the march from Tarmstedt to Lübeck in April 1945. As the end of the war approached, German civilians became more amenable and one day some farmers supplied heavy horses and large wagons for our baggage. We were forbidden to ride on the wagons ourselves, yet as the last one left the field, the solitary figure of the Chemist could be seen asleep on top of the kit-bags. Nobody bothered to protest. After the war I met someone who knew the Chemist and I asked what he was doing. I was told he was making a fortune on the Black Market.

25

Epic Moments

We returned to Stalag Luft III from Schubin at the end of March 1943, a fortnight after my recapture, to find that the camp had been greatly expanded in our absence. The sergeants, who had occupied the neighbouring compound to ours the year before, had been transferred to east Prussia, and their place had been taken by American officers. A new British compound, known as the North Compound, had been constructed beyond it and beyond that another for Americans. We returned to the East Compound. By the end of 1944 the whole complex housed ten thousand British and American Air Force officers.

It was a period in which many famous escapes took place, notably 'the Wooden Horse' and 'the Great Tunnel', about both of which several books have been written. Since I played a peripheral part in both it may be worth recording some aspects which are only briefly mentioned in my book *Escape from Germany*.

The Wooden Horse was a hollow wooden vaulting horse with a padded top. It was constructed by expert carpenters among the prisoners in the East Compound from the plywood sides of the packing cases in which the Red Cross sent us food parcels, and its ostensible purpose was to enable us to keep fit. As the Nazis had elevated physical fitness into a cult, the German authorities were always delighted when we seemed to be following their example. However, the real object of the horse was to enable prisoners to start a tunnel as near as possible to the perimeter fence. In this sense it fulfilled the role of its famous predecessor at Troy.

The first and greatest problem presented by all tunnels was the entrance: how to dig a vertical shaft without being seen and without leaving any trace. Normally, therefore, tunnels had to begin under a building, and since all buildings at Stalag Luft III were at least sixty yards from the perimeter fence, this meant that they had to be anything from two hundred to three hundred and fifty feet long to give the escapers a chance to get away without being seen or heard. Immense ingenuity went into the camouflage of tunnel entrances. They were constructed beneath cooking stoves which were constantly alight, beneath washbasins which drained straight into the ground, under solid cement platforms. But even if they survived the inspections at which the Germans became increasingly skilful, tunnellers were then faced with months of work before the tunnel was completed and during that time any mistakes – in disposing of the earth or making a noise which the German listening devices might pick up – could bring the whole enterprise to a sudden end. Shorten the tunnel and build its entrance where the Germans would least expect to find it and the chances of success were multiplied many times.

The idea had come suddenly to a prisoner called Mike Codner. Codner was an artillery man who had been captured while working with the Royal Air Force. Since he was both a gymnast and a classical scholar it was perhaps inevitable, as he pondered new ways of starting a tunnel, that he should think of the Trojan Horse: a disguise which could be used out in the open and placed as close as possible to the enemy defences – in this case the warning wire guarding the perimeter fence. The horse must be not equine but a hollow vaulting horse which could be carried out to a point near the fence with a tunneller wedged inside and carried back with the addition of several sewn-up trouser legs full of sand hanging beside him. (The soil at Stalag Luft III was about 70 per cent sand.) Codner enlisted two friends, Eric Williams and Oliver Philpot, and between them they persuaded the escape committee, of which I was a member, to let them try.

The horse was light and strong. When not in use it was kept in a passage between the camp kitchen and the canteen for the cooks. As I was still camp Intelligence Officer, I was also still in charge of the kitchen and it often fell to me to help carry out the horse when 'gymnastics' were to begin and to carry it back when they were over. This was not as easy as it sounds. The Germans had examined the horse and knew that it was light. However, it was rather cumbersome and was therefore carried on two poles, held by four men, the poles passing through the ends of the horse rather in the style of a palanquin. Because the horse was much wider at the bottom than the top, those manning the pole were forced into an awkward gait, which helped disguise the fact that they were often carrying something far heavier than it looked. Before digging began, the horse was carried out several times and put over the spot from which the tunnel was to be started. Groups of prisoners then lined up to practise gymnastics under the guidance of Mike Codner, who stood by the horse like a gym instructor. Several had been chosen for their clumsiness and frequently collided with the horse, knocking it over on to its side to the amusement of the German guards. But this allowed them to see that the horse was still hollow and devoid of any sinister feature.

When the tunnel was started, one of the three diggers climbed inside the horse, braced his back against one end and put his feet on the ledge which ran round the bottom. In front of him hung several small empty sacks which could each hold a carefully measured quantity of earth. When full they amounted to 140 pounds, the weight of a small man. On the first day that we carried a man out, a German 'ferret' was standing by the steps down which we had to carry the horse from the kitchen.[1] I could hardly believe that he would not notice that our load was much heavier than usual. But we kept up a steady banter about our bad gymnastics and he merely laughed. Sometimes, when the state of the tunnel demanded it, we carried out two men inside the horse, but in that case they would leave the sacks of sand below ground so as not to make our load too heavy on the return journey. The sacks could be picked up later when only one digger was at work.

The entrance to the tunnel was usually covered by a rectangular plywood sheet. When work was finished the sheet was replaced and covered first with eighteen inches of new sand and then with a layer of dry sand which had been set aside under the horse. When the horse was taken away it was impossible to see where the tunnel entrance lay. We were able to locate it as we knew that it was opposite a certain post in the perimeter fence and roughly a pace from the inside edge of the perimeter track.

What went on in the tunnel none of us on the surface knew; there were rigid rules about never talking about anything to do with escape because too many plans had been given away by casual gossip. But by the middle of October we learned that the tunnel was under the wire and that there was only ten feet left to reach the ditch in which it was hoped to emerge. The tunnellers were now to be sealed in and do a 'mole' to get out. This meant blocking the tunnel behind them by pushing the sand back with their feet and hands and at the same time pushing up air holes as they neared the surface so as to be able to breathe. On October 29th, having tunnelled 120 feet in four and a half months, they broke out, and after many adventures all three reached Sweden and were eventually repatriated to Britain.[2]

'The Great Tunnel', as it has been posthumously christened, was known to those who built it as 'Harry' and was dug, not from our East Compound, but from the North Compound, which had only been opened in April 1943. The driving force behind it was Roger Bushell, who had been in 601 Squadron before the war. Every now and then German guards who visited the camp kitchen in the East Compound for cups of tea used to bring me messages from Roger asking if I could let him have some equipment – electric cable, bed boards, even blankets – which I learned later were used to deaden the noise of the trolley wheels on the wooden railway lines along which each prisoner was carried down the tunnel. I realized that Roger had successfully bribed these guards to carry out his instructions and when I could find what he wanted I used to pay them to carry the equipment back to him in their little Luftwaffe vans.

Unknown to me, the escape took place during the night of March 24th to 25th. By five a.m. seventy-nine men had got away, when a patrolling sentry, walking wide of his usual beat, almost fell into the tunnel mouth as the eightieth prisoner was emerging. Dazed for a few seconds, the guard fired a wild shot into the woods and rounded up the four prisoners who had been waiting for their controller to give the word to move on. Of the seventy-six who escaped, three reached England, five were sent to the concentration camp at Sachsenhausen, three to another Air Force prisoner of war camp and fifteen returned to Sagan. Fifty were shot on Hitler's direct orders, including Roger Bushell. The shootings took place in different parts of Germany and all were shot in the back so that the Germans could claim they were trying to escape.

On March 26th, the day after the escape was known, we heard in the camp that the Kommandant, Colonel von Lindeiner, had been relieved of his post and was facing a court martial. We began to get some idea of what might have happened to those who escaped from the fifteen who returned. Yet even they still did not know for certain the fate of their friends. About a week later, our Senior British Officer, Group Captain

Willis, was summoned to the office of the new Kommandant. He asked me to accompany him as interpreter and witness. As we walked out of our compound he said he was afraid we were going to hear bad news. There was only one other German officer with the Kommandant and two or three guards. After he had acknowledged our salutes and asked us to sit down the Kommandant made the following announcement in German: 'I have been instructed by my higher authority to communicate to you this report. The Senior British Officer is to be informed that as a result of a tunnel from which seventy-six officers escaped from Stalag Luft III North Compound, fifty of these officers have been shot whilst resisting arrest.'

I translated and Group Captain Willis asked at what places they had been shot and how many had been wounded. The Kommandant replied, 'My higher authority only permits me to read this report and not to answer questions or to give any further information.'

Willis persevered and said, 'But can you not on your own authority tell us if any were wounded?' I translated and the Kommandant, who looked embarrassed and ashamed, replied that he thought none had been wounded. For some minutes neither of us spoke as we walked back to our own compound. Then Willis asked me what effect I thought these 'murders' would have on our future escape plans. We agreed that for the moment the escape committee should be asked to suspend all operations. Later, fifty urns containing the ashes of our friends were sent to the camp and within a few weeks a stone memorial bearing their names and housing the urns had been built in the woods nearby. After the war the urns were taken to the British Cemetery at Posen and put under the care of the Imperial War Graves Commission.

*

The success of the allied landing in Normandy changed the attitude of most prisoners towards escape. The end of the war began to seem so close that it appeared folly to risk death for the sake of a few extra weeks of freedom. General Eisenhower's order telling prisoners to stay in their camps until they were formally relieved was heard over the radio and obeyed. After the failure of the Allied offensive at Arnhem, prisoners in Germany braced themselves to face another winter and those in the east, like ourselves, prepared to receive – and hopefully be relieved by – the Russians. By the middle of January 1945, the Russians had reached the River Oder forty miles to the east of Sagan and the sound of their guns grew louder every day. All prison compounds were put on an emergency footing. Since a trainload of Red Cross parcels had recently arrived, we were given extra rations and went into training round the camp circuit in case we had to march; a tunnel was constructed for use in case of an emergency, for none of us was sure how the Russians would behave if they overran us. On the morning of January 27th the Senior British Officer was told confidentially that we were to stay where we were. Six hours later that order was counter-manded and we were told we had to leave that evening.

Since the temperature was 20 degrees below zero, those hours were spent making sledges from planks ripped from the barracks and loading them with food, clothes and whatever might be useful as barter. We marched for ten days and two nights to reach Spremberg, just under a hundred miles to the west, where we boarded a train of cattle trucks. It was so cold marching that men would often fall asleep immediately we stopped to rest; but we did not lose a man. I spent much of my time knocking on the doors of houses in the villages we passed through, and bartering with housewives, offering coffee and chocolate for bread, eggs, chickens and anything else we could find. Our train took us to Bremen where we ended up at a camp called Tarmstedt which had hitherto held only naval officers. For the next two months we watched the Royal Air Force flatten Bremen and Hamburg. We expected every day to be relieved, but to our annoyance our troops did not appear to know of our existence. Then history repeated itself.

On April 8th the Naval Intelligence Officer in the camp informed the Senior Officer of the Royal Air Force that one German officer and forty soldiers were to be left to guard us until the British Forces arrived. The news was not broadcast to the prisoners but it seemed so probable that most of those who had been told believed it. The message was repeated next morning. This time the news leaked out and the camp went wild with excitement. Then the German Area Kommandant, who was cut off from his superiors, changed his mind and at one o'clock we received the order that the camp was to be evacuated that same evening.

In the belief that we were bound to be overtaken by our own forces at any moment, the order was given that we were not to walk at more than two miles per hour. In fact we managed to go much more slowly. The weather was glorious and this time, as a sort of barterer-in-chief, I traded tinned food for fresh, but above all for perambulators in which we packed our food pacels and gear. In the end, our column of three thousand officers must have had more than five hundred of these excellent trolleys. We presented a most unusual sight.

Although the German Army was disintegrating all round us, our guards had automatic weapons and we could not persuade them to desert. On April 16th we crossed the River Elbe by ferry and headed for Lübeck. Two days later we passed a German infantry training school near a village called Tangstedt and watched boys in uniform rushing about and firing blank cartridges like members of an Officers' Training Corps on a field day in England. We camped nearby and when several of them visited our camp in the evening I was called over to talk to them. They were pathetic, some only fourteen years old, and wanted desperately to know if the war would end before they were sent to the front. They knew that their radio did not tell them the truth. I told them that Berlin had almost been surrounded and that most of Germany was already occupied by the Allies. I doubted whether in a few days' time there would be any front to which they could be sent. They were so relieved one felt they wanted to cheer.

The Senior British Officer had daily meetings with the Camp Kommandant who was accompanying the march. When told that we were to go to Lübeck, Group Captain Willis refused to obey the order because he had heard that typhus had already broken out in that town. With the full support of a Senior German Medical Officer, he was able to take over two large farms called Trenthorst and Wulmenau which lay in the beautiful valley of the Trava and belonged to a Mr Raemtsma, director of the Hamburg America Shipping Line. Mr Raemtsma had been living in Lübeck and came out himself to meet us, delighted to have British prisoners occupy his farms before the battle swept over them. We moved in on April 27th.

The farms contained two herds of pedigree Friesians. As most of the Polish workers had left, several of us helped them and took what milk we needed in payment. We slept in barns, washed our clothes in the Trava and lay on its green banks in the sun, which had not stopped shining since we left Tarmstedt.

On May 1st we heard some desultory rifle fire near Trenthorst. Then, in the morning of May 2nd, two Comet tanks arrived in

Wulmenau and a little later a single armoured scout car in Trenthorst.[3] The moment when I heard the scout car commander telling his brigade headquarters over the radio that he had found three thousand Air Force prisoners on a farm near Lübeck was certainly one of the most thrilling of my life. We all shouted and cheered and tried to shake the young lieutenant's hand. A great weight had suddenly been lifted off our backs. Even the most lugubrious among us was laughing and grinning. Brigade headquarters came through again to the scout car commander to say that we were to stay where we were and that a column of lorries would be sent to fetch us as soon as possible. But far from being an anti-climax, the next few days were eventful and dangerous.

No sooner had the scout car gone than not only our German guards, but army units from all over the neighbourhood came in to surrender. We made them pile their arms in the courtyard of the farm and sent them off down the road to Lübeck along which we were told a 'cage' was being established for German prisoners. The sight of so many arms and so much ammunition was too much for many ex-prisoners who grabbed what they fancied and went off into the woods and fields to shoot at every bird they could see. The air above our farms was whistling with bullets and an around-the-clock guard of our own had to be organized to see that no more arms were taken. Luckily no one was hit. Group Captain Willis took over the houses belonging to the farm manager and his assistants, most of whom were women. The cellar contained some excellent wine and the ladies cooked for us and waited on us. When a British infantry unit arrived and tried to empty the cellar, we defended our loot stoutly. Over a drink we explained that we had waited for this for a long time and there were other houses they could visit. After five days during which the farms were filled with motor cars confiscated by members of our camp who drove far and wide over the countryside, a column of army lorries arrived and took us westwards back across the Elbe and then on a pontoon bridge over the Rhine. On May 8th and 9th we were flown to England in Lancaster bombers.

26

Political Missionaries

Our reception in England was startling. The Lancaster, packed with liberated prisoners of war, landed at the Royal Air Force station at Wing in Buckinghamshire, a part of what I hoped would become my constituency after the general election. We had not taken more than a few steps from the aircraft when men and women in uniform stopped us, put nozzles under our trousers and blew a nasty-smelling white powder up inside our clothes. Before we had time to protest they had apologized and explained that we had been deloused. Tea and buns and the smiling faces of the Women's Voluntary Service cheered us up and we were then sent by train to another Royal Air Force station near Liverpool to be medically examined and sartorially re-equipped.

As the train ran northwards through the night the skyline was illuminated by bonfires on hilltop after hilltop, celebrating the Victory in Europe. We all suffered a feeling of anti-climax. Our departure from Germany and the air-trip home had been exciting; we felt we held the centre of the stage. Now we had taken our rightful but insignificant place as part of the great machine that had won the war. Watching the bonfires and fireworks from the train, I felt curiously detached, as if the general rejoicing was for something in which I had had no part. Twelve hours at the Liverpool depot, a reassuring medical examination, the realization that even after the food we had eaten on the march in Germany I still weighed only eleven instead of thirteen stone – then a brand new battle-dress outfit and a telephone call to my parents at Windsor restored morale. Another night journey in the opposite direction and I was home.

Surprisingly, the feeling of unreality persisted. On both sides the anticipation of meeting had been so great that words failed. My mother and father could hardly believe I was really there and I sat in their charming but unchanged drawing room realizing that I had very little idea of how they had lived the past four years and not knowing where to begin. I had read in the newspapers that families had been warned by the Ministry of Defence that prisoners of war might take some time to adjust to peacetime surroundings and had dismissed it as absurd. I soon saw that the warning had been sensible. My parents, I learned later, had hoped to take me away alone with them for a week or two, but I was too restless; the last thing I wanted to do was to sit still. Within a week I was going up to London to see friends, particularly Virginia Cowles.

I had first met Virginia in 1937 just after she had returned from the civil war in Spain. It was her first foreign assignment as a journalist: she had been just twenty-six years old when the war started in 1936 and was the only foreign correspondent to have visited both the Republican Government front near Madrid and General Franco's armies to the north. Her reports, syndicated by the North American Newspaper Alliance, had had a wide circulation in both Britain and the United States. At the time of our first meeting she was writing articles for the *Sunday Times* and *Daily Telegraph* and living in a mews flat lent to her by a friend. I used to go and breakfast with her and take her out to lunch at pubs or grills. We were both living on what we earned. I began to see a lot of her. She was not so much pretty as fascinating to look at, with large brown eyes far apart which held one's own steadily, a broad forehead, wide mouth, tapering chin and a slender figure. She was neither flirtatious nor coy but could enter into one's own thoughts quickly and sensitively. Philosophic or metaphysical ideas bored her; she was practical and, as a reporter, scrupulously honest in her search for facts. She was exciting to be with and I thought seriously of asking her to marry me. But we were both sure that war was coming and thankfully I did not; if she had accepted me we should have been separated for our first five years.

Before I saw her again in 1945 I already knew she had become famous. Her book, *Looking for Trouble*, published in 1940, had quickly sold out; paper rationing prevented it being reprinted. She had seen more theatres of war as a correspondent than any combatant, and she did not report wars from the rear. Lloyd George had quoted one of her unsigned articles in the House of Commons and had asked Randolph Churchill to bring the author to see him. He was taken aback when introduced to a young woman. In 1940 she had gone on a lecture tour through the United States explaining to her fellow countrymen why they must enter the war, and had been awarded the OBE when she returned to London. She had served for a year as a special assistant to Gil Winant, the American Ambassador to the Court of St James. I knew she could be ferocious, but she was also warm and enthusiastic. At no time did she make concessions to her surroundings: she looked immaculate in her American war correspondent's uniform and always wore high heels and make-up, even in the desert.

When we met we began where we had left off in 1939. There was so much to talk about. She took as great an interest in my doings as I in hers and before the end of May, in the Belle Meunière restaurant in Soho, I had asked her to marry me. She said two things: first that she would never marry me unless I had my teeth fixed – several were missing in front because our camp dentist could extract but not replace; second that she wanted a fortnight to make up her mind. I realized that my parents would find it hard to be sympathetic to such a sudden move and went to stay with David and Minty Lubbock at Farnell, near Brechin in Scotland, where David was re-acclimatizing to his own family life. It was there that, at the end of May, Virginia telephoned to say yes.

Meanwhile political life in England had suddenly resumed. The Prime Minister and the Conservatives had hoped that the coalition could continue until the war with Japan was over, but at a conference on May 24th the Labour Party under Harold Laski's chairmanship stated that under no circumstances would the party enter a coalition with the Conservatives after the general election which was to take place on July 5th. Polling days were to be staggered to allow time for members of the forces in distant countries to have their votes recorded; the majority were to vote on July 5th, but for twenty-three constituencies July 12th, and for one July 19th, were to be polling days. The count in all cases would take place on July 26th.

Desmond Donnelly of the Commonwealth Party had already telephoned me to say that although he had been keeping warm my candidature in north Buckinghamshire (a fact of which I was ignorant) he had already withdrawn as the local Labour Party was solidly behind me. To fight the election I had persuaded two former camp inmates to come and help me: Robert Kee and Philip Moore (later to become Secretary to the Queen), both ten years younger than I and keen

Labour supporters. We went down to Buckingham to find somewhere to live. I rented for a month Lone Tree Cottage, about two miles outside the town, belonging to a Mrs Lynes. It was ideal, no electric light or mains water but very cheap, with three bedrooms and a hand pump in the garden at which we would wash and shave. After being away so long we all had the zeal of missionaries, canvassed every village in the constituency, held meetings in the evenings, usually in the open air because the weather was fine, visited Working Men's Clubs, factories, the railway wagon works in Wolverton and Co-operative stores wherever they existed. Teams of enthusiastic local supporters accompanied us, including more than one member of the then secret but now famous code-breaking organization in Old Bletchley. Walter Ettinghausen – who later became Walter Eytan, head of the Israeli Foreign Service – joined our ranks, as did some of the assistant masters at Stowe School.

Our opponents did not take the onslaught lying down. Their candidate, Lionel Berry, son of Lord Kemsley, was respectable but staid; some of his supporters less so. One of our posters was a larger-than-life picture of myself wearing a Royal Air Force cap. Lionel's cousin, Pamela Berry, who lived in the neighbouring constituency, went round painting my lips red wherever she could reach them. We were not supposed to put posters on telegraph poles because they were government property and therefore neutral, but enthusiastic canvassers sometimes broke the law. At Hoggeston, a small village near Winslow, one of my posters was stuck on such a pole just outside the gates of the manor house. Next day, one of Lionel Berry's posters appeared above it. Another one of mine followed and then another of Lionel's. My supporters were intrigued to know who in their village was showing such persistence and waited up the next evening to watch. Soon after dark they were rewarded. Out of the gates of the manor came two men carrying a ladder, a lady following them. The ladder was placed up against the telegraph pole and held firmly while the lady climbed it and stuck Lionel's poster once more above mine. They recognized Mrs Nubar Gulbenkian, wife of the squire. Years later, meeting the Gulbenkians in Le Touquet, I reminded her of the incident. She laughed and said, 'But I could not have your poster outside my gate. I hated you!'

The climax of the campaign was the eve of poll meeting in the Town

Hall of Buckingham. More than a thousand people had crammed into the hall, many of them standing. In my speech I had just said that I thought it was time that cottages in Buckinghamshire were supplied with mains water and electricity, implying that a Labour Government would see that they got it, when a very large old lady whom I recognized as my landlady, Mrs Lynes, got up at the back of the hall and said that she owned many cottages in the constituency and could assure Mr Crawley that all of them were equipped with electric light and mains water. I said quite gently, 'Mrs Lynes, I think you must have forgotten that at the moment I am living in Lone Tree Cottage, which belongs to you. I must tell the audience that it has no water, except for a hand-pump in the garden at which my friends and I wash and shave, and no electricity.' The whole audience roared with laughter and Mrs Lynes left the meeting very angry. When Robert, Philip and I got home later that night, we found all our bedding, sheets, blankets, towels and pillow cases festooning the bushes and trees in the garden. Mrs Lynes had been in and thrown them all out of the windows.

Three weeks later the result of the election was declared in that same room where we had held the final meeting. We had won by a majority of 3,845. The Labour Party had a majority of 158 over all the other parties combined, with a few seats still outstanding. Four days later Virginia and I were married by my father in St George's, Hanover Square. Esmond Rothermere gave us a splendid wedding lunch and Barbie Wallace lent us her house at Laverstoke in Sussex for a weekend honeymoon. It had been a momentous month.

*

The mood in the Labour Party was euphoric. We were not only going to build a new world, but we could see no reason why we should not be in power for the next thirty years. The Conservatives were a party of the past. The Liberals were composed of people who could not make up their minds and their party was finished; to us it seemed pathetic that it would not lie down and die decently. We were arrogant and cocksure. Years later I said to one of my brothers that I must have been insufferable just after the war and he laughed and told me I was.

Parliament was exciting. With almost four hundred Labour members, of whom only around ninety held office of any kind, there were bound to be pressure groups. Having been away for five years I felt out of touch and spent most of my time listening. I found I was constantly being approached by colleagues who wanted to abolish hanging, public schools, the Stock Exchange, university seats in the House of Commons, the House of Lords and even the monarchy. Right from the start there were people who thought that the Prime Minister, Clem Attlee, was so uninspiring that he could not be allowed to stay as leader. Maurice Webb, a popular back-bencher, gave a lunch in the House of Commons for Mrs Attlee to which about forty Members were invited and, although it was intended to be friendly, at the end she said that, after listening to us all, she felt that the only person in the room who was in favour of Clem was herself.

I never shared the urge to supplant Clem, particularly after Ernest Bevin had made it clear that he would never take his place. All the other Labour leaders, Morrison, Dalton, Bevan, even Cripps, were prima donnas in their way and most indulged in a good deal of in-fighting. Clem Attlee was the only man around whom they could all rally. His lack of glamour was his strength. He was scrupulously honest, courageous and quite unambitious. He never thought in terms of being a great Prime Minister or of taking credit when it really belonged to others; he simply did the job as he saw it. Virginia, who kept a diary spasmodically at this time, felt he was not really interested in politics; it was 'a task by which he earned his daily bread, the same way other people run factories or sell eggs and butter'. She noticed that if she sat next to Herbert Morrison, Hugh Dalton or any other minister she argued about ideas and theories. Attlee did not want to 'talk shop'. He was much happier discussing people, reminiscing about the First World War in which he had been an infantry officer, or about his early days in the Labour Party. He thrived on small-talk.

Attlee was without self-importance. Virginia and I used occasionally to go to tea at Cherry Tree Cottage, near Great Missenden, where Clem and Vi Attlee lived. Vi, good-looking and well dressed, was very much in charge. She was always saying, 'Clem, we need more hot water', or 'Clem, will you get some more sandwiches', and Clem would trot off to the kitchen without a murmur. On the other hand, he could be curt and even inhuman. There are many stories about the way in which he dismissed members of his government. When Fred Bellenger asked him why he must leave the War Office, Attlee replied simply, 'Just not up to the job.' At least two junior ministers learned that they had been sacked by reading it in the newspapers. Clem had never seen them or said anything.

I only once attended a Cabinet (it must have been in 1950) when I stood in for the Secretary of State for Air, Arthur Henderson. The discussion was about American air bases in the UK, over which I had recently reached an agreement with Lew Douglas, the American Ambassador. After an hour or so, during which it had seemed to me that the Cabinet was agreed about the action which should be taken, Clem summed up and came to exactly the opposite conclusion. To my surprise no one uttered a word. After the Cabinet had finished, Norman Brook (later Lord Normanbrook) the Cabinet Secretary, came across to me and asked me to repeat what I had said. He wanted to be sure he had got it right. I repeated it and he thanked me, but it was Clem's summing up that went into the minutes.

Clem Attlee inspired loyalty but seldom affection. He was probably closer to Bevin and later to Cripps than any other colleagues and he loved George Hall. He disliked Herbert Morrison and mistrusted Nye Bevan. One Sunday when Herbert and Clem were lunching in our house at Steeple Claydon in Buckinghamshire, Herbert commiserated with him about some disobliging articles in the press. I cannot remember the reason, but Clem was being attacked personally and Herbert said he thought the articles unfair and inaccurate; he hoped Clem had not taken them too seriously. 'Oh,' replied Clem, 'I never read the newspapers.' It was not meant to be a rebuff, simply a statement of fact. I doubt if he ever read anything but political news and as far as that was concerned, he now made the news himself. Comment did not interest him. Clem left shortly afterwards and, as we settled down to discuss his visit, Herbert said, 'You know, I'm never sure whether to believe that little man or not.' It was so unthinkable to Herbert not to read anything written about himself that he really imagined Clem might have been pretending indifference.

*

We had been lucky in finding places to live. In London our family solicitors told me of a lady who had a house in Romney Street, just off Smith Square in Westminster, which she wanted to sell to someone who had had a 'difficult' war. I did not think being a prisoner would qualify, but applied and was accepted. It was a freehold with a vacant bombed plot next door and we got it for five thousand pounds, which my father provided. Virginia, who was still technically entitled to wear an American war correspondent's uniform, hitch-hiked a ride in a Fortress bomber over to New York, where she stayed with her father and bought furniture, linen and kitchen utensils of a quality not easily available in London. 52 Romney Street was a little house less than five minutes' walk from the House of Commons and Virginia made it charming. We found a German refugee called Caroline to cook for us.

In Buckinghamshire we were almost equally lucky. One of my staunchest and most amusing supporters was a man known as 'Maggot' Bryant who lived in Gawcott, a village outside Buckingham made famous by its resistance to enclosures in the eighteenth century. He kept a maggot farm about half a mile outside the village, the product of which he sold to anglers who fished the Great Ouse which ran through the constituency. The smell from the farm was so strong that no one except Bryant ever went near it. He owned several cottages, one of which, an 'island' site in Gawcott just opposite the laundry, he rented to us for a pound a week. It had a big sitting room, three bedrooms, a kitchen and a small dining room, and we furnished it by going round the junk shops in Buckingham and Winslow. After Andrew arrived on Midsummer Day in 1947, we would put him in his pram in the little front garden and girls from the laundry would come across and play with him during the lunch hour. He was very greedy and soon became very fat.

We used to go down to Gawcott almost every weekend and visit some part of the constituency. I was particularly interested in the railways. During the election I had been taken round the railway wagon works at Wolverton by some trade union supporters who had explained to me how they priced each job of piece-work. It was a matter of give and take. The management wanted the maximum production for a reasonable wage, the union a tolerable level of production for a good wage. The negotiations hinged on the conception of 'tolerable'. The union did not base their case on the slowest worker, but had to make sure that the slowest worker could earn a living. The variation in productivity was surprising; a good man on a lathe could produce five times as much as a slow one and earn perhaps six times as much money, with bonuses. But such a discrepancy would put pressure on too many people so the fast workers were forbidden to produce more than a maximum laid down by the union. Relations with management were quite amicable but the system meant inevitably that wagon repairs took longer and cost more than they need have. I had wondered whether the union would change its attitude when the railways were nationalized and the men were theoretically part-owners.

Their attitude did change, but not in favour of higher productivity. Since all railwaymen had seemed to want nationalization, I was surprised at how quickly they became disillusioned. Within six months I heard nothing but complaints. Under their former company, the men said, they used to see their local managers regularly. Since nationalization they saw nobody and had become cogs in a wheel run from London. They were expected to do what they were told. They still spoke of management as 'they' and had even less sense of a common interest than before. Their disillusion struck at one of my chief expectations of socialism.

In Parliament two questions were paramount. How could Britain pay its way? How could we prevent the Russians from dominating Europe? The first question seemed insoluble. The effect of the sale of our foreign assets and the fall in our exports due to arms manufacture had been cushioned during the war by Lend Lease. When this was suddenly cut off in 1945, we had insufficient dollars to buy the food we needed. Every cultivatable acre of our own land was in production and an American loan, which was immediately sought, could only be a stop gap. Stafford Cripps, who had succeeded Dalton as Chancellor of the Exchequer after the latter's gaffe in leaking an item of his budget to a journalist, produced an austerity plan which made further cuts in our food imports and in capital investment. Rationing was increased and the outlook was grim. People talked openly of our being reduced to a standard of living as low as that of the Balkan countries.

In the House of Commons the only meat on the menu was whale or seal steak, both disgusting. However, I was less gloomy than some, partly because I was inured to a shortage of food and because, to my surprise, in Gawcott one could buy fresh vegetables, eggs, fish and sometimes even a chicken. That Britain survived was due mainly to three things: the willingness of the people to endure even greater privation than during the war (bread was rationed for the first time in 1950); the revival of the coal industry, which, under nationalization not merely recruited thousands of new miners but raised production to a level which made us self-sufficient and able to begin exporting coal again; and Marshall Aid.

Today Marshall Aid is a phrase from history, like Lend Lease or the New Deal. At the time it was one of the most imaginative and beneficial gestures made by any country to its former allies. Its origins were enshrined in a phrase used by General George Marshall, the former Chief of Staff of the American Armed Forces who became Secretary of State after the war (that is, United States Foreign Secretary), in a speech at Boston in October 1947: 'We are faced with the danger of the actual disappearance of the characteristics of Western civilization on which our government and our manner of living is based.'

Initially Marshall's offer was to the whole of Europe including the Soviet Union; some of the countries of Eastern Europe gave it a warm welcome. But Stalin rejected the whole idea and insisted that his satellites withdraw their acceptance. Ernest Bevin, on the other hand, seized on the offer and led a discussion within the Labour Party and in Parliament about how best to organize Western Europe to take advantage of it.

27

Return to Poland

At the time of General Marshall's Boston speech I was in Jamaica in my capacity as Parliamentary Private Secretary to the Colonial Secretary, winding up the first conference on the proposed Federation of the West Indies. Arthur Creech-Jones, who had succeeded George Hall at the Colonial Office, had opened the conference but as he had to go on to the United Nations, he asked me to stay and look after it. It was my first experience of an overseas conference and it could not have been more lively. There were at least five delegates, including Norman Manley, Chief Minister of Jamaica; his cousin, Sir Alexander Bustamente, leader of the opposition; Dr Eric Williams; his opponent, Albert Gomes of Trinidad; and Robert Bradshaw of St Kitts, whose command of English and power of invective was as high as the best in the House of Commons.

As it was a preliminary conference to decide the broad outlines of federation and the steps by which it should be achieved, they all felt they could let themselves go. I was in the chair and they soon began to ignore me and to abuse each other directly across the table. I had to deliver a little lecture saying that, as I was sure they were aware, in the House of Commons we had a tradition that personal abuse was unacceptable. Every Member had to address 'Mr Speaker', and in consequence could only refer to another Member in the third person as 'the Honourable Member for so-and-so'. No one wanted to insult the Speaker, and, since invective in the third person is diluted and unsatisfying, abuse is normally kept under control. As all the delegates to the Montego Bay Conference were Parliamentarians, even though they represented different islands, I said I hoped they would adopt a similar procedure in this conference and address the chairman rather than each other. To my surprise, they all agreed at once and adopted House of Commons practice, with which they were obviously familiar.

From Jamaica I flew to New York to join Arthur Creech-Jones who had been attending the debates in the United Nations on Britain's fulfilment of the Mandate for Palestine. As I well knew, nothing we could have said or done would have satisfied both Jews and Arabs since, when Britain was fighting for its life in the First World War, we had made irreconcilable promises to each race.

Virginia had joined me in New York and at the end of October 1947 we sailed for home on the liner *Queen Elizabeth*. Her diary reads:

Thursday, October 23rd. On board the 'Queen Elizabeth':
We are now in English waters with the cliffs of Cornwall showing in the distance. A pale sun is shining and the ship is travelling towards Southampton at 29 knots. I cannot help but feel a sense of drama. One has approached Europe so often at such fateful times in the last ten years, yet this winter may seal the destiny of Western Civilization. Can Europe survive without help from America? Will she get that help? These questions will be answered in the next six months.[1]

The most interesting passenger on the ship is Lew Douglas.[1] Aidan and I have lunch with him nearly every day in the Verandah Grill overlooking the bows. He is a shy, quiet, serious man with great personal integrity. He thinks that Europe, particularly Italy and France, must have aid within the next three months or the communists will get control.

He seems to have a deep and genuine affection for England and thinks the Marshall Plan, quickly implemented, is essential for her recovery. He told us in confidence that he did not think that Cripps' plan would work; that because of the high cost of British goods, the country would not be able to sell sufficient exports to pay her way.

We talked a certain amount about America and the difference between the standard of values and outlook as compared to Europe. 'Do you feel you are leaving the real world or returning to it?' Aidan asked. 'Returning to it,' replied Douglas. 'To me, reality is struggle!'

Friday, October 24th. 52, Romney Street:
Back into the fray again. Awoke this morning to be plunged at once into the problems of the crisis with headlines saying that Stafford Cripps had announced in the Commons cuts in food to restrict dollars and £200,000,000 less is to be spent on capital construction.

It is real austerity but everybody seems to be so relieved to have someone at the helm with a plan, they are taking it reasonably well. All the papers refer to Cripps' 'statesman-like speech'.

Sunday, October 26th. Gawcott:
Aidan and I drove down here yesterday morning. The country was looking beautiful and in spite of the shortages, the complaints and the restrictions, we said a dozen times how lovely it was to be back in England, facing the problems of the real world again. England is the only country I have repeatedly returned to without any qualms or reservations. The very fact of being on English soil has a magic of its own for me.

The Russian refusal of Marshall Aid had accentuated the fears which had been growing in every Western European country since the end of the war. When I returned from Germany in May 1945, I shared the general sympathy for the Russians. They had lost twenty million people, their country had been devastated and in spite of everything they had fought well. We had to help them in every way we could. But as the weeks went by, it became clear that the Soviet Government was seeking not the help but the domination of Europe. It ignored the agreements reached at Yalta, Moscow and Potsdam that free elections should be held in all Balkan countries, and installed communist regimes in Hungary, Rumania, Bulgaria and Albania. Even Tito, in Yugoslavia, who owed his position entirely to British support, had joined Stalin's camp and had tried to seize Trieste and Venezia Giulia. Poland, for whose sake we had gone to war, was in a similar plight.

I had been sent as one of a British parliamentary delegation, along with Leah Manning and Bessy Braddock, two massive ladies whose sympathies were with the left wing of the party, to observe the elections in Poland which had been held in January 1947. A foretaste of what the election would be like had been given in a referendum held on the policies of the Polish Committee of National Liberation (the Lublin Committee to which the Russians had entrusted the provisional Government of Poland after the war) on June 30th, 1946. The committee obtained large favourable majorities on the questions of the Oder–Neisse Line, the new Polish frontier in the west, and abolition of the Senate and the nationalization of all basic industries. Mr

Mycolaczyk, head of the London Polish Committee and leader of the Polish Peasant Party, had protested against the result, alleging rigging of the votes, the arrest of many members of his party, the closure of twenty of their offices and widespread intimidation. He demanded that the referendum be set aside.

Between June and January the situation had worsened. Thousands of Poles were arrested without trial, thirteen members of the Peasant Party Executive had been imprisoned, twenty party branches had been forcibly closed and several party members killed. In November 1946 both British and United States governments had sent notes to the Polish Government protesting at the repressive measures it had seen fit to employ against the democratic elements in Poland.

The British delegation stayed with our Ambassador, Mr William Bentinck (later Duke of Portland), and on polling day he led a motor cavalcade around as many polling stations as he could, his own car flying the Union Jack. Wherever we went, crowds would gather, some cheering and some in tears. One felt overwhelmed by their despair.

Guards armed with sub-machine guns stood outside and inside each polling station. How valid the count was can be judged from the fact that at several stations the presiding officer told us what the result would be while voting was still in process. These officials treated the whole voting procedure with disdain. While he had been Prime Minister, Sir Winston Churchill had made innumerable representations to Stalin about Poland, all of which had been ignored. The British Labour Government met with the same treatment.

At one stage during our drive, two young members of the Polish Security Service came and sat in the front of the Ambassador's car, allegedly for our protection. Both spoke some English. In the course of conversation they began to pour scorn on whisky as a very feeble drink compared with vodka. Knowing that the Ambassador had a bottle of whisky in the car, I suggested they try some. They tasted it, liked it and drank a considerable amount neat. We then began to ask them about their job. Their tongues loosened, they told us they hated it but it was well paid and gave them many privileges. They then went on to explain some of the methods by which the election was rigged, the chief of which was by sending the ballot boxes uncounted to a government office in Warsaw where they were not even opened. Later that afternoon, when the effects of the whisky had worn off, they came to us when we were preparing to get into the car and begged us not to repeat what they had said. 'Whisky', they added, 'is stronger than vodka.' They knew they had said things which, if repeated, might get them shot.

Next day Virginia and I, accompanied by Sefton Delmer, the *Daily Express* foreign correspondent, made a journey of a very different kind. We motored to Sagan to visit the site of the camp of Stalag Luft III. Before leaving England I had consulted David Lubbock about some forged documents which he had buried in a tin box, hoping to recover them later as a record. He had drawn me a map showing the spot. The camp looked much the same. The wire and the watch-towers were still there, the barracks also, but without windows. There was a thin covering of snow on the ground, which was frozen hard. The three of us walked in a line backwards and forwards over the spot David had marked but could detect no hollow sound which would indicate a trap door. Sefton weighed sixteen stone and finally jumped along our tracks like a kangaroo, but to no avail. We learned later that after the 'ceasefire', thirty thousand German prisoners of war had been quartered there in a space which had held only ten thousand British and Americans. We concluded that they had found the 'hide' and filled it in. I felt curiously detached wandering about a place where I had so yearned for freedom and had spent so much time and effort trying to get it.

We then drove north through Schubin to Nakel and on to the village where I had stayed with the Kowalskis during my escape. I was hoping they would be there. But although I found the farm, nobody even knew their name. Our policemen, with whom we were now friends, asked many questions but all they could discover was that in 1943 a great many people had been shot; probably the Kowalskis were among them.

Before we left Warsaw, the American Ambassador, Mr Arthur Bliss Lane, resigned so as to be free to tell the world the truth about the elections. In the House of Commons Christopher Mayhew, then Under-Secretary for Foreign Affairs, said that because of all the 'irregularities' the British Government could not accept that the elections had fulfilled the undertakings given by the Provisional Polish Government and that it therefore 'had to be assumed that those elections were not a true reflection of the will of the Polish people'. But neither the United States nor Britain broke off diplomatic relations.

Even though the Americans had the atomic bomb and the Russians did not, neither the United States nor any country in Western Europe was prepared for a confrontation with Stalin. It was a point of view which a few members of the Labour Party, of whom I was one, accepted with reluctance.

28

The Division of Europe

The division of Europe was almost complete. Ernest Bevin had made it clear that he regarded the Russians as the enemy; Sir Winston Churchill, as leader of the Opposition, had made his famous Fulton Missouri speech on the Iron Curtain. The left wing of the Labour Party still supported the Soviet position but the great majority of Members of Parliament were trying to decide how Europe could best organize itself to make the most of Marshall Aid.

According to Virginia's diary, a stream of people, mainly Labour Members, came to Romney Street to lunch or dine; there was also a smattering of Tories: Duff and Diana Cooper, John and Nancy Hare, Esmond and Ann Rothermere, even Nigel Birch, although Virginia noted that 'it is the fashion now for Tories to say that they can scarcely control themselves when speaking to socialists'.

Being one of those who felt that a European Union of some kind was essential if we were to stage an economic recovery and withstand the onslaught of communist propaganda, I was constantly writing memoranda and promoting meetings to persuade our leaders to take action. It was an uphill task. Ernest Bevin wanted a Europe free of passports, where people could live, travel and work wherever they pleased, but hated the idea of any joint organization to bring this about. Attlee shared much the same outlook. Dalton felt that Continentals had never understood democracy and was pathological about the Germans; Cripps was still unwilling to face the fact that the Russians were now our opponents. The people I collaborated with most closely were Kim Mackay, one of the twenty-seven Labour MPs to attend the European Congress in The Hague in May 1948, at which Winston Churchill delivered the opening speech, and Dick Crossman. Kim was an out-and-out European federalist, Dick a European socialist who wanted the internationalization of all basic industries. The 'European'

Tories, on the other hand, wanted trade treaties, the lowering of tariffs, defence agreements. Even though we professed a common purpose, violent disagreement between the parties must have erupted in the end. Virginia's 1947 diary gives a picture of the comings and goings.

November 1st:
Today Andrew was christened by Canon Crawley at St George's Chapel, Windsor. His name is Andrew Hayward. Andrew behaved very well. He slept all the way to Windsor in a basket in the car, had his bottle and went back to sleep again until the time for the christening at 4.00. He didn't like being put into his christening dress, a wonderful, very long, white lawn hand-done affair with lots of ruffles. Aidan said no doubt his tears were due to being dressed up like a girl. However, he was fairly quiet in the church. He squawked at the appropriate time to let the Devil out, began to whimper when Canon Crawley took him in his arms, but stopped immediately the water was put on his forehead. He loves his baths and he probably thought that was what was going to happen.

Back to Gawcott at about 8 in the evening. At 10 we went to Buckingham to hear the result of the local election. We stood in the square for about an hour. At last Mr Small, the mayor, appeared and declared that the four Independents had been elected. Aidan was very disappointed. However, on reflection, it was not as bad as it seemed; first of all it was 'no change' for Buckingham for it has always been a Conservative council. Secondly, Labour polled more votes than it has ever done before. If Aidan can hold these figures, he ought to be all right in a General Election. At any rate, things cannot get worse. The abolition of the basic petrol ration has just come in and it is rumoured that potatoes will also be rationed. Perhaps next year there will be better issues on which to fight.

Wednesday, November 12th:
Yesterday Megan Lloyd George and Hugh Gaitskell came to lunch. Hugh came from No. 10 Downing Street where he evidently had had a row because he said he was furious at his colleagues. Aidan gave him a stiff rum cocktail (the last of our bottle from Jamaica) and he relaxed. He thinks the miners may just reach their target of 200,000 tons of coal for this year.

With the tiger I shot in Bhopal,
India, 1934

One of the gates of Peking, 1934.
(Most of these gates have now
disappeared)

Esmond Rothermere at Daylesford,
Oxfordshire, 1965

Breakfast in the garden of the Bishop of Jerusalem, 1937.
Left to right: myself, Diana Carroll, Norman Spurr,
my sister Anstice

Camping in the Bishop's garden, 1937

My younger brother Kenneth and myself, 1939

A room in the East Compound, prisoner-of-war camp Stalag Luft III, Sagan, eastern Silesia, 1943. The photograph was taken by a German officer on the camp staff

With Virginia at our wedding at St George's, Hanover Square,
July 30th, 1945

A victory group of party helpers, Bletchley, July 1945

*

Hugh Gaitskell had become my greatest friend in the House of Commons. I think he was a little surprised at his own political success and therefore retained a certain diffidence which made him easy to talk to. Once he trusted you he was completely open and never worried about being discreet. He would say what he thought about his colleagues in Government and discuss any point of view, even if it ran counter to accepted Labour doctrine. His wife, Dora, was more reserved and sometimes tried to restrain him. She was observant and clever enough to protect without annoying him. Once, after an agument at some meeting, Hugh said to me, 'You speak with such passion; I really envy that.' It was something he was to learn. In the later debates over nuclear weapons, the reform of the Labour Party Constitution (Clause Four), unilateral disarmament, Suez, the American bases, few Labour leaders have spoken with such contained passion and overcome so many opponents within his own party. I shared to the full his conviction that only if it remained democratic could a Labour Party govern Britain, but I gradually came to the conclusion, not only that the Marxist wing of the party would continue to divide it even under Gaitskell's leadership, but that socialism, even when democratically based, would ruin the country.

We left Romney Street to go to hear Dalton's Budget Speech. Next day Virginia commented:

Thursday, November 13th:
We have just heard the news that Hugh Dalton has resigned as Chancellor of the Exchequer due to the unfortunate slip he made yesterday in revealing some item in his budget to a reporter on *The Star* ten minutes before he made his speech. *The Star* was on the streets fifteen minutes before the Stock Market closed. I first heard this story this afternoon when I went to tea at No. 11 with Ruth Dalton. She seemed quiet and nervous and told this tale three times, first to me, then to Betty Younger, then to Nicholas Davenport. I realized it was an indiscretion of some consequence and that Dalton would have to apologize to the House, but thought that would be all. Tonight Aidan said he made an apology in the House and Winston Churchill accepted it graciously. Nobody quite understood why he has gone. Rumour is that Cripps will take his place.

A little later I asked Hugh Dalton why he had insisted on resigning when his apology had been accepted. 'I could feel pounds [sterling] escaping through my pores,' he replied dramatically. 'I could not sleep, I could not go on.' The truth was that ever since the Government had taken office, dollars had been draining out of the country at an alarming rate. Without Lend Lease, the cost of the armed forces was insupportable, yet Bevin and Attlee had refused to reduce them while the war with Japan was going on. Convertibility of sterling had been suspended in August and rigid controls on the amount of money that could be taken out of the country imposed; food rationing had been tightened; but military necessities still had to be paid for. Even as economic overlord, Cripps had been unable to stop the drain. I realized that Dalton was at breaking point and felt sorry for him. He had warned his colleagues of what was happening and they had not helped him. Now Cripps was to take over and impose greater austerity than the country had ever known.

Thursday, November 20th:
Today the Royal Wedding. Aidan had forgotten to apply for seats so we took the opportunity to do some work. Felt rather like Peter Quennell who was said to have read Thackeray during D-Day, undisturbed by telephone calls. Only two blocks away the crowds around the Abbey were thousands deep but we were not tempted to move out of the house.

Friday, November 21st:
Morgan Phillips [National Secretary of the Labour Party] and Kim Mackay came to lunch. We had a big discussion about the union of Western Europe. The argument is that even if the Cripps targets are reached, Britain may not be able to sell her goods abroad because other countries may not have recovered sufficiently to buy them, in which case all Western Europe will start on a downward spiral in the spring. The only remedy, according to Kim, Aidan, Dick Crossman and many other back-benchers is to form a union of Western Europe in which heavy industry is socialized and the whole block is one market, not many markets of separate countries. Morgan Phillips said the difficulty vis-à-vis the Labour Party is to try and persuade them that this is not a deliberate line up against Russia.

Dick Crossman was an irrepressible talker. Sometimes he would stick to a theme and use the company he was with as a sounding board to try and clear his own mind; in that mood he could become a bore. At others he would flit from subject to subject being provocative and amusing. He told me more than once that he preferred journalism to politics and that what he most enjoyed was to write an article one week arguing a case and then follow it the next week with another arguing exactly the opposite.

Dick was a delightful guest. He used to bring his wife to stay at Kingsbridge, the farm we had just bought in Buckinghamshire, and was my only Labour friend to take any interest in the running of it. He was impressed by the fact that at weekends I would do the milking and he would ask many questions about the planning of cultivation and finance. I believe it was as a result of these visits that he finally bought a farm himself. He told me that he kept a diary and no doubt he wrote some of it while with us, but I never expected a book of more than one million words!

Monday, November 24th. Romney Street:
Returned from Cambridge where we spent yesterday and last night with Victor and Tess Rothschild. Aidan spoke to the Cambridge University Labour Party, who are violently left-wing. They were incensed that Aidan should put democracy before socialism, even though he tried to tell them that without democracy it was impossible to have socialism at all.

Monday, December 8th:
Tonight Philip Jordan and Robert Kee came to dinner. Philip is Attlee's new public relations officer. He seems very bewildered by the job. He has been writing about foreign affairs for 15 years and has paid no attention to domestic issues. He says it is pretty formidable to be confronted by hardened 'lobby correspondents' all firing technical questions about which you know nothing.

Wednesday, December 10th:
Last night Aidan took part in a public debate sponsored by the Fabian Society at Conway Hall, Red Lion Square. Harold Laski was in the chair, Dick Crossman and Zilliacus were on the platform

with Aidan. The subject was foreign affairs.

Zilly had the straight fellow-traveller line. Everyone was wrong except the Soviet Union. He saw the present conflict as the working class v. the capitalists; therefore socialists and communists must line up together against the democratic capitalists. Aidan of course took the other view; that it was not possible to have socialism without having democracy. Dick was somewhere in the middle.

I was reminded of Attlee's famous reply to a memorandum sent him by Zilly a year or two ago. 'Dear Zilly. Thank you for sending me your memorandum which seems to me to be based on an astonishing lack of understanding of the facts. Yours ever, Clem.'

Friday, December 12th:

Mr Attlee came to dinner last night. Also George Hall, Chris Mayhew and Megan Lloyd George. Mrs Attlee is in a nursing home, having had a minor operation.

The evening went extremely well, much better than anyone would have hoped. Attlee is so tremendously shy and difficult to 'draw out', hates to discuss politics or current subjects and has always been a problem as far as entertainment is concerned; this time we have found the secret: old cronies. George Hall is one of his best and oldest friends, Megan has known him ever since she was a little girl, and he therefore could discuss his favourite topic, 'old times'. He told one story after another and told them with relish. He told of the early days in Limehouse when he was pelted with rotten tomatoes, about the first time he met Bevin, the occasion of a speech when the latter said 'far be it me from it to protrude my personality . . .'

Megan was wonderful. She matched him story for story and was witty and charming. I liked best her story about the time her father, Lloyd George, and Winston Churchill, went to North Africa on what was, I believe, a holiday. She described a wonderful Arab dinner where everybody sat in a circle on the floor while in the middle was a huge cauldron of delicious food. Her father, she said, adored it. He always flung himself into new things with enthusiasm. He followed his Arab hosts and plunged hands into the cauldron and drew out a chunk of meat. Winston sat there hating it. He refused to speak and remained quite motionless, glowering at everyone. Winston loves luxury and comfort and this sort of picnic is the last sort of thing that would appeal to him. Suddenly he gave a tremendous sigh, rolled up his shirt sleeves, turned to Megan and said: 'Well Megan, to hell with civilization' – whereupon he plunged his arm in.

Thursday, December 18th:
Ann and Esmond Rothermere came for dinner. Ann attacked Aidan for voting on a £5,000 cut in the allowance for Princess Elizabeth. Aidan said the 165 Labour Members who voted as he did, did so because they were not told what her expenses were; they refused merely to agree £50,000 carte blanche. In other words, their vote was a protest to show that the Commons cannot be chivvied around. I think it is a very silly thing to do. If you have a monarchy it seems to me the least you can do is vote them the cash to do it well.

My mother raised the same subject with me at Christmas. She felt I had embarrassed my father who was a chaplain to the King. If I were asked my opinion today I would say that the monarchy is a unique institution which cannot be subject to detailed parliamentary scrutiny. Either it is worth many times more than the taxpayer spends on it, which I believe it is, or it should be abolished.

Wednesday, December 24th:
Diana and Duff Cooper with their son, John Julius, came for supper. They were in excellent form. They are going to Ann's for Christmas and rather dreading it. Diana did not talk about France much. How they are going to manage for money, I do not know. Aidan thinks Diana is still ravishing; so do I.

Virginia had become a friend of both Duff and Diana during the war. She had stayed with them when Duff had been British Ambassador to the French Committee of Liberation in Algiers and they both admired her. We stayed with them at the Embassy in Paris when he was Ambassador in 1946. At almost any other time it would have been irritating to Duff to have an ardent socialist under his roof, but it was Ernest Bevin who had kept him at his post and he would patiently listen to my views. Although occasionally I detected the warning sign of a tightening of his jaw muscles, he never lost his temper or was even rude to me. Perhaps the bewitching Lulu de Vilmorin, who was staying with them, kept him in a good mood. I was then a little frightened of Diana but she went out of her way to be charming and in all the next forty years during which she came frequently to our house, I never heard her make a cruel or malicious remark. She was a marvellous guest, putting everyone at ease and telling fascinating stories. Once, when Diana was in her nineties, Virginia rang her up and said that we had a very sticky lunch the following day and could she come and help. Diana drove herself in her Mini from Little Venice to Chester Square, arrived wearing trousers and a large felt hat, and kept us all laughing for the next two hours. There has been no one like her in my lifetime.

Sunday night, December 28th. Gawcott:
Two days of looking after Andrew and not dead yet; in fact he is much easier than before as at last he will sit and amuse himself; he has a doll he likes, also a squeaky duck and a bell. The great attraction is anything that will go into his mouth. He can get a toy telephone of considerable dimensions in now and seems quite happy every time he performs this feat. Aidan has given him lots of bottles, fed him spinach, even changed his pants. He at last recognizes Aidan and is full of smiles whenever Papa appears.

Suddenly the whole political horizon darkened. In February 1948, our worst forebodings about Russian intentions were borne out by the Communist coup in Czechoslovakia. In March, Jan Masaryk, son of one of the founders of the Czechoslovak state, was alleged to have committed suicide by throwing himself from the window of his office into the courtyard of the Czernin Palace. However, it was noted by many witnesses who had been with him shortly before his death that he had been in no way depressed and seemed his usual ebullient self, and the suspicion has always persisted that he did not commit suicide but that the communists forced him to jump or threw him out of the window.

It was in these tense circumstances that Virginia and I went on a parliamentary delegation to Paris. It was an unreal occasion. Champagne flowed and the food at the various banquets was such as none of the English had tasted for years. The French wanted to honour and thank the British, yet on the way Virginia and I for the first time found ourselves discussing what we should do if England succumbed to a dictatorship. We agreed to wait and see what character of man or men took over; we must stay and fight as long as we could, but if the dictatorship looked like becoming rigid we would leave and go to Australia or America. We both realized how extraordinary it was to be discussing such a subject seriously so soon after a resounding victory. Virginia was still keeping her diary.

March 6th, 1948:
Aidan and I stayed with Betty and Bobby George. Very comfortable house in Neuilly which belonged to a *collaborateur*. The 'loo' has those walls that allow the person sitting on it to see outside, whereas none of those passing by can see in. Betty said that practically no one in Paris is in the New Look, despite all the publicity; some women who had started wearing it had abandoned it because they were hissed in the streets and people cried 'Where did you get the money?' All this because the French dressmakers are charging as much as £100 a dress.

Paris saddened me and at the same time delighted with its beauty and wonderful food. Warm spring weather and sunshine with everything looking calm and guileless and yet, underneath, the current of fear running once again. Every French person we met, no matter what his allegiance, would welcome a real union with England; common citizenship, common ownership of industries, etc. You feel that they realize it is the last possible hope. I do not believe I have ever seen people so aware of living through days that mark a great turning point in history and it applies to everyone from the most intelligent and well-informed to the humblest waiter or taxi driver. They are all waiting for a positive lead from Britain or America; they feel as we do, that unless Western Europe unites against Russia, Communism will be the victor and within the next few months.

In May of 1949 a decision was taken by ten European nations to establish a Council of Europe. The Council was to consist of a Committee of Ministers whose decisions on 'matters of importance' had to be unanimous and a Consultative Assembly in which each country was allotted a certain number of representatives according to its population. The Ministers alone had the power of decision but the

Assembly could make recommendations and debate any matter referred to it by the Ministers. I was among the eighteen members of the British delegation composed of Labour and Conservative Members of Parliament, including the House of Lords. The first meeting, to which Virginia accompanied me, was held at Strasbourg in August of that year.

It was an exciting moment. Once more the French, our hosts, set out to make it a great occasion. They served us the best champagne even at breakfast and guided us through all the gastronomic delights of Strasbourg and Alsace. Politically they led the field. Robert Schuman, Georges Bidault, André Philip, Guy Mollet and Maurice Schumman, who had become well known in England through his broadcasts on the BBC during the war, were all enthusiastic for a European Federation. It was we, the British, who held back. Although many of us had adopted the phrase 'functional union' as our watchword, meaning a combination with other members in basic production, defence, transport and so on, in fact our leaders refused to join in any of the French initiatives. I have always reproached myself for not having supported them openly.

The Schuman plan for merging the coal and steel industries of Western Europe was joined by France, Italy, the Netherlands, Belgium and Luxembourg, but not the United Kingdom. Ernest Bevin, guided by Sir Gladwyn Jebb of the Foreign Office, turned a deaf ear to all the pleas made by the Labour delegation in the Assembly to give some encouragement to our European colleagues. Bevin set a pattern which was to be followed through the coming decade, not only by members of the Labour Party but by the Conservatives who succeeded them. Even Sir Winston Churchill, in spite of his speech at the European Congress in The Hague in 1946 which gave such impetus to the idea of a European Union, failed to follow it through when he returned to power. The United Kingdom refused to join the European Defence Community, the Monetary Union, and finally the Treaty of Rome.

Our meeting at Strasbourg, therefore, was a diverting social occasion, but little more. When 'alternates' were appointed to the original delegations, we found ourselves joined by Jim Callaghan, Julian Snow, Stephen Taylor, Freddy Birkenhead, Selwyn Lloyd and John Foster. We dined in succession at all the best restaurants in Strasbourg and took many motor trips through the Vosges mountains and down the

Rhine. Sheila Birkenhead came out to join Freddy, and John Foster, who had been earning quantities of blocked French francs and German marks as an international lawyer, spent them lavishly in entertaining us all. We learned to appreciate 'Mirabelle' and 'Framboise', the liqueurs distilled by Alsatian farmers, and went to Bob Boothby for pills to cure our headaches and save our livers.

I was to return to Strasbourg again the following year when a delegation from the newly formed Federal Republic of Western Germany had been invited to attend as observers. It was the first time since the early 1930s that I had met them as equals rather than as their captive or their conqueror. I found them agreeably at ease and not at all cowed by defeat.

29

The Air Ministry

It was from Kingsbridge that we fought the 1950 election. There had been rumours of an election in the autumn of 1949 but the sudden need to devalue the pound caused a postponement. In the absence of Stafford Cripps, who was in hospital in Switzerland, Hugh Gaitskell as Minister for Economic Affairs, had played a major part in the devaluation, keeping it secret until the actual announcement was made and carrying through the necessary controls to prevent inflation taking hold. Although I cannot remember the occasion, I think I was the first Labour Member to say publicly that I hoped he would succeed Attlee as leader of the party. When Randall was born in July 1950, Hugh was a godfather.

The election was fixed for February 23rd. We had a series of helpers and speakers to stay, including Frank and Elizabeth Pakenham, Hartley and Joan Shawcross, Professor A.J.P. Taylor and my old prisoner of war friends, Douglas Bader and Ralph Ward. Clem Attlee came to speak for us at Wolverton.

My helpers excelled themselves. Both Alan Taylor and Elizabeth Pakenham went round the village meetings preaching a gospel so far to the left of my own that I had to follow them up, explaining that they represented a small but vocal minority in the party. Many of the meetings took place in schools, the squire and his friends occupying the front desks, their servants standing with the farm and other labourers in the village at the back. Elizabeth would speak directly to those standing, telling them not to be bullied by those sitting in front, who no longer held power, an assertion whose truth was more evident at Westminster than on the parish council.

Hartley Shawcross made a speech in which he bemoaned the lack of variety in the food he ate, whether at the House of Commons or at home; before the meeting was over he rushed to the telephone to tell his cook, in case his remarks were reported over the radio, that of course he was not referring to her. Frank Pakenham, who answered for Germany in the House of Commons and who had joined the Roman Catholic Church during the war, would begin his speech with a few earthly observations but very soon address himself to God. It did no harm. Douglas Bader and Ralph Ward told stories about being prisoners of war which made everybody laugh.

On February 23rd the Labour Party actually polled 1,300,000 more votes than in 1945 and 800,000 more than the Conservatives, but because of the way the constituencies were divided (and still are) only had an overall majority of five. There had been a revision of constituencies in 1949 carried out by the Independent Boundaries Commission which affected no fewer than 500 seats, but the Labour vote is so concentrated in Wales and the industrial North that the party has to poll many more votes in the country as a whole than the Conservatives in order to win a majority. It was calculated that had the Conservatives received the same numbers of votes as Labour in 1950, they would have had a majority of 69.

In North Buckinghamshire my majority was reduced by more than half, but I was still 1,500 ahead of my opponent, Frank Markham, who had himself once been a member of the Labour Party. We celebrated far into the night at Kingsbridge, playing ninepins with the champagne bottles that our supporters had brought.

When we returned to London, we found the Parliamentary Labour Party in a state of gloom. The days when Prime Ministers, like Menzies in Australia or Wilson in England after the election of 1964, could govern successfully with a majority in single figures had not arrived. Forty was considered the minimum necessary and a few Members of Parliament thought Attlee should refuse to form a government and let Winston Churchill try with a minority of followers, an improbable hope. Attlee, however, decided to continue. He sent for me on the day we reassembled and said he hoped I would help Arthur Henderson as Under-Secretary at the Air Ministry. I went across to King Charles Street to see Arthur, whom I hardly knew. He gave me a warm welcome, indicated the sort of subjects in which he hoped I would take an interest and said that he would leave me to make my own decisions; if ever I wanted to see him, I only had to walk across the passage. Before he left, he added that when he had to go away, he would always see me beforehand to let me know what was likely to crop up in the Cabinet or elsewhere which I might have to handle for him. It seemed, and turned out to be, an ideal partnership.

I embarked on a new kind of life. In the previous four and a half years, the House of Commons had been the centre of my existence. My time had been taken up with committees, either party or parliamentary, with debates and with the many groups who used the tea room or smoking room as a base for the prosecution of their special causes. Now the House took second place. I attended Question Time on most days, and if in London went along in the evenings to listen to the winding up of debates and to vote. I sat jammed in between other junior ministers on the bench behind the Front Bench. Most of my time, however, was spent either in the Air Ministry or visiting units of the Royal Air Force in Britain and around the world.

An Under-Secretary has been described as 'the lowest form of political life', debarred from speaking in the House on any subject other than that for which he holds responsibility, unable to make a mark as an individual except when answering questions or winding up a debate on matters affecting his own ministry, and, although a member of the Government, so lost in the hierarchy that not one person in a hundred thousand remembers his name. Nevertheless his life is highly organized, particularly in the Service Ministries.

The Permanent Under-Secretary, in my case Sir James Barnes, made himself responsible for the organization of my office, selected the civil servant, Frank Cooper (later the Rt Hon. Sir Frank Cooper, GCB, Permanent Under-Secretary for the Ministry of Defence), who was to be my secretary and instructed me in my role as Vice-Chairman of the Air Council.

This body, chaired by the Secretary of State, is the ultimate authority on all matters concerning the Royal Air Force. It was manned by an array of Air Marshals, all of whom had been well-known figures during the war: Slessor, Dickson, Cochrane, Sanders, Hollingworth. Because of my office, they treated me with respect and went out of their way to answer my questions and generally educate me. I could guess at their politics but none of them ever gave the slightest sign that they allowed political considerations to influence their views. Frank Cooper, himself a Spitfire pilot during the war, used to encourage me to write papers for my colleagues on the Air Council on any subject about which I felt strongly. Some of my successors have told me that a few are still on the files. I do not remember the subjects on which I wrote, but I do remember that one of the most difficult problems of the Air Council was to decide on future types of aircraft. The gap between the time when a new design appears on the drawing board and when the first production model comes off the line is a minimum of three years and can be as much as ten. Meanwhile the whole political and therefore strategic and tactical map of the world may have changed, and what seemed like a brilliant idea when first put forward is no longer applicable in the new situation. We all knew that Herr Heinkel had produced a successful jet aircraft in 1939 and that if Hitler had ordered it to be mass-produced as a fighter the result of the war might have been different. We also knew that Sir Frank Whittle had himself test-flown the first jet aircraft in Britain in 1941, but that delay in ordering it meant that we had no jet aircraft until after the war. We were constantly asking ourselves whether we were making the same sort of mistakes. The decisions had to be informed guesswork. The later arguments over Barnes Wallace's swing-wing and the T S R 2, thought by many to be the most advanced military aircraft ever produced, only emphasized the difficulties of making such decisions within reasonable financial limits. The same is true of every advanced type of missile in the 1980s.

In 1950 I soon realized that the most useful thing I could do was to visit the Royal Air Force commands in Britain and abroad. Direct contact enabled me to try and explain the reasons for decisions which serving officers often found incomprehensible and allowed me to keep Arthur Henderson and other members of the Government in touch with the opinions of those who had to execute their decisions.

Whenever I visited a Royal Air Force station, I was accompanied by a serving officer in uniform, Squadron Leader 'Sandy' Johnson, like Frank Cooper a wartime Spitfire pilot. He was the ideal companion, often able to correct or supplement my impressions because people sometimes talked more freely to him than to me. Together we visited, always by air, the headquarters of Bomber, Fighter, Transport, Coastal and Training Commands, the Royal Air Force Headquarters in Scotland, and the two chief instructional colleges, Cranwell and Halton.

At Cranwell I flew a glider for the only time in my life and found the silence disconcerting. In Scotland we stayed first with the Senior Air

Officer, Scotland, who had a charming house on the banks of the Firth of Forth, and then flew up to Kinloss, a station on the far northern coast, famous because when all the rest of Scotland might be fog-bound, the skies over Kinloss were always clear. There we were taken on a patrol over the Orkney and Shetland Islands in a Halifax bomber. At one moment the pilot asked me to take over the controls. We had just flown over Lerwick, the capital of the Shetlands, when the outer port engine stopped. I was surprised how easily the aircraft adjusted to three engines and continued northwards. But no sooner had we reached Herma Ness, at the northern tip of the Shetlands, than a signal came from the Air Ministry saying that we must return immediately to Kinloss. I protested in vain and we landed without mishap. The Halifax was the biggest aircraft I had flown and I had much enjoyed it. After all these trips we were always flown back to the Royal Air Force station at Bicester, at that time a grass airfield next door to Charlie Kelly's gallops which I had known so well at Oxford, and only twelve miles from Kingsbridge. Virginia used to bring Andrew and Harriet out to meet me.

Our trips abroad spanned half the globe. The Royal Air Force had several squadrons in Western Germany, some in Cyprus and Egypt, a unit at Makulla in Oman, several squadrons in Malaya, another unit in Hong Kong and pilots operating in Korea, whose headquarters were in Japan. In Germany we stayed with Air Commodore 'Paddy' Bandon, who commanded No. 2 Group at Fundern. Paddy was a typically Irish character who held that as our forces were in a sense ambassadors in a now friendly Germany, the appearance of the wives of all ranks was as important as that of their husbands. He used to hold what he called 'hat parades', and pass judgement on the general appearance of the ladies – and particularly their hats – before any big occasion. He did it with such charm that no one took offence.

Some military exercises were being held by the army of the Rhine in which the Royal Air Force was co-operating. Group Captain Donald-son took me up in a two-seater Meteor trainer to see what was happening. After a little while he handed over the controls and told me to fly low to see if we could penetrate the army's attempts at camouflage. It was the first jet aircraft I had piloted. We were below a hundred feet and saw a lot of trucks standing amid pine trees without any attempt at camouflage. The troops waved at us. I was told later we had also passed over some tank units but we certainly did not see them. Their camouflage must have been good.

In September, during the parliamentary recess, we went to Malaya where British forces were fighting the Communist guerrillas. We stayed with Air Marshal Sir Francis Fogarty in Singapore and were then sent into the Sultanate of Johore, where Air Vice Marshal Melhuish was in command, and taken on a jungle patrol for which I was armed with a revolver. The jungle looked impenetrable and I remember thinking what sitting ducks we were for any guerrilla sniper hiding in a tree. On the other hand, if the sniper had exposed himself he would almost certainly have been caught and killed. Melhuish thought rightly that we were winning the guerrilla war by our policy of resettlement. In the north, where Communist units came across the sea from Vietnam or secretly filtered through from Thailand, villagers were at their mercy because there were not enough troops to defend them. The guerrillas, heavily armed, descended on a village, forced the inhabitants to feed and hide them for as long as necessary, and then often left as suddenly as they came. The Government therefore had decided on a wholesale removal of the population from exposed areas and their resettlement further south where our troops could protect them. A few months after we had left Malaya I read that Melhuish, a cheerful and natural commander, had been killed by the blade of a helicopter; I never learned how a man with such experience had got himself into a position where such a thing could happen.

We flew to Japan, in not a Royal Air Force but an American aircraft, the pilot of which, under the pooling arrangements between those taking part in the Vietnamese War, was a British Wing Commander. On board was the United States General Stratemeyer and an Australian, General Robertson. The weather was appalling, the cloud base often as low as two hundred feet and the landing at Iwakuni air base, without radar or blind-landing aids, a remarkable feat of airmanship. Being an international load of passengers, we all did our best to hide our anxiety, but I noticed a look of great relief on every face as we landed.

In Tokyo, the visit was made memorable because I had been asked to luncheon by General MacArthur, the Supreme Commander of American Forces in Japan, and of the United Nations forces in Korea. It was a wonderfully staged event. When I arrived at the great palace from which the General ruled Japan, I was ushered into a vast hall, at one end of which was a low stage. On it, mixing dry martinis, was Mrs MacArthur, alone. Along the walls below the stage, American Marines in white helmets and white gloves stood at intervals and, at the far end, two Marines guarded large sliding doors, which were shut.

Mrs MacAarthur told me that her husband was in a meeting but would arrive shortly. We stood chatting for perhaps five minutes when suddenly, at some invisible and inaudible signal, the Marines sprang to attention and the sliding doors parted, revealing MacArthur standing in front of a line of officers in khaki. The Marines presented arms and MacArthur marched up the hall with the khaki line behind him, mounted the steps up to the stage in the same formation and greeted me warmly. He then turned to the line of khaki figures and said, 'Mr Crawley, I want you to meet my General Officers.' I was formally introduced to each one in the line and only when the last had shaken hands did they relax and enjoy their martinis. At lunch the General was excellent company. The United Nations Forces, of which 90 per cent were American, had just finished the campaign which drove the North Korean and Chinese out of South Korea and back to the 38th Parallel. There was now a pause in the fighting while the two sides discussed a ceasefire. MacArthur praised the performance of the British contingent of the United Nations Forces, which numbered a little over two thousand men, and British pilots. He also said that the South Koreans had recovered their morale and fought well in the recent campaign.

I then plied him with questions about Japan. Japan, he said, was no longer an occupied territory but an ally in a state of tutelage. Few people had greater potential, and he was doing all he could to restore their self-respect and direct their energies into new enterprises. They showed an almost childlike gratitude as well as aptitude and he had no doubt they would become one of the most productive of the free nations.

Then he commented on Britain. He was full of admiration for our enterprise in producing the first jet airliner, the Comet. 'As a people you have brains and that is the way you should use them.' As I had already flown in both the Comet and that other experimental airliner, the Brabazon, the largest aircraft ever built and powered by piston engines, I was able to tell him something about them. In the Brabazon you felt you were in a hotel rather than an aircraft; it had a large cinema and a sort of central lobby where passengers could meet and walk about. But whenever I looked out of a window and saw the vast wings bending under their loads, I felt nervous. As Nathan Rothschild had said of the *Titanic*, one felt the Brabazon was just too big. It was not developed further.

Having met MacArthur I could not help being affected by his sudden fall six months later. On April 11th, 1951, he was dismissed by President Truman for authorizing his troops to cross the 38th Parallel in Korea 'if tactically necessary for their survival', and for advocating an extension of the war into China. I have no doubt President Truman was right to insist that his foremost military commander obey the instructions of the Government and Chiefs of Staff; MacArthur had to go. Whether the strategic thinking behind his dismissal was sound will be debated so long as men retain the freedom to argue. This was the last occasion on which the possession of nuclear weapons gave the United States the strength to force the Communist powers to climb down. If the opportunity had been taken, it is possible that the division of the world into blocs based on opposing ideologies might have been ended, but that is crystal gazing. The facts were that President Truman was acting as the agent of the United Nations, an organization which would certainly not have sanctioned any extension of the war. Neither the United States nor its allies were prepared to risk the confrontation which MacArthur was proposing.

*

Throughout the first nine months of 1951 the Labour Government in Britain was in difficulties. Ernest Bevin died at the end of March; Stafford Cripps, still Chancellor of the Exchequer, was dying in Switzerland; Nye Bevan resigned in April, ostensibly over charges for health prescriptions (which he had approved in principle the year before) but really over fury that Gaitskell had been made Minister of State for Economic Affairs and was clearly designated as the successor to Cripps. Harold Wilson and John Freeman followed him. In April, Mussadeq became Prime Minister in Persia and nationalized the Iranian Oil Company. In Egypt, Nahas Pasha denounced the Anglo–Egyptian treaty of 1888 as a result of which an international condominium ran the Suez Canal. In Parliament there was a general feeling of depression among Labour Members. There was no parliamentary reason for Attlee to consider a dissolution, but we all knew he was thinking that way; on September 19th he announced that Parliament would end on October 5th, and that polling day for the new Parliament would be on October 26th. He gave as his reason that after governing for eighteen months with a very small majority the Government felt the time had come to ask the electors for a renewal of confidence.

It was a curiously flat election. There were no major issues; Labour fought on its record and the Conservatives on the theme that it was time for a change. One sensed a general irritation among people over rising prices and continued shortages, but although Virginia and I canvassed every town and village and worked as hard as ever, by polling day we had no idea what the result would be.

At the count we could see that the piles of voting papers were almost level, but when we were told that the last box had been counted we were 1,500 votes ahead. My opponent, Frank Markham, came and sat down beside me and said he was ready to concede, but at that very moment his agent came up to him and said that the supervisor had found one more unopened ballot box. There was no reason to suspect it would drastically affect the result, but as we watched the piles of voting papers, the Conservative votes increased until they seemed to be level with our own. My agent, Ray Bellchambers, then told me that Markham was 50 votes ahead. We were allowed two recounts, but although the results differed by two or three votes, the final tally put Markham 54 votes ahead. That last ballot box had been an Aladdin's cave for him. We stayed to hear the final announcement of the result and I was able to thank my supporters, who were inevitably downcast. Then Virginia and I went home sadly to Kingsbridge.

*

The loss of his seat is the politician's great hazard. At one moment he is a public figure, part of a great machine and perhaps a leader; the next he is not merely just a private individual but probably out of work. I was lucky in having the farm. Virginia wisely said nothing about the future, but went on writing and looking after the children, the youngest of whom was eighteen months old. She was waiting for me to recover my balance.

At first I was on the look-out for a by-election, two of which occurred quite quickly. I went to see members of the committee at Islington, but realized that they were uncompromisingly left wing. Much more hopefully I went to Reading and was put on the shortlist. But although as I made my speech I could tell that I had many supporters, the key questions were all slanted. Twice I was asked in different ways whether I was in favour of abolishing the American air bases in Britain and when I said no I sensed that I had lost. I was told later that my opponent, Francis Noel Baker, whom they chose, had said yes and that if I had done the same I would have been selected.

We concentrated on the farm and put our little house in London up for sale. I felt completely cut off from politics and the world to which I had grown accustomed. Then suddenly one evening after we had finished the harvest, Virginia said to me, 'You told me you used to make documentary films before the war. Do any of them still exist?' I had to confess that I had no idea but said I would find out. My father had told me that he had given all the educational films to the Religious Film Society and I still had the address of the company which had bought *Between Two Worlds*, the documentary on modern Palestine, which was one of the burning questions of the moment. Although the Religious Film Society had used the educational series extensively, no copies remained. On the other hand, the company which had distributed *Between Two Worlds* not only had a copy but presented it to me and said I could make whatever use of it I liked. Virginia and I saw the film and liked it. Although it dealt with Palestine of the 1930s, it was still topical and to the point.

During my years in Parliament I had made friends with George Barnes, the head of the fledgling BBC television. We invited him to dine and he asked me what I intended to do now that I had lost my seat. I told him about my pre-war television experiences with Philip Dorté and Ian Orr-Ewing and said I would like to show him the film about Palestine which I had made in 1937. Philip Dorté was still working for the BBC and George brought him along to see *Between Two Worlds*. When the titles appeared on the screen Philip said encouragingly, 'I know this is the sort of film I am going to like.' Indeed, they both liked it, George saying that it was just the sort of thing they were looking for. So began a new and fascinating part of my life.

30

India's Challenge

When we visited George Barnes at the BBC we quickly came to an arrangement that Virginia and I would do a series of at least six 50-minute programmes on India, whose independence had been formally granted six years before. I was to be my own cameraman and commentator and Virginia was to do the research. The BBC would pay our air fares to India and back, supply one 16mm camera (I hired a second very light one for use in the hand), all the film – which was only black and white – and all the staff and facilities to do the cutting and editing. We would be paid fifteen hundred pounds to cover travel in India and our own living expenses. Our stay was not expected to be longer than three to four months.

We had chosen India because we had both been fascinated by it in 1934. The teeming life, the colour and immense variety of culture within one civilization made it a natural for documentary films. We realized that our funds were very little for two people to travel round India for four months, so we set about finding contacts through whom we might be able to stay with Indian or British residents. Grindlays Bank wrote to all its local branch managers in India, a kindness which proved invaluable; the Foreign Office wrote to Alexander Clutterbuck, who was British High Commissioner in Delhi; we both knew 'Jai' and Ayesha Jaipur and the BBC gave us the names of its representatives in all the major towns. Then Virginia had a piece of luck. She sat next to Henry Ford at dinner one night and after telling him what we were about to do said, 'I don't suppose you could help us with a car, could you?' To her delight he said that his company had only recently opened an assembly plant in India and nothing could be easier. He thought it would be a prestige advertisement. The car would cost us nothing and would have a driver.

During all these preparations I spent long hours with the BBC, learning all I could about television. The chief Current Affairs Producer was then Mrs Grace Wyndham Goldie, a woman who was to become a legend in her lifetime. Her father was a Scottish railway engineer and, when she was born, was just finishing the railway to Mallaig in the Western Highlands. He then took his family to Egypt. Grace was sent to a French school in Alexandria, then to Cheltenham Ladies' College and finally to Somerville College at Oxford. She joined the BBC in 1944.

Grace had her headquarters in Lime Grove, a street only a short distance from the present BBC Television Centre. Around her she had collected a group of exceptionally bright young men: Donald Baverstock, Alasdair Milne (later Director General of the BBC), Michael Peacock, David Attenborough, Tony de Lothbiniere, to mention only a few of those who began their careers as assistant producers under her. She was an alert and attractive woman with sure judgement and a quick sense of humour. Fortunately she also believed that if television was to deal credibly with political subjects, it must use people who had experience of political life. Of those who had been in Mr Attlee's government and lost their seats in 1951 or later, she selected John Freeman, Christopher Mayhew, Woodrow Wyatt and myself in the early 1950s. 'We had arrived,' Grace wrote twenty-five years later, 'without intention and simply because they were all free and effective, at the extraordinary situation in which four of the most successful commentators and interviewers on television were four men who had all been junior ministers in the Attlee Administration of 1945 to 51.'[1]

Both Grace and we were aware that the appearance on television of so many former Members of Parliament belonging to one party might be seen as a breach of that impartiality in politics which the BBC was bound to observe under its Charter. Grace's argument was that there were plenty of discussion programmes on which Members of Parliament could appear and make their political case and, indeed, earn useful fees. What she wanted for the Current Affairs Department was not argument but exposition, and if the BBC was to carry the weight it deserved, it was often essential that the expositor should have experience of Government. She wrote later: 'They [the four men mentioned above] were able to contribute to political communication by television something quite different from what was being done by journalists and dons. Its quality was realism. They showed a far greater understanding of the difficulties of Government than the more theoretical critics.'

Grace won her battle, but it was not until her book appeared in 1977 that I realized what a struggle she had had. On page 89 of that book she wrote: 'On May 30 1953 the Prime Minister, Mr Churchill, when making a general complaint about the BBC's use of Labour Party candidates in its programmes, gave as an example the fact that the prospective Labour candidate for North Buckinghamshire, Aidan Crawley, was in India preparing a series of television programmes which would be transmitted by the BBC in August.' Fortunately Mr Churchill had been misinformed. Grace was able to tell her superiors that although I was certainly preparing a television series in India, I was not a Labour candidate anywhere and had no immediate plans to become one. The BBC stood firm and 'the gang of four', as we might have been called, were able to continue their broadcasting.

But I have jumped ahead of my preparation for India. As soon as our project was confirmed, I was lent a 35mm camera by the BBC and told to make a short story on film. I did the story of our farm and used Harriet as a milkmaid. Even at the age of five she showed some of the qualities that later made her such a good commentator herself. The film on the farm was considered satisfactory. Then I practised with all sorts of different lenses, mugged up what I knew about the care of film in a hot climate and learned to use all the latest equipment for cutting and editing film. Finally I arranged for the BBC to send us batches of film in India through their representatives in Delhi, Bombay and Calcutta. We were ready to go.

In India we first stayed with Sir Alexander Clutterbuck in New Delhi. He was extremely kind. He told us he could put us in touch with almost any politician we liked to name, but, as our programmes were to deal with the lives of ordinary Indians throughout the country, he strongly advised us to do our filming first and then return to Delhi. He gave us a list of introductions to each of whom he wrote personally. We picked up our car, a large Ford limousine with a Christian driver from southern India who spoke a little English and asked us to call him George. We also arranged, through All India Radio, for the handling of the film we were to receive from, or despatch to, the BBC.

In those days, driving through India, even on the main roads, was quite an adventure. There was virtually no tarmac, except on the outskirts of cities, and the pot-holes were as frequent as shell holes must have been in no-man's land in the First World War. Added to which the passage of lorries, bullock carts and the occasional car corrugated the road's surface in ridges as regular as corrugated iron. Luckily our driver was experienced. To go too slowly was bone-shaking, to go too fast destroyed the car. At between forty-five and fifty miles an hour the wheels skipped from one ridge to another with surprising smoothness. But there was an added hazard. The traffic consisted maily of bullock carts with four or sometimes six bullocks in a team. Their journeys were short in mileage but of long duration and the drivers were often asleep. But asleep or awake they knew nothing of signals, so that when bullock carts were ahead, irrespective of whether they were approaching or going in the same direction, the driver of a car had to be prepared for the bullock team to turn suddenly at right angles across the road, as often as not unguided but at the whim of the leading bullock. Our driver understood this hazard so well that we never came in contact with either bullock or cart, but there were anxious moments.

It was in a village near Tuticorin, south of Tiruchirapalli (then Trichinopoli) that we did our first serious filming and it was there that we learned our first lessons about the untouchables. We stayed with a Mr and Mrs Hogg, a couple who had recently retired from Grindlays Bank. The road to the village ran along the bank of a canal from which an endless line of irrigation poles,[2] worked by boys and girls, were pouring water into ditches. The canal was fringed with palms and some of the fields were green with young rice. Many boats were moored to the shores. After a forty-minute drive along a dirt track one entered the main street of the village which had about a thousand inhabitants. The street was wide, dusty, without paving and pitted with cart tracks. At first the houses were little better than palm-thatched hovels with a hole for a door and without windows, but as we reached the centre of the village, near the well, the street narrowed and the surface became hard and smooth. Many of the houses in this part of the village were white-washed and mud brick with thatched or even tiled roofs; a few had two storeys. Often the walls of the houses were covered with pats of dung, slapped on so as to dry in the sun. The pats were used for fuel on primitive cooking stoves. I came to notice that in India one of the signs of agricultural advance were farms (seldom whole villages) where dung was used as manure. The little white-washed temple had a miniature tower.

This was the caste village. At the top, living together in one street of tiled houses, were the Brahmans, who might be priests, bank clerks working in Trichinopoli, lawyers, schoolteachers, police, accountants or scribes (letter writing was an important function in any Indian village). Living close to the Brahmans were the craftsmen, brickmakers and bricklayers, timber merchants, carpenters, thatchers, wagon makers, wheelwrights, potters, blacksmiths and rope makers. Farmers looked after their own sheep and goats and many of them had a few emaciated cattle. Their mainstay were the water buffaloes which were not only the chief source of milk but were used for the plough and to pull wagons. Even in the houses of Brahmans there was no plumbing. This is not a craft that is necessary in southern Indian villages.

We met the village headman on our first day. He was a small, thin, leathery man in his fifties with a soft voice and a gentle smile. There had been no election when his predecessor had died, but a general consensus had been reached that he was the right man. One could tell at once that the villagers liked and respected him. He spoke enough English for us to communicate. We explained to him that we wanted to film the details of the life of the village, and so each day he would suggest a different family and a different occupation.

One day, as we crossed the temple square, I noticed some men and women sweeping the sun-baked earth. I asked the headman who was responsible for keeping the streets clean and he said, 'Oh, the untouchables. They do not live in the village, they have a village of their own a little way away.' I asked if we might go and see it and he said he would arrange it. I could tell he did not like our going. The untouchables' village was about half a mile away, out of sight of the caste village. The houses were straw hovels sited haphazardly; there was no street and the whole group made an uneven circle. At one side of the circle was the well. No caste Indian would ever drink water from an untouchable well and, even if their own well ran dry, no untouchable would ever dream of coming to the caste well. I had read of people being killed for such an act.

The headman said we could film the village provided we kept at a reasonable distance, but he did not think we should go into the houses. In fact it would have been far too dark to film under the thatch and in any case most of the untouchables squatted or lay about on the ground by the door. A 'house' consisted of one low room, perhaps five yards long and two or three yards wide, with a mud floor. There did not seem to be any furniture. A few untouchables greeted the headman or smiled at us, but mostly they were unwelcoming. I asked the headman if anyone in the main village ever touched an untouchable for any reason at all and he said, 'No, but we might not be able to avoid it in a bus.' Indians do not shake hands with each other; instead they put their hands together as if in prayer and make a slight bow. I never saw a caste Indian make such a gesture to an untouchable.

We found that some Brahmans in the village employed untouchables as gardeners. I asked one how he paid his man. 'Oh!' he said demonstrating, 'I throw the money on the ground and he comes and collects it.' He was quite happy to let me film him doing it.

The headman told me that most southern villages had satellite untouchable villages close to them, although sometimes one satellite would serve two caste villages. On our travels we saw several satellite villages but we never filmed another. Untouchables were not forbidden by law to own land or property and I was given several instances of untouchables who had emerged from their environment, received an education and made fortunes. This is not as surprising as it sounds. Except in Kerala, Christians are untouchable and, by association, all Europeans, North and South Americans, Moslems and Jews. Yet caste Indians do not refuse to meet them or even to shake hands.

I have related elsewhere how the Maharajah of Alwar boasted that he had never shaken hands with an Englishman without wearing gloves, but he was untypical. More revealing was an incident which occurred in a large house in Calcutta where four generations of the same family lived together. The head of the household was the senior lady. It was she who had invited us to come and film the house and family, and she who took us round. Tall and thin with aquiline features and bright black eyes, she wore white with an embroidered white hood over her head and spoke a little English. Towards the end of our tour she took us to see the larder. It was gleaming white, with fresh meat and vegetables, flour and rice and a mass of tins on the shelves. It was too dark to film but, to please her, I took a few shots of the old lady lifting things from the shelves. As we left the house shortly afterwards, her eldest son, a man of about fifty, also dressed all in white, said with a smile, 'I think it might interest you to know that my mother has gone back to the larder and is now busy throwing away a lot of food. She noticed that as you were filming, your shadow fell across some of the shelves. Wherever your shadow fell the shelves will now be empty.' And he added, 'This, of course, is because you are an untouchable and, although I did not notice and would not have taken any notice even if I had, the elder generation is still very strict about religious observance.'

One other scene in our village remains in my mind. Virginia had talked to the headman about childbirth and he had introduced her to a woman whose daughter was within hours of having a baby. She was lying on a heap of warm, fresh dung covered with straw which had been specially collected and put in her hut. The headman told us that the family considered that the dung had life-giving qualities. The girl's mother introduced Virginia to the midwife, a fine-looking woman who was just off to harvest some wheat in one of her little plots. She had a sickle in her hand. By gesture and with a bright smile she indicated she would come back soon with the sickle. Not quite understanding her gestures, Virginia asked the headman what she could have meant. He said, 'She meant she would come back to cut the umbilical cord with the sickle.' So I went out and filmed the midwife sickling the wheat, taking a close-up of her sickle, and then filmed the mother-to-be lying on her bed of straw and dung. The baby was born on the following day.

Our stay in the village ended in a touching way. We had told the headman the day when we expected to complete our filming and he said that he hoped we were satisfied. He paused and went on, 'The day after tomorrow is Independence Day. Several of the villagers have asked me if you would be prepared to raise the Indian flag at our ceremony. They would consider it a great honour.' I accepted immediately. We had got to know so many people in the village during our two weeks of filming that we felt part of the community. We had been almost as pleased at the birth of the baby as the family into which it had been born.

For the flag-raising ceremony a little dais made of hard mud had been constructed in the temple square and a few rickety chairs stood in a line on the dais behind the flagpole. The flag was hanging loosely at the bottom of the pole. Virginia and I sat immediately behind it and behind us sat several of the village elders. The headman made a speech, at the end of which he clearly referred to Virginia and me;

villagers standing in front of us clapped. Then the headman turned to me and asked in English if I would raise the flag. I said, slowly and in English, that as an Englishman I considered it a great honour to be invited to raise their flag of independence. I then pulled the rope and the flag waved boldly in the breeze. Everybody seemed happy.

31

Bombay Races

From Trichinopoli we went south to Madurai where we filmed details of the beautiful carvings on the gopurams of the Meenakshi temple. The temple is certainly one of the wonders of the world. In the outer courtyard priests were sacrificing kids and lambs which pilgrims had brought them as offerings. I can still hear the soft thud with which the knife cut through their necks and see the pathetic little heads rolling on the ground. Outside, the temple was in wonderful condition, built of that smooth grey stone to which we had grown accustomed. I am told that many of the carvings have now been restored to their original violent colours, fascinating but also rather horrifying.

From Madurai we motored down to Cape Cormorin, the very southern tip of India. All 'Land's Ends' arouse a romantic pang and it is true that from the point at Cape Cormorin you can see the waters of the Arabian Sea meet those of the south Atlantic and the Indian Ocean. There was some sort of small pavilion on the edge of the point and the point itself is clearly defined. There were no concessions to tourists and nothing to tempt them in the way of food or drink. We drove on north up the west coast towards Trivandrum, the capital of Kerala (which used to be known as Travancore). Kerala had a new Premier, Mr Nambudiripad, who had won a recent provincial election for the Communist Party. He was then engaged in a bitter dispute with the Bishop of the Church of India, whose four million followers had one of the highest literacy rates in the country and were very articulate. At that time the Church of India was also in dispute with the Anglican Church, but the Bishop told me that his own Church was going from strength to strength. The country round Trivandrum was lush, a maze of palm trees, rice and corn fields and canals. It was also heavily populated. There were then more people per square mile in Kerala than anywhere in India except Bengal. On Sundays the people dressed all in white, the women with white flowers in their hair, and went to their churches in thousands.

By this time we were a team. On the road to Bombay, which ran some way inland, we decided to make good all the road scenes we had so far missed. At a crossroads just before we entered a village we saw half a dozen men squatting on the corner while a barber shaved them. George stopped the car and took the tripod out of the back. I got out with the camera, Virginia followed with her 'dope sheets' (the sheets on which are recorded all the details of the filming, exposures, location, date, and so on). George came with me to act as far as possible as interpreter plus assistant. Nowhere in southern India did we meet with any objections to our filming. I would call out to Virginia the number of the film reel, the lens on the turret head which I was using, the exposure, whether it was a facial close-up, a mid or long shot, and at the end, the length of footage I had taken. She would note the place, date and time and add any points that she herself felt interesting, such as the price of a shave, and the number of people the barber managed to shave every day. When we had finished we gave the barber and his clients a few rupees between them – George was very firm about not giving them too much – and went on our way.

One of the most difficult shots to take on the road was the turning of a bullock cart. We saw plenty of drivers fast asleep and line after line of carts; but to be in the right place when the bullocks took into their heads to make a right-angled turn was almost impossible. George solved the problem for us by finding out from one or two drivers how far they were going and where they were turning off the main road. We would then station ourselves at the turning and film away. Sometimes we mistook the turning and the carts went slowly past us; sometimes we were lucky and got a line of motor cars putting their brakes on furiously while the drivers leaned out of their windows swearing at the bullock carts. The only thing that was never difficult was to film the driver while he was asleep. As one of them explained to George, the bullocks knew their own way home and the drivers didn't have to bother.

It may have been on the way to Bombay, or later, that we visited a famine area. There are few years in India when some areas do not suffer famine and it is easy to discover where the areas are from reading the local newspapers. This area was only a day's drive away. We had been given the name of the village where famine relief was being distributed. As we drew near we began to pass a line of people on foot, dragging themselves along the dusty road. Occasionally a cactus grew by the roadside and, if the family had a spade, it would stop to dig the plant up so as to get at its roots, some of which might be edible. Many men were almost naked and some so thin one felt their stomachs must be hitting their spines. We drove slowly on until a gap in the line of stragglers allowed us to film those we had already passed.

In the village, relief workers were doling out soup, rice, sugar and flour. There were also some water carts. It was clear that even with this help many people would not have the strength to get home, and an impromptu open-air camp was being formed. Further down the village street men were distributing wheat and barley from sacks. I asked an official how many people had the strength to carry a sack home even in a wheelbarrow. He agreed it was a major problem but explained it was only their second day in this village and they had already begun to collect bullock carts and any other suitable form of transport from fringe areas. The Indian Red Cross had already established a post in the village rest house and a team of doctors and nurses were hard at work. They faced an overwhelming problem. It is not uncommon, even in India, to hear people say that, terrible though it is to see people starving, it is nature's way of keeping down the population.

*

We had been looking forward to Bombay. Both Virginia and I had seen it first – but separately – from the sea in 1934, with the sun rising behind its hills and shining on water that was like glass. There was, literally, a 'gateway to India' in the form of a ceremonial arch which had been put up on the shore at the point where King Edward VII landed on his visit in 1905. Behind it was the Taj Mahal Hotel, ornate, air-conditioned and expensive, an hotel we both disliked but could endure for a change. We gave ourselves three nights there; if we stayed longer in Bombay we would have to move. And we had friends, the Talyarkhans; Russi, a Parsee who had been at Harrow with me, and Indira, his wife, who was a Bonarjee from Bengal, beautiful, amusing, forthright. Her elder sister, 'Minnie', had married an Englishman named Lindsay Emerson, then assistant editor and later editor of *The Statesman*, Calcutta's prestige newspaper.

For the first few days Indira took charge of us. We dined with her the day after we arrived and when I rhapsodized over the beauty of southern Indian women, she said, 'Tomorrow I will take you to the Bombay races. You will see more beautiful women in half an hour than you have ever seen in your life.' I asked if I could bring a movie camera and she said she would find out. If it was a small hand camera she thought it would be all right. It *was* all right and Indira had not exaggerated. The Bombay racecourse had trees and flowers which put Ascot or Longchamps to shame. Elegant Indians in tropical European suits with panama hats, or in that Indian dress which allowed them to wear silver buckles on their shoes and silver buttons on their long tunics, walked with women whose saris outshone the flowers. I filmed so fast that Virginia could not keep up with her notes.

During a pause when we stood talking to Indira, a tall dark girl walked past whom I thought without question the most beautiful I had ever seen. I said so to Indira as I raised the camera. Indignantly and spontaneously she exclaimed, 'You cannot call her beautiful. She is black.' I was taken aback. I thought I understood a Brahman's feelings towards an untouchable, but that someone as gentle and civilized as Indira should be colour-conscious in a country where no one except a foreigner was white, shocked me. I upbraided her at once. She laughed and said, 'But we all feel like that.' Over the years we have discussed it. At first I thought it must be an Aryan prejudice against a Dravidian; the beauty, whom Indira knew and liked, did indeed come from the south. Indira herself was a Bengali Aryan whose ancestors came from Kananj in the United Provinces; but the vast majority of Bengalis are Mongolo-Dravidian, so that her prejudice must have been purely due to colour. I have had the same thing said to me in Italy by a northern woman about a Neapolitan and have since wondered whether there is some innate sense of superiority in those who have to withstand cold climates towards those who are lucky enough always to be warm; a mixture of jealousy and disdain. Certainly neither colour nor racial prejudice is rational. If it were, it would not be so strong.

We had an introduction from the High Commissioner to the Premier of the State of Bombay, whose capital was Bombay city, Mr Moraji Desai. The first meeting was extraordinary. We had an appointment in his office at eleven a.m. and arrived punctually. We waited for an hour, during which one of Mr Desai's secretaries came in two or three times to say that Mr Desai was terribly sorry but he was being unavoidably detained, and hoped we would continue to wait. Then after another half-hour his private secretary came in and sat down. 'A most unusual thing has happened,' he said. 'This morning the sari of Mr Desai's daughter was caught in an electric fire and she was burned to death. Mr Desai is certainly going to see you and he had hoped until now it would be possible today. But he asked to be excused. He hopes to see you tomorrow and I am to telephone to you in the morning.'

We expressed our shock and sympathy and went back to our hotel. It was a disappointment because we had hoped to persuade Mr Desai to let us film the Bombay Parliament. We had been told in Delhi that there was no question of our filming the Lok Sabha (the Federal Parliament) but that it was quite possible that Mr Desai would agree in Bombay. The premiership was his first major political position and, besides having a great respect for Britain, he might welcome the publicity. Now it looked as if it would be impossible. We had limited time and money and could not, so we thought, wait for him to recover from his tragic loss. We were wrong. The next morning the telephone rang and the Private Secretary asked if we could be at Mr Desai's office by eleven a.m.

When we arrived Mr Desai was waiting for us. He was dressed all in white, a long white coat, with those white chuvidai pyjamas so popular in India, white slippers and a white Congress cap – like a military forage cap which has been pressed down so as to cover the whole of the top of the head instead of being worn on one side. Just turning sixty, he was tall and thin, his face handsome with aquiline features. He apologized for failing to keep his appointment. 'I know that my daughter is happier now than she has been and that it would be wrong of me to grieve. But the manner of her death affected me more than I should have allowed it to. I beg you to forgive me.' He went straight on to ask about our trip and to know whether he could help us. He was so calm and practical that we at once disclosed our hope of filming a session of his legislature and I added that I had hoped to film an interview with him. He agreed to both propositions and asked his Private Secretary to make the necessary arrangements. We then talked about India generally. Mr Desai was a vegetarian and something of an ascetic. One of his passions was prohibition, which had already been introduced in Bombay and which he hoped to spread over the whole country. To my suggestion that it might increase corruption and damage respect for the law, he replied that there was corruption everywhere and he had not noticed that America had become less corrupt or more law abiding since prohibition had been abolished.

32

Along the Ganges

Our next target for prolonged filming was Calcutta, which we planned to reach in stages, passing through Delhi and taking the well-worn route along the Ganges through Agra and Benares. Our long and dusty drive through Rajasthan was broken at Jaipur, where we stayed with Ayesha and Jai whom we knew in England. They had been married in 1940 and Ayesha was still shocking some of Jai's more elderly subjects by wearing jeans in public. In middle age she is still a beautiful woman; then she was breathtaking. Nothing had been allowed to spoil the seventeenth-century city with its buildings of pink and white stucco grouped around the old battlemented fort. We stayed at the Rambagh Palace (now a hotel), had tea at the medieval castle in the centre of the city whose bare brown stone announced its age, picnicked at the hunting lodge late in the evening, played tennis, swam and watched polo. There were no boards to mark the limits of the polo ground which was of very bare grass, so the referee's whistle blew much less often than in England. The standard of play was such that there was never any question of the ball straying among the spectators.

There was a routine at the swimming pool where we gathered when the polo was over. The guests all bathed first while Jai was massaged. Then four men came to the swimming pool carrying a long pole, from which hung a green velvet curtain. The men stood either side of the pool – two men at each end of the pole – unfurled the curtain and then dragged it slowly up and down, allowing it to trail in the water. Only after the water had been cleansed in this way was the Maharajah allowed to immerse himself. Ayesha, although Jai's third wife, was our hostess; Jai's second wife, a Princess of Jodhpur, lived in the house as well. Jai visited her every day and was very fond of her. But she never mingled with his guests and we never saw her.

On a later visit to India we stayed again at Jaipur when Jai was

Rajpramukh (Governor) of the Province of Rajasthan. Ayesha was already a Member of Parliament and they were doing a lot of official entertaining for the Government of India; while we were there the Shah of Iran's brother and his wife came to stay. One of Jai's ADCs gave me some statistics of Jai's household at the time. There were twenty-two cooks who worked in relays, some thousand servants in all, of whom three hundred were gardeners; seventy-five polo ponies all with their grooms, and nearly a hundred cars. The gardens were a dream, great blocks of pink and white flowers to match the walls of the palace.

By coincidence, Ayesha had fought a by-election in Rajasthan on the same day in June 1962 as I had fought one in West Derbyshire. She had won with a majority of 175,000 and I with one of 1,200. Ayesha had joined Rajagopalachari's Swatantra Party and was therefore in opposition, a fact that was to produce an extraordinary sequel. Fifteen years later, long after both Nehru and Jai had died, Ayesha was still a Member of Parliament for Rajasthan. Mrs Gandhi, whose Congress Party had suffered a severe defeat in elections in the State of Gujarat in June 1975, was under pressure to resign and, when she refused, many opposition leaders called for a campaign of civil disobedience. Then on June 12th, after a law suit which had lasted four years, the High Court of Allahabad annulled her election in 1971 and charged her with electoral malpractice. In law she was no longer a Member of Parliament nor could she legally carry out the duties of Prime Minister. In retaliation, without consulting the President of India or the Indian Cabinet, she declared a 'State of Emergency', suspended all civil liberties including habeas corpus, assumed dictatorial powers and began a systematic suppression of all opposition. Within two weeks, more than a hundred thousand prominent Indians were in gaol, including Ayesha and most Opposition Members of Parliament.

However, retribution overtook Mrs Gandhi. In March 1977 she not only lost the general election to the Janata Party, but she and her son Sanjay lost their own seats. There was nationwide jubilation. But the members of the Janata Party quarrelled among themselves and Mrs Gandhi was able to return to power in 1980. Her humiliation, however, had taught her not to abuse her trust so flagrantly.

*

Calcutta was a challenge. In 1952 it was a city of some eight million inhabitants of whom between two and three million lived in a sprawling petrol-drum shanty town which surrounded the city proper. There were more beggars and there was undoubtedly greater poverty in Calcutta than in any other Indian city, and yet I found Calcutta inspiring. When people have nothing except the dhoti in which they stand and nowhere to sleep except in the street, it is astonishing to find them so proud and passionate. It used to infuriate us to see a cow knock over a vegetable stall in the street and then eat the water melons while the owners, who depended upon these things for their livelihood, sat and watched. But the cow was sacred and we were told that if we shooed it away we should be attacked immediately. This was the only city in which we had to hide in order to film street scenes. We would hire a bullock cart, lie on the floor covered in straw and film scenes as we passed them. George sat up with the driver and passed on our directions. Whenever we tried to film on our feet we were assailed by indignant passers-by, although we did manage to film people sleeping in the streets because we arrived while it was dark and filmed them as they woke up. There must have been several thousand people lying on the pavements. As it became light, they would get up and go to one of the taps on the kerbside to wash and shave. I would stand in a doorway with a long lens and shoot as soon as there was enough light. Sometimes people saw us filming and came towards us, shouting menacingly. We would then decamp around the corner and try another street. We kept the car out of sight, but close enough to be a refuge in case of emergency.

It was an introduction from my father which provided us with the most unusual film sequence of the whole trip. At the turn of the century, when he was preparing himself for entry into the Church, my father had visited the Oxford Mission to Calcutta, a leper colony which was run by a young priest called Father Douglas. The Mission was staffed by young men from Magdalen College, Oxford, some of whom had already been ordained, others being candidates for ordination. Enquiries at Magdalen, which was also my father's college, had revealed that Father Douglas was not only still alive but still in charge of the Mission. My father had written him a letter.

My impression of the Mission from outside was of low wooden huts alongside compounds bounded by chicken wire. In the centre of one of

258

these compounds was a tall, straight figure in a long white cassock held at the waist by a black belt. Several other figures in white cassocks and black belts were moving about among dark, near-naked people, most of whom crawled or squatted rather than walked. I do not remember any flowers or trees and the earth was brown, hard-baked mud. The tall figure was Father Douglas, now more than eighty years old, with grey-white hair and a classically handsome face with eyes that twinkled. He had received Father's letter and clearly remembered him quite well. The next two days were among the busiest of our trip.

Neither Virginia nor I had been in contact with lepers before. Father Douglas explained the nature of the disease, which he assured us was not contagious, calling lepers to him so that he could touch them and we could examine them, or just walking among them with us and talking to them. They all had complete trust in Father Douglas and would answer any questions. Only confirmed lepers were allowed to stay in the Mission. Those in the early stages of the disease would have lumps on their arms, legs or faces, and fingers or toes which had become stumps. Advanced cases were sometimes difficult to look at, faces in which the lips had been eaten away and the eye sockets had become sunken or where the whole face had been distorted into that leonine expression which is characteristic of the disease.

The most surprising discovery was the lepers' cheerfulness. We filmed many groups and finally came to one which was preparing itself for a begging expedition. They had low wooden carts, only an inch or two from the ground, which they would either propel with their hands or in which one leper would pull another. Father Douglas got some of them to show us how they made a perfectly sound leg or arm look like a stump. Indian limbs are, or so it seemed to me, much suppler than ours; when a man or boy in a cart unwound a leg which had been doubled underneath him, it was difficult for us to believe what we saw. He was greeted with applause and laughter from all his companions. Begging, Father Douglas explained, was an important source of income because, although the Mission could supply shelter and some medical care, its funds could not provide pocket money for the hundreds of lepers who wanted to stay there. We asked Father Douglas to dinner, but he said he would far rather we entertained his staff, so on several evenings we had as companions young men who had only recently left Oxford. Again, what surprised us was their gaiety. All had good degrees and gave the impression that to spend their lives in a leper colony was a privilege beyond price. The conversation ranged widely late into the night. We left feeling in their debt.

*

Our Indian adventure ended in Delhi. The High Commissioner had arranged for us to film interviews with Pandit Nehru and Dr Ambedkar, the untouchables' leader, and also to meet Vice-President Dr Radakrishnan who, after a distinguished career in several Indian universities, had been a Professor of Eastern Religions and Ethics at Balliol for many years until Independence drew him back to his own country. Dr Radakrishnan had aroused animosity by merging all the Hindu gods into one in his teaching. Orthodox Hindus thought he was emasculating the religion. He was, therefore, a controversial figure at the time we met him.

Amita Malik of All India Radio had arranged for an Indian cameraman to take the sound interviews. Nehru was one of the easiest men to film. Dressed in white jodhpurs, a long black tunic with silver buttons and a white Congress forage cap, he sat down and talked to us as if he had known us all our lives. I asked him about his time at Harrow, which he had not much enjoyed, though he was lyrical about Balliol. When I asked whether the fourteen years he had spent in gaol under the British had made him bitter, he replied that if he had been the Viceroy he would have done exactly the same. 'You had your timetable for the granting of Independence and the right to stick to it, but we were in a hurry.' His main preoccupation at that moment was the problem of linguistic States. 'I do not want linguistic States,' he said. 'There is only one common language in India and that is English. No one speaks Hindustani in the south and if we are to hold India together we must not only maintain the use of English but spread it through education. To redraw the boundaries of Indian States on the basis of race and language is to risk the fragmentation of the country. Yet politically I fear I may have to give way, at least in some instances.'

A few years later we were to meet Nehru again when I was doing another series for the BBC called *The Inheritors*, the theme being the progress made by countries which had recently achieved independence not only in Asia but in Africa and the West Indies. Then he was most concerned with China. We talked in his office which had a large map of

Asia on the wall behind his desk. I remember him getting up at one point and running a pointer along the whole two thousand miles of India's northern frontier. 'This is what haunts me night and day,' he said dramatically. 'If China decides to attack us she can do so at more points than we can defend.' He went on to develop the theme that for India friendship with the Soviet Union was the only safeguard. I asked him if that was why he was taking a neutral stance towards Hungary, which at that moment was struggling to assert some independence from the Soviet bloc. His reply was surprising. 'You speak of Europe. Europe does not mean much to me. The Europeans have never helped us. If you talk of England, that is quite another thing. You have educated us politically.' And he went on to talk of England with a warmth that was captivating.

One evening Nehru gave a dinner party for Lady Mountbatten, who was staying with him. The warmth of his welcome was touching. He took her arm and led her into the marquee where a buffet supper was waiting, and stayed with her the whole evening. The tent was divided into two, one half for carnivores who liked alcohol and the other for vegetarian teetotallers. The only person to make for the latter half was Lady Cripps, Sir Stafford's widow. When it was seen that she was alone, several people joined her. Virginia and I had visited her daughter, Peggy Appiah, in Kumasi in Ghana. It was at the time when Nkrumah had put Joe Appiah in prison and Peggy's house was surrounded by hundreds of sympathizers sitting silently on the ground. Peggy had won their hearts by carrying her babies on her back, African style. While we sat and talked, two beautiful children had come into the room, a boy of about six and a girl a little younger. Virginia had exclaimed at their beauty. Peggy had smiled and said, 'Yes, God has been very good to me. I am ugly and Joe is not very good-looking, but God has allowed me to produce these children.' Lady Cripps told us that Joe was now out of prison, but added that she was afraid that Peggy did not see much of him. Joe, we knew, had the reputation of being an inveterate womanizer and spent most of his time in Accra, the capital, where he practised as a lawyer.

Is my memory playing tricks, or did Dr Ambedkar greet us in a brown toga and sandals? He was certainly not in European clothes, which I had been told he might be. We met him at his house and talked on the verandah. Everything about him was larger than life. He was a big man with a large round head, a loud voice and a tremendous laugh. As an untouchable boy he had been taken up by the Maharajah of Baroda, who made him his ward, and eventually had become a qualified lawyer and a Doctor of Philosophy and Science. Yet his childhood experiences had coloured his whole life. In his Hindu school he was not allowed into the classroom but was hung in a basket outside the window from where he could listen to the lessons. The caste Hindu boys neither ate nor played with him. Similar incidents occurred throughout his life. Even when he started practising in the Bombay High Court, the canteen superintendent refused to serve him tea.

Ambedkar's hatred of caste brought him into conflict with Gandhi, who upheld caste but wanted to integrate the untouchables into Hinduism by opening the temples to them. Gandhi worked for a change of heart among caste Hindus and believed that once the untouchables were accepted within the Hindu system their social and economic position would rapidly improve. Ambedkar held that only if caste was abolished would untouchability disappear. The two leaders finally reached a compromise when Ambedkar accepted that the untouchables were part of the Hindu community but obtained special representation for them in provincial assemblies. This caused resentment among many Hindus, particularly in Bengal. There was a sparkle about Ambedkar that was truly Churchillian. One feels the richer for having met him.

We left many friends in Delhi: Amita Malik and her husband, Iqbal, of All India Radio, had been trained by the BBC and vigorously upheld the tradition of independence from Government control; Kushwant Singh, who had written a history of the Sikhs; Frank Moraes, the editor in turn of the *Times of Ceylon*, the *Times of India* and later the *Indian Express*. I interviewed them all, getting them to talk about their lives in the new India.

When we reached Bombay to catch the boat home we received a shock. A cable had arrived from Grace Wyndham Goldie saying that nothing we had filmed in Calcutta was usable. Mortified, we took an aeroplane and in twenty-four hours refilmed the leper colony and the street scenes. We had two or three days in hand and were still in time to take our passage home when we got back to Bombay. In London we were met at Lime Grove by some rather shame-faced young producers who confessed that they had only viewed two tins of the Calcutta film, each of which was scratched; the rest were perfect. We were so relieved that we had no time to be angry.

The BBC had sorted out the film before we arrived home and it did not take long to get the programme into shape. A crisis came when I started to lay on the commentary. I had been watching a good many BBC documentary programmes and noticed that the style of commentary was impersonal and the tone rather flat. In the belief that I should win approval, I decided to adopt the same approach. At the end of the first reel I waited hopefully for some comment from Grace, who was supervising in the gallery. There was a long silence. Then her voice came into the earphone.

'Aidan, that was terrible. If you can't do better we shall have to reconsider the future of the whole series.'

I asked what was wrong.

'Everything!' she said. 'You were dead. I wouldn't have known it was you speaking.'

'Oh,' I replied. 'You want a bit more of *me* in it?'

'Everything you can give.'

We went through the reel again and I spoke as I felt, remembering details as the picture appeared. This time an entirely different voice came into the earphones. Grace was pleased, made several suggestions and said we should go straight ahead through the programme. The series was shown during the year 1953.

33

A Decade of Documentaries

India's Challenge launched me on a television career which lasted almost for a decade, mostly with the BBC. As the television audience was steadily increasing, I also found myself in demand as a feature writer for the newspapers. There was still a good deal of inverted snobbery about television. Many readers of *The Times* or of the *Manchester Guardian* boasted that they did not own, or wish to own, a television set. But feature articles on India or Persia which appeared in the *Sunday Times* under a caption saying that I had 'just returned from a study of those countries undertaken for the BBC' went some way to counter the argument that television was only a mass medium unworthy of the attention of well-informed citizens. And the scope, both of the television programmes and the articles, began to widen. Visits abroad alternated with programmes which dealt with industrial efficiency in Britain, management, restrictive practices, salesmanship, the colour problem and the civilian use of nuclear energy. In January 1957 a series of articles in the *Sunday Times* was introduced by the editor as 'by Aidan Crawley, whose television documentaries have given him a pre-eminent reputation as a commentator on current affairs'.

All this was heady stuff. I began to realize that I was becoming well known when people came up to me in shops and said, 'I know your face so well, yet I can't remember where we met.' Once, when I was crossing Piccadilly and had reached the central island, a taxi pulled up and the driver leaned out and started arguing about something I had said on television the night before. It took a policeman to move him on because he was obstructing the traffic and I could not help feeling flattered. Yet I think I had always been suspicious of television fame, partly because of my experience in the House of Commons. Members of Parliament did not like television personalities because, without representing anyone but the producer who chose them, they could command such huge audiences. Bob Boothby and Michael Foot had aroused considerable jealousy by their success in the discussion programme *In the News*. Both were Members of Parliament but by their skill in front of the cameras were achieving acclaim out of all proportion to their political importance. Grace Wyndham Goldie had pointed out that programmes like *In the News* were in danger of supplanting Question Time in the House of Commons itself. Feelings against people who were not in Parliament but dealt on television with political subjects were even stronger, and for some years television was subject to what was known as 'the fourteen-day rule', which laid down that nobody should discuss on television matters which were to come before the House of Commons within the next fourteen days. The rule did not last long, but it illustrates the attitude which Members of Parliament had towards television, and having been a Member myself, I felt considerable sympathy with them.

More important, for me, was the presence of Virginia. In the ten years from 1935 to 1945 before we were married she had attained great distinction as a war correspondent. She was now writing biographies. Her book on Winston Churchill, which came out in 1949, was often recommended by members of the Foreign Office to foreigners visiting England. More than thirty years later, when William Manchester came to write *The Last Lion*, he told her that he considered hers still the best book about Sir Winston and quoted it many times. She remained always a professional writer. Although she was thrilled with any success I might have – unknown to me she kept and dated most of the articles I wrote – when I asked her to read something I had written, she would always say, 'Are you sure it is ready for me to read?' Even when I knew it was not, I would sometimes persist and would then get the reply, 'You should never show me anything as badly written as that. It destroys one's confidence in you.' Crestfallen I would return to my desk.

She was an equally severe critic of my television programmes. The number of words in a television commentary is so small that it is a question of condensation rather than writing. Style lies in the way you say the little you have to say. If I missed a point or failed to give it the right emphasis, she would pounce on it at once. And she would be equally quick to spot a false note in my voice or a false gesture. She would tell me if I looked down when she knew I should be looking at the person I was talking to, or failed to look at the camera on the rare occasions when it was necessary. Of course I continued to make many of the same mistakes and Grace or one of her assistants had plenty to do, but I was well protected against any temptation to exaggerate my own importance.

Working for the BBC meant spending a lot of time in London and we decided we needed a house large enough to hold the children as well as ourselves. We noticed that many large houses were either still inhabited by evacuees or were empty. No one really thought that such houses would again be occupied by private individuals. Virginia agreed with me that a large house was probably no more difficult to run that a small one, so we started examining Belgravia. Some of the big corner houses in Belgrave Square were empty and could have been had for a song, but we decided they were too grandiose. A few minutes away in Chester Square we found what we wanted. Number 19 had a thirty-one-year lease for which the Grosvenor Estate was asking a premium of three thousand pounds. It had been on the market for three years and no one had made a bid.

True, almost every room had a square of cement in the middle of the floor on which a family evacuated from the East End had done their cooking from 1940 to 1947 or 1948. There had been dry rot in the basement which the estate had burned away and our surveyor warned us there was dry rot in the top storey. Nevertheless we had sold 52 Romney Street (a freehold) quite well and decided to offer three hundred and fifty pounds for the lease. To our surprise the offer was accepted.

We signed a lease and started putting the house in order. Every pipe, all the electric wiring, all the plumbing needed renewing; central heating had to be put in. As the work proceeded we realized that the dry rot in the top floor was serious and might spread. It was the seventh storey (counting the basement as floor one) and made our house the highest in the square. The four top rooms had been servants' rooms and we did not need them. So I went to the Grosvenor Estate and said that I would like to take off the top floor, burn out the dry rot and put on a new roof. If I did so, I hoped they would give me an extension of the lease. I fancy they were having great difficulty in finding tenants and were pleased to have one who would actually live in a house rather than ask leave to turn it into flats. In any case, they agreed to my plan but said, rather apologetically, that they felt as a matter of principal they should charge me something. Within twenty-four hours they suggested another hundred and fifty pounds. That meant we had a fifty-six-year lease for a premium of five hundred pounds. I accepted at once and within six months the new roof was in position, the dry rot cured and we had moved in. We had decided to send the children to the French Lycée for the next year or so and to engage a French *au pair*, Madeleine Husson. We then embarked on another BBC series, this time on the Middle East. It was the last in which I was my own cameraman and which Virginia and I did alone together.

*

The political structure of all Middle Eastern countries was changing rapidly. Wherever we went we found existing regimes frightened by the new nationalism. In Iraq, which was linked with Turkey, Pakistan and Britain in the Baghdad Pact, we interviewed young King Faisal and his Prime Minister, Nuri Said, who had once been a sergeant major in the British Army. The King, during his long minority, had been at Harrow, and like his Uncle Abdul Illah, who had been regent from 1933 to 1953, spoke perfect English. Nuri was openly pro-British and highly suspicious of President Nasser, whose agents were active in Iraq. 'He is a revolutionary,' he said, 'and wants to destroy all the old Arab regimes.' Before we left, Nuri became sombre. 'They will get me in the end, I know, but I have good Intelligence and shall keep going as long as I can.' In fact he remained Prime Minister for another five years.

It was the same in Kuwait, which outwardly seemed calm and secure. The Sheikh's family, who manned the Government, were always accessible to their people. One sat on benches among a queue of Kuwaitis and visitors waiting to be led up to the Minister in his white silk robes. The streets were washed daily at great expense by special carts using water from the desalination plant whose chimneys one could see along the seashore. The new hospital had all the latest equipment and five hundred beds, not twenty of which were occupied when we visited it. One reached the hospital along tarmac roads, interrupted every few hundred yards by wide roundabouts across which one rarely saw another car.

There were then only 325,000 indigenous Kuwaitis; the poorest we met (and filmed) was a boat builder whose slipway was on the shore. He earned more than twice the wage of his English equivalent and I believe that today the discrepancy is even greater. Yet in the *souk* (market), we heard dark mutterings from the merchants about young revolutionaries coming out of school echoing Nasserite slogans and vowing to destroy all feudal regimes. Their following lay not among the Kuwaitis but among the Turks, Persians, Kurds and others who flocked to the oil-rich sheikhdom for work, and already outnumbered the indigenous inhabitants. Their wages were low and some of them were beggars.

When we visited Persia, which was once more officially so called, the Shah had not long returned. Dr Mussadeq had been elected Prime Minister by the Majlis and approved by the Shah in April 1951, but their partnership had been uneasy. The Shah, who was only twenty-five, approved the law nationalizing oil production but had found Dr Mussadeq's radicalism difficult to control. Mussadeq was allegedly a right-wing nationalist, but his utterances antagonized the allies on whom Persia depended and encouraged every form of extremism within the country. In August 1953, after the failure of an attempted coup by the Imperial Guard, Dr Mussadeq's supporters and a crowd of Communists demonstrated in Teheran against the Shah, tearing down his portraits, destroying statues of his father and demanding that the Shah be brought to trial as a traitor. On August 16th the Shah and Queen Soraya fled by air from North Persia, where they had been on holiday, and arrived in Rome.

Before he left his country, the Shah had appointed General Zahedi as Prime Minister in place of Dr Mussadeq, who had illegally dissolved the Majlis. On August 19th, Zahedi, who had made a proclamation from his hiding place saying that he was the only legal Prime Minister, overthrew Mussadeq's government with the help of the army. He arrested Dr Mussadeq (who was still in his pyjamas) the following day and formed a new Cabinet. The Shah returned on August 22nd.

It must have been about six months later, in February 1954, that I again went to Persia for the BBC, this time not with Virginia but with Anthony de Lothbiniere, who was to be my producer for many years. The Persians appointed a delightful man called Golestan (whom we at once called Golly) to be our guide and interpreter and he managed to persuade the Minister of Court, Mr Ala, to arrange for me to interview the Shah. It was the first time the Shah had ever appeared on television, but he was completely at ease. I knew that Dr Mussadeq was under house arrest and when I asked the Shah about him he said the doctor faced certain charges but that he was old and ill and might have to go to hospital. He had already announced that Mussadeq's life would be spared and that he was allowed to see people. The subject the Shah most wanted to discuss was the distribution of Crown land to peasants, which he had begun on his own initiative two years before and was now continuing. He hoped that by setting the example on the royal estates, he would be able to persuade the large landlords to do the same. In this he was largely disappointed.

We went to the Caspian Sea. Golly said the journey would take six to eight hours. It took twelve and we arrived as the sun was setting. Our taxi was an old Buick, large, comfortable but dilapidated. All four tyres went flat in turn and we sat shivering by the roadside while the owner mended the punctures. There was snow and ice on the roads and no heating in the car. Then suddenly we came to the lip of the great amphitheatre of mountains which forms the southern edge of the Caspian Sea. The sun was still shining and it got warmer and warmer as we went down. People in bright cotton clothes were out in the fields below. As we drove along near the edge of the water, we saw people sunbathing on grey sand. The houses we passed were made from mud and wattle with reed-thatched roofs, some of them on stilts for protection against heavy rains. Eventually we came to a smart tarmac esplanade bordered by a row of large, round electric street lamps. We had reached the Shah's seaside resort and were to stay in the only hotel as the guests of the Persian Government. There was literally no one on the esplanade and we were the only guests at the hotel. The whole place seemed dead.

As the hotel staff were preparing supper, Golly, whose spirits never flagged, came in smiling and asked if we liked caviar. He added that Persia had just terminated the Fishery Concession under which the Russians ran the caviar industry (under a Persian chairman) and the Persians now ran it themselves. We said that we did like caviar and for the next week we were never without it. It came, that first evening, in a tureen with a huge ladle. The eggs were big and grey and fresh. We ate literally until we could eat no more, washing it down with local vodka mixed with juice from fresh limes. We slept like logs and awoke to find the same tureen, freshly filled, awaiting us for breakfast. After that we never had a meal without caviar, even when picnicking. Luckily Tony de Lothbiniere and our cameraman liked it as much as I did. In between, we filmed the semi-tropical life around us, motored up to as near the Russian frontier as we were allowed to go, filmed a caviar factory, learned the elementary facts about sturgeon and bathed in the Caspian Sea. The waves were quite big and the water, which tasted a little like the Dead Sea, was buoyant. As our old car chugged its way up the mountains again on the way back to Teheran, we put on our fur hats and were full of regret for something we suspected we would never see again.

In Oman we stayed with David Smiley, the Commander of the Oman Scouts, and his wife Moyra. Muscat, the port and capital, is the perfect pirates' lair, better even than St Malo on the Normandy coast. You enter the bay through a narrow cleft flanked by two high, jagged rocks on top of each of which stands a stone citadel. A heavy chain could close the harbour, which became known to Arab sailors as 'the Hidden Port' because it is almost invisible from the sea. Inside the bay houses crowd the shore. In front of a large house on the left stands a tall flagpole: this is the British Consulate, and in those days the tradition still obtained that any slave who managed to reach the flagpole and cling to it earned the right of manumission. The Consul-General, who was an Englishman called John Phillips, told us that the tradition was becoming an embarrassment because there were very few slaves left; nowadays the people he found clinging to the pole – and he found them quite often – were simply beggars who wanted a meal. They got their meal, but he had begun to question whether the tradition still served a useful purpose.

We played cricket in Muscat on a ground of sun-baked mud, the boundaries of which were marked by white-painted rocks. The pitch was of matting and I played for the Sultan's Forces team. Our opponents were mainly Indians who were in commerce in Muscat or in the Sultan's employ. Local knowledge was vital in this game. Within the boundaries were several rocks standing vertically, which counted, not as part of the ground, but as extra fieldsmen. I am sure I was warned of this but I still remember being surprised when, having hit a ball rather hard and about chest-high past cover-point, I saw the turbanned fieldsman turn round and catch it off a large rock which stood behind him. The applause told me that I was out.

David Smiley was a local hero. Recently he had won a decisive victory in a mini-war instigated by Saudi Arabia in the hope of capturing the Buraimi Oasis which belonged jointly to the Sheikh of Abu Dhabi and the Sultan of Oman. Smiley's campaign was as bold as General Wolfe's at Quebec. The operation involved scaling a precipitous mountain with sheer cliffs of a thousand feet, to reach the six thousand feet high plateau where the guerrillas had their bases. The troops under Smiley's command included not only his local troops but two squadrons of SAS (Special Air Services), one squadron of Life Guards and the Trucial Oman Scouts. The cliff was considered impassable but the SAS, using ropes, climbed it and found the summit unguarded.

34

The Eternal Fires

The story of the Anglo-French occupation of Port Said, Ismalia and Suez on October 31st, 1956, has been told often and in great detail. I had forgotten, however, that Virginia and I went to the Middle East as early as November. Fortunately Virginia kept a diary whose existence I only discovered as I was rummaging through a box of papers looking for something else. She must have told me she was writing it, but she began more than one diary only to stop after a few weeks or even days. She never spoke of this one afterwards, and I did not imagine she had preserved it.

Virginia's diary began on the day we flew out from Heathrow: November 7th.

November 7th:
George Jellicoe was at the Baghdad airport to meet us. He speeded everything up through the Customs and on the way to his house we talked about Egypt. He said he thought Eden's action was disastrous folly and that it was touch and go whether the Iraq government could hold their position as a friend of Britain. It was so late that we did not argue the point and went to bed.

Thursday:
We got up about 10.00 in the morning. The hotel is charming. Our rooms look over the Tigris. There are a lot of little boats on it and far down the river is one of the big refineries which account for the smell of oil which hangs over the city. It was warm and sunny and I put on a frock and sweater. Baghdad is a fascinating city. Despite its romantic name, it looks as though it has recently been bombed. Everywhere you go roads are dug up and building is going on. Pavements are

mostly holes and caverns. The streets are thronged with a strange medley of people, Arabs in traditional Arab dress, boys in striped pyjamas which is apparently also Arab dress, and dozens of huge American cars. Baghdad is a booming oil town. In the last few years, ever since the Shah nationalized the oil refinery at Abadan, Iraq has been getting £80,000,000 a year from the pipelines alone. This explains the feverish building and the shining cars. The truth is that there is full employment in Iraq and the people have never been so well off. We walked up to the bridge that goes across the Tigris and Aidan took some camera tests. As usual people gathered around laughing and pointing, but they were very friendly and everybody seemed delighted to pose. The situation is supposed to be very tense but certainly, wandering about as we did, we got no such impression.

Iraq is under martial law. Every now and then you see white jeeps patrolling the streets with machine guns on the roof. The schools have been disbanded for the week and probably will not be allowed to open next week either. George tells us that the British Embassy is practically in quarantine. They do not see any of their Iraqi friends. In the afternoon Aidan and I went to the Iraqi Government office to see Khalil Ibrahim, the Government 'spokesman'. He was very friendly and said he would help us all he could. Despite the British gloom, the friendliness of the people here in Baghdad is amazing.

Friday:
We went to the British Embassy to see Sir Michael Wright, the Ambassador. I had known him 25 years ago in Washington or Paris. He seemed afraid to see us by himself and was flanked on one side by Mr Jacomb and on the other side by Mr Kellas. Before he began speaking, he made it clear that if we wished to have any secret information, we must regard it as completely off the record. He then talked for half an hour and, of course, gave no information at all. One is so used to this type of person it is hard to suppress a smile. Apparently he is the one who has been spreading all the gloom and despondency. He electrified me by saying: 'If only the British Government had been more sensible it would have dropped a bomb on Tel Aviv to show the Arabs that we were not trying to support the Jews but taking impartial police action.' I retaliated by saying that if

we had ever done such a fantastically stupid thing we would not only have had the whole of public opinion in London and New York against us, but we would have certainly ruined the situation beyond hope.

Naturally, he looks at the whole situation from the Iraq point of view and thinks of nothing but of keeping the goodwill of the Arab world. He said it was touch and go whether Nuri would be able to retain power. However, the opinion Aidan and I have already formed is that Nuri will remain in power and the country will be kept calm. Michael Wright admitted that the Israeli statement last night to the effect that they would withdraw from Egyptian territory was bound to help as it was believed that this was due to pressure from the British. He asked Aidan, as a special request, to talk to absolutely nobody for two days. This seemed to us ludicrous because if the Iraqis want to put their case, what better means can they have than television where they can reach an audience of 8 million. Nevertheless, Aidan and I decided that since he had a lot of background shots to take in the next few days, we would not do anything until Monday and then, if the British Embassy is still unco-operative, we will go straight to the Iraqi Government.

The Iraq Petroleum Company arranged for us to fly to Kirkuk, their main pumping station. Virginia's diary continues:

Saturday:
It was fascinating flying over the desert. The minute we rose into the air the flatness spread out below us on all sides as far as the eye could see. The one mosque of Baghdad gleamed in the sun. Little mud villages and patches of cultivated land continued for ten minutes and then suddenly gave way to nothing but desert. We were leaving the Tigris behind and there was now only an infinity of sand. After flying for an hour we reached K3, which is the Iraq Petroleum Company's largest pumping station. It has huge diesel engines – the kind the Syrians blew up last week. Oil from K3 is pumped right through Jordan and Syria to the Mediterranean port of Tripoli. Its executive houses look rather like suburban villas, other employees' houses a bit smaller. There is a cinema and a golf course. Once again, we were off. An hour of flying and we were at the Kirkuk airfield.

It is difficult to describe these oil places. You see so few people. All the pipes lie on the ground and it looks the epitome of automation. Everything above the surface is painted silver which shines in the sun – the great oil tanks and gasometers. Oil drilling and pumping is the cleanest work one can imagine; one never sees oil, one only sees men tending dials and polishing sparkling machinery.

We drove into the city of Kirkuk before it got dark. The old city is on the hill and the modern one follows the course of the river just beneath it. As usual, the Arab streets were dirty and crowded, with every sort of thing being sold including bread in the middle of the road. You see donkeys and horses pulling carriages past parked American cars, Western dress, Eastern dress, everything mixed together in noisy, smelly, crowded streets. In the modern part of the city there are hundreds of shops selling spare parts for machinery, tyres and sparking plugs, and it seems to be a very thriving community. In the evening we dined with Mr Taux, the Frenchman who was general manager of the petroleum company.

Sunday:
It is now Sunday morning about 9 o'clock and I am going downstairs to have breakfast. It is dry but bitterly cold. Aidan came in frozen. He had taken shots of the 'eternal fires' (the flames which burn the gas escaping from the oil wells which one sees all over the desert as one flies across it at night) and the oil installations. We started out about 1.00 p.m. and a man who works for the IPC and speaks Kurdish, Arabic and English came with us. We went into a little village close to Kirkuk. The little huts were made of mud and straw, exactly the colour of the ground, a sort of brownish-red. What surprised me was how colourful the clothes were. All the women were wearing Arab skirts and head-dresses with beads around their wrists; the children were a blaze of red and purple and orange.

Wednesday, Baghdad:
We met Dr Creighton, who is advisor to the Public Health Department in Baghdad. He took us to the outskirts of the city, only five minutes from our hotel but the most disgusting slums one can imagine. Thousands of mud huts built out in the desert, no hard-

surface roads, only dust. The worst part of the whole thing is that the Baghdad sewerage scheme pumps all the sewage from the city into the canal straight through these poor quarters. The stench is unbelievable. Each hut contains perhaps two rooms and usually eight or ten people sleep on straw mats on the floor. They have little mud ovens in the courtyard where they bake their bread. There are many children running about. None of them go to school because the schools are too crowded. Typhus is rife because of the stinking water. Just outside the huts you see hundreds of birds and stray dogs going through the rubbish. Often children fight over the garbage. All the children have eczema or trouble with their eyes; their hair is falling out and they have horrible-looking sores on their bodies.

The Egyptians are still pouring out the most incredible lies. Long after we got here they were claiming that the British were still bombing Cairo, that hundreds of aircraft had been shot down, that fighting was going on from street to street, and that thousands of British and Egyptian soldiers had been killed. The fantastic thing is that the ordinary person here has no idea that Egypt has suffered a defeat of any kind.

Friday:
Our last day here. Aidan spent it interviewing people, one of whom was an Arab, formerly Prime Minister, who had said previously that he would not dream of being on television. I did not arrive until Aidan had almost finished the interview with him, but when I appeared he waved me inside the house to talk to his wife. She is a wonderful character, very rich, very voluptuous with jet black ringlets and brilliant black eyes. She had huge rings and a sort of black and green flowing robe. The minute I walked into the room she boomed at me, her voice even deeper than my own: 'What is England doing? I cannot sleep any more, I am so frightened of the Russians. It is all the fault of England.' Then a servant came with a huge tray of Turkish coffee, Turkish delight and an enormous box of chocolates, and although she had a very ample figure, she took three or four of each sweets. I suppose that is the way she spends most of her millions. She was such a marvellous character that I adored the whole scene.

We returned to the hotel at 2 o'clock in the morning and Aidan still had a lot of work to do. He started at about 3 o'clock. We were not due to leave the hotel to catch the aeroplane for Istanbul until a quarter to five – but suddenly there was a knock on the door and one of the porters said that the woman next door was not feeling well and hoped we would not make too much noise. Aidan finally decided the only thing he could do was to take his tape recorder down to the bar on the ground floor, which was deserted, and finish his commentary there. He had only been gone about 20 minutes when he came back, steaming with rage. Just as he had got going, the door was opened and a little Arab peered at him silently and then walked forward rather politely and said, 'I think you are a spy!' Aidan had said, 'For heavens sake, shut up! I am trying to do a commentary for the BBC.' But the little man was very stubborn and plonked himself in a chair saying that he had to listen. Aidan went on and after five minutes the little man said, 'It is very lucky for you that what you say is good, not bad, because I came into this room determined it was your life or mine.' Aidan said the man was stinking drunk so didn't take the threat very seriously. However, he couldn't work in peace with the interruptions and so he brought the tape recorder back to the bedroom, sick woman or not, and spent another fifteen minutes finishing his recording.

*

Eighteen months later, Virginia and I were back in Iraq. A revolution during which a group of officers, led by General Abdul Karim Kassem, killed the young King Faisal, his uncle Prince Abdul Illah and the Prime Minister, Nuri Said (who nearly escaped disguised as a woman), had transformed the whole scene. Humphrey Trevelyan[1] was now our Ambassador in Baghdad and with great skill he arranged for me to interview Kassem. Kassem himself had been the target of an assassination attempt six months previously and we were shown the exact spot in one of Baghdad's main streets where the assassins, hiding behind some pillars, had opened fire with sub-machine guns. Kassem was hit several times but fired back out of his car. He was out of hospital in three months.

Having been firm supporters of both King Feisal and Nuri Said, the British were not in good odour with Kassem; but he needed help in selling the oil produced by the former Iraqi Petroleum Company and he did not want to antagonize all his feudal Arab neighbours. Colonel Nasser had already denounced him for his links with the Communists and he was having trouble with the Kurds in his northern territories. He needed friends. Although Kassem was accepting help from the Soviet Union, he refused to include Communists in his Government and blamed them for the massacres of Turkomans in Kirkuk.

Humphrey, who was having difficulty in seeing Kassem himself, was keen that I should do so. It was a strange meeting. The BBC producer and myself were fetched from our hotel by an officer in uniform carrying a revolver. As we entered the military headquarters, other armed officers flanked us. In each ante-room the officer who greeted us had a revolver on his desk. The room in which the interview was to take place was a large hall with rows of empty chairs lining long tables. Only two chairs were to be occupied. The General sat at the end of the long table and I sat round the corner on his right. Behind him on a wall hung a picture frame which contained the shirt, still bloodstained, which he had been wearing in the car when the assassins opened fire.

Kassem himself was an extremely handsome, very English-looking man, his fair hair greying, his eyes very blue and his complexion fair. He had classical features. I began by saying that I had only once before seen a bloodstained shirt preserved in a frame, and that was in the library at Windsor Castle where hung the shirt in which King Charles I had been executed. Kassem said that his shirt was there to remind people that the revolution was indestructible. Looking past me down the long hall as if he were addressing a large audience, he then began a speech which lasted several minutes and echoed all the slogans about the revolution which one had read in the world's press. I tried to ask him questions, but he took no notice. When he had finished his speech, he rose, shook my hand, thanked me for coming, and left the room. We filmed a few of my questions because, although none had been answered, it would help indicate the atmosphere in which the interview had taken place. We then made our way past all the revolvers again, back to the hotel.

Humphrey did not want me to go to the Embassy in case he could be held even indirectly responsible for anything I wrote or said so we arranged to meet in the house of one of his staff. I remember telling him that I felt Kassem was mad. I think he agreed. I also felt that the situation in the Middle East would remain unsettled so long as Kassem was there and that no good would come to Iraq. These very obvious conclusions were soon borne out because within a year Kassem was laying claim to Kuwait and causing continual friction in the Arab world. Although Kassem in his turn was executed in 1963, I had been wrong in thinking his removal would bring stability to that part of the world.

*

The epilogue to these Middle Eastern experiences came many years later, in 1983. Virginia and I had been to Kenya with Jack and Drue Heinz.[2] As none of our children had seen the Nile, I suggested that we meet them in Khartoum. Virginia and I flew from Nairobi; two of our children came from the ends of the earth, one from Hong Kong, one from Texas. We stayed a night in Khartoum, where some of the Kontomikolos family came and had a drink with us, delighted that their old house on the banks of the Nile had been restored to them. Their family had done business in Khartoum for many generations.

I had my father's 1929 Baedeker of Egypt with me and spent much of the evening regaling the family with the advantages of approaching Egypt from the south rather than from Cairo. In particular I expatiated on the interest of seeing Wadi Halfa, the town founded by Kitchener and the terminus of the railway from Khartoum. Few people, I pointed out, got as far as Wadi Halfa if they came from the north and Baedeker spoke of Coptic, Greek and English churches as well as of the beautiful mosque and an interesting souk. We set out by train the next day, having acquired one first-class compartment between the five of us. Every now and then the train would stop for no apparent reason. While daylight lasted we would get out and stretch our legs. Andrew, my eldest son, then aged thirty-two, pointed out that each stopping place was marked by a slanting white board with a number on it, attached to a low white post. As the British had built the railway, we assumed that the number had some significance – perhaps to indicate a point at which the engine's boiler could be filled with water. There was seldom any sign of a station. As night descended, we arranged ourselves for sleep. Claiming to be the hardiest traveller, I chose the floor and had an excellent night. Andrew and the two girls shared a seat between them and were full of complaints. It was nothing compared with what followed.

Truth to tell, I was sadly out of touch. I knew that the temples of Abu Simbel had been moved to a new site because of the formation of Lake

Nasser, and my travel agent in London had told me that it should be possible for the boat which took us across the lake to stop and allow us to see them. But I had made no enquiries about the boat itself, which I assumed would be something like the one I had recently seen in the film made from Agatha Christie's book, *Death on the Nile*. I also knew the boat started from Wadi Halfa, but had not realized that the town of Wadi Halfa no longer existed. The three churches, the mosque and the souk had all been swallowed up by Nasser's waters and only the name remained. This was explained to us by the driver of the lorry which came to collect our baggage when the train finally stopped. There was literally nothing in the way of building except a row of mud huts. The train had ended up in the middle of the desert.

Virginia said she thought she could see the quay, but the ship did not seem to be in yet. We got the lorry to take us to the quay. On the way we stopped at a mud hut labelled 'Tickets'. I bought five tickets and was delighted at their cheapness, but when I asked about cabins, the ticket salesman said that was a matter for the captain. I asked when the ship would arrive and he looked surprised. 'The ship is there now,' he replied.

The truth then began to dawn. What we had thought to be the quay were two fairly large tin barges, one with no superstructure at all and the other with a row of six plywood cabins above the hold. The barges were to be pulled by a tug, the only craft in sight with an engine, all the two hundred and fifty miles across Lake Nasser. The journey would take fifty-six hours.

We went on board the barge with the superstructure and at once occupied two cabins, which gave us four berths. We asked about food and were told that it was Arab food and the only drink was tea. Our informant said, however, that we could buy tins of food 'in the village'. Virginia, who had borne it all stoically, said she would go to bed; the rest of us went off to the mud huts and bought tins of sardines, soused herrings, tinned pineapple and a few biscuits. When we got back, we were met by the captain, a turbanned Arab who spoke quite good English and told us that all the cabins were booked and we would have to move. The children agreed to give theirs up to an Indian lady who looked as if she would have a baby before we got to Aswan. Virginia and I resolutely refused to quit our cabin and told the captain that he would have to throw us out by force. In the end he caved in. We were left, therefore, with two very narrow bunks, the floor, and the floor of a little cubby-hole which was called the 'sitting room'. The hold of the barge was crammed with Arabs squatting or lying on the floor, playing cards or sleeping. The food, we soon saw, was inedible, a form of soup with lumps of fat floating in it. The only good thing was the tea, which was hot and sweet.

I confess that during the next two and a half days I suffered some qualms about my family. Virginia, resolute and practical as always, had one look at the 'loo' – two holes in the deck which were filthy and stank – and said she would stay in bed and neither eat nor drink until we got to Aswan. Andrew, the most equable, made up his mind to enjoy himself and was persistently cheerful. Harriet struggled to see the funny side but ended by nearly having us all arrested.

Two things surprised me. The first was the cold. Lake Nasser is large and one is often out of sight of the banks. The wind, in spite of the sun, can be icy and there were no spare blankets. The second was the squeamishness of my children. Sardines and soused herrings are nourishing food; with biscuits, rather good. After the first meal they all refused to touch them. I hate shaving in cold water, so I shaved in tea. Andrew thought there was something unclean about tea and would not shave at all. We got within sight of the High Dam at the end of the second day, but the captain decided to lie up in a cover and land next morning. When we reached Aswan, all our passports were taken ashore and with them our health papers. We then paraded on the barge in front of Egyptian doctors who insisted that we eat four pills each to prevent us from catching all the diseases against which we had already been inoculated. We protested that if they would get our passports they would see that we had no need of pills. To no avail. Harriet lost her temper. Thumping the table in front of the doctors, she complained of scandalous inefficiency: 'How dare you claim independence?' she shouted. 'You couldn't run a kindergarten, far less a country. What you need is to be run by the British and the sooner you get them back the better!'

The doctors looked surprised and I murmured to Harriet that if she did not stop we would all end up in jail, but I do not think the doctors had understood what she had said and she left the barge without having to swallow anything. She recovered in the taxi which took us to the Temple of Edfu.

35

Americans at Home

The fifties were a successful period for us. Both Virginia and I were earning a lot of money from writing books and articles, the farm was paying its way. Chester Square had become an attractive London house and I was still doing a lot of television. We expanded the farm, buying another five hundred acres, and began growing wheat and barley.

In London the children had left the French Lycée, the boys going to the Westminster Junior (day) School and Harriet to the Francis Holland, both schools within walking distance of Chester Square. The boys left our house at eight o'clock in the morning, and although they called to us as they raced past our room down the stairs, they also always stopped on the pavement outside the front door to shout at our open window, 'Goodbye Mummy, goodbye Daddy,' before they crossed the road. We installed an upright piano for Harriet in the basement and a miniature billiard table for the boys.

A change came in our domestic regime when Andrew went to Harrow at the age of thirteen. Mr Campbell, the headmaster of the Westminster Junior School, agreed with us that Randall would not be happy there without Andrew, so I rang up Alan Barber, my old Oxford friend who had become headmaster of Ludgrove Preparatory School, and asked him if he could possibly find Randall a place. Without a moment's hesitation he told me the date on which term started and said, 'Send him along. I shall look forward to having him.' So began an enjoyable three years for Randall, and for me the renewal of a friendship with Alan which nothing ever marred.

In London Virginia filled the house with people for lunch and dinner, politicians, writers, visitors from the United States. An evening with one of the latter led to my next television series. Ed Murrow, famous as CBS's television war correspondent, was at that moment being sponsored by ALCOA (the Aluminium Company of America) in a controversial and highly popular series called *See it Now*. While in London he had watched one of my *India's Challenge* programmes. After dinner he said he would like me to do a programme about America and asked if I would take one of his *See it Now* slots. The slots were half an hour long, and apart from a sentence introducing me, he would take no part whatever. He added that I could go where I liked, see whom I liked, film what I liked, using the camera crews that CBS always employed, and have all expenses paid. It was a dreamlike offer. I accepted at once and then rang up Grace Wyndham Goldie to find out how I could fit it in with the plans I was making with the BBC.

Grace was thrilled. 'You *must* go,' she said. 'But ask Ed if we may re-edit some programmes for the BBC out of the film you take. Of course we will only show it after you have appeared in America.' Ed was delighted at the idea which would give *See It Now* free advertisement. The editing of the last programme of *India's Challenge* was finished at the end of July 1953 and within a week I was in New York. Virginia was to join me later.

Ed Murrow, well over six feet tall, dark, clean-shaven and hand-some, was a workaholic. 'Work never killed anybody,' he used to say; he never stopped. Chain-smoking, he would walk about as he talked, take telephone calls, then see his shadow and producer, Fred Friendly, and throw out ideas. Fred was always making jokes; Ed was rather sombre. We worked in the CBS offices in New York and within a few days had the outline for the programme. I was a young Englishman, former Member of Parliament, looking at post-war America. There was no time-limit. It did not matter if I filmed a subject and then scrapped it because I had found something better. 'The ALCOA budget is enormous,' I remember Ed saying, 'and film is the cheapest thing we have.' We sketched out an itinerary and timetable so that Fred could alert the film crews: Washington, Virginia, South Carolina, Texas, Kansas, Chicago, Detroit, Buffalo, Indiana, Ohio, ending up in New York. I was to pick people's brains in each city and go into the country whenever I thought it was worthwhile.

In New York I stayed with Virginia's father, Dr Edward Cowles, who lived in a house between two churches at 591 Park Avenue. It is still standing and is likely to continue to do so because, unless a developer gets permission to pull down one of the churches, any rebuilding is impossible. Dr Cowles was an unusual man whom I had got to know when Virginia and I went to New York together soon after we were married. I had accompanied the Colonial Secretary, Arthur Creech-Jones, to the United Nations to prepare a way for our surrender of the Mandate for Palestine and Hartley Shawcross had come too. I remember a dinner, at which Professor Hayek was also present, when Dr Cowles got so angry at our socialist approach that he bawled me and Hartley out and put an end to the discussion.

Entering his house, one would find people sitting in couples all the way up the stairs waiting to see him. He was a remarkable doctor, a psychiatrist who believed that mental and physical illness were always linked and that psychoanalysis without medication was criminally wrong. He frequently quarrelled with the medical profession for being too rigid with regard to mental illness. He had a fashionable clientele and charged them through the nose, but he also ran a clinic for the poor, whom he hardly charged at all. I had been to a party at his clinic attended by about two thousand previous patients and was amazed at the number of people who told me how my father-in-law had transformed their lives. Some had had 'paralysed' limbs, and had been to one specialist after another without results; Dr Cowles had diagnosed the disease as partly mental and cured them completely. He had done the same for literally hundreds who suffered from nervous disorders. I discussed with him what I should film in New York. He recommended the waterfront, a world of its own that was always giving trouble, and he promised to organize this through a detective who worked there.

I spent three months in the United States and shot more than forty thousand feet of 35mm film for a programme which could only use three thousand. Ed gave the BBC a print of all the footage, which they re-edited into four 40-minute programmes of four thousand feet each, called *Americans at Home*. They must have been some of the cheapest foreign programmes the BBC ever made. One of the most curious facets of filming in the United States was the difference in the rules under which one operated in different states. In Washington, for example, where I interviewed politicians, the local union rule forced us to use a crew of eighteen; in Chicago, two men were able to do the whole job, including sound and lighting; in New York we used eleven men (the ideal unit for filming on location anywhere in the world is four); in England we usually had five or six, including the producer.

I remember filming a negro tobacco share-cropper on a farm in Virginia. When I asked him what he thought of President Roosevelt, his eyes filled with tears. 'Ah,' he said, 'what a man! To me he was all man.' We filmed the University of Virginia at Charlottesville, where the old slave quarters, little red-brick bungalows, had become undergraduates' lodgings. Sadly, I was unable to visit Cowlesville, near Williamsburg, where Virginia's ninety-year-old uncle, Carter Cowles, still lived. Our first visit to the city a few years before had been a great family occasion. Dr Cowles in New York had spoken of the family home at Cowlesville, near a village called Toanna in Virginia, as a great colonial mansion. Three thousand acres had been granted to the Cowles family on the banks of the James River in the year 1607 by Captain John Smith, and some member of the family had lived there ever since. After the Civil War, Virginia's grandmother had brought up eight children, four sons and four daughters, at Cowlesville. All the boys except Carter, the eldest, had gone away to make their fortunes. Virginia had visited Cowlesville once as a child but could remember nothing about it, so her father had insisted that we drive down to see his brother, a journey of several hundred miles.

When we got to Toanna, a small, not very interesting village, I went into the store and asked the way to Cowlesville. The shopkeeper scratched his head, repeated the name once or twice and then said, 'Oh, you must mean the place where old Carter Cowles lives,' directing me to it with a warning that the road was not very good. We drove past one or two quite large farmhouses and then saw on our left a large red-brick colonial mansion at the end of an avenue of trees. Feeling this must be the house, I turned down the drive to be met by a pack of Great Danes. A farmhand called them off and I asked if this was Cowlesville. He laughed and said that if I wanted old Carter, I should go at least two miles further down the road I had just left. 'You can't miss it,' he said. 'The road ends at his house.' Disappointed, we retraced our steps. The road soon turned into a muddy track and after a while I saw to our left what looked like a large negro shack. It had a portico with rough wooden pillars and the paint had peeled off the wooden walls. Behind the house there were several large sheds and in front, on a sort of grass plinth, a tractor standing as if it were a statue. 'This must be it,' said Virginia. 'I know my father gave his brother a tractor and I know that he has never used it.'

We walked up the rickety steps to the front door, pigs scattering from under our feet. A wizened negress – obviously of a former slave family – opened the door. 'Oh,' she said in answer to my enquiry. 'You will find Mr Carter with the mules. You must drive round to the big shed at the back.'

Like all Cowleses, Uncle Carter was small, his brown hair only slightly grey. He emerged from between the legs of the mules and gave Virginia a great hug. 'How wonderful!' he said as we walked into the house. 'I must let everyone know.' Our room had a large bed but I noticed that in the bathroom the bottom had fallen out of the washbasin. I never saw a bath. Uncle Carter put on a bow tie, a tweed coat and some smart twill trousers and looked every inch the squire. He explained that the early Cowles settlers had cleared fifteen hundred of the three thousand acres they had been granted, but that the rest was still woodland. From his conversation I gathered he spent more time 'huntin', which meant shooting, than farming, but he was a charming host. We had fried chicken for supper and, as we had had a long drive, went early to bed. Soon after midnight, however, we heard cars driving up and there were loud knocks on the door. There was no telephone, but somehow Uncle Carter had informed his relations and they had all come to see Virginia.

We dressed again and came down to a room full of people. They spoke in strong southern accents, but were immensely friendly and treated me as one of the family. The thing they most wanted to know was whether we were going to 'the weddin'. I asked which of them was getting married and they laughed. 'No,' they said. 'The weddin' of Princess Elizabeth and Prince Philip.' Their engagement had just been announced. It was not until four o'clock that they began to go. As one of them left, she kissed Virginia and in a slow drawl said, 'We think your husband's mighty cute but we can't understand a word he says.'

If I could have reproduced that scene, it would have been perfect for the programme, but Uncle Carter was now ill and without him it would have meant little. Instead we went to a ranch in Texas and filmed a cattle round-up and then visited the great cattle yards in Kansas City where men with sledge hammers stood above the lines of cattle passing in single file below them, hitting them on the head as they passed. In Indiana, we stayed with old friends, Tom and Mary Sinnock, who lived in a village called Mount Summit, near Newcastle. During the course of the evening we learned that in a few days' time a debate was to take place in the state parliament at Indianapolis on a motion to ban *Robin Hood* as book or film because of its subversive tendencies. I immediately rang Ed Murrow and told him that I proposed to make this debate the centrepiece of my programme. 'I am sorry to disappoint you,' he said. 'I am doing a special programme on it next week myself.' I did not see Ed's programme, but it was widely reported; the motion was carried. My 'end piece', as Fred Friendly called it, was done on a ferry sailing past the Statue of Liberty, as hundreds of thousands of Americans have done this century to fight in Europe's wars.

After Virginia had joined me in New York, we went to see one of Senator McCarthy's hearings on Un-American Activities. Ed Murrow had been filming the sessions since the beginning of the year and was planning a whole programme on them. He said that he would give me a ten-minute clip to try out on the BBC. He wanted to test public reaction before showing it in America.

The courthouse was crowded, but we had good seats. McCarthy, dark, heavy-jowled and with at least a day's growth on his chin, was already seated. His committee had been reduced in numbers because the three Democratic members had resigned in protest at his claim that he had the power to appoint whomsoever he pleased as chairman of the sub-committee. Only one man was being questioned while we were there, a former university lecturer who had friends who were or had been Communists. McCarthy was ruthless. I cannot remember his exact questions, but his line was that anyone who could be a friend of a Communist must in his heart accept their views. No one who appeared before the committee was allowed counsel. There were no rules of evidence, nothing to prevent any imputation being made, however unfounded. There was not a shred of evidence that the lecturer had ever propounded Communist doctrine or even appeared sympathetic towards it. He stuck manfully to his position, which was simply that his friends included people of all shades of opinion, mostly opposed to Communism. In a university, above all, it must be possible to air any opinion, even if only so that it may be countered. His answers had not the slightest effect upon McCarthy, against whom our feelings grew more intense the longer the hearing went on. He was certainly the most odious man in whose presence I have ever found myself, and that includes Gestapo interrogators. The lecturer had already lost his job;

his name had been blackened and his life probably ruined. McCarthy could lick his ugly chops.

The clip of the McCarthy hearings which Ed lent me was dramatic and the reaction in England everything he could have wished. It was not for several weeks that his full programme was presented in America and I never saw it. I was told it was devastating, but it was a pity it could not have been shown earlier. It might have saved the reputations and careers of a few more innocent people.

36

African Odyssey

Our travels in Africa had comparatively little to do with television. Between the years 1934 and 1983, Virginia and I visited thirty African countries, sometimes for pleasure, sometimes because of the war, but mainly to report either by pen or through broadcasting or for official political business. Each of us went there first in 1934, quite separately and before we had met.

I had returned to Egypt in 1941 to join 73 Squadron of the Royal Air Force in the desert. A year later Virginia flew into Algeria as a war correspondent to report 'Torch', the allied invasion of North Africa. The First Army was advancing on Tunis from the west. Having watched the battle of Kasserine Pass, she attached herself to the Irish Guards who were operating near Gafsa. With Captain David Henecker, a peacetime pianist who had been deputed to look after the press, she visited a farm at Thala where some French troops were billeted. When German bombers were seen approaching, the French commander ordered everyone to take to the slit trenches outside the farmhouse. Fortunately both Henecker and Virginia had decided to stay in the farm, as the slit trenches received direct hits.[1] Shells then began to fall round the farm and the French commander told everybody to leave as General Rommel was reported to be on his way to occupy the place.

Virginia and Henecker got into his car, but as they started to leave another air attack began. They dived into a ditch but their car was badly damaged. Disconsolately they began to walk until a lorry came up behind them, driven by a British tommy, who gave them a lift. Virginia sat between the driver and Henecker and was amazed at how cheerful the driver was. Shells were falling all around, but when she asked him if he liked North Africa, he said, 'Oh yes. You see, I like travelling, really.' He told her he was married and had children. Used to the American

GIs who all seemed to carry photographs of their wives and little ones, she asked him if he didn't miss his family. 'Oh,' he said, zig-zagging violently when a mortar landed near them, 'they'll keep.' By driving skilfully, he soon took them out of range of the guns and dropped them back at their unit where they were told that Rommel had indeed arrived at the farm. Everyone had assumed that Virginia and Henecker had been taken prisoner.

Another incident Virginia liked to relate occurred somewhere near Algiers. She had been to visit a unit and was walking along a road, hoping to thumb a lift. As a war correspondent, she was wearing American uniform. A British staff car drew up beside her and a red-tabbed Brigadier in the back seat asked her to get in. As she sat down he said, 'I must tell you that the only reason I am giving you a lift is that I disapprove of any woman being allowed up at the front and am on my way to headquarters to have you all recalled.' He then told her about some nurses whose boat had been torpedoed and who had been rescued only after several hours in the water. Someone had ordered them up to the front, but he had countermanded the order and was keeping them doing nothing in Algiers, awaiting repatriation. Shortly afterwards, the Brigadier reached his headquarters, got out and told the driver to take Virginia wherever she wanted to go. Virginia learned from the driver, who disliked the Brigadier, that his name was Cowell and that he was in the Army Medical Corps. Instead of going to her billet she then got the driver to take her to see the nurses, who were fuming with rage and disappointment.

From the press camp, Virginia then sent a telegram to London. She had recently attended the christening of the baby Winston Churchill as his godmother, and knew the Prime Minister and his wife well. Before she left London, Mrs Churchill, as she then still was, had told Virginia that if ever she wanted to report anything important to the Prime Minister personally, she should send Mrs Churchill a personal message and she would pass it on. In her telegram Virginia told how the nurses, desperately needed at the front, were being prevented from going there and were even being threatened with repatriation. Within a few days a message came back that the nurses were to go to the front immediately.

The story ends with a curious twist. Some years later, headlines in the newspapers reported that a general's son had turned into a girl. Pictures showed an elegant platinum blonde, to be known in future as

'Miss Roberta Cowell', daughter of Brigadier Cowell of the Army Medical Corps. It was difficult not to feel that the Brigadier had met with a just reward.

＊

I next went to Africa in 1946 as Parliamentary Private Secretary to George Hall, the Colonial Secretary who was attending the West African Council, an organization mooted by the war-time coalition government to try and co-ordinate the economic development of the West African territories, which included Nigeria, the Gold Coast, Sierra Leone and the Gambia.

We then flew in the Prime Minister's York, a noisy but comfortable high-wing monoplane, to Bathurst, capital of the Gambia, where we stayed with Sir Hilary Blood, a man who was as outspoken and robust as his name led one to expect. The Gambia was a freak colony consisting of a narrow slice of land, nowhere more than ten miles deep, running along both banks of a river for a distance of two hundred miles inland. It had come into existence because the Gambia River was the largest navigable waterway on the whole west coast of Africa. From the fifteenth century onwards, traders had sailed up it in the hope of tapping the largely mythological 'riches' of the interior of the continent. The Portuguese were the first to establish a trading post there to which Africans would come from as far away as the Sudan, bringing ivory and grain for sale. By the 1450s, however, the main trade was already in slaves. Sir Hilary pointed out the islands at the mouth of the river which had been used as assembly points for slaves. They were inhospitable and insalubrious and the water around them was so full of jellyfish, in particular the poisonous 'Portuguese man-of-war', that no one dared bathe.

On a later visit I made with Virginia and Tony de Lothbiniere of the BBC, the then Governor, Sir Percy Wyn-Harris, took us on a tour of the river in a little steam yacht. This was not an extravagance, but a necessity: indeed, it was the Governor's chief form of transport, for there were few roads and the river was by far the quickest way to visit the people, almost all of whom lived on its banks. Wyn-Harris was a legendary character, being the man who had found Mallory's ice axe (or Irvine's) on Smythe's Everest expedition in 1933. He told us that he had been only nine hundred feet from the summit of Everest at the time and could easily have climbed the mountain that day, for the weather was perfect; but it was not his turn. He had no oxygen and did not need any. He was slightly contemptuous of all the modern equipment, saying that if one was properly acclimatized, one should not need it.

Yet on the torrid Gambia River he was equally in his element. His joy was a little brass cannon which was mounted in the bows of his yacht. Whenever he came to a village he would load the cannon with fireworks and then, approaching the rickety pier alongside which we were to tie up, he would fire it off, straight over the heads of the crowd which had assembled on the bank. He knew the range exactly and the fireworks would explode above the people to their huge delight. Wyn-Harris would then disembark and walk among them.

It was when staying with him that I first saw a District Commissioner hold a Court. Wyn-Harris did not accompany us but told me that he thought it was worth filming. We were driven in a jeep to a point on the river bank where the ground inland was flat and covered with tall grass. After waiting for perhaps a quarter of an hour, we saw a procession of men walking through the long grass. In front was the District Commissioner, a young man in his twenties, wearing a topee, shorts and a bush shirt and carrying a short cane. He was followed by Africans in robes and then by a long file of khaki-clad porters, each carrying a box or bundle on his head. The bundles were unloaded first, under an enormous banyan tree. A trestle table and an assortment of camp chairs and stools were set up. Then the boxes, which contained endless files, were unloaded and the files piled near the table. By now several hundred Africans were sitting in a semi-circle on the ground in front of the table. In the centre sat the District Commissioner, flanked by robed Africans – advisers and assessors.

The Court was declared open by an African. Then the first plaintiff was called forward and stated his case to the District Commissioner. Witnesses followed, then the defendant and his witnesses came forward. The advisers and assessors knew the details of each case and explained the background to the District Commissioner. The cases were mostly about land, women, theft or family quarrels. The proceedings were cheerful and informal. The crowd often laughed and sometimes clapped; one felt it was a day out for them. At the end the District Commissioner would ask the opinion of several of his advisers and then, having listened to the assessors, who suggested a suitable punishment or fine, gave his verdict slowly and distinctly in English, from which it was translated into the vernacular. The cases were all recorded in the files. Nobody questioned the District Commissioner's judgements.

We felt we were seeing the Empire at its best; it was a moving scene. There were no soldiers and no one carried any arms. I was told there were one or two policemen but they kept discreetly in the background. This scene was to be re-enacted up and down the Gambia River for another twenty years. Then, in 1965, the Gambia became independent.

*

In Sierra Leone the Governor, Sir Maurice Dorman, told us about diamond smuggling in the interior and suggested it might be something we would like to film. Diamond digging took place in the swamps. A family would pay a few pounds' rent for perhaps fifty square yards of swamp in which they were then allowed to 'dig' for twenty-four or forty-eight hours. Digging was really a primitive form of hand-dredging. The dredge was a bowl, usually made of earthenware or matted straw, to the sides of which were attached two cords of plaited reed. The 'dredger' would dip the bowl into the water, bring it up full of mud and gravel and then swing it over to the dry land, where the contents were deposited in a heap. Other men and women, squatting on their haunches, then sieved the gravel and mud until only the smallest stones were left. These were sorted individually by hand. The dredger went at an incredible speed, often in rhythm to a song, and the sorters had to work fast to keep pace. We saw several groups find more than one diamond, which looked like a small grain of silica. The diamonds were taken to a thatched hut nearby where representatives of the South African Diamond Corporation sat at a trestle table and paid cash for any stone which they approved. One tiny stone might make a family rich for several months.

But although the digging was controlled and policed, Sir Maurice had told us that several million pounds' worth of diamonds were smuggled out of Sierra Leone every year. Small stones were easy to conceal, even beneath a finger-nail, and it was impossible to patrol every jungle path. The smugglers showed great ingenuity. Little caches had been found in every conceivable part of the coachwork and chassis of cars and lorries, including the interior of air vents and tubeless tyres. Women would carry diamonds hidden in their plaited hair.

On the other hand, smugglers ran considerable risks. Cannibalism was still common in certain parts of the country in the 1950s and 1960s and smugglers crossing the territory of an alien tribe were often attacked. We flew to Kenema, in the Eastern Province, to visit a hospital. The doctor told us that he had first become aware of the extent of cannibalism in a curious way. He often had to perform surgery and was relieved, after his first amputation at the hospital, when an African orderly came to him and offered to dispose of the limb. Thereafter, whenever the doctor had to amputate, the same orderly was always at hand. Eventually the doctor's curiosity was aroused and he made enquiries. He discovered that all the other orderlies were jealous because the one who disposed of the amputated limbs had been selling them at a high price to cannibals around the airfield. Although human flesh is the same pale hue whatever the colour of the skin, it seemed that flesh with a white skin was preferred. When I recounted our experience back in Freetown, a Creole lady said to me, 'Did they tell you also that the day of boiling their victim in an iron cauldron is over and that they now eat us "tartar"?' At first I thought she was joking, but I was assured that it was true.

37

Nkrumah's Ghana

Meanwhile my life in England was undergoing a subtle change. My television programmes, and more particularly some of the articles I had written on industrial relations, had begun to attract the attention of Conservative politicians. For the most part, since I had joined the Labour Party in 1937, I had seen very little of my old friends. A few, like Peter Cazalet, John Cowdray and Esmond Rothermere, had always refused to allow politics to disturb our relationship and I had occasionally visited them and taken the children. Fairlawne in particular was a favourite. Peter's sons were almost the same age as mine, and Zara, his second wife and a great beauty, was always welcoming.

It was not only the games of tennis and croquet which were fun but also the riding. Peter used to let me join the string of steeplechasers who went out in the early morning, and sometimes ride a school over fences. When the Queen Mother was staying with him – he trained her horses – she too would get up before breakfast and watch us all gallop past. There was one other treat. In those days Peter and Zara had a chef whose name was Michel Roux, now famous as the owner of Le Gavroche restaurant in London. The food he produced was usually irresistible. Peter used to remind me of an occasion when, having eaten two *Oeufs Benedict* and an immense portion of saddle of lamb, I regretted as I surveyed the *Baba au Rum* that I had lost my appetite. Only once do I remember daring to criticize a dish, a sort of meat loaf which contained (or so I thought) large lumps of lard. It was a pity, I suggested, to spoil good beef in that way. Zara replied that it was even more of a pity I was such a philistine as to be unable to appreciate one of France's greatest dishes.

However, it was still necessary to earn a living. In the late 1950s I was to embark on a television series for the BBC called *The Inheritors*, which dealt with the same theme as our Indian series: the progress made by former members of the Empire since they had achieved independence; and also an investigation, jointly with Virginia, into Communist penetration in Africa, commissioned by a group of companies some of which had interests in Africa and Britain.

The Gold Coast was at that time in the vanguard of constitutional change, having received a new constitution in 1951 under which elections were to be held for an African Assembly. The Convention People's Party, of which Dr Kwame Nkrumah was leader, won a resounding victory. Nkrumah, who had been imprisoned in 1948 after leading riots in the capital, Accra, was released and asked to form a government, the first to have an African leader. Nevertheless, there would still be a British Governor, as in Sierra Leone and Nigeria, and Departments for Police, Security, Foreign Affairs and Defence were still reserved for British officials who were members of the Government.

Sir Charles Arden-Clarke, the Governor, was one of the great pro-consuls of the Empire. He had had an interesting career. In 1919, while still in the army, he had been sent with three other Englishmen on a military mission to the White Russians who were then fighting in the Ukraine. The Cossacks had achieved considerable success and were taking a lot of prisoners, many of whom willingly changed sides. The only people not given such an option were the Red Army Commissars, who were immediately executed. Sir Charles described how one evening in the officers' mess four Commissars were led into the dining room during dinner. The Colonel rose from his seat at the dinner table, and, offering his curved sword by the hilt to the young Englishman, said that, as the only foreigner present, he would do them great honour if he would decapitate the prisoners. Arden-Clarke was able to decline the honour on the grounds that under the terms of his mission he was not to take part in any fighting. Whereupon the Colonel himself took the sword and with four rapid backhand strokes performed the executions. The heads rolled on the carpet and, while the orderlies cleared up the mess, the officers continued with their dinner.

It was Sir Charles who had appointed the nationalist agitator Kwame Nkrumah Chief Minister of the first elected government of the Gold Coast, an experiment which at first looked as if it might succeed. Although his contemporaries at London University spoke of Nkrumah as a Communist, he began by showing himself a model pupil administrator. He dutifully banned all Communist publications from the Gold Coast, stated that although he was a Marxist-Socialist he was also a friend of Britain, and reaffirmed the political goal he had announced during the general election of Dominion Status within the Commonwealth. He agreed to give the new constitution a chance and, while criticizing as 'bogus and fraudulent' the provisions which allowed Permanent Secretaries (that is, Colonial officials) to take charge of all the key Government departments, he accepted the position of 'Leader of Government Business'. On March 5th the following year, 1952, as a result of further amendments to the constitution, Nkrumah was appointed Chief Minister with precedence over all Permanent Secretaries. In 1954 he was able to appoint the first all-African Cabinet in British Africa, exercising complete control over every department of government. On March 6th, 1957, Ghana achieved full independence as a Dominion within the Commonwealth, the first African colony to do so, and in 1960 it became a Republic with Nkrumah as Head of State and Prime Minister.

Virginia and I visited the country in 1960, by which time the deviousness of Nkrumah's true nature was beginning to become apparent. It first showed itself in an unexpected way. Arden-Clarke had a personal secretary, Erika Powell, an attractive and intelligent woman whom we both liked. One day a security officer told Arden-Clarke that Miss Powell's car had been parked outside Nkrumah's house after dark. The Governor sent for Erika and asked her if this was true. Erika replied that it was, and that she was in love with his Prime Minister. Arden-Clarke then said that in that case she could no longer continue as his personal secretary and he must send her home. Erika accepted his decision. However, the ship in which she sailed called at Freetown and, while lying in the harbour, it was boarded by members of Nkrumah's staff who told her that she must accompany them back to Accra because, in spite of her dismissal by the Governor, the Chief Minister had appointed her as *his* personal secretary. Erika returned and Arden-Clarke accepted her new position – wisely, as it turned out – because, although Erika continued her affair with Nkrumah and often sat at the head of his table, she kept in close touch with the Governor's security service and, without being disloyal to Nkrumah, often played a useful role.

Her African career came to an end after one of Nkrumah's visits to

China. Erika occupied a room in Peking next door to Mr Adamafio, one of Nkrumah's ministers. The walls were not very thick and in the course of the night she overheard a conversation between Mr Adamafio and a colleague, the gist of which was that now that General Alexander, the British Chief of the Ghana Defence Staff, had been forced out, they must get rid of the 'last of these white faces, particularly this bitch who is with us here'. His tone of voice was so menacing that she told Nkrumah. Since he could not afford to quarrel with Adamafio at that stage, Nkrumah agreed that she should leave Ghana when they returned. Erika returned to England and lived in seclusion.

However, Nkrumah was now playing a double game. To the British he appeared the loyal Commonwealth colleague, enjoying attendance at Commonwealth conferences where he had a certain *réclame* as the first independent African Prime Minister. He collaborated in economic projects and encouraged foreign and particularly American investment. Among his own people, however, he was becoming increasingly tyrannical. Within a few years of his coming to power, all opposition leaders in Ghana and several thousand of their supporters were in gaol or in voluntary exile. At the same time, Nkrumah was turning Ghana into a base for the Afro-Marxist movement whose ultimate aim was the unification of the whole continent under Marxist rule, with himself at its head.

The Afro-Marxist movement was founded in the 1950s when it became clear that Britain was continuing the course she had followed in India and bowing out of the African part of her Empire as well. To take advantage of such an opportunity, the Soviet leaders had reorganized their Foreign Office. Until the 1950s there had been hardly a Russian in Africa; African affairs had been relegated to a sub-department of the section dealing with the Middle East in the Kremlin. When Khrushchev appointed Professor Potekhin his chief adviser on African affairs, things began to change. Professor Potekhin had asserted repeatedly that the new states of Africa were bound to reject capitalism and become part of the anti-Imperial democratic camp led by the Soviet Union. Khrushchev agreed with him and began to plan ahead. A new Afro-Asian department of the Soviet Foreign Office was created and an African Institute added to Moscow's Academy for Science, with Professor Potekhin as its head. A special news service was set up to provide background information for African newspapers and magazines, and a relentless radio offensive was launched mainly in English and French, covering the whole continent much more audibly than the BBC.

In the mid-1950s, Cairo had seemed the natural headquarters for this verbal campaign. President Nasser had turned to Moscow for help, both military and economic. The Russians were to build the new High Dam at Aswan; Russian tanks replaced British in the army and about three thousand Russian 'experts' came to instruct Egyptians. At home, Nasser was turning Egypt into a Marxist state. He had confiscated most of the land, had nationalized more than five hundred companies and made Cairo the centre for all African dissidents who had had to flee their own countries. The African Association, whose headquarters were at Africa House in Cairo, was their centre, the Afro-Asian Solidarity Committee their operational command.

But Nasser's pre-eminence was short-lived. Ardent Moslems in his own country resented his dependence upon the atheist Soviet Union; his feudal Arab neighbours became alarmed at the revolutionary ideas his agents were spreading; his African admirers were quick to recognize that his real interests lay not in the African continent as a whole, but in the Arab world. When we visited Africa House it had already ceased to be a revolutionary centre and had become a sort of displaced-persons' club where an ill-assorted mixture of refugees, occupying rooms labelled 'Kenya', 'Northern Rhodesia', 'South Africa', sat around talking. Most of them had already been disowned by the nationalist organizations in the countries they claimed to represent and, although their club was still being paid for by the Egyptian Government and Iron Curtain Embassies, there was a general feeling that its days were numbered.

In Moscow Professor Potekhin changed his tactics. He quietly bypassed the African Association in Cairo and dealt directly with the Russian Embassies which were being set up in each newly independent African state. Since the intoxication of independence had plainly made African nationalism too strong to be immediately subverted to Communism, the African Institute in Moscow adopted an interim policy, in which all forms of African nationalism were encouraged as a means of destabilizing the regimes of those countries still under the influence of Western colonial powers. This meant supporting a feudal monarchy

like Haile Selassie's in Ethiopia, where the Russians had just undertaken to build an oil refinery at Assab on the Red Sea, a military
dictatorship like the Sudan or a tribal dictatorship like Somalia. It also
meant breaking off relations with dissident refugee groups which the
Soviet Union had previously supported in Cairo but which were now
an embarrassment. At the same time, the Russians were preparing for
the future by encouraging a stream of students to leave their own
countries and enrol in universities, either in Moscow or in the satellite
countries of Eastern Europe.

As we wrote in our report on the penetration of Communism in
Africa, no one could begin to understand the Africa of the 1950s and
early 1960s who did not appreciate the passion for education which
obsessed the young. Education was the way up, particularly in Government service, which was the source of all promotion and power and
often also of money. Marxist ideas had captivated many young Africans; to them, capitalism meant nothing, because they had never had
any capital. The development of capitalism would simply mean an
increase in foreign investment and therefore in foreign domination.
Russia, on the other hand, populated overwhelmingly by backward
peasantry in the 1920s, had reached the front rank of world power and
was rivalling the American scientific achievement in the short space of
thirty-five years. As Julius Nyerere, the leader of Tanganyika (as it still
was) said to us: 'It cannot be such a bad system.' That the application of
Marxism produced dictatorships was often an attraction to the African.
Although tribal customs offered many safeguards to families, African
tribal chiefs ruled autocratically. The idea of individual liberty seldom
aroused strong feelings. Indeed, the only time we heard it discussed
with emotion was among the Ghanaian refugees in Togoland who had
fled from Nkrumah's rule. Although theoretical Marxism might be
attractive to young Africans educated in the West, the appeal of the
Iron Curtain countries was of a quite different calibre. The qualifications for entry into Western universities were usually too high for the
vast majority of young Africans, yet however primitive their background or limited their intellectual capacity, boys with any spirit would
do anything to win an educational label. They therefore turned to the
countries behind the Iron Curtain, where the authorities, more interested in indoctrination than education, demanded no academic qualifications at all.

The one country to which the Russians could look for enthusiastic co-operation was Dr Nkrumah's Ghana. Nkrumah had established three institutions, all of which were responsible to a Cabinet Committee over which he himself presided, through which to pursue his African-Marxist dream: an African Affairs Centre, the All African Peoples' Conference and a Bureau for African Affairs. The last was by far the most important, but we were surprised to find that no member of the British or American missions in Accra had visited it. Getting in did not prove difficult. The building which housed the Bureau stood behind a high wall in the centre of the city, an armed policeman at the gate. When we drove up in a taxi and asked for Mr Badern, the Director, we were immediately allowed in. Mr Badern was away but a young man called Dzima who described himself as his deputy invited us into his room. He explained that the Bureau was Ghana's Intelligence Centre for the whole of the African continent. Any refugees entering the country had to be screened by the Bureau before they were allowed to remain. If they passed the test they were sent to the African Affairs Centre, which was little more than a transit hostel where immigrants could be held under supervision.

Nkrumah himself was a curious mixture. Joe Appiah, Peggy Cripps' husband, had been with him as a student in London and used to describe how Nkrumah was sometimes seized with terror when crossing the street. Appiah had to take his hand and coax him first to the island in the middle of the road and then, after much persuasion, to make the final dash. Arden-Clarke admitted that Nkrumah possessed personal magnetism but felt he was unstable. Sir Robert Jackson, a man of wide experience as an international consultant, who was appointed Commissioner by the Americans to advise on the Volta Dam Project, was a warm admirer. Once, I was sitting in Sir Robert's office at Flagstaff House with the door open, when Nkrumah, whose room was next door, walked past and greeted him from the passage. It was plain from Sir Robert's voice and manner as he replied that he regarded Nkrumah with veneration.

Nkrumah's attempts to assert total control over the economy led to chaos. Needing money, he introduced a system of forced savings, only to discover that it would take the one printing press capable of doing the job two years to print the forms needed to administer the scheme. It was the same with import-export control; the necessary administrative machinery simply did not exist. Yet Nkrumah spent recklessly. Twelve Iluyshin airliners were bought from Russia; the first two were so uneconomic that Nkrumah tried to cancel his commitment to the other ten. The Russians refused to allow this and when we were in Accra the aircraft, their jet engines still cocooned, stood deteriorating on the tarmac. Nkrumah also spent millions on himself. He had numbered accounts in Swiss banks. He owned villas in Cairo and Rabat, an hotel and other property in London.

By the time we left Ghana the Government was heavily in debt and inflation was soaring. The price of food and clothing had doubled in two years while wages had been reduced by taxation. As a result there were strikes throughout the country. In the port of Takoradi, where the strike had lasted longest, we were told that feeling was so strong that no bar-keeper dared put up a picture of Nkrumah on his walls for fear of having it torn to pieces. We witnessed one minor riot. As we were passing the police station a free fight was going on in a doorway. Apparently, a hundred people had been arrested the night before and because the prisons were full they had been locked in the police station. One man had turned out to be a soldier and his comrades had driven down from the local barracks and were in the process of rescuing him.

But Nkrumah's unpopularity at home and in other African countries had not weakened his standing in the Communist world. When he visited Moscow or Peking he was given a dazzling reception. Streets were lined for miles on end, vast auditoriums were packed with cheering supporters. The profusion of food and drink at banquets was almost embarrassing in contrast to the drab life of the ordinary citizen. All this was not only because Nkrumah proclaimed himself a Marxist, but because he allowed his country to be used as a base from which the Soviet Union could develop its long-term strategy for the whole of Africa, a strategy which coincided with Nkrumah's pan-African dreams.

The truth about Nkrumah came out in February 1966. While he was visiting China he was deposed by a group of Ghanaians led by the former chief of the Defence Staff of the Army, Major General Joseph Ankrah. The action was carried out by two army brigades, the only resistance coming from Nkrumah's presidential guard of two hundred men at Flagstaff House, twenty of whom lost their lives. The government was taken over by a National Liberation council on whose behalf a spokesman said in a broadcast to the nation that 'the myth surrounding Kwame Nkrumah has been broken'. Although Nkrumah would not believe that a coup had really taken place until told officially by Zhou Enlai, the Chinese Prime Minister, there was general rejoicing in Ghana. Large numbers of Russian and a smaller number of Chinese 'experts' were sent home, the camps at which 'freedom fighters' were being trained to 'liberate' other African countries were closed. Hundreds of political prisoners were released, exiles returned. The support given to dissidents in Nigeria was withdrawn. The staff at the Chinese and Russian embassies were dramatically reduced and a new constitution proclaimed. Nkrumah took refuge with M. Sékou-Touré in Conakry.

38

Independent Television News

It is curious how uneven memory is. When I started looking back at my life in television, I gave little thought to the *Viewfinder* series which I did for the BBC between June 1954 and April 1955. The reason for this lapse became clear when I looked at the newspaper cuttings which had been kept by the producer of the series, James Bredin. *Viewfinder* covered a wide range: interviews with King Faisal of Iraq; the first television interview ever granted by Eamonn de Valera, the Prime Minister of Eire; the proceedings of the Trades Union Congress in England; the Health Service; Field Marshal Kesselring and Willy Messerschmitt in Germany; British Rail; the hydrogen bomb, to name only a few. The series was interlarded with programmes under other titles like *Panorama*, so that although I remembered most of the subjects we covered, I had forgotten the particular vehicle. Yet it was the *Viewfinder* series which earned me one of the most interesting opportunities of my life: the founding of the news service for commercial television which had been established by Act of Parliament on July 30th, 1954.

The reviews of *Viewfinder* had been favourable. Hyperbolic phrases like 'the near-perfect screen reporter', or 'the ace-investigator of BBC television', outnumbered those who found me 'depressing', 'humourless' or 'pedagogic'. Nevertheless, the invitation in February 1955 to meet a sub-committee of the companies which had been granted licences to broadcast commercial television came without warning. At that meeting it was explained to me that the new Independent Television Authority favoured a common service of national and international news for all the 'independent' companies, that it was to be financed by the companies but would be non-profit-making, and that the Authority itself would have the right to send a representative to the board meetings. The news must be presented without political bias.

The name suggested for this service company was Independent Television News and I was asked if I would like to become its first Editor. There was some urgency as the companies hoped to be on the air later that year, and I agreed to let the committee know within a few days.

Fundamentally it was not a difficult decision. I had been in favour of commercial television since the idea was first mooted, mainly because I believed, contrary to the opinion of those who opposed the Act, that competition would raise rather than lower the standard of television as a whole and would in many respects improve the output of the BBC.

In particular, I had always deplored the impersonal presentation of news on television. Certainly the dead-pan voice of an invisible announcer prevented sensationalism, but it also dehumanized the news, throwing away every advantage that television offered and making it look as if news had nothing to do with people at all. This belief had been powerfully reinforced a few months before when, working for Ed Murrow in New York, I had watched Huntley and Brinkley presenting the news for the Columbia Broadcasting System. There was a vitality and sharpness in their performance which derived from the presence of two intelligent, informed men conveying to the audience their own understanding of what they were saying. I had bored many of my colleagues in the BBC with my views ever since I returned.

However, my experience of newspapers made me cautious. Life for an editor with only one proprietor could be difficult enough, but with four or more companies and a statutory Authority looking over one's shoulder it would be impossible unless one was given complete editorial control. At my next meeting with the sub-committee, therefore, I not only made this plain but insisted that, besides being Editor, I should also be Chief Executive of the News Company and have a seat on the board. I wanted to be party to all the discussions, both on policy and on performance, and ultimately responsible for the management of all departments. When all this was granted without demur, I said I would accept their offer with great pleasure and would be able to start when my present *Viewfinder* series finished at the end of March.

I knew that some people would reproach me for leaving the BBC, which had given me so many opportunities, but if one believed its monopoly should be broken, it was surely right to help the new organization. I had accepted the one job in commercial television which I thought I could do well and where I felt I had something new to offer.

The period from March to September 22nd, 1955, turned out to be an exercise in improvisation. We had no base and moved from one building to another, beginning at York House, Queen's Square, London W1. We had no studio or television monitors and to carry out screen tests had to use studios in Hampstead and Highbury. Philip Dorté, with whom I had worked in those very early days of television in 1935, was seconded from the Associated Broadcasting Company to become Director of Operations, which meant that he was in charge of the whole technical side of the operation. Jim Bredin,[1] who besides being my producer in *Viewfinder* had also won fame with *Asian Club* and *Press Conference*, came with me to ITN as senior producer, and Richard Goold Adams, who for many years had been Foreign Editor of the *Economist*, took a real plunge into the unknown and became my Deputy Editor.

Our first job was to find 'newscasters'. The name indicated the difference I envisaged between their role and the 'news readers' of the BBC. They would not only appear on the screen but would play an active part in both the collection of the news and the drafting of its presentation. This was an extension of the roles of Huntley and Brinkley in New York and meant that our newscasters would not only appear in person on the programme but would go out with the cameras on at least one news story a day and when they returned in the evening would work with the sub-editors so as to get the report written in the way they wanted to speak it. This would inevitably involve them in disputes with film producers, cameramen and sub-editors, but I thought it would add life to the whole proceeding.

Altogether, I believe we watched more than three hundred news-caster tests, of which I saw at least a hundred myself. We had advertised for applicants who would be 'involved in helping to prepare and appearing on the screen to deliver, the daily news bulletins for the new Independent Television service due to start in the autumn'. We had said that previous experience was not necessary, that the requirements were a knowledge of current affairs, the ability to think on one's feet and a good presence. An indication of the way my mind was working was given by the sentence 'the work might appeal to a barrister thinking of giving up the Bar'.

The applicants divided themselves into four broad categories:

barristers or those with experience of the Bar; actors; journalists and authors; those with experience in the BBC. Only a few women applied and no politician or prospective political candidate that I can remember. Several of the BBC candidates were good but their manner had a BBC stamp which was exactly what we wished to avoid. The actors often had beautiful voices but listening to them one had the feeling that they were indeed acting; they did not convince me that they were really interested in news. The best were the journalists and the barristers.

One rather curious fact emerged: those watching the tests usually agreed quite quickly in their judgements. I suppose we were all looking for something not easily definable and, although it might sometimes be there, it was very obvious when it was not. Our shortlist included Robin Day, who had been a barrister until recently when he had joined BBC as a producer; David Lloyd James, a freelance broadcaster who had been at school at Haileybury and then went to Trinity College, Cambridge; Barbara Mandell, who had been on the staff of the South African Broadcasting Corporation for many years; Rex Keating, who began in the Near East Broadcasting station in Beirut and then became Director of Broadcasting for the Government of Cyprus; and Christopher Chataway, one of the first four-minute milers who also held the world record for three miles, who belonged to no category but was chosen because his style and personality appealed to all of us.

Several directors of our board attended the final tests, and it was only then that any serious difference of opinion emerged. Sidney Bernstein, head of Granada Television, for whom I had great respect, did not like Robin Day's appearance or manner. In addition he said we really could not have a newscaster who had to wear spectacles. I realized that Day's rather acerbic tone and aggressive manner might irritate some people, but to me he was the ideal antidote to Chataway's film star looks and boyish charm. I told Sidney I really did not think that spectacles could be allowed to be a bar to a newscaster but added that I would get Day to wear some that were less obvious. I explained why I felt Day was the right man for us, and when Sidney seemed adamant and said he would have to raise the matter at the board, I said that in that case he would have to find another Editor; I had made it absolutely plain that I must have total discretion in the selection of news and the manner in which it was presented. Sidney gave way at once and from then on proved one of our staunchest supporters.

There have been several descriptions, notably by Robin Day and Reggie Bosanquet, of the Heath-Robinson nature of our rehearsals. For several weeks before the September D-Day, our entire team worked each day as if we were on the air. Having gutted the newspapers, Arthur Clifford and Max Caulfield, the news editors, would discuss with me what stories we should cover and how: with film, filmed interviews, discussion before the camera or straight announcement. Then John Cotter and his assistant manager of 'film input' would make arrangements for transport, locations, interviews on location, informing the police, lining up those who might take part. Cyril Page, the senior cameraman, would allocate camera crews to each story. Clifford or Caulfield would brief reporters like John Hartley or Lynne Reid Banks. When they all came back to the office in the evening, they would present their reports to the sub-editors and often argue long and hard about the amount of space or film coverage their particular story should be given.

All that was pretty straightforward. It was the actual presentation that was so make-believe. We had virtually no proper equipment until the week before we were to go on the air and the last and vital mechanical part was installed only an hour before Chris Chataway was due to deliver his first bulletin. Neither he nor Robin Day had seen themselves on a television monitor, and since we had no 'teleciné' machines, no film had been televised either. The practice bulletins were delivered in the newsroom, with a wooden mock-up taking the place of a camera; film was shown on a white wall behind the newscasters, sound effects and background music were supplied on a gramophone disc and captions were written on a blackboard.

So as to help people understand what we were trying to do, I used to make the entire staff come into the News Room to watch the rehearsals and encourage comment. They were not often enthusiastic. It required a real effort of the imagination to transform the disparate assembly of gadgets and people into something as compact as a performance on a television screen. I was not depressed myself because I could see that the team was beginning to work together and I believed that when the equipment arrived they would all be astonished at how everything fell into place. But there were bad moments. Once, morale sank so low that Richard Goold Adams told me there was a move to get me to ask the Television Authority for a postponement. Nothing could have been more fatal. Philip Dorté kept me constantly informed about what equipment was reaching the companies, and although some had studios where drama production could be rehearsed under proper lighting, we were all virtually in the same boat. Although I realized that the News Company was at the bottom of the list for deliveries, I also knew from fellow directors that none of them would want to open the service without the News. I did not believe they were hiding anything from me.

One day I made everybody stay on for a few minutes after the bulletin rehearsal and gave them a pep talk. I well understood how bewildered they must feel that such an important operation should be so inadequately prepared, and I said so. I went on to explain the whole position in regard to equipment, to point out that ours was a comparatively simple operation and that it would be far worse if we were presenting a music-hall spectacular, which I gathered from the press was to be one of the features of the opening night, without being able to see what it looked like on a television monitor. I pooh-poohed the idea of postponement, saying that we had never been misled by our suppliers and I continued to believe in them. Finally, I promised them unlimited champagne after what I knew would be a spectacularly successful opening night. I was told afterwards that people had been cheered by what I said, and we had no further trouble. When the telecinés and monitors did arrive, even the most critical sub-editor seemed pleased with what he saw.

As we all expected, Christopher Chataway was the star of the opening night and next morning the newspapers were full of him. 'Independent Television pulled its first new "star" out of the hat last night – four-minute miler, Chris Chataway,' was a typical comment. But Robin Day did everything I hoped and Sidney Bernstein, as well as our Chairman, Captain Thomas Brownrigg, RN, came round to our studio during the evening to congratulate us all. In an aside to me, Sidney said warmly, 'You were quite right about Robin Day.'

It is curious to think that there was ever any doubt about Robin. By the time he was knighted in 1981 he had become an institution, yet he has not had an unchequered career. Robin is not always amenable or tactful. After a certain number of years in a job he gets restless and he has often had rows with his employer. He quite rightly sets a high price on his work; he has strong likes and dislikes. As a result he has oscillated between Independent Television and the BBC according to the people he had to deal with and the sort of programmes and money he was offered. He has also occasionally suffered from what I call 'Commentator's Disease', which means that he suddenly feels ashamed of always commenting on what other people do instead of doing something himself. Even Ed Murrow caught the infection.

Fortunately Robin had at some point joined the Liberal Party, and when the disease took hold and he tried to enter politics, he did so as a Liberal candidate. He was unsuccessful. But he was also un-Roman enough never to burn his boats, and was able to return to television. Gradually he learned, which I never did, that in a world in which general knowledge, particularly about politics and current affairs, comes overwhelmingly from radio and television, a fearless commentator has a role more influential than any but an outstanding minister and more durable than any politician. Robin has had to endure domestic tragedy, an assault by thugs in which his jaw was broken and a heart attack which entailed five 'bypasses'. Nevertheless, he has achieved a unique position in television and remains as acute, irrepressible and delightful as ever.

*

In general the main ITV programmes were politely, but not enthusiastically, received, whereas the News was frequently picked out as the one 'original' or 'refreshing' feature of the new service. The staff of ITN heaved a sigh of relief and set about improving its performance. Within a week, the BBC had paid us the compliment of engaging Roger Bannister, a doctor and Chris Chataway's predecessor in running a four-minute mile, as their athletics commentator.

However, the honeymoon was short. The character of Independent Television News had been altered during the summer of 1955 by several events. The entry in April of Cecil Harmsworth King and the *Daily Mirror* group into the ATV consortium; the withdrawal in July of Esmond Rothermere and his Associated Newspapers from the Rediffusion Group, which became almost wholly owned by British Electric Traction and Associated Rediffusion under John Spencer Wills; the failure of Kemsley-Winnick Group to materialize; and the substitution of the Associated British Picture Corporation, with Howard Thomas, formerly of Associated British Pathé, as managing director: all had altered the composition of the ITN board. Stuart McClean and Gerald Sanger, both of whom I had known on the *Daily Mail*, Lord Kemsley and Denis Hamilton, with both of whom I had had a long association as a journalist, all left, to be replaced by Paul Adorian, a talented scientist from Rediffusion, Howard Thomas and Eric Fletcher, the latter a former Labour Member of Parliament and fierce opponent of the whole concept of commercial television, from Associated British Picture Corporation.

Unknown to me, Robert Fraser had been in correspondence with Eric Fletcher about the obligation of ABC Television to join the News Company, which was an integral part of its contract. Fletcher had declared himself 'appalled' at the 'reckless' capital expenditure which was contemplated and protested also that the running costs were unwarrantably high in view of the results, which were 'disappointing in the extreme'. In his view, the present organization of the News Company needed such drastic overhaul that ABC were disinclined to join it and felt they could prepare their own news items at much smaller cost and with much greater efficiency. This latter view was upheld in further correspondence by Howard Thomas, who, as a previous chairman of Pathé News, had considerable experience.

I had been aware that some members of the board were unhappy about the film with which we were illustrating the bulletins, but they were knocking at an open door. We needed more cameras and more of the sort of exchange agreements that Philip Dorté and I had negotiated with CBS in New York just after we had been appointed. The first intimation I had that there were more serious criticisms came in November, when the board insisted that the seven o'clock bulletin should be reduced from fifteen minutes to seven and that the ten o'clock bulletin should be put back to ten forty-five. Although the reason given for this latter move was that many viewers waited up for the news and then switched off and went to bed, we in the company felt that the alternative was too late and that many of our present viewers would not wait up.

As a result of my protests at these changes, I became aware of an entirely new undercurrent among the members of the board. Howard Thomas continued to question the need for any separate News Company at all and was unconvinced of the necessity for more than very occasional use of film. I remember a suggestion made during a board meeting that there should be no formal bulletins but that news should be 'slipped in' between other programmes in two-minute 'snippets'. Thomas was a powerful advocate and some of the weaker members began to waver over what had hitherto been a fundamental agreement. I warned the board that if any of these suggestions were adopted, I should be obliged to resign.

According to Bernard Sendall,[2] the official historian of Independent Television, the Authority agreed at a meeting on December 20th, 1955, on three propositions: first, the News Company ought to be solely responsible for the national news, only regional news being undertaken by the individual companies; secondly, there should be a minimum of twenty minutes of news a day; and thirdly, the news must involve 'visual' presentation, including some use of film. Since all three of these items had been agreed at the foundation of ITN and had been the basis of the offer to me of the editorship, it is strange to read that they were now spoken of as 'propositions', apparently never thought of before. Nothing was said to me, either of the meeting or the propositions when members of the Authority visited the offices of ITN that same evening. Their visit provided one comic moment. As I was leading our visitors out of the lift to go to the News Room, I noticed two men rolling about on the floor of the passage having a fight. It was so unusual a sight that I stopped to identify them. The only one I could see clearly was the man on top, Arthur Clifford, the News Editor, whom we were just about to visit. I turned to my guests and said, 'At the moment the News Editor seems to be engaged in a rather heated argument with one of his staff. We will visit the sub-editors first.' By the time we had finished talking to the sub-editors Arthur was back at his desk and gave such a lively account of his job that his recent 'argument' was forgotten. Next day the chairman, Sir Kenneth Clark, wrote me the following letter:

This is to say two things. First, how much impressed all the members of the Authority were by what they saw in your department last night and, secondly, to say how glad and relieved I am to learn that for the time being, your resignation is withdrawn. The news that it had been tendered was a very great shock to the Authority. They are entirely behind the News Company and I do hope you will not take such a step again without having given me the opportunity of putting your difficulties to them.

*

However, the Authority's letter had changed very little. At the next Board meeting, on January 5th, 1956, new times and lengths of the news bulletins were agreed but the newsreel was to be discontinued and become the responsibility of the companies and, most important of all, the budget was to be cut to cover 'news programmes only'. In fact the newsreels added only fractionally to the budget because the film used was mainly what was intended for the bulletins but had been left out for considerations of space. The cut discussed at the meeting, on the other hand, was of more than one third, a crippling reduction from £350,000 to £200,000 per annum. In addition, a sub-committee of the Board was to be set up to supervise our preparation of a budget. We had been through the budget with a toothcomb and I realized at once that such a reduction would reduce the amount of film used to a negligible quantity and turn the bulletins into a recital, which would not interest any newscaster of the type I had recruited. It would mean the destruction of ITN as we knew it.

Since Sir Kenneth Clark had asked me to warn him if I thought of resigning again, I asked him to see me immediately. He received me with Bob Fraser and no one else. I told him that it was quite plain that the companies were out to destroy the News Company as we had conceived it and that I was not prepared to preside over its destruction. I then turned to Bob Fraser and said that I held him largely responsible for what had happened. In November, when the companies halved the length of the main news bulletin and put back the late one from ten p.m. to ten forty-five, he had made no protest nor had he said anything to discourage the ideas put forward since then to emasculate the bulletins and the company itself. I had thought I had the support of the Authority but had come to the conclusion that he, Fraser, was on the companies' side.

Fraser did not reply but Clark intervened to say that the Authority was going to insist on a minimum of twenty minutes' news a day. I am positive that this was the first time I had heard such a statement and I was immensely relieved. I replied that in that case I felt my resignation had achieved its object. I urged the Authority also to insist on a budget which made such a presentation of news possible. At the end of our talk Clark asked me if I could not reconsider my resignation in the light of what he had said; I replied that things had gone too far. I no longer had any faith in the intentions of the Board and they had plainly lost confidence in me. I agreed to stay on for six months to help find a successor.

In my letter of resignation, which was published next day, I said: 'It is clear that the board has no intention whatever of meeting my views and that our attitudes are too far apart to allow me to continue.' Richard Goold Adams resigned with me and Chris Chataway followed soon afterwards. That night, January 13th, 1956, Kenneth Clark made the unusual gesture of allowing himself to be interviewed by Robin Day on the subject of my resignation. It was a first-class interview and Clark answered all Day's questions. He made it plain that the Authority did not like the reduction in length of bulletins or the proposed cuts in the ITN budget. He was going to insist on a 'full and responsible news service of at least twenty minutes a day'. If necessary the Authority would consider taking over the News itself. There was such an outcry in the press the following day that the Authority felt it necessary to reaffirm its faith in the Independent Television News organization, which it described as 'one of the outstanding successes of commercial television'. At last I felt I had won my battle and that the future of ITN was safe.[3]

39

The Edge of Success

Most resignations are followed by anti-climax, but having stayed on at ITN to see Geoffrey Cox into the saddle, I felt I had served it well, and left without regret. Not having to go to an office I spent more time on our enlarged farm, planted a small orchard, embarked on a considerable drainage scheme on our new land and did penance cleaning out the muck from the battery hens (as manure it is over-rich and smells accordingly). In London I used to steal away some afternoons and watch the boys playing football and cricket in a far corner of the Westminster School ground in Vincent Square on which I had so often played myself.

When I left ITN, a writer in *The Economist* had remarked that commercial television had been lucky in having as its first News Editor someone who was rich enough to resign on a matter of principle; but the farm could not support us and when, after a few weeks, John McMillan, Programme Controller of Thames Television, asked me to act as consultant to a series of foreign programmes called *Intertel*, I accepted gladly. The programmes took me to France and Canada, working with Elkan Allan as producer. Not long afterwards, Leonard Miall, 'Head of Talks' at the BBC (which really meant head of documentary films and talks), to whom Grace Wyndham Goldie was deputy, rang up and I was able to resume my two-year rolling contract with the Corporation. The wolf was a little further from the door.

My first assignment was an enquiry into the state of British industry to see how far it was making use of new methods and how successfully it was competing with its European rivals. There were to be seven programmes entitled *The Edge of Success* and Donald Baverstock, a fiery young Welshman recently discovered by Grace, was to be the producer. We liked each other from the start.

We made one immediate discovery. Chairmen and managing directors of British businesses showed extreme reluctance to appear on television. 'Publicity' for them was a dirty word, and many refused to allow cameras into their factories or offices. I spent hours on the telephone trying to convince them that I was not seeking to pillory or even criticize them but to give them an opportunity to describe their business; if they had difficult problems it would be up to them, not me, to expound them.

We were lucky in one or two instances: Imperial Chemical Industries had been pioneering 'time and method study' at its great northern works at Billingham near Middlesbrough with the full co-operation of its trade unions. We spent a most rewarding day with Mr Russell Currie, one of the pioneers in this field with an international reputation who, although not a member of the company, was responsible for the introduction of Work Study throughout ICI. He was happy to explain his system in front of the cameras. On the same theme, we found a printing firm in the Midlands whose proprietor had called in the 'time and method' experts; by charting the movements of every employee during the day and then rationalizing them, they had not only saved the company thousands of pounds but made the work less tiring and enabled the workers themselves to increase their earnings by improving productivity.

Not unnaturally, those who were most successful were keenest to appear. A furniture manufacturer on the outskirts of London had taken infinite pains with the layout of his factory, had full order books, paid high wages, and enjoyed trouble-free labour relations; a department store encouraged its employees to make suggestions, and made use of a surprising number. In some of the new coal pits, new machinery had not only revolutionized output but made it possible to keep clean areas which had previously been covered in black dust. I remember being astonished to find beautiful flower beds within sight of the entrance to the coal shaft, and shower baths which would have made Wimbledon look to their laurels.

However, most of the old industries were declining. During a programme on British Railways I discovered that engine drivers had to keep time by their own watches. There was no sort of equipment to tell them whether they were running late or what speeds they had to attain to catch up. When I asked the chairman, General Sir Brian Robertson, whether this might not account for some of the unpunctuality for which

British Rail was always being reproached, he accused me of 'bowling him a fast one'.

One of the most dismal records emerged from the shipbuilding industry. Almost all shipbuilders refused to take part in any programme, but eventually we persuaded a small family firm on the Clyde to receive us. In other industries we had been able to establish that enterprising management could overcome seemingly crippling restrictive practices; failure to invest in new machinery and methods was not the fault of the unions. In shipbuilding, however, the demarcation lines drawn between different trades seemed to reduce the opportunities for ingenious management almost to zero.

One of the operations we filmed was the welding of steel plates on to the deck of a ship. However accurately the plates were cut they never fitted exactly and several things had to be done before they could finally be welded together. As we filmed, we noted that men from four different trades, one of whom had to bring a mate with him, came to do a job which, we were soon to discover, was done by one man in Sweden, Germany or Holland. The resulting delays seemed interminable. All work stopped for one or more hours while the welders waited for a particular tradesman who was finishing a job elsewhere, perhaps on another ship. When he came and did something which took a few minutes, there would be another wait for his successor. After several hours only one job remained: someone had to knock away the wedges with a hammer. It was something that any of us, given a hammer, could have done in five minutes. But the right tradesman was busy elsewhere and, when he had still not appeared by three-thirty, workers knocked off for the day because the shift was coming to an end. During the making of our series we went to Altona (near Hamburg), Stockholm and Rotterdam and found a striking difference of attitude among the unions. The questions they were asking their yard-owners were not related to demarcation but to why this or that piece of new machinery had not been installed so that the men could do the job more quickly, earn more money and ensure the continuity of their jobs by winning further orders.

Most stagnant of all was the newspaper industry. By its very nature this industry has always been particularly susceptible to sudden strikes. For a mass-circulation national newspaper, failure to print a day's issue means a loss which, if not crippling, may take months to recoup. A sudden stoppage, so easily brought about by a break in a reel of paper flowing over the presses, puts management at a great disadvantage. Rather than forfeit not only the price of several hundred thousand copies of the paper, but the advertising revenue which is earned by each page, editors and managers given way to sudden demands, often made while the paper is being printed. In the early days of the century, when mass-circulation papers made huge profits, this did not seem to matter greatly, but as costs rose and competition increased, particularly after each world war, the threat of a stoppage became more and more serious; for over the years the unions had established many 'practices' which, while they may have eased the daily life of the printer, made it more and more difficult for managers to make a profit.

In the autumn of 1957 I was asked by the *World's Press News* (the newspaperman's newspaper) to do an enquiry into the state of the Press in Britain. I was given every help by most proprietors and many unions, largely because they had watched the *Edge of Success* programmes. Surprisingly, the articles are still of interest because they show that the struggles which have taken place between Messrs Murdoch, Maxwell, Rowland, Shah and the print unions were foreshadowed thirty years ago. Already in 1957 photo-composing machines were eliminating the need for metal typesetting and therefore threatening the existence of linotype operators in newspapers. The teletype-setter had emerged and was enabling publishers to cast slug-set type in offices all over the country by typing in one office only, again reducing the demand for typesetters. New electronic devices were greatly improving the reproduction of half-tone and line blocks and therefore of pictures and advertisements. A string-tying machine had been invented which could replace the packers who tied newspapers into bundles and whose singing I had so much enjoyed in South Wales. But although all these machines were in use in ordinary printing houses, the resistance of the unions had prevented them being adopted in newspaper offices, in some of which the string-tying machines, having been bought, were lying unused in the cellars. Many more men were in fact being employed in the press and publishing rooms of daily newspapers in 1957 than in 1939.

By the 1970s, few national newspapers were making a profit, by the 1980s only one. The others were being paid for either by provincial newspapers, if the national daily proprietor was lucky enough to own any, or by new proprietors who were prepared to spend millions annually for the prestige of owning a well-known title. Such a situation could not last. Either the unions had to come to terms with modern techniques or several newspapers would disappear and with them thousands of jobs, not only among printers.

But while the print unions were digging their own graves, other events had been rocking the wider union world. At the same time as my *Edge of Success* programmes had been appearing, Woodrow Wyatt[1] had become a star of a revamped *Panorama*. Rather as I had done for *Viewfinder* a few years before, he travelled to the world's trouble spots. Then in May 1946 he turned his searchlight on the British trade unions.

Bill Carron (later Lord Carron) had just won a seat on the National Executive of the Amalgamated Engineering Union (which had a million members) in an election in the Sheffield and East Midlands area. During the election it had been discovered that in areas which had Communist officials and members, the signatures on many of the ballot papers had been forged, and that names of men appeared who had not even been present on the night the votes were cast. It was only when the false votes were disqualified that Carron scraped home. Next he was running for the presidency. Woodrow decided to devote the whole of a *Panorama* programme to the affairs of the Amalgamated Engineering Union, addressing himself directly to the members. He told them that in a democratic country they had the right to elect as many Communist officials as they pleased, but asked them if that was really what they wanted. While making the programme he discovered that most union members knew little about the candidates and many were unaware that the elections were being held at all. His programme was a sensation. The proportion of members voting increased from about 7 per cent to 11 per cent (still a pathetically low figure) and all three Communist-backed candidates were defeated.

But Woodrow had only just begun. As a result of that programme he was approached by Jock Byrne, the only non-Communist member of the National Executive of the Electrical Trade Union, and was shown confidential documents which revealed how the Communists had maintained control of the union since the war by falsifying election returns. Woodrow's devastating *Panorama* programmes, and the articles he wrote exposing the frauds, brought the issue to the High

Court. Finally, after a struggle lasting five years, the Communist General Secretary, President and other Communist members of the Executive were forced to resign. In 1961 Jock Byrne was made General Secretary of the union. One of his first acts was to introduce postal ballots for the election of the Electrical Trade Union officials; the members have been represented by moderates who truly reflect their views ever since.

I was soon able to supplement what Woodrow had begun. On my return from one of our African trips, Denis Hamilton, the Editor of the *Sunday Times*, asked me if I would do a series of articles on the penetration of Communists into British trade unions as a whole. The articles appeared in the *Sunday Times* in the autumn of 1962 under the title 'The Hidden Face of Communism', and were also printed by the newspaper as a pamphlet. The objects of the series were first to describe what had happened in the Electrical and Engineering Unions since Woodrow Wyatt had exposed Communist fraud six years before, and to discover what was going on in other unions; second to describe the organization of the Communist Party and the methods it was using in its campaign. The results were disturbing.

The Communist Party had made a surprising recovery in Britain since the Soviet occupation of Hungary in 1956 when it lost seven thousand members almost overnight. John Gollan, the new General Secretary, a small, gentle-looking, soft-spoken Scot with whom I had a long talk in his office in King Street, Covent Garden, had shown great skill in adhering to Lenin's maxim that the early stages of anti-capitalist revolution must be carried out without the intended victims being aware of what is going on. Communists must pose as reformers and, by the use of tactical language, disguise the organizations through which they gradually undermine confidence in the value of a free society. Titles like 'Teachers for Peace', 'The Medical Association for the Prevention of War', various 'Friendship' societies for countries under Communist control, above all 'The Society for Cultural Relations with the USSR', all sound so civilized that people who regard their professions or cultural pursuits as 'above politics' are apt to join them. They soon find themselves feeling guilty if they do not support Soviet proposals for nuclear disarmament and embarrassed when others raise questions such as the abuse of human rights in the USSR.

Gollan had also improved the organization of the party, particularly by the use of 'Advisory Committees' through which officials of the party advised Communist trade unionists how to handle elections for the union office. Where the candidate supported by the Communist Party stood a good chance, members of the party would be paid to enter the area to help canvas and to orchestrate the denigration of any strong non-Communist candidate. All this was contrary to the rules of every trade union, and had members of the Labour Party done it they would immediately have been denounced; but Gollan could rely on the loyalty of his party members never to betray what was happening.

By these methods, Gollan had been making steady progress. Membership of the Communist Party had increased and several prominent professors and intellectuals had joined. Penetration of the trade unions – the prime objective of Communist strategy in Britain ever since the visit to Moscow in 1926 of the first British Communist leader, Harry Pollitt – had steadily expanded. The Communist Party had never really believed it could win power through the ballot box, but realized that this was not necessary. The trade unions had founded and still financed the British Labour Party and through the block vote dominated the party conference. Capture the key positions in the main trade unions and you could force the Labour Party openly and legitimately to adopt Communist policies. Participation in elections was merely a smokescreen.

At the time that I was writing the articles, the situation was deteriorating. The moderate Electricians were more than holding their own but the cherubic-faced and cheerful Bill Carron was fighting a desperate battle in the Engineering Workers' Union. The non-Communist vote had been falling and it seemed likely that within months the moderates would lose control, a gain for the Communists which would more than offset the loss of the Electricians.

Several other unions were being threatened: among draughtsmen, teachers, post office workers, cinema and TV technicians, woodworkers, plumbers, painters, civil servants and bank workers, there were branches and areas under Communist control. A particular drive had been laid on against unions in the communications industries, dockers, seamen, motor car manufacturers, BOAC. Frank Cousins, General Secretary of the Transport and General Workers' Union, whose wife had been a member of the Communist Party and was still a sympathizer, was openly advocating militancy, which was exactly what the

Communists wanted. A crucial test would come when the elections for the Yorkshire branch of the National Union of Mineworkers took place in 1963. The margin between the moderates and the Communists and their sympathizers was narrow. If the Communists won they would then dominate the National Executive of the National Union of Mineworkers and alter the balance of the Trades Union Congress.

The people who resisted this onslaught were either former Communists who had been sickened by the dishonesty and ruthlessness of their former colleagues or who had suffered at their hands, or stalwart members of the Labour Party – and I gave a list of names – who felt that the Communists were destroying the movement the unions had founded and spent their own time and money travelling round the country warning men and women what was happening. But dedicated, and in many cases successful, though the resistance had been, it had not been able to halt Communist penetration of our society.

Ten years later I was commissioned by Harold Evans, then Editor of the *Sunday Times*, to write a sequel to 'The Hidden Face of Communism', bringing my account of the degree of Communist infiltration up to date. An election for officials of the National Union of Mineworkers in the Yorkshire area was imminent and in my article I repeated the warning I had given ten years earlier. I delivered the article punctually and was promptly paid. A few days later I received a letter from Harold Evans saying that he was very sorry but that all his young men told him that I was wrong and he could not publish the article. I then sent it to Michael Berry (now Lord Hartwell) and to my surprise received an identical reply. Knowing that Sir Gordon Newton, Editor of the *Financial Times*, was not only independent-minded but powerful in his organization, I sent it to him. He rang me up and said that no doubt he would have difficulties with his staff but he was determined to publish the article, even though he might not be able to give it the space it deserved. He kept his word. Within a week the NUM elections were held and my fears were confirmed. A day or two later I had occasion to telephone Harold Evans about a quite different subject. As soon as he heard my name he said, 'I know, you are ringing to say I told you so.' I replied by telling him what I was ringing about and never discussed the articles again. Nevertheless, his reaction and that of Michael Berry showed that left-wing infiltration among junior editors and executives could paralyse the will of editors who at other times and over other issues had shown courage and independence. It was to need Mrs Thatcher's legislation and a new generation of proprietors to break the stranglehold that the Marxists and their fellow travellers had succeeded in imposing upon newspapers through trade unions.

40

The Fruits of Independence

The next phase of our enquiry into the Communist penetration in the African continent took us to the Congo just when the United Nations forces were trying to establish order and prevent the newly independent country from being dismembered. Mr Tshombe was still in control of Katanga, Mr Gizenga of Stanleyville and Orientale Province, Mr Kalonji had declared Kivu independent and others were trying to do likewise in other provinces. Air services had been disrupted. We must have flown into Leopoldville either from Lagos or Yaoundé. There were some United Nations troops on the airfield and all seemed quiet; we took a taxi driven by an African. As we entered the city, however, and slowed down for some traffic lights, two boys who cannot have been more than fourteen or fifteen but were armed with sub-machine guns began walking alongside the car and waving the muzzles of their guns at us, shouting to the driver. We waved and smiled back and fortunately the driver was able to calm them and shake them off.

At the British Embassy a member of the staff who was doing his best to be friendly said to us quite seriously that we would find out much more about the situation in the Congo if we stayed in Leopoldville than if we went into the interior. Two or three heads of European businesses echoed his views, pointing out that the Congo's foreign trade had held up surprisingly well since independence and that work on plantations abandoned by the Belgians had been resumed. However, there was something about the general atmosphere in the city which made us both apprehensive and suspicious. The suspicions were confirmed by M. Kamitatu, the French-speaking Premier of the Province of Leopoldville, who did not pretend he was having an easy time. He admitted that he was faced with famine in a large area and that the southern part of his province was claiming independence. 'My chief difficulty,' he said, 'is that my people still take the word "independence" literally. They think it means that they need do no work. I am in the odd position of trying to reimpose the laws the Belgians made.'

Fortunately we had an introduction to some Belgians who, although still living in the capital, were in touch with some of their countrymen elsewhere. On their advice we went to Luluabourg, the capital of Kasai, about a thousand miles east of Leopoldville where a few months previously there had been fighting between United Nations forces and mutinous Congolese troops. Our Belgian friends arranged to put us on a flight and have us met the other end. Since conditions in the Congo proved too chaotic for us to draw any conclusions useful for our report on the penetration of Communism, we put our experiences in an appendix, from which I quote:

It is impossible to assess the degree of Communist infiltration in the Congo while the country remains in a state of anarchy. The Congolese army is a rabble. Until it is disarmed and a much smaller force created which has European technical advisers and, if possible, some European officers as well, the massacres of Kongolo will be repeated elsewhere and orderly government in the provinces or at the centre will remain a dream. Congolese troops not only attack Europeans, they rob and pillage the countryside, take food from villagers at gunpoint, steal lorries and supplies from civilian contractors and United Nations forces, sell their arms on the black market and, when the local banks receive their currency from the hard-worked printing presses in Leopoldville, drive into the towns in lorries and take what they consider to be their pay.

In such circumstances it is a miracle that life continues as it does. It is due entirely to the few remaining Europeans, mostly Belgians, who continue to run hospitals and businesses, and their loyal African staff, who often go in danger of their lives. The difficulties are enormous. Trains and aircraft run intermittently and lorries have to run the gauntlet, not only of bad roads, but of the Congolese soldiery. Almost all the Bedford lorries belonging to the United Nations are unserviceable and the British Colonel in charge of the Nigerian detachment, Col. Dunbar, told us that this was due to a well-known weakness 'in their generators'. An ex-English Sergeant

Major in charge of the only garage able to do the repairs explained that the real 'weakness' was simply that all the spare parts and often the generators themselves had been sold by the United Nations troops to black-marketeers. Forty lorries had disappeared altogether. When goods arrive in the European-owned stores, they disappear the same day. Most European firms continue to charge normal prices but their Congolese distributors are making fabulous profits. The black market thrives on P.X. goods sold by United Nations personnel.

We visited the hospital in Luluabourg which the Belgians had built for the Congolese, and found it in an appalling condition. It is run by the local government with the help of four doctors supplied by the United Nations. The Israeli doctor who took us round told us that a year before (July 1961) when she came, the hospital was magnificently equipped. As we went through the children's wards she pointed out that nearly all the mattresses and blankets had been stolen and the children had to lie on the bare bedstead. Most of them were dying of malnutrition, yet that very morning the cashier had absconded with about £50 and there was nothing with which to buy food. Later that day the wife of a Belgian businessman managed to buy six sacks of rice to keep the hospital going for three or four days. There was no oxygen or gas in the hospital and no operations could be performed. Smallpox had broken out.

Meanwhile the officials of the local provincial government were enjoying the fruits of 'independence', living in the smartest hotel or the houses the Belgians had left empty. We visited the hotel and discovered that no whites were accepted. In the evenings the Terrace Bar was crowded with gaily dressed African women parading up and down and doing, we were told, better business than they had ever known.

Perhaps the worst feature of Luluabourg was the bad feeling between the three hundred and fifty-odd Europeans who kept the city going and the United Nations troops and officials. The Europeans were convinced that the UN knew of the 'search' which resulted in the rape of many European women, and could have prevented it. The head UN official denied this and pointed out that he could not properly object to a search for spies being carried out. But even if he was prepared to accept such a flimsy excuse, he should have been on the alert to see that it did not endanger life, and it is difficult to believe that none of his staff was aware of what was going on. An Englishman who was being marched down the street called to some Nigerian soldiers and told them what was happening, but they turned their backs on him. A group of Scandinavian technicians belonging to the United Nations were seen drinking with Congolese officers in the bar of an hotel while women were being raped upstairs. While they were sitting there, one woman jumped from a balcony to the pavement and broke her arm and a rib. It is true that the United Nations officials lived in the residential quarter which is perhaps half a mile from the centre of the town, but it was in that quarter that some of the worst atrocities were committed.

Our departure from Luluabourg was indicative of the state of the country. The Belgian merchant with whom we stayed had warned us that although they had reserved seats for us on one of the unscheduled flights to Leopoldville, they could not guarantee what would happen at the airport. Our hosts said that the first hurdle was to get our passports stamped and added, 'I know the man in control of passports and I think I can manage that for you. I will come with you.' When we reached the airport we were led to a large room at one end of which an African was sitting behind a trestle table, flanked by civilian assistants and guarded by several armed soldiers who stood round the walls. The Controller, we were told, had been a porter at the Luluabourg railway station under the Belgians and after independence had become Controller of Passports. Everyone had to get their passports stamped, not only to leave the country, but to leave the Province of Kasai. Our host took our passports, told us to stay where we were near the door, and gradually made his way round the room which was filled almost entirely with Belgian men and women, all of whom were trying to leave. The woman standing next to me said she had been trying to leave for a week but had never been able to get near enough to the Controller to have a chance.

After a few minutes we saw our host squeezing himself past those at the back of the trestle table until he was standing directly behind the Controller. The latter continued to examine passports, stamp some and give back others with a curt refusal. The atmosphere was tense and one woman who met with a refusal burst into tears and began to plead, only to be led away by a soldier. The Controller paused after stamping one or two passports, and I saw our host bend over his shoulder, say something in a low voice in his ear and put our two passports on the table in front of him. The Controller glanced at him, then stamped our passports without comment. As our host made his way back to us, the Controller suddenly rose, said he would stamp no more passports that day but would be back at the same time tomorrow. There were groans and objections, but he marched out, followed by his guards. 'That is how it always is,' said the lady next to me in a resigned voice.

Our host led us out and showed us where the flight desk was. 'I am afraid I cannot help you any further,' he said. 'I do not know the man who controls the flights, but I am told he is unpredictable. The only thing you can do is to show him your tickets and passports and wait. You should be all right.' And with that, we said goodbye.

We were at the end of a short queue and all those in front of us were given boarding cards. I began to be hopeful. But when we reached the desk the man looked at our passports and said that we would have to wait because he was not sure whether there would be a seat. I wondered whether to offer him money, but thought it might cause trouble. We waited while several more people were given cards and I approached him again. 'Not yet,' he said, although we were the only people waiting. At that I lost my temper. In French, which became less grammatical as I got angrier, I expostulated. It was our first visit to his country, I said. We had travelled to almost every African country during this year and this was the first time we had been treated with such discourtesy. What sort of impression did a newly independent country want to make? And so on and so on. At first he looked surprised, then annoyed, and then suddenly he began to laugh. 'What strange people you English are!' he said. 'You always think you deserve special treatment. Well, this time you shall get it.' He then gave us boarding cards, took us out to the aeroplane and wished us a good flight. After we had taken off, Virginia turned to me and said that when she saw me losing my temper she had felt sure that we would end up in gaol. 'I have not been so relieved to get out of a country since being behind the Iron Curtain,' she added.

From Leopoldville we went to Katanga. Again, there were no scheduled flights but as Mr Tshombe still had Belgian advisers, our Belgian friends were able to get in touch with them. We received a message that Mr Tshombe would be delighted to receive us at Elizabethville. For the only time in our lives we were received in state.

328

An emissary was at the airport to greet us and an escort of at least twenty black-suited motor-cyclists was waiting to accompany us into the city. At a speed of sixty mph we were taken straight to Tshombe's house. On the way it occurred to us both that such a reception of two journalists must be a sign of desperate uncertainty.

Mr Tshombe was friendly. A large man with large gestures and a broad smile, he said he was honoured that we had come to see him. He then talked intelligently about the situation. He felt that the determination of the United Nations to destroy all links between Belgium and the Congo was a huge mistake. The Belgians may not have been ideal colonists – who were? – yet they had done much for the Congo and were the only people whom the Congolese people knew and trusted. Like M. Kamitatu in Leopoldville, Tshombe was far more forthright than any European or representative of the United Nations.

I forget where we stayed, but I have photographs of shell-pocked walls of the British (or American?) Consulate where I met Mr McGee, the American emissary to Katanga, and an English colleague. Mr McGee explained his Government's attitude towards Tshombe and Katanga and said, 'We have nothing against Katanga, in fact we would be quite happy to see it independent, but we know that if we do not conquer it for Mr Adoula [recently appointed Prime Minister of the Congo] Russian jets will be here within a few hours.' We protested at what seemed to us such a naive view. The Afro-Asian bloc in the United Nations was no more likely to invite Russian combat units into the Congo than American, nor was it conceivable that the Russians would risk a major war by sending troops to the Congo without the support of the United Nations. Would it not, we asked, be better for the United Nations to concentrate on restoring law and order rather than in expelling Mr Tshombe from Katanga, almost the only part of the Congo where some semblance of law and order still existed? But perhaps we in our turn were being naive. Mr McGee replied that the Americans feared that if they gave any support to Mr Tshombe, they would at the same time be encouraging every other separatist movement in the Congo, including Mr Gizenga's pro-Marxist government in Orientale Province. This would give the Soviet Union just the pretext they needed for interference and would have led to even greater chaos than already existed. We realized before we left that Tshombe was doomed.

41

From Cairo to Casablanca

We first went to Morocco as a family; I think it must have been in 1958, when Randall was eight and the other two children ten and eleven respectively. I know we flew, because Randall made friends with an Arab boy in the aeroplane who asked us all to lunch with his uncle when we reached Fez. His name was Omar el Kostali and he was going home after the Easter term at an English private school. He liked his school, loved England and spoke perfect English. We did not reach Fez until towards the end of our tour, but Randall had kept in touch with Omar, who had given us exact instructions on how to reach his uncle's house. We left our car a short distance away and walked through some dirty and smelly back-streets until we reached a tall, brass-studded wooden door in a high wall. The door was opened by a slender, beautiful black girl in Arab dress, who we learned later was really a slave but nevertheless lived as part of the family. We found ourselves in a large courtyard with tiled floor and walls, a fountain playing in the middle and many flowers against the walls in formal beds. As we followed the girl across the courtyard, Omar joined us and took us to his uncle.

Sheikh el Kostali was of medium height, wearing a white turban, a striped jellaba and Moroccan slippers. Through Omar, who inter-preted, the Sheikh gave us a warm welcome and took us to a tiled room leading off the courtyard, where we all lay down on divans round the walls. There were no doors, each room leading to the next through open archways. After a rest and some sweet tea drunk from small glasses, we were summoned to a gargantuan feast, of which I remem-ber only three dishes out of at least six. The food was brought in by black servants on large round brass trays and put on a stone table around which we stood to help ourselves. For the third course there was a whole roast chicken each, laid in rice; this was followed by a huge bowl of couscous with lamb, marrows and other vegetables – and this was followed by melons, figs and oranges. As I remember, we ate with our fingers, sitting on the edge of divans or occasional chairs, and talking little. Our host talked endlessly to an Arab friend or occasionally to Omar. Between each of the main courses we were invited to lie on the divans and relax. The Sheikh himself set the example from a neighbouring alcove which resounded with hugely satisfactory belches. Omar encouraged us to do the same.

Earlier in our trip, we had lunched in Tangier with David Herbert and Peggy Hulbrecht, a Dutch friend of Virginia's sister Mary. The boys discovered a café where they could play with slot machines, but one morning they got into a fight. The café owner had objected to their playing with the slot machines without ordering anything to eat or drink and had tried to throw them out. The boys resisted and the proprietor threw Andrew through the plate glass window in the front of the shop. Whereupon Randall went for the shopkeeper and butted him in the stomach with his head, temporarily winding him. Meanwhile Andrew had picked himself up from the pavement, fortunately unhurt, and the boys ran away.

Shortly afterwards we left for Rabat, where we paid the equivalent of one pound each for a bed and were interested to discover during the night that our hotel was also a brothel. We went on through Mogador to Marrakesh. At Mogador, a charming coastal town of which some of the old walls remained, our journey nearly came to an abrupt end. We were hot and the beach was empty, so we parked the car and walked down to the sea. When we returned, the car had gone. At the police station I was told to wait. A quarter of an hour later, a smiling policeman drove up to the door – in our car. He spoke enough French to tell me that it had not been driven very far – the next street to be exact. He had found the young men who had taken it, and had frightened them with dire threats, but as the car was undamaged he felt that we would rather have it back than press charges. We thanked him warmly.

The weather was glorious, so next day we motored on the road to Taroudant down the other side of the Atlas Mountains until we reached the desert beyond. When I said that this was the beginning of the Sahara the children were so excited that they leapt out, rushed into the sand and rolled around in it. We drove back through Beni-Mellal, where the temperature was nearly 120 degrees, and an Arab lady warned us to stop Randall walking bare-headed in the street; through

Khenifra and Azrou to Meknes, where we stayed the night, going on next day to Fez for our feast at the home of the Sheikh el Kostali. It was a trip none of us would forget.

A few years later, Virginia and I were to return to Rabat for our study of infiltration of Communism in Africa. King Hassan had only recently survived the attempt on his life made by members of his Air Force. We saw several of the opposition leaders, who spoke freely about their plans to introduce a socialist state; they admitted, however, that they were forbidden to organize political parties and did not think they would come to power until the King abdicated or was forced off his throne. Abdul Razzaq, on the other hand, one of the Moroccan trade union leaders, was openly using his union as a weapon through which to bring the country under Communist influence and was, apparently, without hindrance, sending all student members of his union to Iron Curtain countries for their higher education. Although King Hassan has shown himself one of the world's most buoyant monarchs, it is still too early to say for certain that Abdul Razzaq's efforts have been unavailing.

But the main interest in this visit lay in the Ambassador with whom we stayed at the British Embassy. Sir Charles Johnston at Aden had told us about Ronald Bailey and his wife Joan, who were the miraculous survivors of an assassination attempt in Ta'izz, the capital of North Yemen. The Baileys told us their story. Ronald was on the staff of the embassy at Ta'izz, and had come home one evening to his flat, which was at the top of a five-storey building, when the doorbell rang. All the inside doors were open because of the heat and Ronald and Joan could see the front door from where they sat. They were not expecting anyone. Ronald got up and went to the door. When he opened it, he saw in front of him an unknown Arab of about his own height, who at once attacked him with a knife, stabbing him several times in the neck and chest.

Joan, who had been a Wren during the war, heard him cry out, saw what was happening and dashed across the room at top speed, hurling herself at the Arab whose arm was raised to give a final *coup de grâce* to her husband. She hit him with such force that she not only knocked the knife out of his hand but sent him reeling backwards down the stairs. She picked up the knife, shut the door of the flat and bent down to tend to her husband, managing to drag him into the bedroom and help him on to the bed. She wrapped a scarf around his neck, which was bleeding badly, and staunched the other wounds with anything else she could find. Ronald was groaning and at one point murmured that he feared he was going to die. 'She flared up at me,' he said, 'and almost shouted that I was damned well not going to die, that I had a wife and three children and that she was going to save me. She then sat by me until the doctor came, holding the veins from which most blood seemed to be coming. It is entirely owing to her that I am still here.' The Arab was never seen or heard of again. Five years later, Joan was still slim and athletic and both Virginia and I felt that if anything similar happened she would do exactly the same again.

*

In Tunisia we stayed with Leo and Edwina d'Erlanger at their palace of Nejma Ezzohra in Sidi Bou Said, a village on a hill about eight miles from Tunis. The palace was built by Leo's father at the turn of the century and overlooked the sea. It was on several levels; one door from the street led straight on to the flat white roof. Old Baron d'Erlanger had employed all the best craftsmen he could find in the Arab world to embellish the house, and it was rich in carvings, stone trellises and tiles of all kinds. On one level, channels in a marble floor carried water through every room, in many of which fountains played. There were no right-angles in the palace, apparently because of the Arab belief that symmetry and perfection belong only to Allah. The blue and green tiles were of magical beauty.

Most of the diplomats accredited to Tunisia and several members of the government, including the young Bourguiba, came to lunch or dine. Conversation was in French, but although Leo and Edwina were greatly admired by the Tunisians, I always felt a slight constraint. Leo's pride had been a valley which he had bought and planted with a special type of olive tree. Spanish or Italian olives ripened late and the crop was liable to be devoured by migrating birds, but Leo had discovered that the Californians had developed an olive tree the fruit of which ripened several weeks earlier, before the birds came. (It had first been grown by the Romans.) With great care he had cultivated this tree and planted his valley with it. But in the first flush of independence the Tunisians, recognizing the value of the trees, had 'nationalized' the valley and taken over what had been a remarkable example of individual

333

ingenuity. The subject was taboo when members of the Tunisian government came to the house.

*

In Khartoum we stayed with the British Military Attaché, Major Hook, and his wife. They loved the Sudanese and helped us to meet many of them. But a military dictatorship breeds an uneasy atmosphere. The Government had imprisoned not only those who had left-wing views but former political leaders who wanted to return to parliamentary government. The trade unions had been disbanded and new labour laws made any genuine form of trade unionism impossible. Press and radio were heavily censored and the only publication still bold enough to criticize the government was a magazine edited by a frail but beautiful Sudanese school mistress. As we talked to her in a tiny, dilapidated office, a white-robed, turbanned figure came silently into the room, looked at us and walked out again. The school mistress told us that he was one of the spies the government employed to watch her. The only explanation she could give of why her magazine was still allowed to appear was that there was still some chivalry towards women; but she lived in daily expectation of arrest.

As in so many African cities, Russian diplomats in Khartoum lived in a compound surrounded by walls, to which an extra four feet had been added to the height when the embassy opened. Except for one gardener, the Russians employed no Sudanese servants and not even tradesmen were allowed within the gates. Once, when the milk boy could get no answer at the gate and was rash enough to walk inside, he was kept there for four days. Thereafter he left his bottles on the pavement. Because the Russians were building two hospitals in the Sudan, and accepting more than two hundred students a year at Moscow University, the Sudanese government did not object to their behaviour. A minister told us that the Moslem religion was so strong that Communism would have no attraction for Sudanese students, even after five years' indoctrination behind the Iron Curtain.

The Hooks took us to Omdurman, where we struggled to reconstruct the battle from the maps in the museum. There were even some photographs, the typewritten captions of which were so faded as to be almost unreadable. They had obviously been written when the British were still paramount in the Sudan and spoke enthusiastically of a handful of British defeating thousands of 'the enemy' in various actions. It was an interesting commentary on the Sudanese character that nobody had bothered to change the captions since independence.

*

From Khartoum we flew to Addis Ababa. In 1962, Ethiopia, still officially a Christian country, was the most backward in Africa, corrupt, feudal and savage, ruled absolutely by Haile Selassie, the King of Kings. One hundred miles outside Addis Ababa most natives carried spears, and when we visited a leprosarium near Lake Awasa, a hundred and fifty miles south of the capital, which was run by a British woman doctor, Mrs Fitzherbert, she told us that she had had four cases of severe spear wounds in the hospital in the last month. She also told us that it was not safe for anyone to walk alone on the road after dark.

Although Haile Selassie spent the war in Britain and was restored to his throne by British arms, he had seized the excuse of a dispute over Greater Somalia, in which the British supported the Somalis, to move away from the West and embrace 'non-alignment'. This involved making a trip to Moscow. His visit was successful, for soon an announcement was made that two hundred Russian geologists were coming to Ethiopia to search for minerals and a large new technical school would be built by the Russians on the shores of Lake Tana. There were other results: both the Yugoslavs and the Czechs were allowed to embark on large-scale experimental schemes involving the growing of groundnuts and sunflowers.

We visited the Yugoslav plantation which was not far from the malaria-infested Lake Awasa, and found that the experiment had been a total failure. About five thousand acres had been planted and we drove past miles of neatly laid out fields with rows of healthy-looking plants ready for picking, but unfortunately bearing no nuts. The despairing Yugoslav manager who was the head of the agricultural college in Belgrade told us that he had never undertaken such a back-and heart-breaking operation. He had only five Yugoslav assistants and relied solely on Ethiopian labour. The Ethiopians were not a race who liked manual labour and all his fellow Yugoslavs had worked themselves to a standstill. The Yugoslav in charge of the mechanical repairs had literally dozens of trucks, tractors and harvesters waiting in his

335

workshops, and had nearly had a nervous breakdown. The manager had never heard of the British groundnut scheme at Kongway, but had made the same mistake of planting on a large scale before trying an experimental strip.

There was widespread, almost violent, unrest among the young, educated Ethiopians. They told us with reckless frankness how appalling the corruption was, how the whole country operated on a basis of élitism and privilege, how justice was waived if any member of the oligarchy was involved, how dozens of people were flung into gaol for political offences and often died because of appalling prison conditions before being brought to trial. These young men, civil servants, teachers or community workers, said they did not know what they wanted but that anything would be preferable to the present system. They admitted that the Emperor had the following of most of the tribes in the country but hoped that when he died changes would take place. No one knew for certain who his successor would be, but there were divided loyalties in the army and fears of bloodshed.

Why did Haile Selassie, a feudal and absolute monarch, allow the Russians to set themselves up in Ethiopia? The answer was both historical and political. There was an old connection between the two countries: in Tzarist days Ethiopia was the only African state where Russia was represented. More recently, the Soviets backed the Emperor in his plans for Eritrea. More important still, Haile Selassie longed to play a leading role in the new Africa. He built a huge United Nations Assembly Hall in Addis Ababa in order to induce the Economic Commission for Africa to make their headquarters there; he then invited the left-wing Afro-Asian Solidarity Committee to hold their next meeting there. By such gestures he had hoped to rebut accusations that his regime was feudal and out of date, and since he did not allow Ethiopian students to study behind the Iron Curtain, he apparently believed that he was safe from subversion.

The Emperor ruled for another fourteen years. As in so many African countries, rebellion finally came from the army, which first relieved him of his power and then, a few months later, deposed him. Severe famine had added to the general discontent. Since Russian advisers were already established, it was not difficult for them to influence the military governors, who faced appalling problems. Within a few years, Ethiopia had become the first wholly Marxist

African country. Today, over a decade after Haile Selassie's death, Ethiopia's leaders, having ignored the warnings of the United Nations and other specialist organizations about the faults in their agricultural methods, face one of the worst famines in the country's history.

42

A Dairy Farm

Meanwhile the farm which had been the basis of our family life for fourteen years was running into trouble. It was called Kingsbridge and lay in the parish of Steeple Claydon, about four miles south of Buckingham. The farm had belonged to two sisters by the name of Hubbard. Hilda, the younger sister, was a socialist and I had often been to see her. Tall, fair-haired, angular and down-to-earth, she ran the farm with her elder sister, who was a staunch Tory. Both sisters being in their seventies, the farm had become too much for them, and they had decided to sell. The house had charm: long, low, red-brick and red-tiled roof, part built in the late seventeeth century but added to by the sisters' father a hundred years ago. Six bedrooms, a large drawing room with long windows, a study, big hall, good dining room and kitchen all looked south on to a lawn with the fields beyond.

The house stood at the end of a lane running down from the main road which was a dead end. Another, smaller house stood on the other side of the lane, also a farm, which belonged to a Mr Lowe. The lane stopped at the River Ouse (the Great Ouse eventually reaches the sea at the Wash in Norfolk), which ran through the back of the farm and across which there was only a footbridge. Beyond the Ouse lay the hamlet of Hillesden where a battle was fought in the Civil War. The King's men had held the bridge (hence the farm's name) but the Roundheads had captured and burned the big Tudor house on top of the hill. Only the chapel remained, with an inscription saying how many men were killed within its walls during the battle. In 1947 there was a farmhouse on the site of the Tudor house, lived in by a man named Cotton, also a Labour supporter and a Non-Conformist preacher, who farmed some three hundred acres. The only traffic down the lane came either to Kingsbridge or to Mr Lowe. It seemed the perfect place to bring up a family.

Virginia's 1947 diary tells the beginning of the story:

Sunday, October 26. Gawcott:
This afternoon we went to see Cotton, a charming farmer who lives at Hillesden, and discussed with him the possibility of buying Kingsbridge, a 100 acre dairy farm which joins his land. We got down to hard figures; he had been over every inch of the land for us and said it was not in good condition as it had been badly farmed, but with money spent on it could be turned into a fine dairy farm. He said £6,000 was about the right price for it, perhaps a bit more because of the house. He figured up stock and equipment and said that would probably cost another £6,000. Very expensive, but he assured us that we ought to be able to cover interest on the borrowed money and our wage bill. We left, unable to think of anything else and we will probably make an offer next week after Aidan has a chance to discuss it with his father.

Sunday, November 2nd. Gawcott:
This afternoon we went over to have tea with Miss Hubbard, the owner of Kingsbridge which we hope to buy. It was a clear, windy day, the country looked lovely. Kingsbridge was looking so pretty it whetted our appetites more than ever. Miss Hubbard, a tall, tweed-skirted, flat-heeled supporter of Aidan, gave us a wonderful tea and told us how much she hoped we would become the owners of the farm.

Monday, November 3rd:
This morning on our way to London we stopped in Winslow and saw Mr Wigley, Miss Hubbard's agent, and made an offer for Kingsbridge of £7,000. He is a delightful man and told us that a farmer had already made the same offer and his duty as a businessman would be to make one of us put up more. He said he knew that Miss Hubbard wanted us to have the farm, so if it was close, the preference would certainly rest with us. He told us to think it over.

Thursday, November 13th. 52 Romney Street:
Great news. We have got the farm. A letter from Mr Wigley, the agent, to say we can have it for the price we offered, £7,000. The other man has withdrawn his offer as he does not want to wait until

next September, the earliest date we can move in. I looked after Andrew, who is growing fatter every day and more and more greedy. He has begun to have cereal and vegetables, but my guess is that shoe leather and grass would be received with equal enthusiasm.

Sunday, December 14th:
Today Cotton walked over our farm with us. He told us the good fields and the bad and said that the land should be excellent dairy land eventually. It will take at least three years to put it into shape. It is very good of Cotton to help us so much; I feel we are imposing on him and am rather embarrassed.

Sunday night, December 28th, Gawcott:
Yesterday Aidan and I went over our farm. It looked very pretty outside and it is always a thrill to set foot on one's own land. However, what a lot there is to do inside. Lots of ceilings need redoing, all the walls need paint and wallpaper. We are going to try and get a permit to have a couple of bathrooms put in, which is essential.

Sunday, March 7th. Romney Street:
Went to the farm this morning with Mr and Mrs Clark, potentially our farm manager and his wife. They are both very nice and Aidan is terribly pleased with Clark whom Cotton recommended to him. Clark is a cricketer and wants to come to us. His wife seemed to like the house so I think it will all be settled in a week or so. It was a nice day and I am getting keener on the farm all the time; it is only in the winter that it looks so terribly bleak!

Aidan has already bought five heifers and looked at six more today for which he will make an offer. They have been running with a bull for six weeks so we hope they are in calf. We will therefore start farming with 11 Friesians which ought to mean about £5 worth of milk a day.

There was a lot of work to be done on the farm buildings, installing a milking machine, enlarging the cow byre, repairing the bull pen. We had an estimate of six hundred pounds for a central heating system of twenty-five radiators, which we accepted. We moved in on time, transporting all our furniture and belongings from Gawcott to Kings-bridge with our new Ferguson tractor and trailer. It was a journey of about three miles and we made several trips. The Clarks lived in the old part of the house, Virginia and I in the new and the children in the middle. Harriet was born in London on September 10th. The doctor was swimming in the sea off Brighton when she began to arrive and the only person to help was Mary Holtz, Virginia's blind sister who was married to a Dutch airman and living in London. We took the baby straight down to Kingsbridge. Mary's old nanny came for Harriet's first six months.

The herd gradually grew to sixty milking cows and their heifer followers, for which we used to hire grass 'keeping' from our neigh-bours. Our best cattle-buy happened in the House of Commons. I was telling Rob Hudson, a former Tory Minister of Agriculture, about the farm and when he heard I had Friesians he said he might be able to help. He had a top-class pedigree herd, some of which had produced red and white instead of the normal black and white calves. He could not register the red and white, but they would probably have black and white progeny and in any case would be first-class cows. If I wanted them I could have them at the price of commercial cattle, a hundred and twenty pounds each. I took four of them at once and hoped they would form the basis of our herd.

For a year or two we kept a Jersey cow for the house but, as the butter-fat content of our milk improved, David persuaded me to buy a separator; our great luxury then became lashings of Friesian cream with our porridge. We kept free range, and deep litter, chickens, ducks, a goose and a gander and turkeys. The ducks moved about the farm as a flock and I could never bring myself to kill one for the table. The geese made a terrible mess, but the gander was a great character: whenever any car went down the drive he ran alongside hammering on the door panels with his beak. The turkeys did well and roosted on the posts of a barbed wire fence, but the gipsies soon learned about them and one night silently stole six. In 1950 we bought Fergus, a Friesian bull, who at two years weighed a ton and three quarters. The farm was so isolated that we often turned him out among the cows.

Success, failure and accident alternated. The milk cheque was the basis of the operation, but we sometimes got two tons of wheat to the acre and we sold all our bull calves. I became my own spare milkman

341

and would bully any member of the family to help me over Christmas or Easter when David had a few days off. My younger brother, Kenneth, recalls a bitterly cold Christmas morning when I got him up at six o'clock, gave him a bucket of ice-cold water and a rag and told him to wash the cows' udders as they waited their turn for the machine. Our worst shock came out of the blue. The Electricity Board had a small transformer in our back field for which they paid us a little rent. One morning when David came to milk he saw three dead cows lying near the transformer. They were Rob Hudson's red Friesians. There was a fault in the earth wire and all three had been electrocuted. Any person or other animal going within five yards of the transformer would also have been electrocuted. The Board engineers rushed over and we were paid compensation, but my dream of a pedigree herd had vanished. We would never be able to afford such good cattle again.

Minor accidents happened frequently. At that time there was no law preventing young boys from driving tractors and Andrew became quite expert. One day, however, he fell off and the disc harrow ran over him. Fortunately he lay still and was not even scratched. Andrew also loved operating the pronged lift which we used for loading bales of hay or straw. One day, as he was raising it, Randall rushed up, caught hold of the prongs and was lifted to the full height of ten feet. I saw him hanging there, told Andrew not to move the lift, stood underneath and lifted Randall down. If Andrew had panicked we might both have been badly hurt. By the age of six, Andrew could drive the combine harvester and we earned quite a lot of money hiring ourselves out to neighbours, Andrew tying the sacks as they filled and I driving the harvester. One evening a motor-cycle roared up to the field where we were working, with a message for me to telephone the House of Commons. I apologized to the farmer whose wheat I was cutting, and who was sitting alongside me, but told him that Andrew would drive while I was away if he himself would do the sacks. He looked surprised but I gave him no time to protest. When I came back an hour later, he was all smiles and told me that Andrew was a better driver than I was.

For ten years, with fairly regular injections of our earnings from the BBC and journalism, we broke even or made a small profit. Virginia kept the accounts and we led a life which in retrospect seemed wonderful to both of us. Of course, many hours were spent agonizing over bills and wondering how to make ends meet, but somehow we always managed. To come down after a tense week in Westminster and look out of our bedroom window in the early morning to see the steam rising from our cows' backs as they waited to be taken to the milking parlour, made everything worthwhile. The climax to the year was the harvest, when we would have competitions to see who could load the most bales in the shortest time. Every now and then Virginia or one of the children would let in the tractor clutch too quickly and all the bales and those of us sitting on them would be hurled to the ground in a heap.

We made improvements. A contractor who was building a section of the M1 near Bletchley came and repaired our drive for us. He built us an asphalt tennis court, and followed it up by using his mechanical diggers to make a swimming pool. As we had a cricket net and a croquet set on the lawn, the boys learned to play their games before they went to school.

People came to stay. Herbert Morrison came to open a village fête. When he went up to bed that night, I noticed that he left his shoes outside his bedroom door as if he were in an hotel, so I took them down quietly, cleaned them and put them back. Others who came were Dick and Zita Crossman, Douglas and Peggy Jay, Hugh and Dora Gaitskell, Ann Fleming, Mary and Carl Holtz, Frank and Elizabeth Pakenham. My father made a special trip to see Harriet when she was a month old. I think he had a presentiment that he might not live long, and he died a month later, while making a speech at an old comrades' dinner of the Brigade of Guards.

Then tragedy struck. We had bought some more land jointly with Eric Dudley (who used to hunt with the Whaddon Chase) at the other end of the village of Steeple Claydon and the Clarks had gone to live in their own house. One morning Mrs Clark rang up and asked me to go round quickly. David was upstairs in the bathroom and the floor was covered in blood. He had had an internal haemorrhage and had almost collapsed. I got him to hospital, and after some months he had recovered enough to run a little farm of his own with his son; but he could no longer do the work he had done for me. We persevered for four years but never found a satisfactory substitute. As the children were now in their teens and at boarding schools, they did not always want to come down to the farm in the winter at weekends, but preferred to stay in London. So, sadly, we sold the farm in 1962 to our old friends Jack and Frankie Donaldson.[1] The sale of all our farm machinery in the field beside the house is one of the saddest things I can remember. Harriet felt she had lost the only home she ever knew, but by then much else in our lives had changed and there was no time for regret. We still had not completed our African Odyssey.

43

Communists Foiled

After being thwarted in Ghana and the Congo and stalled by the Emperor of Ethiopia, Professor Potekhin and his Soviet masters seemed suddenly to have been presented with an opportunity to subvert an African territory when, in 1964, revolution broke out on the island of Zanzibar, a British Protectorate. The revolution, engendered by groups of Communists working, for once, under the influence of both the Russians and the Chinese, was more racial than political, an uprising of an African majority against Arab landowners and Indian traders and shopkeepers. There was a massacre, as a result of which the park and beach in front of the Sultan's palace was littered with thousands of bodies. 'Field-Marshal Okello', a Ugandan who had played a considerable part in the revolution, claimed that 11,995 of his 'enemies' had been killed in the first twenty-four hours of the uprising. Communist hopes of a new African base were dashed when President Nyerere, within three months of the outbreak of violence, managed to persuade the new revolutionary President Karume of Zanzibar and Pemba to sign an Act of Union with Tanzania. President Karume stepped down, and in so far as Communist policies were adopted at all, their effects were confined to the islands.

Virginia and I had visited Zanzibar six months before the revolution. It was then certainly one of the most attractive islands in the world: flat but pervaded by the scent of cloves, which provided one of its main exports, endowed with marvellous shallow beaches of silver sand on which it was possible to walk out to sea for half a mile and then sit down in warm water a foot deep and allow the ripples to pass over one's body. It seemed a haven from the turmoil of the rest of Africa. In the old city of Zanzibar the brass-studded wooden doors hid spacious courtyards with tiled floors and walls and fountains, and the streets were so narrow that one had to squeeze into a doorway in order to allow a single car to pass. The English Club, where the windows looked straight on to the sea and the wide rooms were kept fresh by gently swinging punkahs, took one back to the India of the Raj. Turbanned waiters in scarlet uniforms and sashes like those at Viceroy's House in New Delhi silently served breakfast. A lawn and a concrete slipway led down to the beach where a fleet of small sailing boats lay at anchor. There were regattas almost every weekend. In the evening the townspeople spilled out on to the park by the sea and strolled in front of the Sultan's palace. The flowing white robes of the Arabs and the saris of the Indian ladies made a beautiful peaceful picture. Nothing could have been more deceptive.

We visited the two main Communist headquarters, small, shabby bungalows covered in Marxist slogans. Piles of books and magazines – almost all in English – were stacked against the walls. Young Africans sat around on the books or squatted on the floor. For the first time in Africa we found that the Chinese were competing with the Russians on almost equal terms, each country having penetrated one political party and one of the rival trade union federations. Each had supplied their 'contact' with large sums of money; each had invited trade union leaders to Moscow or Peking and had made an unforgettable impression. In Moscow the Zanzibaris had been awed by a sense of power; in Peking by the friendliness of the people. One man who had been on a tour from Peking to Shanghai, and had visited factories, trade union headquarters, communes, People's Courts and 'Palaces of Leisure', said: 'One can make no greater mistake than to imagine that the people of China are not behind the government. I have never seen such enthusiasm anywhere.'

As we talked, we realized that these young Africans had felt at home in China because the life of the Chinese peasant was so close to their own and because the Chinese loved to laugh. However, if it ever came to a struggle for power between the two Communist factions in Zanzibar, there was no doubt in our minds which country would exercise a dominant influence. Three times as many students from Zanzibar had already gone to Russia or Iron Curtain countries than to China. The Chinese were inhibited by an almost impenetrable language barrier. They spoke neither Arabic, Swahili nor any other African language. Students going to China had to spend at least two years learning elementary Chinese. They could not hope to write it.

We visited several Chinese embassies in African countries, where the diplomatic language was English, and found no one with whom we could really communicate. One smiling First Secretary answered all our questions with the words 'Of course'. We suspected that they were the only English words he knew, so we decided to test him. 'Do you agree,' we asked, 'that the Chinese People's Government is a harsh dictatorship with little or no contact with its own people?' He gave us the same answer with the same tooth-revealing smile. In all the thirty African countries we visited, we found only one Chinese project in the field, and that was in the Cameroons, where it had been a failure. Although several Russian and East European projects had also failed, Russia was in a position to supply far more and better equipment than China and had wider industrial experience. The Chinese had organized several trade exhibitions but they had become almost a joke in Africa because of the poor quality and narrow range of the goods on offer. While we were writing our report we read several articles in English and French newspapers suggesting that the Chinese were likely to supplant the Russians as both advisers and suppliers in the newly independent African countries. This we found to be nonsense. Perhaps the Chinese are a more sympathetic people to both Africans and Europeans, but during this period they were far too preoccupied with maintaining the impetus of their own revolution to be able to take more than a superficial interest in other continents.

*

We did a lot of motoring in West Africa, visiting Senegal, Mali, the Ivory Coast, Guinea, Sierra Leone and Nigeria. I have a photograph of Virginia and me in a Land Rover embarking on a chain ferry across a river near the frontier between Guinea and Sierra Leone. It reminds me of one thing about that long journey. In the last village in Guinea – to judge from a map, it must have been Kukura – we passed a statue in the little square which was garlanded with flowers and found it was of Patrice Lumumba: a black stone head on a plinth with real hair on the head and face and a pair of spectacles on the nose. The lenses had been broken. Flowers were scattered at the base of the plinth. We asked a young man whether Lumumba had lived in or visited this village. He said he did not think so, but that he was a great hero in the region.

We also drove from Lagos to Lomé, the capital of Togo, crossing the state of Dahomey (now Benin). Until 1960, Togo had been the eastern part of Togoland, a former German protectorate divided in 1922 into territories administered by British mandate (west) and French (east). In 1957, the western half of the country was incorporated into Ghana, just before the latter achieved independence, and in 1961 Togo, the eastern half, became an independent country.

Lomé was a pleasant little town, lying along a palm-fringed stretch of coast. In the middle of the town stood the square white German schloss where the newly elected President, Mr Sylvanus Olympio, lived. Born a member of the Ewe tribe while the country was still a German colony, Mr Olympio was educated in English and French schools after the British had conquered the country in the First World War, and had taken a degree at the London School of Economics. For many years he had been the manager of the United Africa Company, a subsidiary of Unilever in Togoland. He was pro-Western and pro-British and welcomed us warmly.

Surprisingly, he was also welcoming a growing number of Russian salesmen. 'My Unilever training makes me think in terms of prices,' he explained, and went on to say that the price of Russian goods was so much below those of any Western country that although the quality was inferior, he considered them a good buy for his people. Russian cement and bicycles were doing well and the only available matches in Lomé were also Russian, although you normally had to strike at least eight before one would light.

There were also bookshops in Lomé, supervised by two Russian women whom we saw driving about in a jeep. The books, mainly in French, were the ones we had seen in every Communist bookshop in Africa, including the *Collected Works of Lenin*, *Lives of Russian Revolutionary Heroes*, *Das Kapital*, the *Communist Manifesto* and a few modern tracts attacking the Common Market and NATO. The shops also stocked Chinese children's books like *La Route Etincelante*, *Hon Li* or *Grand Lin et Petit Lin*, well printed and illustrated and far more attractive than anything the British or Americans were offering. Yet when we visited the reading rooms, the Communist room was always empty while the American room, in a different building and containing English and French classical novels and technical magazines, was quite crowded.

Mr Olympio disliked Nkrumah, President of Ghana, whom he

described as a man 'obsessed with fears'. He said that Togoland was giving refuge to more than six thousand Ghanaian refugees and they were still coming in at the rate of sixty a week. We talked to many of them and learned more about what was really going on in Ghana than we had in Ghana itself. Nkrumah's tyranny, they told us, reached down into every station of Ghanaian life. All those to whom we talked had relations in prison and many had seen members of their family killed. The hatred for Nkrumah was such that they were convinced he could not last.

We warmed to Mr Olympio. He was original and refreshing, yet we felt that like so many other African leaders thrown up by the convulsions of independence, he was doomed. He had quashed the opposition parties in his recent general election and, indeed, the groundswell of unrest which we sensed then was to end two years later in his assassination. It was not until after a second military coup in 1967 and the election of M. Eyadema as President, that Togo knew any stability.

*

I do not remember whether we travelled by boat or by air to Duala, the port of the Cameroons, but we went there because the country had been a minor East–West battlefield for the past six years.

The French Cameroons were granted independence early in 1960 and the western province of the British Cameroons elected to integrate with the new republic. The Federation was formed in 1961 and, a few months before we arrived, British troops were withdrawn. A large section of the Union of Cameroon Peoples, led by M. Mayi Matip, broke away from the terrorists and was recognized by President Ahidjo as the official opposition. They subsequently won twelve seats in the Federal Parliament at the general election. We arrived in Duala at the end of November 1961 and after a few days flew to the capital, Yaoundé, which lies in beautiful hilly country about two hundred miles to the east.

There was a considerable discrepancy between what we had been told in London and Lagos about the Cameroons and what we discovered when we arrived in Yaoundé. The inhabitants of the western Cameroons were said to be living in terror more of the Cameroonian Army than of the Communist guerrillas; in one unofficial report, we read that Cameroonian soldiers had killed a hundred

349

thousand Cameroonian civilians. But in Paris, before leaving for Africa, we had been warned that the French advisers of the Cameroonian Government considered British fears of disorders greatly exaggerated, and we found that the French were right.

The Cameroonian troops had in fact behaved admirably. A British businessman from Victoria, the port of Buea in the former British-administered province, told us that his business had been unaffected by the change of regime, and added that much of the misinformation which was reaching Lagos and Whitehall was due to resentment felt by former British officials at the choice made by the Cameroonians to join the Federation rather than Nigeria. Most of these officials had now gone home. M. Foncha, the leader of the former British Cameroons, had insisted on retaining the forms of British parliamentary democracy in his province, and his opponent, M. Endele, was still allowed to campaign freely in favour of joining Nigeria; but M. Foncha and his colleagues had become loyal supporters of President Ahidjo. The truth was that the new Federation had got off to an excellent start.

Kingsbridge Farm, Steeple Claydon, Bucks: our home from 1948
to 1962

Kingsbridge, 1951. Virginia and myself with our three children:
Andrew, Randall, Harriet. (My mother had used the swing chair
when she was a child)

A patrol in the Malayan jungle, 1951. I am in the white hat,
carrying a revolver, on an official visit as Under-Secretary
of State for Air

Filming for a *See It Now* programme for Ed Murrow, 1954. We
were visiting a privately owned oil well in a Texas back garden

Farnborough Air Show, 1951. *Left to right*: Air Marshal Sir Basil
Embury, Princess Elizabeth and myself

Farnborough Air Show, 1951. *Left to right*: Secretary of State for
Air, Arthur Henderson; Air Marshal Sir Ralph Cochrane; King
George VI; Queen Elizabeth; myself

Virginia, myself and Harriet in Parliament Square on the way to
take my seat as Member for West Derbyshire, June 1962

44

Turbans and Robes

Nigeria was then and still could be the most important country in West Africa. We went there many times. My first visit was in 1946, after the West African Council meetings in Freetown; then eleven years later I went again for the BBC series *The Inheritors*, accompanied by Virginia and Tony de Lothbiniere, our producer. Wherever we went, the local managers of Barclays Bank kindly put us up. These were the last days of Nigeria as the British had known it. The Sardauna of Sokoto, an Emir of great dignity and authority, was still the Premier of the Northern Province, Chief Awololo led the Western Province, and Dr Azikiwe the Eastern Province. Dr Abubakar Balewa was the Federal Prime Minister, and Chief Festus Obote-Eboe had just been appointed Finance Minister.

I interviewed both Chief Festus and Dr Balewa. The Chief wore a Nigerian robe and a straw boater with a white feather in it. He was a buccaneer in the sense often used in British politics: large, genial and unscrupulous, with a tremendous laugh and total confidence. I had been told that he was corrupt and had already amassed more than a million pounds. We discussed the coming of independence and he was optimistic, believing it was Nigeria's destiny to lead West Africa in the coming decades.

Dr Balewa was a great contrast. He was known to be incorruptible and several stories were circulating in Lagos about European and American businessmen who had had the temerity to offer him money in return for a contract. They did not remain in the country long. He was temperamentally and religiously opposed to Communism and socialism because both, in his opinion, involved intimidation, but he had a profound belief in the future of Nigeria. After patiently answering our questions for some time, Dr Abubakar suddenly interrupted the interview, saying it was time for him to say his prayers. He then withdrew to the next room leaving the door open and we could hear him praying. After five minutes he returned and continued the interview.

Three years later, in 1961, when he had become Sir Abubakar Tafawa Balewa, I talked to him again. It was after we had seen the left-wing leaders of the Nigerian trade unions and the Youth Congress as part of our enquiry into the infiltration of Communism. The Youth Congress, under the leadership of Dr Otegbe, had claimed fifty thousand members throughout Nigeria and were considering forming a new political party, hoping that 'Zik' (Dr Azikiwe) would become the Nigerian Marxist leader. Sir Abubakar dismissed our suggestions that belief in socialism was spreading, saying that all those to whom we had been talking were 'subversives'. Nigeria, he added, was a predominantly Moslem country and would having nothing to do with Marxism or socialism.

One afternoon I interviewed the Governor, Sir James Robertson, a Scot as robust in appearance as in character. It was a memorable day, because the Chief Justice, Sir Stafford Foster-Sutton, had lent me two ponies to join in a game of polo. It was a scratch game on iron-hard ground. Two of our opponents were Emirs from the Hausa country in the north, and both wore blue cloaks which, at full gallop, billowed out and made them look like ships in full sail. It also made it hard to see the ball if one was coming up from behind. My interview with the Governor was at four-thirty p.m. and I stopped playing polo in plenty of time, as I thought, to have a bath and change; but although I did both, I had underestimated the humidity of Lagos and when I presented myself I was still sweating so profusely that Sir James suggested we postpone the interview for a couple of hours. When we talked he was mainly concerned with how many British civil servants would accept the offer of the Government to extend their tour of duty so as to give the newly independent Federation a good start. Whitehall had made a foolish financial arrangement under which most of them were paid to resign immediately.

We went to Ibadan to see Chief Awolowo, the Premier of the Western Region, and also to attend a ball at the university. The ball was enchanting; dozens of young Yoruba women in blue robes with voluminous turbans danced to drums in the open air with that slow, erotic rhythm which I had hitherto associated more with Hawaii than Africa. Some of the young men wore European dress, but none of the couples touched each other, moving their hips and hands in unison while their shoulders remained steady.

The Yorubas are one of the ablest and most volatile of Nigerian peoples. Chief Awolowo was a worthy representative. He spoke better English than most Nigerians, who are sometimes hard to understand. (I remember once in London at some Colonial Office gathering asking two men in Nigerian dress what language they were speaking and being surprised at the rather indignant reply, 'English, of course.' I also found debates in the Federal Assembly in Lagos hard to follow.) Chief Awolowo had accepted the federal constitution which was to follow independence with the clear intention of achieving maximum autonomy for the Western Region. He was more radical than the other provincial premiers and one felt he would not hesitate to ally himself with Nkrumah if he felt it would enhance his freedom of action. But he was intelligent and entertaining.

From Ibadan we drove to Ife and then on to Benin City. The Oni of Ife reminded me of Ambedkar in India. He was larger than life and twinkling with fun. I had been told that many of his people regarded him as a god and, in front of the camera, I asked him if that was how he thought of himself. He laughed loudly and said, 'No, I know I am not God, but many of my people think I am. They expect too much of me and that makes life difficult.' The Oba of Benin, on the other hand, was a rather sinister character. He had invited us to his palace at six-thirty in the evening and we were led straight to a large room where he was playing billiards. The full-sized table was surrounded by boys, who I was told were slaves, acting as markers, picking the balls out of pockets and if necessary putting them on spots. The Oba at once invited us to play. He was thin, of medium height, unsmiling and dressed in white. He was also very short-sighted and more than once missed his cue ball. Luckily neither Tony de Lothbiniere nor I, nor the English civil servant who was accompanying us, were any good, so we had an amusing match. Both the game and dinner were made unusual by a diminutive figure in a large straw hat carrying a solid wooden fan with a long handle (rather like a deck-tennis bat) who turned out to be the Oba's 'joker'. At any moment he would wave his fan, bow to the Oba, and then utter piercing sounds which echoed through the palace; he was apparently reciting poetry, or simply commenting, often unfavourably, on the Oba's guests. The Oba took no notice but made no effort to

353

stop him. Like jokers of old in Europe, this one had licence to do and say what he liked.

When we left the city next day our guide pointed to a column of smoke which was rising from behind the palace walls and told us that it was probably due to the sacrifice of some young girl. The Oba, we gathered, was neither Moslem nor Christian but pagan, and given to pagan rites. No one had been able to catch him red-handed, and none of his servants dared speak, but it was known in the city that some girls had mysteriously disappeared.

For our BBC series we drove north to Jos, where Tony and I played golf on what must be the rockiest course in the world, and so on to Kaduna, Kano and Katsina. The Hausa people, who number some fifty million, are Moslems, and their country – a vast arid plateau in which villages and towns are built of mud bricks sometimes painted ochre-red – is far more like Iraq than southern Nigeria. One felt once more in the Arab world. The Emir of Kano, one of the most powerful chiefs in Nigeria, received us in a red palace with crenellated walls, but would not give an interview. The Emir of Katsina, however, who lived on the northern border where Nigeria marches with the former French Niger, was friendly and impressive. Young, small but athletic and smiling, he was every inch a ruler and plainly commanded the allegiance of all around him. At the time he was one of the best polo players in the world, with a handicap of ten. One could easily see why. Horses abounded and, as there were few roads, the normal way to travel was to ride. The country was flat and treeless and it was possible to gallop for miles in almost any direction. The Emir was hopeful about independence, but nervous that people in the south might be influenced by Ghana and try to destroy the influence of the hereditary chiefs. 'Up here,' he added, 'it might be necessary to secede.'[1]

It must have been on a subsequent trip that Virginia and I visited Enugu, the capital of the Eastern Province, because 'Zik', formerly Premier, had by then become Governor-General of the Nigerian Federation. As Chancellor of the University of Enugu, he was granting degrees to some sixty undergraduates, several of whom were women. It was a splendidly scholastic occasion with all the undergraduates in gowns and 'Zik' in full Chancellor's robes with gold embroidery and a gold tassel on his mortar-board. He performed the ceremony with great dignity. We were, however, surprised that only two out of the sixty

354

degrees were in agriculture, where the need was greatest. 'Zik's' acceptance of Governor-Generalship had come as a shock to all the young Afro-Marxists who had been hoping to persuade him to become their leader. He disappointed them still further by criticizing Nkrumah in uncompromising terms and emerging as the leader of the Monrovia Group of West African countries who pledged themselves to uphold democracy. The Ibos, who dominated the Eastern Province, were generally considered the cleverest of the Nigerian peoples and provided civil servants and accountants for the whole Federation, particularly the Northern Province.

Back in Lagos we stayed with Antony Head whom I had known for many years. He was British High Commissioner in Nigeria from 1960 to 1963, and a delightful host. It was he who arranged for us to listen to a debate in the Federal Parliament. Although informal and intimate in debate, the robes and turbans worn by the members gave the occasion a dignity not easily matched in Europe. Antony had a marmot which used to twine itself around his neck as he ate breakfast and was always turning up in odd places. His wife, Dot, knew many talented artists and sculptors. She gave us a beautiful wooden head of a girl which still sits in our drawing room.

The hopes which we, in common with most other foreign observers, entertained for Nigeria, proved illusory. In January 1966, a revolution occurred not through Communist or other left-wing agencies but because the army commanders could not control mutinous troops. Two of the most respected men in Nigeria, Sir Abubakar Balewa, Federal Prime Minister, and Sir Ahmadu Bello, Sardauna of Sokoto and Premier of the Northern Province, were shot dead on the first day by mutineers, and many others were to follow. General Aguiyi-Ironsi, the Commander-in-Chief, took charge, abrogated the constitution and declared a military government. He in turn was ousted after three months by Lieutenant-Colonel Gowon. Since that time Nigeria has alternated between corrupt civilian rule and military government and has lost much of its influence in the African world.

45

Kenya and Uganda

I felt I knew Kenya even before we went there. My cousin Eliot Crawley, who had captained the Harrow XI in 1924 and had given me my 'flannels', had gone out there to work on a farm. He used to write long letters to my father, describing the life. Interspersed with details of the crops they were growing – sisal, alfalfa, pineapples, avocados, maize and fruits such as citrus and mangoes – were stories about his 'boys', as he called his African farmhands, and of cricket and polo matches. It was the heyday of the white settlers who, with encouragement from the British Government, went out in their thousands after the First World War. The country sounded glorious and the life idyllic for an athletic young man.

Superficially, the reality lived up to the imaginary. Soon after we first arrived in Nairobi, Virginia and I got up just before dawn and drove out into the game park on the edge of the town. We had promised our hosts that under no circumstances would we get out of the car. Our first and greatest thrill came quite soon. We were driving slowly up a rise in the open plain when we saw, about fifty yards in front of us, a herd of impala crossing the road in single file. We crept on a little and stopped, and saw that they were not just crossing the road but playing a game; they galloped in a circle and when each animal came to the road it made a glorious leap, clearing the tarmac with a margin that took one's breath away. They must have been doing this for at least ten minutes while we watched, only moving away as the sun began to show above the horizon. I had seen fox cubs playing at first light in England, but it had never occurred to either of us that a whole herd of deer would do such a thing just for the joy of being alive.

A little further on we saw four pairs of eyes and four pairs of fluffy ears looking at us from a scrubby knoll about ten yards to our left. They were lion cubs; their mother must have been with them, but was out of sight from the road. We all sat quite still looking at each other. Then we drove on. After perhaps half a mile we saw a signpost saying 'Hippo Pool'. We drove towards it and stopped under some trees by a small river. Several hippopotomi came to the surface and stared at us from the water. Suddenly there was a thump on the roof of the car, and then another. We could not think what it was until we saw red behinds loping away from us. The baboons were also playing a game, galloping at us and jumping on and off the roof of the car just for the fun of it. During the next twenty-five years we were to return many times to Kenya but nothing ever quite equalled the delight of that first morning.

In Nairobi we stayed with Michael and Susan Wood. He had been a pupil of Sir Archibald McIndoe, the most famous plastic surgeon in Britain who had performed wonders for wounded servicemen during the war and whom Virginia had known well. Michael was now a consultant surgeon at Nairobi's King George VI Hospital (now the Jomo Kenyatta Hospital). Susan had been a Buxton, eight members of which clan had been at Harrow with me. Her parents were Alfred and Edith Buxton, he a missionary and both of them pioneers in Africa. As a baby, Susan had been carried in a hammock on a safari from the Congo to Juba on the Nile. She has the bluest of blue eyes and red hair of a particularly beautiful shade and is a remarkable woman in her own right. I think it was she who first told us about Michael's visit to Dr Albert Schweitzer, one of his great heroes, when Schweitzer was running a medical mission deep in the jungle in the Gabon. Michael owned a single-engined aeroplane and had set off from Nairobi with Susan as his navigator to find his way to the doctor's hospital at Lambarene. It must have been a hair-raising journey through Zambia and across the Congo, because the rain forest is monotonous, maps were inaccurate and landmarks difficult to pick out. But after several days' flying they succeeded.

In that same aeroplane Michael flew us up to his farm at Ol Molog in Tanganyika on the slopes of Kilimanjaro just below the tree line. There were eight farms round the mountain, all of which had been leased by Englishmen from the Tanganyika Government. We landed in standing corn and walked up to the house, which stood close to the forest looking north towards the Equator across Amboseli and the Masai Jami. It must have been one of the most beautiful farming sites in the world. Our neighbours were Bill Stirling, who had commanded the

SAS in the war after his brother David had been taken prisoner; Derek Bryceson, another Englishman, who became Minister for Agriculture in Tanzania; and Robin Johnston, who had been with me in 73 Squadron in the desert. He reminded me that the last time we had spoken was over the radio at Sidi Hanish on the day I was shot down.

Below Ol Molog, on the edge of the plain, we could see the *manyattas* of the Masai, circles made of thick thorn hedges into which the tribe and their cattle withdrew at night for protection against lions and other predators. Michael took us to visit some of them. Their huts were made of rough sticks and mud with earth floors and no furniture. Inside there was an overwhelming smell of dung. One manyatta was inhabited only by young men and women between the ages of sixteen and nineteen who, according to Masai custom, had been segregated for two years from their families. Venereal disease was common and the Masai population was steadily falling. The young men and women were tall and thin and all wore a long red-ochre cloak called a *shuka* which came almost to their ankles. The women wore beads and the men carried spears. They were semi-nomadic, moving across a wide area of Kenya and Tanganyika, a proud and independent people, unsmiling and not very friendly. According to the custom of the tribe, the young men attained manhood only when they had killed a lion, alone and armed with a shield and a spear. A week or so later, in Michael's waiting room in the hospital at Nairobi, I saw one of these young men with long, bleeding claw marks down the sides of his face, waiting patiently to be treated. He spoke to no one and regarded us all with proud disdain.

It must have been on a later trip that Michael allowed me to film an operation. He had a five nation team including a Portuguese anaesthetist. I was doing the camera work myself, and after about an hour I took a rest. Looking through the lens, I had concentrated on trying to make what was happening intelligible to a television viewer and had felt totally detached, but when I sat down and watched from the side of the room I suddenly felt faint. I murmured to Michael that I was afraid of passing out and thought I ought to leave. He replied severely, 'Pull yourself together. I am not going to have you disgracing me in front of my team.' His words acted like an electric shock and I watched and filmed the operation through to the end.

On January 4th, 1959, we drove north to stay with a cousin of mine who lived in a house near Naro Moru at the foot of Mount Kenya. She had been born a Gibbs, daughter of my mother's eldest brother, and married Charles Bathurst-Norman, whose fag I had been at Harrow and who was now a District Officer in the Colonial Service. They drove us up Mount Kenya in a jeep to the top of the tree line, getting stuck in a bog on the way from which even the four-wheel drive had difficulty in extricating us. At eleven thousand feet we got out and walked a little, but the stretch between us and the rocky summit six thousand feet above was treacherous mountain bog and the rocks themselves could only be tackled by a trained mountaineer. One of the first men to climb the mountain had been Sir Percy Wyn-Harris, our host in the Gambia and a great friend of Charles.

1958 was an uneasy time in Kenya. Sir Evelyn Baring, the Governor who had seen the country through the whole of the Mau Mau rebellion and was trusted by a majority of Africans and Europeans, had had his term of office extended by eighteen months to the spring of 1959. But people were worried by what might happen when he left. The metamorphosis of Jomo Kenyatta was under way, but no one was sure how far it would go. It was widely feared that he was only waiting for independence to embark on an orgy of property confiscation and the eviction of Whites and Asians, though in fact this never happened. Mr Oginga Odinga, who was thought to have received as much as seventy-five thousand pounds from the Russians and to have paid Mr Kenyatta's debts, was still a leading member of the Kenya African National Union and possessed enough influence in some constituencies to determine who should become a candidate for the Assembly.

These fears were fanned by the constant agitation, led by Mr Tom Mboya, to have Kenyatta released from house arrest in the northern province so that he could take his place as President of KANU and lead his country into independence. However, Mboya need not have worried. When independence came in December 1963, before Kenyatta's release, it was not his but Oginga Odinga's influence which was in decline. Kenyatta was to emerge as the true father of his country and it is due to him and to Europeans like David Stirling and Michael Wood, who succeeded David as President of the Capricorn Africa Society, that Kenya is one of the few states in the world in which a White minority lives in harmony with a ruling majority of Blacks. Mr Oginga Odinga is still alive, but his name is seldom mentioned.

*

We drove to Uganda, spending a night in the former Government House at Entebbe, the old administrative capital overlooking Lake Victoria. The lawn running down towards the lake was still mown and the view was enchanting, but the house felt unlived in and gloomy. The next day we drove to the commercial capital, Kampala. In the diary from which I have already quoted, I wrote: 'The most peaceful country we visited was land-locked Uganda, half-modern, which has not yet made up its mind what policy to pursue.' It was not to be peaceful for long. Independence had come in 1962 and the first general election towards the end of that year had thrown up Mr Milton Obote, leader of the Uganda Peoples' Congress, as Prime Minister. He was an unusual-looking man, small and lithe, with a prominent forehead and a shock of black hair parted so that it stood out to one side of his head. He had very bright black eyes and the most beautiful hands. His long, delicate fingers were constantly moving to express what he wanted to say.

Mr Obote had inherited a political dog's dinner. The Kabaka of Buganda, Sir Edward Frederick Mutasa (or 'King Freddie', as he was known in the British Brigade of Guards of which he had been an officer), having failed to persuade either the British Government or the United Nations to grant independence to his own Bugandan kingdom, which comprised a third of the Ugandan population, became Federal President of the new republic. Nevertheless, he was determined to retain his rule over his own kingdom which included the two major cities of Entebbe and Kampala. The rulers of the three smaller kingdoms, Ankole, Bunyoro and Toro, also wanted a federation which left them their tribal autonomy. When we talked to Mr Obote, who had been in office only a few weeks, he was clearly unsure whether he should align Uganda firmly with the Commonwealth or look for aid to the Communist world; but his immediate problem was the unification of the country. In the end it was to take him five years to merge the four tribal kingdoms into the republic which the Ugandan People's Party demanded. As President, the Kabaka had refused to sign the constitution incorporating the four kingdoms, and eventually a pitched battle took place around his palace between his guards and the Ugandan Army. About a thousand people were killed. The Kabaka fled and died in London in 1969. After that, Mr Obote came out in his true colours as a left-wing autocrat, nationalizing every activity in the country, including the banks, and suppressing opposition through emergency powers. In January 1971 he was overthrown by an army coup led by General Idi Amin. It is perhaps a measure of the horror of the regime instituted by his successor that Mr Obote again became President in 1979.

46

The Inheritors

The last of my television series was the most ambitious. It was an extension of the theme of *India's Challenge*, a view of the progress made by several former colonies since the granting of independence. Antony de Lothbiniere was the producer and, since the programmes would span the world, we decided to spread them out over two years. This did not prevent either of us from doing other less demanding jobs in between. We decided also that to give us some basis for comparison, we would include one of the older Dominions which had been operating as an independent country within the Commonwealth for several generations. We chose Australia. Besides Australia, we planned to cover East, West and Central Africa, the West Indies, and Malaya. We also included a second visit to India to take a rather more political view than had been possible in *India's Challenge*. There were to be seven programmes in all, scheduled for transmission in the last two months of 1958. We started filming in 1957, in the West Indies.

Our first stop was Jamaica. Having been left in charge of the conference on the Federation of the West Indies in 1947, I was delighted to be returning to Jamaica in 1958, when the Federation was actually coming into being. Ian Fleming, an old friend, had told me that I could use his house, Golden Eye, at Ocho Rios on the north coast. It was a bungalow with a separate building where Ian used to work on his James Bond stories, and there were several patios. The main point of interest, however, was a little bay cut off from the sea by a coral reef which ran straight across its mouth, just below the surface of the water. The reef was about sixty yards from the boathouse. We would paddle out on lilos, put on snorkelling goggles and ease our way across the rough coral until we could look down into the ocean below. It was about seventy feet deep beyond the reef, and if one was patient one could see a great variety of fish, including barracuda. On two occasions, Jamaicans came along and, without goggles or masks, dived down to the bottom, speared a fish and carried it away. The whole operation took them between one and two minutes.

A Sword of Damocles hung over the Federation from the start. Jamaica, the largest and by far the most populous island, was separated by fifteen hundred miles of sea from Barbados and by almost as much from the Windward and Leeward Islands in the east, which formed the bulk of the Federation. Jamaica had little in common with the other islands and was always afraid of being dragged down by their poverty. Yet if Jamaica left, the Federation would collapse because none of the small islands wished to come under the domination of the second largest, Trinidad, which was their neighbour. In 1958, the Federation included Jamaica, but there was a general feeling that Norman Manley, the Prime Minister, would not stay in very long. There was therefore an air of unreality about the whole situation. Everyone was thinking more about what would happen when the Federation broke up than about how to make it strong and durable. As it turned out, both Jamaica and Trinidad left the Federation within four years, at the end of 1961. It was dissolved at the end of May 1962, a new Federation of the smaller Windward and Leeward Islands taking its place.

From Jamaica we flew straight to Trinidad to interview Lord Hailes, the Governor-General of the new Federation, and Sir Grantley Adams, the Federal Prime Minister who had been to Oxford and had been called to the English Bar. He was a delightful man and loved cricket, but one had the feeling that he was too gentle a soul to cope with buccaneers like Alexander Bustamente, Eric Williams and Albert Gomes. His premiership lasted little more than four years.

We then set off in a light aeroplane, hopping up the Windward Islands: St Vincent, like a garden with beautiful small beaches; St Lucia, with its Pitons like the alps of Jura; Dominica, whose range of mountains reached a height of nearly five thousand feet; and Antigua. In St Lucia we stayed with the Governor, Lord Oxford, a son of Raymond Asquith who had been killed in the First World War, and grandson of Herbert Asquith, the Prime Minister who resigned in 1916. Lord Oxford had married Anne Palairet, a member of the famous cricketing family; their two teenaged daughters, Annunziata and Katie Asquith, were with them. It was refreshing to be in a family and the visit cast long shadows. A decade later my youngest son,

Randall, fell in love with Annunziata when both were at Oxford, and our two families became close friends. The two girls joined my children in the family art business which still flourishes.

We had been inadequately briefed about Antigua. No one had told us that we had timed our visit to coincide with a four-day fiesta during which the entire population took a holiday. No one did any work, nor went to bed. We learned this from the taxi driver who took nearly an hour to reach our hotel. Every street in St John's, the capital, was jammed with people dancing the calypso to a succession of steel bands which were spaced at intervals of two or three hundred yards. When we got to our hotel we dumped our suitcases, armed ourselves with cameras and went back into the town.

It was impossible not to dance. The rhythm was intoxicating and men and women swept one into their line or circle with irresistible enthusiasm. For the next three days we never saw anything but laughing, smiling faces and never took a step that was not in time to music. The instruments of the bands were all home-made, including the drums, and consisted mostly of old bits of iron beaten with other bits of metal. I cannot remember anything like a saxophone or a trumpet. We would drop into bed when we could dance no more and awake to the sound of the bands which never stopped. In the end the crew left their cameras behind because they had shot enough footage, but still we danced.

One of the objects of coming to Antigua had been to meet Mr Byrd, the Chief Minister. He was said to be an engaging character who, as head of the island's one trade union, was at that moment leading a general strike against himself as head of the government. It was impossible to set up a meeting until the fiesta was over as no one could find Mr Byrd or any of his assistants. When finally one afternoon we ran an assistant to ground, he said the Chief Minister was asleep but would certainly see us the following morning. Mr Byrd turned out to be a tall, genial man with slightly greying hair. When I asked him, in front of the camera, whether he found any incompatibility in leading a general strike on behalf of his trade union against himself as Chief Minister, he laughed loudly and replied, 'None whatever. The strike is going well, but of course, the Government will decide what to do.' He held both offices simultaneously for many years.

Barbados was our last port of call. The sugar-cane was standing and there was a cruise liner in Georgetown Harbour, but the three-hundred-year-old Parliament was not sitting and Sir Grantley Adams, the Chief Minister, was away in Trinidad. We foreswore politics and filmed the parishes and their people. The difference between them was marked. In a small parish called St John's we filmed poor whites, a group of families who lived exactly as their co-villagers but did not intermarry. When I asked them about their ancestry, none of them seemed to know from whom they stemmed. They had been poor whites for several generations and were becoming in-bred, but although they were not increasing in numbers, neither were they disappearing.

When I started to write these reminiscences I went to the Commonwealth Library in Great Smith Street and tried to find some account of their origins from old histories and parish records, but without success. However, since I had to spend a night in Barbados on my way to join a cruise through the Windward Islands at the beginning of March 1985, I took the opportunity to drive out to St John's and see if I could discover more at first hand. The village had not greatly changed over the years. Some of the houses looked smarter, but the inhabitants were obviously poor. Immediately, I noticed black and white children walking and playing together; the keeper of one of the stores was a white woman who might have been doing the same job in any English village, but she was too busy to talk. A few houses further on I saw a very handsome young white man with a beard and blue eyes doing some carpentry. He said that I would find white Barbadians scattered all over the island, not just in St John's. When I asked him if he knew anything about his ancestors, he said, 'I don't even know who my own father was. A lot of us don't. Nowadays we intermarry with blacks much more than in the past, so you'll find a lot of mixed families. No one thinks anything of it. We are just white Barbadians.' Two of his neighbours said they had white relations, but it was not a subject of any particular interest. The probability is that seamen or convicts settled in considerable numbers and lay low. This happened not only in Barbados but in most of the other islands as well. Even the phrase 'poor whites' has now died out.

*

In picking Australia as the old Dominion to be used as a basis of comparison with the new independent colonies, we had chosen well.

Isolated from the mainstreams of migration over the centuries and also from the competitive assault of colonizing powers, it has a homogeneity which even the influx of three or four million immigrants from Europe after the Second World War has been unable to disturb. Australia is still a country in which it is possible to study the development of British characteristics and institutions, unalloyed by more than a smattering of external influences.

In 1958, when Tony de Lothbiniere and I arrived to complete the last programme of *The Inheritors*, the prospect was exciting. After prospecting in northern Australia for twenty years, Jack White had found large deposits of uranium. Sir Ian Clunies-Ross, having relieved Australia of its plague of rabbits through the deliberate spread of myxomatosis, was rendering thousands of barren acres fertile by the application of 'trace elements' derived from cobalt and copper. At the same time he was carrying out experiments in rain-making; in areas where a certain amount of cloud existed, he was increasing rainfall by a quarter. Professor Marcus Oliphant, Australia's leading nuclear physicist, was continuing experiments with 'Zeta', the application of nuclear energy to sea-water, by which he believed it would be possible to irrigate tens of thousands of square miles with fresh water for sixpence per thousand gallons – far less than I paid for water on my farm in Buckinghamshire. Emptiness, Australia's overriding problem, seemed on the point of being conquered.

In Canberra people talked of making the bush blossom. They said that a new kind of immigrant would be needed: not peasant farmers from Indonesia but people capable of farming on a large scale. Rum Jungle in the Northern Territory and Mary Kathleen in Queensland, where uranium had been found, would become great new industrial centres based on the use of nuclear power. Europe and the United States would provide the machinery, skill and credit.

Not everyone shared this intoxicating dream. More than three-quarters of the ten million people who then inhabited Australia lived in the great cities and their outlook was bounded by their surroundings. Even today, tens of thousands of citizens of Melbourne and Sydney have never been further afield than the most convenient beaches and only a tiny proportion of the people know or care about the outback. But in any country only a small proportion of the people have the urge to be pioneers and, as we crossed and recrossed Australia (we flew more than forty thousand miles in three months), we never doubted that the Australians would meet any challenge which science could set them. We were constantly meeting people who were buying land in the interior or forming syndicates to start some new enterprise. When we landed at Brisbane airport we were met by a crowd of journalists and prospectors whose first question was 'How much money have you got?', followed by an assurance that the questioner could double it in a week. Some of them came from Surfers' Paradise, a stretch of beach to the north of Brisbane which had once belonged to a retired Group Captain of the RAF. Some years before, he had bought the land at about sixpence an acre, built himself a small two-storeyed house and waited for the developers. None came, and he was rapidly running through his savings when a journalist friend told him that what he needed was 'a name'. After talking through the night they came up with 'Surfers' Paradise'. The Group Captain then spent the last of his money on a series of advertisements.

As we walked along the beach, every shop and ice-cream stand was doing a roaring trade. Most of them changed hands every few months as the owners took their profit. In some parts of Surfers' Paradise, sites on the beach for which the Group Captain had paid sixpence an acre were selling for a thousand dollars a square foot. He himself had sold out and gone to another part of the country.

From Brisbane we began a whistle-stop tour of the continent. The signs of Japanese bombing were still visible in Darwin, the capital of the Northern Territory. What I had not realized was that Darwin was not part of a state but a colony, governed directly from Canberra, nearly two thousand miles away. Instead of the cattle men, prospectors and geologists I had expected to meet, my hosts were a very bored group of government servants. 'It's like being sent to Siberia,' said one. In all the Northern Territory's half a million square miles there were only thirty-one thousand inhabitants, and of those half were aboriginals. It was also one of the most expensive places in the world. Beer in Darwin cost five shillings a bottle and a room at the airport hotel rather more than its counterpart in Sydney. It was only on the racecourse that one got a glimpse of the outside world. Australians like betting but in the Northern Territory it is illegal except on the racecourse. So races there had to be. Every Saturday during the racing season the same group of horses plodded round the Darwin course at the advertised times, while the crowd stood with their backs to them facing rows of television sets and betting on the races in Sydney, Melbourne, Adelaide or Perth at the other end of the continent. On the day I was watching, four horses shared the six Darwin races in pairs and by the end of the day neither pair could get out of a trot. Nobody even seemed to know their names.

Much of our tour was kaleidoscopic. Near Darwin we filmed an aboriginal boy shooting a sitting duck with a catapult on the edge of a pond in the bush. We visited an orderly sheep station in the mountains of New South Wales. We were dissuaded from going to what we were told was the largest ranch in the world in Queensland (eleven thousand square miles) because it would take us too long to find anything to film. In a cove on the coast of New South Wales we picked oysters off the rocks and ate them while we swam. We flew over the great Victorian Desert on our way from Adelaide to Perth, where it rained torrents for four consecutive days. We visited the vineyards in the Barbarossa Valley, went racing in Melbourne with a member of the committee and were taught a lesson in comfort and elegance. The rooms in the grandstand and the food were worthy of a great country house. In Melbourne I spent an afternoon with an elderly cousin, Rose Merivale, who pointed out from her window the slopes on which, as a child, she had watched chain gangs working in the fields. Finally, we flew to Alice Springs, which stands rather surprisingly at the southern end of the Northern Territory. Having read Nevil Shute's *A Town Like Alice* we knew a little of what to expect. It had been built square, like a grid, and was still a frontier town. Some of the characters in the book were still alive but we were not there long enough to meet them.

Our real object in going to Alice Springs had been to visit a station called Hamilton Downs, as we had an introduction to the manager, Mr Pryor. He lived about sixty miles away. The metalled road went only part of the distance but we were told that we would have no difficulty in following the tyre tracks afterwards as there was nowhere else that they could lead. We left Alice Springs after lunch. Unfortunately, no one had warned us that it had recently rained in the area and that in places the track had become soft. In one such patch our car stuck axle-deep in the mud. We dug the soft, sandy earth away with our hands and by uprooting part of the surrounding bush – which was astonishingly easy – we made a floor of branches from the car to the nearest stretch of hard sand. After three hours we got the car out.

Although the tyre tracks were distinct, we had to make frequent detours to avoid soft patches and did not arrive until around midnight. We had seen the lights of the homestead for some time and Mrs Pryor was still up to meet us. Since that day I have met several people who know her, and all agree that she is a woman in a million. Buxom, handsome and cheerful, she took no notice of the time, gave the six of us a tremendous supper and sat down to enjoy the evening. By Australian standards Hamilton Downs was a small station of only fourteen hundred square miles, holding about nine thousand head of cattle. Mrs Pryor showed us a large-scale map on the wall and pointed to some hills about fifty miles away. 'I haven't seen my husband for three days,' she said, 'and I don't expect to see him again for another week. He and the cowboys are moving cattle from one part of the ranch to another. But he's somewhere between us and those hills. If you persevere you're bound to find him.' She advised us to leave soon after six o'clock in the morning, adding that when her husband called her on the radio she would tell him we were on our way. Then we talked about her life.

The Pryors had married while he was working (I think, as a lawyer) in Alice Springs, and they had two children, the eldest, Gary, being ten years old. But her husband (I do not remember his Christian name so I will call him Jim) had always wanted to live in the outback and so when, a few years before, the job of manager of Hamilton Downs had become vacant, he had applied for it.

'For eight months of the year,' Mrs Pryor said, 'he lives in the open, sleeping under the stars, riding all day, cooking his food on an open fire and drinking tea. In the school holidays, if he is not too far away, I go with him. We wouldn't go back to the city for the world.'

Knowing that her nearest neighbours were sixty miles away in Alice Springs, I asked about the school. Mrs Pryor said it was a radio school run from Alice Springs, with fifty pupils scattered across an area about the size of Britain. 'If you get back here by Friday evening,' she said, 'you can film Gary doing his lessons next morning.' It was then three o'clock on Wednesday morning so I suggested we get three hours' sleep. I don't think Mrs Pryor cared whether she went to bed or not.

We found Jim about an hour before sunset the next day. He was sitting by the truck, which was his daily home, the bridle of his horse Brenda looped over a branch nearby. A group of aboriginal cowboys wearing wide-brimmed, battered straw hats, were squatting on the other side of a large bonfire, their horses tethered nearby. Jim said he liked the 'Abos'. They were good cowboys and understood what had to be done without always having to be told. They did not have much to talk about but this did not worry him. 'When you're running only six beasts to a square mile, you have to cover a lot of ground. At the end of the day I have a lot to think about. By the time the fires burn low I'm ready for sleep.'

Jim had known we were coming and had killed one of his beasts to give us supper. A row of raw steaks was lying on front of the fire. We each chose one and laid it in the red-hot ashes. We had brought bread and beer. We ate and talked under the stars. Jim was worried that city life was making Australians soft. He was the only White in his team of cattlemen and he would not have had it otherwise, but he did not think that young men brought up in the cities could stand the life. And yet if Australians lost interest in the outback, they missed the whole point of their country. He knew about Clunies-Ross and Oliphant and felt that they were pointing the right way. 'Australia should process its own uranium ore rather than export it,' he said.

We had filmed the scene around the fire and taped some of the conversation, and gradually the silences lengthened as one by one we dropped off to sleep. The cattle were so thin on the ground that we accepted Jim's advice to return to his house next morning rather than follow him for an occasional shot of a steer. Mrs Pryor was surprised to see us a day early, but said we could make good use of it by going to meet the Flying Doctor who was due on the landing strip at one-thirty. 'No one is ill, but he will bring the mail,' she explained. The doctor, a man in his early thirties, got out of the aircraft cabin, gave Mrs Pryor her mail, asked after everyone and flew off. The next station at which he was calling was more than a hundred miles away. The rest of us went back to the house to film Gary, whose radio lesson that day was at three-thirty.

Gary had his desk on the verandah. The cameras were ready, and at twenty-five past three exactly we filmed him speaking into the microphone: 'William Easy calling. Good afternoon, Mrs Pearce. Are you receiving me? Over to you, over.' Mrs Pearce, sitting at her switchboard at Alice Springs, took each pupil in turn. In two or three minutes she was ready and Gary started reading aloud. Mrs Pearce interrupted with corrections. Then Gary handed over to a little girl about a hundred miles away and listened while she went through the same routine. Isolation, far from being a handicap, had been turned into an advantage by the radio school. Having to talk and listen over the air gives the children confidence and, because they get individual attention, pupils from the radio school are often ahead of those from primary schools in the town when they go on to their secondary boarding schools.

In the evening, after Gary had gone to bed, we played gin rummy. Then Mrs Pryor suddenly asked if we had seen the egg trick. She led us to the kitchen table, which was good and solid, fetched a tumbler half filled with water, an egg and a round tin tray about fifteen inches in diameter with a low rim. She ten asked us for a packet of ten cigarettes. She put the tumbler at one end of the table, about three inches from the edge, and placed the tray on top of it, taking care that the tumbler was as near the middle of the tray as possible. The tray overlapped the edge of the table by some inches. She then emptied the cigarettes from the packet, squeezed the sides until it was nearly round, and placed it on top of the tray, over the centre of the tumbler. Then she stuck the egg into the top of the empty cigarette packet. Satisfied with her work she returned to us and said, 'How much will you bet against my getting that egg into the tumbler without breaking it and without touching anything on the table with my hands?' We examined the set-up from every angle. We knew the tray was solid, the tumbler normal. The cigarette packet had belonged to one of us. Without lifting the tray, the feat looked impossible. We each put a pound on the table.

Mrs Pryor then went to a cupboard and took out an ordinary household broom. She stood at the end of the table by the tray and told those of us who were at the bottom end to get out of the way. She then put the business end of the broom on the floor and stood on it so that the handle came up vertically in front of the table, exactly opposite the tray. Taking the broom handle with her right hand about six inches from the top, she moved it towards her chest and then suddenly jerked it forward so it hit the overlapping edge of the tray. The tray shot across the table and hit the floor; without even having time to notice what had happened, we saw that the egg was floating in the tumbler, quite whole.

The great joy of the egg trick is that anyone can do it. When you jerk the broom handle forward you have to be careful not to hit the edge of the table as well as the tray or you spoil the impact. Otherwise it is a question of seeing that the tray and cigarette packet are as near dead centre over the tumbler as possible and that the tray protrudes about four inches over the edge of the table. The tray should not be too heavy, and if it has a rim it must be a low one. You can do the trick with a gramophone record if you do not mind risking it breaking. For most of the rest of that night we took turns doing the egg trick, and I doubt if more than two eggs were broken. Later we all did it in different parts of the world, almost always with success.

The more we saw of Australians, the more we liked them. They can be touchy. They itch to stamp on the slightest hint of superiority on the part of any Englishman; they do not grant that English as spoken by educated Englishmen is in any way preferable to that spoken in Sydney or the Wild Western films. They are shrewd, direct and energetic. To see literally hundreds of floodlit courts where tennis is being played in the middle of the night as you fly into any major city is an eye-opener. Although Australian tennis and cricket have had their lean years, some other sport – yachting, rugby football, bowls or swimming – always bobs up to take a place at the top. From the point of view of our programmes for the BBC, perhaps the most relevant impression we gained was that, of all the countries we visited, Australia was the least likely to succumb to a dictatorship. Australians are good grumblers, but they are open to reason and express themselves vigorously. A bully will get a bloody nose.

On that first tour for the BBC, I had been lucky enough to spend half an hour talking to the Governor-General, Field Marshal Slim. On his appointment in 1953, he had warned Sir Robert Menzies, the Australian Prime Minister, that he had 'a considerable facility for dropping bricks'. Field Marshal Slim dropped his heaviest brick soon after his arrival when addressing the National Congress of Returned Services League, which had become a sort of sacred cow. Even Prime Minister Menzies had granted it formal access to the Cabinet Committee concerned with repatriation and rehabilitation. Slim told the National Congress that it was time its members stopped thinking they were a special case and stopped pressuring the Government for special treatment. A howl of indignation went up throughout the country. No politician of any party would have dared to say such a thing for fear of losing votes. But Slim was above politics and most Australians recognized in their hearts the truth of what he had said. Within a month the Member of Parliament who had attacked him most violently made a public apology in the House. Thereafter Slim never looked back. His occasional 'home truths' echoed across the continent and made him arguably the most popular Governor-General Australia has ever had. He was in a good mood the day I saw him because the backwash from his last brick had begun to flow his way. He was nearing the end of his time at Yarralumla (he had been persuaded to accept a two-year extension of the five-year appointment) and was looking back over his years of office. 'I have learned to love these people,' he said. 'They can be marvellous and they can also be infuriating. Rather surprisingly, they can also get into a rut. That is why, about once every six months, I deliberately say something which I know will bring them up with a jerk. If there is truth in it, they will always acknowledge it in the end.'

47

The Monckton Commission

We pursued our enquiry into Communist penetration right down to Cape Town. Kenya was then the last country in which there was any immediate Communist threat, and with the emergence of Kenyatta as a statesman that threat was soon to disappear. In the countries to the south of Kenya, whether under Portuguese or British influence, or in the South African Republic, the immediate political question was not the struggle between East and West, but white supremacy. For how long could a white minority continue to rule large black majorities without the blacks having any say in government? In the Rhodesias the situation was becoming explosive because it had reached a point where the whites could only maintain their position by force. Two years after we left they attempted to do just that. But Ian Smith's unilateral Declaration of Independence was doomed unless it could win South African support; as it turned out, the South Africans did not want to burden themselves with what they felt sure would be an extra liability.

Virginia and I first visited Southern Rhodesia in 1958 when we stayed with David Stirling, whose mother was keeping house for him in Salisbury, the capital. The Governor-General was the Earl of Dalhousie, who had married David's sister, Meg. Dalhousie had been in the House of Commons with me, although on the other side. Virginia's diary informs me that we dined at Government House the night we arrived, January 9th. I remember the evening well. I did the egg trick and then we danced; there were lots of young English and Scottish people staying in the house. Later on I began swinging the girls off the floor, holding one leg and an arm and telling them to keep the other arm and leg outstretched so that they felt as if they were flying. Meg said she wanted to fly and I managed to get her quite high. Simon, her husband, was more difficult as he must have weighed between fourteen and fifteen stone and I could only get him an inch or

374

two off the floor. He used to maintain afterwards that I had failed to lift him at all, but if that had been the case, his suit would have been in tatters.

David Stirling was launching a new drive for the Africa Capricorn Society, the object of which was to bring blacks and whites together in the hope of making a multiracial state possible. In Kenya he had had considerable influence, partly because the whites were so heavily outnumbered and also because the white immigrant in Kenya had a broader outlook than his Rhodesian counterpart. Southern Rhodesia was far more industrialized and a large proportion of its quarter of a million white inhabitants were artisans, with their own trade unions which objected to Africans doing skilled jobs for fear of their members losing their own. These arguments were still being debated when I returned two years later with the Monckton Commission which had been set up by Mr Macmillan, the Prime Minister, to advise on the future of the Federation of the Rhodesias and Nyasaland.

The intention was that the Commission should be all-party. Neither in Northern Rhodesia nor in Nyasaland had the Africans been consulted; the Federation had been imposed by the United Kingdom acting in collaboration with the Government of Southern Rhodesia. The Africans in both northern territories were hostile and the existing colonial governments at best luke-warm. Both territories were demanding self-government as a preliminary to independence, and all their African political parties condemned the Federation as a means of perpetuating white domination. They demanded the right to secede.

Sir Roy Welensky, on the other hand, the Federal Prime Minister, was demanding total independence within the Commonwealth for the Federation with control of foreign affairs and defence and direct access to the Queen. Sir Roy had stated publicly that in his opinion the Commission had no right to consider anything but the future of the Federation. Any question of secession by any member was outside its terms of reference. The British Government had seemed to give qualified support to this view. With Sir Hartley Shawcross, an old friend and a distinguished member of the Labour Party who was also appointed to the Commission, I went to see Walter Monckton.

We told him that since the right of secession was a vital issue for at least two of the three member countries (and for the third under different circumstances) we could not possibly accept the invitation unless he could assure us that *any* subject relevant to the continuation of the Federation would be within the terms of reference of the Commission. He replied that he had been chairman of more than one commission and that he would never accept such an appointment unless he had absolute discretion in his interpretation of the terms of reference. Hartley and I decided that he had given us sufficient assurance to enable us to serve.

As an experience, the Monckton Commission was fascinating. Its twenty-six members, drawn from the United Kingdom, Northern and Southern Rhodesia, Nyasaland, Canada and Australia, included members of several Parliaments, the Moderator of the Church of Scotland, writers, professors, lawyers, farmers, trade unionists and businessmen. There was only one woman, Mrs Elspeth Huxley, who had been born in Kenya and had written nostalgic books about her life there. There were five Africans: Mr Katilungu, chief of the mine workers' union in Northern Rhodesia; Mr Habanyama, Chief Counsellor of the Guembe Tonga Native Authority; Chief Sigola, head of the Ndebele people; Mr Gondwe, Education Officer in the Northern Province; Mr Chirwa, a veteran African nationalist who was an opponent of Federation. Since the African nationalist parties in both Northern Rhodesia and Nyasaland had not only announced a boycott of the Commission before it had even started its work but were shamelessly intimidating all those who might wish to co-operate and give evidence, these men were showing considerable courage in agreeing to serve, and more than one was to suffer for it. Mr Gondwe's son, who was a parson, had his house burned down after he had attended a cocktail party given by the Commission, and his nephew, who also came to see us, had his shop burned to the ground. Twice I saw Africans who had been giving us evidence being beaten up by young African nationalists when they had left the building in which we met. One of them returned to the Commission to ask for protection.

Some excerpts from a diary I kept while the Commission was sitting in 1960 may help convey the atmosphere in which we worked:

February 29th:
The Commission was divided into three parties. I was in the second which left on February 18th for Choma, a little hill station where we were all put up by private individuals. Judge Beadle (Southern

Rhodesia) and I stayed with Dr Naylor, squint-eyed, stocky, efficient and cheerful. Built his own house; wants neither to be promoted nor moved. Case full of guns. He told the Judge that he used a single-barrel, 12-bore shot gun repeater to shoot lion: 'Take them in the throat as they lope towards you, at not more than 15 yards.' The Judge said, 'He's mad.'

Our first 'boycott'; little group under a banyan tree outside the Boma (the District Commissioner's office) with placards. Charles Arden-Clarke went over to talk to them. I suggested taking their evidence outside, under the tree. Arden-Clarke: 'No. That would be a victory for them. Let them come inside if they want to.' He told them that we would be delighted to hear anything they had to say if they chose to come and give evidence, but they refused.

February 22nd, Ndola:
This is the capital of the Copper Belt. We are hearing evidence in the new theatre; the acoustics very bad. Placards outside saying, 'Monkey go home', 'Get Sir Roy another job', and so on. The people holding the placards peaceful but silent. We sat as a whole Commission.

February 24th, Kitwe:
Another copper mining town. We hear evidence in two parties. I was with Walter. In view of the fact that there were some 30,000 Africans in the town of Kitwe to 3,000 Europeans, and the Africans had no representation on the town council, a Commissioner asked the mayor, who was giving evidence, whether he thought it right that the Africans should have no representation. The mayor took offence and did not answer.

February 26th, Mufulira:
Another mining town. I noticed that the mayor's wife bowed but did not shake hands with either Mr Habanyama or Mr Chirwa. She said to me when they had passed by: 'I didn't really want to come. You see, I'm a South African and I knew I would have to sit at the same table as Mr Chirwa. I have never done such a thing in my life but my husband said I was now a public figure and had to.' In the evening, at another reception at which she was hostess, she not only shook

377

hands with both of them, but took them in and introduced them to other people. I told her afterwards I thought she had done very well.

It was at this stage that I caught jaundice and had to spend most of the next three weeks in bed. I did not really recover until March 20th. As I received copies of the evidence given to the three parties of the Commission and was able to read it, I remained in touch with what was going on.

March 17th:
I was picked up by Mr Allanson, an ex-Royal Air Force pilot, bronzed and moustached, who had finished the war as second in command at Biggin Hill. During his first two years, he hated all Africans, they lied and stole, he said. The District Commissioner had advised him to leave the country; then he learned their local language and now gets on well. He dropped me at Charles and Cherry Deacon's. The Deacons were an interesting pair. She was a school teacher and one-time socialist, while he was a jack-of-all-trades. For seven years, she taught and he worked in the copper mines, becoming an expert electrician, before they had saved enough money to buy and start their farm. Today they have 3,000 acres.

For two hours they talked about the African; how he could not or would not learn how to farm, even when they showed him time and again. A neighbour drilled maize for an African family with his own machinery but told them they must come and ask for top dressing which he would supply. They never came; they could not be bothered to do the little work involved, and their harvest failed.

Deacon said that if anyone tried to take his land he would fight. He had nothing else to live for. So would she.

March 18th, Lusaka:
Judge Beadle, A.E.P. Robinson, Elman-Brown and Bob Taylor, all South Rhodesian members of the Commission, returned today. They had been deeply impressed by the failure of the Federation in the north. Elman-Brown: 'It simply isn't working. There is no question about it.'

March 21st:

We left Lusaka airport at 8.30 in the morning to fly to Lilongwe, in Nyasaland, where the Malawi Congress Party had told its members to boycott us but not to make any demonstrations, simply to ignore us.

We took evidence in the Boma; several tribal Africans came forward, most of them in favour of Federation. One, a Mr Makomo, who was secretary of the United Federal Party in the District, said he was immune to intimidation because his shop had already been burned and boycotted. Almost all of the witnesses said that members of the Malawi Congress Party had been touring the town during the last few days threatening them if they gave evidence.

The provincial Commissioner, a tall, fair-haired man wearing shorts and an open shirt, was impressive. He said that his authority was being steadily undermined by the Malawi Congress Party. It was impossible to take action against intimidators because none of their victims would give evidence. They were too frightened. The forms of intimidation are either a threat to burn their house, which is very easy because all of them have thatched roofs and are only made of mud and wattle, or a threat that wives and children will suffer, or that they themselves will be beaten or killed. Sometimes the threat is simply a vague: 'If you don't do what we want, wait and see what happens when we are in power.' Intimidators frequently use witchcraft which is very prevalent in this area. It is effective.

Indians are doing well in business and are delighted with Federation because it produced special Indian schools at which there are now more than 2,000 children. Before Federation the Indians had no schools to themselves at all. In the afternoon we drove down to Dedsa.

The road runs along the boundary with Portuguese East Africa [now Mozambique] and it was noticeable how many fewer villages there were on the Portuguese side. Dedsa is nearly 6,000 feet high and clusters round the bottom of a mountain which goes up another 1,000 feet. Nyasaland Forestry Department has planted a lot of conifers and other trees which were very refreshing after the endless bush.

The most disturbing thing at Dedsa were the schools. Discipline in Nyasaland has broken down even more completely than in

Northern Rhodesia. The headmaster of the Dedsa secondary school says that he was having to close down his sixth form because half his staff were leaving. They were all young men who had come out from England, mainly rather left-wing, but they simply could not stand the life in Dedsa. The African boys showed no appreciation whatever of being taught and would often refuse to attend class or to do what they were told. Only two days before we arrived, the son of Mr Matinga, a member of the Federal Legislature, was beaten up by some of the boys because his father had written an article in a magazine in favour of Federation. The headmaster said he had the boys in and beat two of them; but they were not in the least sorry and resented being beaten, asking, 'What are you beating us for?' He also said that the standard was extraordinarily low compared with Fiji where he had been before.

March 26th, Limbe:
One of our witnesses was threatened by four Africans as he left the hotel where we were taking evidence to go back to his office in the Railway Building. The young Africans showed him a piece of paper saying that because he had given evidence to the Monckton Commission, he would be killed. He recognized one of the men and knew where he worked and told the police that he was prepared to give evidence. The police are going to prosecute.

April 1st, Chiradzulu:
A mountain not far from Limbe. DC's house in beautiful position. Chiefs and councillors, again in beautiful robes and scarlet fez-like hats made of silk. One hat had a royal coat of arms on the front, robes black with red edging, rather like degree robes. While we were at Chiradzulu we were told by the DC that Dr Banda had been released.

April 7th, Bulawayo:
Flew to Bulawayo in the early morning. Very wide streets because Cecil Rhodes insisted that a team of 8 oxen (16 oxen in all) should be able to turn round in any part of the town.

April 8th:

Party 3 under Tommy Crathorne, visited Plumtree on the borders of Bechuanaland. Visited a school run on English Public School lines. Tommy asked each of us to make a speech. Visited two missions run by German Fathers.

April 17th, Wankie:

Drove out into the game reserve and saw eleven varieties: giraffe, buffalo, elephant, wart hog, kudu, zebra, wildebeest, sable antelope, roan antelope, lion (2 beautiful male lions lying under a tree). Next morning when we went out, we also saw a Steenbok, a beautiful little buck that raced in front of the car for a long way. Innumerable birds including very large ground hornbills, secretary-birds, eagles, and dozens of others.

The game warden told us that he had seen a giraffe kill a lion with a kick in the face and the two lions that were following it immediately ate their comrade. A lion kills a buffalo by getting on to its back, putting its paws under the buffalo's jaw and then wrenching the head back and breaking the neck. A big bull buffalo is too much for a lion, and the rangers had seen buffalos driving lion away. The ranger also said that he had seen a lion kill a lioness with a single blow. The lioness had come into the pride of a stranger and was killed immediately. The wardens believed that there are something like 10,000 elephant and 10,000 buffalo, both increasing at an alarming rate. When the rangers want to keep down the numbers, they never shoot in the game reserve, but shoot outside.

As an elephant galloped in front of our car with its ears back, a ranger said it might stop and do a 'bluff charge' as we had disturbed it at its drinking. I asked the ranger how he would know that the charge would be a bluff. He said, 'Oh, it's quite easy to tell; the idea that when an elephant is angry it charges with its head back and its ears spread and trumpeting is all nonsense. When an elephant is really angry and serious, it gets right down with its tusks on the ground and charges at that angle so that it can throw you over its head. It moves incredibly fast.'

April 21st, Salisbury:

Went to see Welensky after dinner with Tom Dugdale, Hugh

Molson and Donald McGillivray. Welensky very friendly (his wife came in for a few minutes) and very frank. He said categorically that he would not tolerate any change in the Northern Rhodesian constitution since it had only been introduced last year and must be allowed to run its course. He admitted Nyasaland was a different proposition and he had never wanted it in the Federation. Now it was there, he thought it a mistake for it to go out but he recognized that it was an African country and must have an African government. It was a question of timing.

April 23rd, Kariba Dam:
Sir Duncan Anderson, a very impressive man. The dam is a colossal project and the underground turbine room, which has been tiled like a bathroom throughout, is a truly vast hall. It was all being got ready for the opening by the Queen Mother.

April 26th, Salisbury:
Dinner with Jack Grant who was captain of the West Indies cricket team while I was at Oxford. He is now a missionary. He had asked to meet me. Mr Sithole, an African parson who wrote a book called *African Nationalism*, Mr Shamyarira, editor of the African newspaper, the *Daily News*, and Leo Takawira, the secretary of the Capricorn Society, also came. I had met these last two with David Stirling in 1958. Their wives were also there but, although nice looking, were silent.

All three Africans emphasized the fact that the situation had changed since I was last here. Then, they were all for co-operating with the Europeans and were members of political parties in which the Europeans also took part and, indeed, led. But since they never seemed to get anywhere with the Europeans, they had now changed. Takawira is a leader of the National Democratic Party, which is purely African. Both Sithole and Shamyarira, intelligent and moderate men, are worried by the fact that all educated Africans talk as if there were no hope of them getting any concessions 'unless somebody dies'. They meant that violence is the only way to make the Southern Rhodesians recognize their terms.

In the last week that we were in Salisbury, I got A.E.P. Robinson, Bob Taylor and Sir Victor Robinson, Samkanje and Shamyarira to have lunch with me. None of the Southern Rhodesians had ever lunched with an educated African before. Africans told the Southern Rhodesians what they had told me and I think my colleagues were duly impressed. At any rate, I heard both Robinson and Taylor asking Samkanje and Shamyarira if they would come and dine with them once the Commission had finished its work.

May 10th, Departure:
We left Salisbury at 2 p.m. At Nairobi the Governor met us with members of the East African High Commission and for three quarters of an hour we took evidence from them. It was plain that the Commission was not working very well, and unless it had more financial power it would never be effective.

We landed at Khartoum at midnight with a temperature of 100° and sat out in deck-chairs under the stars while they refuelled the aircraft. We reached Heathrow at 10.30 a.m. and Virginia met me. In the afternoon we went to Vincent Square where the boys were playing cricket. Randall got 52 not out and Andrew 46 not out, the last part of which I saw. What a welcome!

The Commission did its utmost to fulfil its terms of reference but it was clear even before our report came out that no constitutional proposals could assuage the determination of African nationalists to have nothing to do with the Federation. The report was not adopted by the British Government and the Federation was dissolved within three years of our leaving the territories (December 31st, 1963). Within another two years, both the northern territories had achieved independence within the Commonwealth, and Mr Ian Smith had taken Southern Rhodesia out of it by declaring unilateral independence.

From a purely personal point of view the Commission marked another turning point in my life because it ended a decade of current affairs reporting in print or on television and led to my return to politics. I was having a severe attack of 'Commentator's Disease' and feeling the need not only to comment but to share in responsibility. The Commission had been an opportunity to do so. Sir Ian Jacob, the Director General of the BBC, who had been a firm supporter in all my television work, had said to me privately that he hoped I might build a position for myself in England like that of Ed Murrow in the United

States. Had Sir Ian remained with the BBC I might well have continued, because he was a sympathetic and inspiring leader. I was less sure of Sir Hugh Carleton Green. Within two years of serving on the Monckton Commission I was back in Parliament, not as a Labour but as a Conservative Member.

48

Return to Parliament

My decision to change party had been of long gestation. Even during the years of Attlee's Government I had begun to have doubts about the Labour Party. Philip Williams, in his biography of Hugh Gaitskell,[1] mentions a dinner party Virginia and I gave in 52 Romney Street in 1951 to which Hugh Gaitskell, Douglas Jay, Denis Healey and one or two others came, and at which I suggested we drop Clause 4 of Section 4 of the Labour Party Constitution which commits it to bring about the 'common ownership of the means of production, distribution and exchange'. This clause, I argued, which had only been included in 1918 as a gesture towards the Russian Revolutionaries, was an interpolation into the aims of a party whose real origins had been non-conformist and radical rather than Marxist; it committed us to nation-alization on a scale in which no one except the small band of Marxists believed. We had a lively discussion in which Douglas Jay, who within ten years was to be in favour of dropping nationalization altogether, was my most vigorous opponent. Hugh Gaitskell, who was to propose and fail to achieve this very measure after losing the 1959 election, was not hostile but uncertain.

That evening showed the way my mind was working, and I was not alone in my thinking. After the 1950 election, from which Attlee emerged with a majority of only five, many Labour MPs said that the commitment to wholesale nationalization was a millstone around their necks. It enabled the Tories to frighten every shopkeeper, farmer and small tradesman into believing that the real intention of the Labour Party was to take their businesses away from them and build a country like those emerging in Eastern Europe where all pubs, cafés, shops and petrol stations were owned by the state – and as tourists were beginning to discover, these were few and far between. Even those British industries which had been nationalized were not proving to be the success that many of us had hoped and a strong lobby was growing within the party to drop the nationalization of steel. Labour Members were beginning to say openly that anything as amorphous as the state was not a good employer and that officials of great national organizations were often less inclined to listen to their workers than employers whose own livelihoods depended upon the success of the enterprise. We are all gregarious to a certain extent and while I was in Parliament I was carried along by the enthusiasm of friends and the excitement of political life; but when I lost my seat and began travelling the world as a television reporter and journalist, I came under fresh influences.

The United States was always a tonic. I knew from before the war that Americans are apt to welcome new ideas, whereas the English are suspicious of them. In Texas in the 1950s I was particularly struck by the courage of the young men, bank clerks, journalists, mechanics and truck drivers, who slogged and saved and spent their last dollar in the search for oil. Even if they failed, none of those I met regretted the struggle. Gradually I came to the conclusion that it is independence of mind which contributes most to the world and that the most inspiring people have been those who are prepared to go on their own.

It would be absurd to suggest that there have been no robust socialists – the history of the British Labour movement alone is full of them – but the root of socialist thinking (not, of course, of Communist thinking) is egalitarianism. I came to the conclusion that egalitarianism was a false ideal founded on fear and jealousy rather than humanity, and that those who made it their goal spent more of their time holding people back than urging them on. In the early days of socialism great trust was placed in planning. Textbooks and speeches were full of the danger of leaving any organized effort to the 'hazards' of the market. Plans could avoid booms and slumps, prevent unemployment and increase wealth. It now seems to me that planning is the most exacting science, or art, of all. Plans have to allow for changes in taste, new inventions, new discoveries, new habits, and mistakes. In Britain after the Second World War, it was said confidently that we could never produce enough coal and we planned new pits accordingly. Within a decade such huge stocks were piling up at the pitheads that over the following ten years the size of the industry had to be cut by half. Hugh Gaitskell used to say repeatedly that nationalization was a means to an end, not an end in itself. The same is true of planning.

Lastly, I was influenced by what I had learned about trade unions. There have been politicians who have said that we ought to have grown out of the need for trade unions. Understanding within the working population ought to have reached a level at which all are trying to increase productivity and reduce effort. Industry could then take advantage of every new invention, expand indefinitely and employers would pay the maximum wages. It is a wonderful dream, on a par with the dream of Communists who believe that when true Communism is achieved there will be no need for government of any kind.

The number of countries where men can freely associate is ever declining but wherever they exist there will be trade unions. What matters is that they should be democratically organized: by their nature, trade unions can take collective action which directly affects the lives of other members of the community, so they are an obvious target for power-hungry, ambitious men. In a democracy, trade unions are a potential alternative to Parliament as a source of power. It is for that reason that Communists in Moscow and King Street have sought to get control of them for the last sixty years. It is therefore essential that such organizations should reflect the views of their members as accurately as possible. Postal ballots carried out by an independent body, both to elect leaders and to decide whether or not to strike, are the minimum safeguards any trade union in a free society should accept.

A free society should also insist that trade unions do not affiliate to any political party. It is a distortion of the true function of British trade unions that almost all of them are not only affiliated to the Labour Party but finance it and dominate its policy-making conference. Any Labour Government has to struggle not to become an extension of the Trades Union Congress. It is nothing short of grotesque that trade unions, through their political fund, should be able to provide the main income of one party when many thousands of trade unionists feel that their interests are better represented by other parties. In West Germany, where the trade unions were reorganized by British trade unionists after the Second World War, such things cannot happen. It is always said that Will Lawther, Jack Tanner and their colleagues gave German trade unions the constitution they would like to have achieved in Britain. While I was still a member of the Labour Party, I advocated financial divorce from the trade unions and the establishment of individual membership as the basis of party finance. I believe that if this was the rule for all parties our politics would be healthier. Enthusiasm may be harder to generate, but it is worth more than money.

North Buckinghamshire had chosen Robert Maxwell to succeed me as Labour candidate, and I had ceased to be a member of any party. Friends like Robin Day used to urge me to join the Liberals, but having come to believe that private enterprise was the only thing that could lift any community out of apathy and poverty, I felt it was more sensible to throw my lot in with the party that did most to foster it, rather than to enter a halfway house.

Towards the end of 1957, therefore, I joined the Conservative Party in Westminster and a year or so later was enrolled on their list of candidates.[2] I was still doing programmes for the BBC and in 1959 Oliver Poole (later Lord Poole), then chairman of the Conservative Party, asked me if I would interview Harold Macmillan, the Prime Minister, in one of his party political broadcasts. As it would have broken the spirit of my contract with the BBC, under which it was laid down that I should be free of political bias in my broadcasts, I refused.

The Monckton Commission and our enquiry into Communist penetration in Africa occupied the next three years, but there was a lull in the spring of 1962 and once again I began to take an interest in British party politics. I canvassed for the Conservatives in the Orpington by-election in March, which was eventually won by Eric Lubbock, the Liberal. It was one of the greatest swings against the Conservatives on record: Lubbock turned a Conservative majority of 14,700 at the general election in 1959 into a Liberal one of 7,855 in 1962. Then, in June, the appointment of Sir Edward Wakefield to be United Kingdom Commissioner in Malta caused a by-election in West Derbyshire, and I decided to have a go. I was put on the shortlist with Norman St John Stevas and Mr V. Argyle QC, and spent a rather uncomfortable afternoon being kept apart from the other candidates in a very small room in the Conservative headquarters in Bakewell. But I was chosen.

*

West Derbyshire was one of the most beautiful constituencies in England. Its boundaries then stretched from Hathersage, near Sheffield, to Sudbury, near Uttoxeter, a distance of little less than fifty miles as the crow flies. Except for the part to the south of Ashbourne, it was all Pennine hills and moors, chequered with stone walls and cut by steep valleys, some so deep that the inhabitants could not receive television signals and had to be connected by cables. There were only four towns with more than five thousand inhabitants, Ashbourne, Wirksworth, Matlock and Bakewell, but more than a hundred villages. The two great houses, Chatsworth and Haddon Hall – one belonging to the Duke of Devonshire and the other to the Duke of Rutland, whose brother Lord John Manners had a tenancy for life – were in the centre of the constituency and only a few miles apart from each other. They both offered us hospitality and we descended on them with all our helpers.

We fought the campaign by canvassing. I was determined that I should be seen in every street in the constituency and that our canvassers would call on every house. We had some delightful encounters. One lady listened to us carefully in her doorway and then said with a sweet smile that she was sure that I believed every word I said but that in their house they felt that God did these things much better than any politician could. In a village near Hathersage the houses stood back from the road, each with a separate path leading to its door. Virginia and I advanced side by side to different doors. I found letters stuffed in the box in my door and was about to try another when the woman to whom Virginia was talking turned to me and said, 'It ain't no good your trying to get in there. He fell down dead at the bottom of the stairs two days ago and they haven't been in to clear 'im up yet.'

My younger son, Randall, then aged twelve, who came up to help during his half-term, bought a load of squibs which went off with a loud bang, and went round putting them on the doormats of every house with a Liberal poster in the window. He was never in sight when they exploded and I used to follow him as the doors opened and apologize to the indignant householder, assuring them that it was not I who was the culprit but a small boy whom I had been unable to stop. The most rewarding visit was in a village just below Riber Castle, near Matlock, where a lady came to her gate followed by a whole family of English sheepdogs whose wool completely covered their eyes and who all leapt at me at once, covering my suit with mud from their paws. They were the only dogs I have ever really wanted to own and had I bought one she might have voted for me. (She was a Liberal.)

There were four candidates: Mr John Dilks, Labour; Colonel Ronald Gardiner-Thorpe, Liberal; Mr Raymond Gregory, Independent (a candidate financed by Lord Beaverbrook and standing on an anti-Common Market ticket); and myself. Before the count began I heard that members of the Conservative Central Office in London were laying odds of three to one against us.

From the start of the count it was clearly a close thing. The votes were stacked on trestle tables, and although Dilks' stack was always lower, there was very little between Gardiner-Thorpe and myself. One minute he would be ahead; the next I was. After an hour or so Virginia and I went to sit down in a corner. My agent, Ray Allison, came over to tell me he thought there was sure to be a re-count, but when the last ballot-paper had been stacked it was plain that our column was longer than Gardiner-Thorpe's. There was no re-count and I won by 1,220 votes.

With memories of Orpington fresh in their minds, the Liberals had been confident of victory. West Derbyshire, led by members of the Cavendish family, had been a Liberal seat at the beginning of the century and there was still sentimental loyalty to the Manchester School tradition. But I had been encouraged by the fact that Jo Grimond, the leader of the Liberal Party, had not come to speak for their candidate, who was apparently not very popular at Liberal headquarters, whereas both Quintin Hogg and Christopher Soames had spoken well for me. The latter, who was Minister for Agriculture at the time, spent two hours on his feet in Ashbourne cattle market answering farmers' questions, mainly about the Common Market, which the British Government had formally applied to enter.

Champagne flowed that night in Conservative houses, and the next day we formed a motorcade to tour the constituency. The weather had been glorious throughout the campaign and our triumphal ride was one long picnic. That night, however, I received a telephone call from Martin Redmayne, the Chief Conservative Whip. After congratulating me, he asked whether I would consider taking my seat in the Commons on the following Friday. When I asked why, he replied, 'A lot of our fellows won't be too pleased that you have won and I thought it might be a good thing if you took your seat when few people are in the House. You may not get a very good reception.' It was a dampener on our spirits, which were high not only on our own behalf but because we felt we had done well for the party in reversing a disastrous trend. I replied cheerfully that I did not mind about my reception but that I intended to take my seat on Monday, if he could arrange it. Nevertheless the telephone call was an omen.

Either because Conservative Members were not as hostile as he feared, or because the Chief Whip had done an excellent job rallying them, I got quite a warm reception when I took my seat on Monday, June 9th. The Speaker, whom I had known before, greeted me as an old friend. Mr Macmillan sent me a handwritten note of congratulation and Tony Barber, his Parliamentary Private Secretary and my prisoner-of-war friend, seemed genuinely delighted to see me back. However, the Whips' Office soon administered another cold douche, informing me that I had been appointed to the Scottish Grand Committee. Although important to Scotsmen and Englishmen with northern connections, this was otherwise a parking place for Members who had no special interests, so I wrote back politely, thanking them for the honour they had done me but pointing out that as I had little knowledge of Scottish affairs and no particular interest in them, it was unlikely that I would ever attend. I heard no more.

Later I served on the Public Accounts Committee, which, although able to cross-examine senior civil servants in charge of Government Departments, was then handicapped by being limited only to what had already happened. We could neither ask questions about nor hint at what was being done or what was to come. I did, however, make one curious discovery. Knowing that the Committee was going to examine the accounts of the Post Office, I visited the Head Post Office in West Derbyshire. Since many villages in the constituency had been snowed up the previous winter, I asked how, in such circumstances, the Post Office delivered telegrams. I was told that telegrams were always delivered by the postman or by telephone. As only 11 per cent of the houses in my constituency had a telephone, this was plainly an unsatisfactory situation. I also gathered that however urgent the message in the telegram, if the consignee had no telephone there was no other method of delivery, even if the roads were clear. Yet the person who sent the telegram still paid full telegraphic rates and did not know that his or her message would not arrive until the next day.

When the Permanent Head of the Post Office appeared before the Committee, I explained what I had learned and asked him if it was true. He admitted that it was. When I suggested that he was defrauding the public, he was embarrassed. The system was subsequently changed.

My articles on *The Hidden Face of Communism* appeared very prominently in the *Sunday Times* in October and I was invited to join the Ad Hoc Committee of the Conservative Party. The Committee, consisting of MPs, industrialists and professors, was preparing a bill to promote better industrial relations under the chairmanship of Lord Amory, formerly Sir Derek Heathcote Amory, Chancellor of the Exchequer from 1958 to 1960. Its purpose was to establish a fresh legal framework for industrial relations so as to overcome the chaotic conditions being created by strikes organized on the shop floor by militant shop stewards or groups of militant workers, usually in defiance of union officials. Such strikes accounted for 95 per cent of industrial stoppages in the early 1960s and were usually termed 'unofficial' or 'illegal', both of which epithets applied.

These strikes were a symptom of what I had been writing about. Communists who had penetrated the unions, usually disguised as members of the Labour Party, were often elected shop stewards by a show of hands on the factory floor. Then they used their position to undermine the officials of the union and foment trouble. Their activities were destroying the orderly conduct of collective bargaining and damaging the economy by making it impossible for firms to fulfil the delivery dates specified in their contracts. For eleven years Conservative Governments had closed their eyes to what was happening under a policy of emollience towards the unions, but the position was deteriorating rapidly. Union officials were losing control of their members; shop stewards who held no official union position were either provoking the anarchy or losing control of the men on the shop floor. The 'sleeping dogs' which Monckton hoped to let lie were at the throats of employers, union officials and their own union members.

I sat on the Ad Hoc Committee for eight years, during the last two of which I was no longer a Member of Parliament. I agreed with almost all of its recommendations, many of which were incorporated into Mr Heath's Industrial Relations Act of August 1971, although with hindsight I would admit we were trying to do too much too quickly. But I failed to persuade my colleagues on the Committee to accept what I considered to be by far the most important reform of all: the introduction of compulsory postal ballots for the election of national and regional union officials and before the declaration of a strike. One of the chairmen of the Committee put forward the extraordinary argument that because once, when postal votes had been used, a Communist had been elected, it was therefore unsafe to introduce such voting generally; this in spite of the decisive experience of the Electrical and Engineering Unions. Not only are postal ballots democratic, but they are the only way of ensuring that the views of rank and file trade unionists can be heard without risk of intimidation, and that union officials continue to represent the views of a majority of members. If the rule had been introduced in 1970 the leadership of most unions would have been in moderate hands by the early 1980s. Instead, it was to be another fourteen years before this essential reform was finally achieved.

Meanwhile Harold Wilson, Ted Heath and Jim Callaghan had come and gone. The Trades Union Congress, dominated by men who believed first and foremost in the expansion of trade union power, irrespective of whether it was used in the Marxist interest, successfully sabotaged Harold Wilson's and Barbara Castle's one brave effort to provide trade unionism with a more democratic framework in the Industrial Relations Bill of 1970, and went on to declare all-out war against Heath's bill a year later. Both bills were based on Lord Donovan's Royal Commission on Trade Union and Employers' Associations which sat from 1965 to 1968. James Callaghan, although Home Secretary at the time, voted against Mrs Castle in the National Executive of the Labour Party, thereby sealing the fate of the bill and winning the support of the trade unions in any future struggles within the Parliamentary Labour Party. He was paid in full by being elected leader after Harold Wilson's resignation in April 1976, and reaped his harvest when, as Prime Minister, he faced the 'winter of discontent' of 1978 to 1979, during which the country suffered its most sustained attack from trade unionists who had been encouraged by successive Labour governments to believe in direct action. That such an ardent parliamentarian as Callaghan should compromise himself with so many who advocated the use of extra-parliamentary power was surely out of character. He was never able to recover his authority in the country and his lapse cost him the general election of May 1979, after which Mrs Thatcher succeeded him as Prime Minister.

Mrs Thatcher was wiser than Ted Heath. Instead of one massive measure, she spread her legislation on industrial relations over four years. In the 1980 Employment Act, she tightened the laws on picketing, the closed shop, unfair dismissal, and made public funds available to defray the cost of postal ballots held by trade unions. In the 1982 Act she further clarified the law on closed shops, and fixed limits on damages against trade unions in civil proceedings. Following the overwhelming Conservative victory in the general election of June 1983, a Trades Union Bill was introduced. When it became law, it made postal voting the norm for the election of union executives, postal ballots compulsory before a strike, and provided for the holding of a ballot every ten years to determine whether the members of a union wanted a fund for political purposes.

My own contribution to these events was minor. At the Conservative Party Conference at Brighton in October 1962, four months after I had won the West Derbyshire by-election, I made a speech on the theme of power without responsibility as it applied to trade unionists, particularly referring to unofficial strikers. I could tell it was not popular with the platform, and as soon as my five minutes were up the red light appeared in front of me on the rostrum. When I did not immediately stop, the Chairman called me to order. But the Conference made it so plain that it wanted me to continue that I was allowed a few more minutes. Such speeches are only of value if their reception indicates a mood. I was left in no doubt during the rest of the Conference that my words had struck a chord. More important, when Parliament reassembled, I was able to repeat some of the points I had made to the 1922 Committee of back-benchers. There was a good attendance and some Members of the House of Lords took the trouble to come and listen.

I was appointed to the Committee to consider the Contracts of Employment Bill, a mollifying measure designed to ensure that proper notice was given in case of dismissals or resignation and that the terms of employment were fully explained to all employees. When I proposed a minor amendment to one of the clauses I only failed to defeat the Government (with the opposition abstaining) by one vote. Half the Conservative members of the Committee voted with me. There were rumours that I was being considered for the Ministry of Labour, but I had too much experience to take such rumours seriously. The most I would claim is that during those early years as a Conservative Member of Parliament, I did help to make the party aware of the dangers threatening democracy by the infiltration of Marxism in Labour constituencies and the trade unions. Later the threat was spread to certain Labour-controlled municipal councils such as the GLC and Liverpool, where Marxism has been quick to show its ugliest and most sinister face.

*

During that summer of 1963, Jack Profumo occupied the centre of the political stage. Before the next Conference, Macmillan, with whom I had felt bonds of sympathy, had announced his resignation and Sir Alec Douglas-Home had become Prime Minister. I have never subscribed to the view that his lack of economic training disqualified him for the post; on the contrary, he had the detachment and integrity to make a good Prime Minister. Nor do I think his rather skeletal appearances on television were responsible for the loss of the general election in 1964. He always talked sense and very nearly won. I am not sure that any Conservative leader could have done better in the post-Profumo circumstances. I went to the meeting at which Alec Douglas-Home resigned, intending to vote for him. When I asked him afterwards why he had done so, he said he felt it was better to go voluntarily than to be forced to leave later in the year. The Heath bandwagon was already rolling.

White Man's Africa

While I was still in Parliament we completed our investigation into the penetration of Communism in Africa with a visit to the South African Republic. I had first been there in 1958 with Virginia, when the country was peaceful. It was possible to drive around freely, enter African townships unaccompanied, call on farmers and whomever else was willing to see one, without introduction. One discussed apartheid, which was still in its infancy, endlessly. It was not difficult to understand and even sympathize with the Boer farmer. The Europeans who came to the Cape three hundreds years ago did not have to fight: the land was empty. There were no villages or towns. No doubt nomadic tribes claimed grazing rights over vast areas, but the early settlers rarely saw other human beings. They were poor and hard-working; they cultivated the land and made it productive. Soon Africans came of their own accord to work for them.

When we drove from Cape Town to Durban, it was difficult to believe we were in Africa at all. The hills, wearing a mantle of Mediterranean pines, rolled down to the sea in great curves whose contours were like English downs. From the road we could see miles of carefully tilled fields covering rolling hills and green valleys. Flowers grew in gardens on the roadside and white, red-roofed houses suggested southern France or Italy, not the sun-parched bush, desert and jungle which covers so much of the African continent.

In the country districts, there was no colour problem. Isolated from the rest of the world, and from much of their own continent, the farmers still lived much as planters had in Virginia or South Carolina before the American Civil War. We stopped at random at many farms owned either by Afrikaners or people of British descent. One old Boer slammed the door in our faces, but usually we received a warm welcome and, whatever the time of day, were offered tea and biscuits.

When asked if they were having problems with their African workers, they would smile and say we should not believe the newspapers. One elderly Afrikaner couple told us they employed eleven families numbering about fifty people, half of them children. They had not had to look for labour for years. An English couple said they had taken on their last new family seventeen years ago and never expected to have to do so again as they were now into the second generation of farm workers. 'They are part of our family,' they said. The farmers looked after their workers' health, supplied clothes, shoes and most of the utensils they used. Their wives acted as midwives for African women. Some farmers paid their workers partly in cash and partly in weekly rations, others only in cash. We only met one, a rough-looking Afrikaner, who complained of his labour. He called them a 'lazy, good-for-nothing lot' and wanted to replace them with 'coloureds' as soon as possible.

In the towns and cities it was different. Small towns in South Africa are like frontier towns in Wild Western films: low houses, wide streets, shops and a church. In the centre of Johannesburg, on the other hand, you could imagine yourself in New York; in Cape Town, in an Australian or European city. But wherever we were and whomever we talked to – businessmen, newspaper editors, civil servants, lawyers, shop keepers or social workers – every white person wanted to discuss the colour question. The moment we said we came from England the conversation became charged with emotion. Had Britain and America gone mad? Did they not realize that the white man was fighting for his very existence? Were they really prepared to support sanctions against South Africa?

Even English-speaking businessmen, who used to call themselves progressives and in former days constituted the white opposition to the Afrikaner government, told us that when other countries turned their backs on South Africa they had become nationalists. 'Apartheid may seem heartless,' one of them said, 'but it is a straight question of survival. We don't despise the black skin, but if we start giving these primitive people political rights, they will devour us.' A woman shopkeeper said, 'Multiracialism simply won't work and any form of gradualism is the thin edge of the wedge. We have seen it in the rest of Africa. Open the door a crack and we will be overwhelmed. Therefore we say no concessions, and we will fight to the last man before we give up what is rightfully ours.'

In 1960 people with views like these were firm supporters of Dr Verwoerd, the prophet of apartheid who as Prime Minister had recently inaugurated the policy of the 'Bantustans'. In Pretoria, an official from the Ministry of Information showed us a huge map of South and South West Africa which was splashed with black areas which he explained were the areas the Bantu settled after the early Kaffir wars.[1] They covered some 13.5 per cent of the land surface of the Republic and were the home of about three and a half million Bantu, or a third of the black population. The Government's intention, he said, was to make them into wholly Black states, to develop them both agriculturally and industrially and finally to give them complete independence as 'Bantustans'. Eventually South Africa would become a Federation of black and white independent countries.

When we asked him what white South Africans would do for labour when the Bantustans became independent, he replied that the industrialists would 'contract labour in' just as they already did in the mines. 'It will be no different from English people importing Spanish and Italian servants,' he insisted. What the official was really saying was that the African was treated as a foreigner in white South Africa. Even though several million worked for whites in industry, agriculture or commerce, they could never earn the right of citizenship. Even if they worked as domestic servants, they had to have passes so that they could be identified and controlled. Soon after we left South Africa in 1964, servants were forbidden under the Group Areas Act to live in white areas; thousands were thereby rendered homeless and unemployed.

We drove to Pietersburg and on to the African University of Turfloop. The Principal, with whom we stayed, was an Afrikaner in his forties who was dedicated to giving his all-African undergraduates the best education possible. His staff was a mixture of Africans and whites. After dinner, to which some white professors came, we asked if we could meet their African colleagues. The Principal said, 'Of course,' but added that to do so we would have to drive to the other end of the campus. Even in a university the races were segregated. He drove us himself and one of the African professors promised to drive us back.

We must have met at least six African professors, and we sat and talked with them for hours. They told us that while politics was supposed to be a forbidden subject in the university, in practice the

398

undergraduates talked of little else. We asked them what political philosophy they taught and they said it was what they themselves had learned in England, a philosophy based on the importance of the individual. 'We are turning out hundreds of bright young Africans steeped in the liberal democratic tradition. What they will make of their own country when they leave us has yet to be seen.' Our hosts were amusing, articulate and tolerant. They did not inveigh against apartheid, they just did not believe it could continue. They had respect and affection for their young Principal.

So that we could hear the 'spiritual case' for apartheid, we were taken to dine with some pastors and professors who belonged to the Dutch Reformed Church, an institution which has elevated apartheid into a philosophy with a religious foundation. The pastors quoted texts from the books of Genesis, Deuteronomy and The Acts of the Apostles upon which they based their belief in apartheid. At first we were inclined to laugh but our hosts were so obviously sincere that we listened. The key text is contained in verse 28 of the first chapter of Genesis: 'And God blessed them and God said to them be fruitful and multiply and fill the Earth and subdue it.' The Dutch Reformed Church interpreted this as meaning that God commanded the people of the earth to spread and diversify into different races. They regarded it as implicit in this command that the races should each develop their own culture and not mix. There are some fifty other texts which have been called in aid of this interpretation, but it has been refuted by other African Protestant theologians, in particular by the Revd Douglas Bax, and denounced by the World Alliance of Protestant Churches as recently as 1982. But the Dutch Reformed Church reaffirmed its beliefs, and its views are still accepted as the spiritual basis for apartheid. Hence the Bantustan 'homelands' and the general policy of segregation.

We visited several homelands and black townships in the Transkei, then the largest and most developed of all the Bantustans. The country was treeless but beautiful, with majestic hills and valleys; but much of the land was suffering from severe erosion due to over-stocking. The territory supported nearly a million and a half people, about six acres of land per head. Life was organized tribally under chiefs and headmen and the people were poor and primitive. The government officers in charge of the area were doing their best to teach the elementary laws of husbandry, as English colonial servants had done in many parts of Africa forty years before, but doing it with much larger funds. A minimum budget for agricultural rehabilitation in the Transkei alone was ten million pounds for ten years. Nevertheless, they said it would take at least fifteen years before erosion could be cured.

We motored fifty miles to have tea with Chief Matanzima, who was fighting an election to decide who should lead the Transkei into independence, he or his rival, Chief Poto. Chief Matanzima, a tall, thin, aggressive man, had the support of the South African Government because he accepted the 'Bantustan' idea. 'I would allow no white man into the country. They are too greedy,' he said. Chief Poto was attending a funeral so we saw one of his chief advisers, a lawyer named Guzana. He rejected Bantustans. 'We have no hope of development without the money and assistance of the white man. If we accept Bantustans we will be deprived of any rights in the white man's South Africa. We believe in multiracialism.' Matanzima duly won the election, and although he was occasionally a thorn in the side of the South African Government, he helped establish the Bantustan idea which spread to many parts of the Republic. But as Dr Verwoerd discouraged private white investment, and the amount provided by the Bantu Development Corporation has been a mere trickle, Bantustan development has been as slow as Chief Poto feared.

In Soweto, the huge black township outside Johannesburg which we visited more than once by ourselves, we did not find anyone who thought that the Bantustans were anything but a confidence trick designed to debar Africans from the affluence of the white man's Africa. This was not surprising. The black townships contain the city workers, who are the best educated, most skilled and most politically conscious in South Africa. Soweto was a sobering sight. The one- or two-storeyed houses stood in endless rows, bleak and ugly, although they offered far better accommodation than the shanty towns or suburbs which preceded them, many having three rooms, a kitchen and electric light. Most of the townships had football fields, canteens, beer-halls, and nursery schools for the children of working mothers. Some had tennis courts and swimming pools. Although some people said they enjoyed the amenities, the mere fact that under the Group Areas Act they had been segregated destroyed their pleasure. Whenever we entered a house, people crowded in or put their heads through the windows to talk to us. Several wanted to know whether we thought Britain and America would apply sanctions against South Africa. They knew that their own nationalist party organizations had been broken by the police and saw no hope of any relaxation in apartheid except through pressure from outside. Others questioned whether sanctions would really work; a few advocated armed uprising as the only hope.

As we completed our survey in 1963, we felt that the whites had perhaps twenty-five years in which to meet the challenges of their country. Things did not go too badly to begin with. In the reports we wrote in the early 1960s we expressed fears that students returning from behind the Iron Curtain might be able to persuade their Governments to join the Communist Bloc, but by the end of the 1970s it looked as if the drive to capture Africa for Communism through indoctrinated students had failed. Except for two or three doctors in West Africa who had spent as much as sixteen years in Moscow or Eastern Europe, and who explained that if they had not satisfied the examiners in Marxism-Leninism they would not have been allowed to take their medical degrees, none of those to whom we talked had enjoyed their student courses. The pattern was always the same. For the first few weeks they were given red-carpet treatment, but once the honeymoon period was over, discipline became strict. Africans were forbidden to mix freely with Russian students and only saw those who had been ordered to supervise them. Ordinary Russians were no more pleased to see a black face than other Europeans. One Nigerian told us that when he had hailed a taxi in Moscow to escort home a Russian girl, the driver had refused to take them. When the Nigerian protested, the driver called the police, who beat him up.

As a result, the Soviet Union lost ground in Africa during the 1970s. In the 1960s, Ghana, Guinea and Mali were Marxist states; Egypt and Algeria seemed likely to join them, and there was room for Communist hope in Morocco and Somalia. By 1980 Nkrumah had been overthrown and all North and West Africa had rejected Marxism-Leninism; Somalia was looking to the West for help. In Angola and Mozambique, Marxist Governments were only controlling sections of their countries with the help of Cuban troops, while the rest of each country was in the hands of guerrillas. Ethiopia alone, under Colonel Mengistu, was a Russian satellite, and that country, facing one of the most severe famines in its three thousand years of history, and fighting a bitter civil war, was scarcely an advertisement of which Communists could boast. Most African countries remained poor, but they had shown a spirit of independence fiercer and more tenacious than the Russians or most Europeans had expected.

By 1985 the picture had changed again. It began to seem possible that the African National Congress might succeed where thirty years of intense effort by the Soviet Union had failed, by capturing the richest and hitherto most unlikely country of all, the South African Republic. With my niece, Susanna Swallow, I was invited to revisit South Africa by Charles and Margild Fiddian-Green, who live in Johannesburg and have a farm in the northern Transvaal. He was chairman of a company called Rennie for twelve years and is a friend of the Zulu Chief, Gatsha Buthelezi. Charles arranged a trip which began in Cape Town, took us up the Garden Route to George, St Francis Bay, the Transkei, Durban, Bophuthatswana, through Natal to his farm in the Transvaal from where we were to make an expedition to see part of the Kruger Game Park, then back to Johannesburg where we would visit gold and diamond mines.

Scenically it was glorious and, from the point of view of pleasure, exciting. In the Cape we stayed at Fleur du Cap, the guest house of Dr Anton Rupert, an Afrikaner liberal whom I had met before and whose son is a friend of my younger son, Randall. Dr Rupert had originally bought the house for himself but found it was too big and made it into a guest house. It has a famous garden and in the early morning we breakfasted off fruit by the swimming pool in which Susanna would swim twenty lengths. Each day we motored round the countryside.

The Fiddian-Greens drove us through Natal, which I found even more beautiful than the Cape, to Boschoek, a farm which had belonged to a well-known South African who had recently died, 'Punch' Barlow. That night we went to a ball at a neighbouring farm.

At Sun City, another holiday resort in Bophuthatswana, a million-dollar golf tournament had attracted many of the world's top players. It is a fantastic resort with a lake, a game park, lovely gardens, tennis courts, golf course, an auditorium which can hold a thousand people, and several hotels. There must be more slot machines in the casino than anywhere outside Las Vegas and it was packed with Asians and Africans and Afrikaners from all over the Republic.

The Fiddian-Greens' three-thousand-acre farm in the northern

Transvaal could have been in Wales or the border country between England and Scotland: rocky and green, with a four-mile trout stream which he had stocked and dammed. The two best pools were just in front of his house, which was built and tiled with local stone. They had planted eighty thousand trees in the previous twelve years, mostly fir and eucalyptus, which were cut in a five-year rotation and would make fifty thousand pounds a year when in full production. To that he could add another twenty-five thousand from letting the fishing rights on the trout stream. They took us through part of the Kruger Game Park, which is about three hundred miles long by a hundred wide, to lunch with a friend who had a hippo pool. We saw fifteen different mammals including elephant, giraffe and hippopotamus (but no lion) and forty different species of bird. Then back to Johannesburg to dine with Harry and Bridget Oppenheimer at their house, where the rococo Victorian sunken garden was floodlit.

I have dwelt on our tour deliberately to show that despite all the terrorism and police action about which one reads, most white South Africans are still living an agreeable life. Cut off by the rest of the continent from Europe, and, except in the black townships, having a paternalistic relationship with the Africans who work for them, many are still unable to feel that drastic concessions to the blacks are necessary. Black servants in white houses are treated almost as part of the family. Black South African employees in offices, factories or in the mines are learning an increasing number of skills and have a well-paid and seemingly secure career in front of them. Yet all the time we were there we were conscious of an underlying tension, far greater than anything we had experienced before.

Just outside Cape Town there were roads passing black townships along which our driver would not go. For the first time in thirty years, Margaret Vane, who had come to Palestine with me in 1937 and who was manager of a mainly Asian housing estate which we passed several times, had been advised not to go to her office because young Africans were standing at the street corners throwing bricks and stones through car windows. Instead of being free to go into Soweto or any other black township alone and when we pleased, as Virginia and I had done on our first visit, we were unable to visit any township at all. Martin Griffith, a member of the British Embassy, took us to see Mr Quoboza, a black African assistant editor of the *City Press* in Johannesburg. He was an open supporter of the African National Congress and said that he could see no other African party which could represent the majority African view, not merely in the townships but throughout the country as a whole. This, I realized, was the party line and would have been hotly denied by Buthelezi, Matanzima and other African tribal leaders. But when he said that he was in favour of a federation, provided that the ANC was brought into the preliminary talks, one felt he was not unreasonable.

All the whites we met, including Mr Koornof, who had been a member of Mr Botha's Government, favoured federation with 'one man one vote' in every province. Harry Oppenheimer said that he was convinced that, provided intimidation could be contained, such a vote would produce a large moderate African majority. But none of them felt the same urgency as we did. Because Mr Botha had to carry with him his nationalist right wing, almost every concession he made was restricted when put into operation. Thus more and more moderates like Mr Quoboza were turning to the ANC as the only effective means of exerting pressure. When Mr Julian Ogilvie Thompson, the chairman of De Beers, said in an interview that South Africans did not really know what people abroad wanted, he was being jejune. It is perfectly clear that the Russian Communist bloc wants one man one vote in a unitary government dominated by the African National Congress, which in turn will be dominated by Moscow. The West, including President Reagan, wants a faster dismantling of apartheid and a vote for all adult Africans, preferably in a federation which includes the Bantustans or, failing that, within a unitary republican state. And the West wants positive steps, like the repeal of the Group Areas Act, to prove that the South African Government is in earnest.

As every visitor to South Africa knows, all its inhabitants, Indians, coloureds, whites and blacks, are proud of being South African. The blacks rightly boast that they earn higher wages, enjoy better opportunities and practise more skills than any other black African people. Their standard of living and the education available for their children is superior to that in the Ivory Coast or Nigeria. With English as a common language they can see openings for their talents throughout the African world. But because the Afrikaners continue to treat them not merely as a subject race but as an inferior people, they are being forced into an opposition which is becoming more violent and bitter as every month passes.

It is impossible to predict with any certainty how the struggle will end. For some years the white South African army and police may contain black terrorism under a permanent state of emergency. But as the violence escalates more and more blacks will kill blacks because, in spite of intimidation by the African National Congress, there are probably as many black Africans in the townships who are passionately opposed to the idea of a Marxist dictatorship as are in favour of it. In the homelands and tribal areas the proportion of opponents to the Congress is probably larger. If sanctions result in greatly increased unemployment in the Republic and its neighbouring territories there may be such violence between blacks that it amounts to a form of civil war, not between armies but between factions. If there is a blood bath it may be filled mainly with black African blood.

In that case, fewer and fewer of the one and a half million whites who are entitled to foreign passports will want to stay in the Republic and tens of thousands of indigenous whites will want to emigrate. The two million-odd who would remain might endure a state of siege and a steady decline in their standard of living for many years. They would not be the only fanatical minority in the world but might prove to be the most self-sufficient and longest lasting. Even if the whites become confined to the southern tip of the continent, I do not see any combination of black states being formed which would be likely to dislodge them, and there are many powers in the world which would prefer a white enclave round the Cape of Good Hope to a black state which might open its harbours to the Soviet Union. No sane man can wish that apartheid will lead to a nuclear war. In the long run that risk can be avoided only by an eruption of common sense and humanity among South African whites themselves.

50

A Television Franchise

The idea of applying for an independent television franchise had come to me during discussions in Parliament on the Pilkington Report and the Television Bill of 1963. The bill arose naturally from the first eight years of commercial television and was introduced in that year because in 1964 all the independent television companies had to renew their contracts.

As a guide for Parliament, Sir Harry Pilkington had been appointed in 1960 to chair a committee to review the future of broadcasting. Apart from being openly partial to the BBC and critical of the Independent Television Authority for not exercising sufficient control over programmes and advertising, the committee made no radical recommendations. The most controversial clauses of what duly became the Television Act of 1963 were those which postponed the introduction of a second channel for Independent Television but supported its immediate introduction for the BBC, and the alteration of the basis on which the companies paid the Treasury a special financial levy. The rest was designed to tidy up the system and make sure that the monopolistic tendencies inherent in it (for no television or radio company can take advertising unless it is under the control of the Independent Broadcasting Authority) did not obliterate competition.

Not surprisingly, therefore, new contracts had been granted to all the existing companies (with only minor alterations) in 1964, but a further review was announced for 1967, preceding another new round of contracts in 1968. It was for this round that I began to prepare. My motives were not particularly lofty. Like many people who had a professional interest in television, I thought I saw many ways in which programmes could be improved and felt strongly that unless changes were made among the contractors in 1968 the existing franchise holders would establish an irreversible right to commercial television –

something which had never been contemplated by those who founded it. There was little point in breaking the monopoly of the BBC in order to create a rival monopoly in perpetuity. I also felt that some of those at the 'sharp end' of television, programme makers and producers, should have seats on the board of directors of the companies and be able to share in some of the profits which their efforts generated for their backers. I therefore recruited a team of executives and producers, almost all of whom worked either for the BBC or an existing commercial television company and wished to remain anonymous.

The business of making an application to the Independent Television Authority was well organized. The Authority advertised for applications, sent out forms which set out the financial and technical requirements, and made suggestions about the kind of programme output they were looking for. I hired a small office in Queen Street, Mayfair, and found a man who had already made television franchise applications and knew the technical and other information we should have to provide. For the best part of a year we worked on our written application. Meanwhile I visited the chairmen of several major companies to get financial backing. Only one company which we approached was not interested. Eventually we had been guaranteed five and a half million pounds in shares and unsecured loan stock and could present an impressive list of names from industry and finance in our support.

Weekend Television in London, which had hitherto been confined to Saturday and Sunday, had been extended to include Friday evenings from seven o'clock onwards. In our application we said we were willing to undertake either the four and a half Monday to Friday franchise or the weekend in London, but expressed a preference for the latter because we felt audiences were more relaxed at the weekend and might therefore respond more readily to what we had to offer.

In the course of our preparations we had learned of more than one rather similar consortium to our own which was applying for the same franchise. It came as no surprise, therefore, when the Authority, of which Lord Hill (once famous as 'the Radio Doctor') had become chairman, suggested that we merge with another group. It transpired that David Frost, well known for his satirical BBC programme *That Was The Week That Was* had approached several of the same financial backers as ourselves, chosen the same managing director – Michael

Peacock, then controller of BBC1, who had agreed to come to either of us – and would welcome me as chairman if we won the franchise. The merger took place amicably. David and I got on well and we duly presented ourselves to the Authority.

The meeting in Brompton Road on May 5th, 1967, was dramatic. Although the Authority had stipulated that applicants should name the chief officers of their proposed company, there were several instances in which this proved impossible without endangering the current job of the person in question. One could, however, give such names secretly to the chairman. It was a 'hole-in-the-corner' arrangement but none of us could see any alternative. In our case, for example, the proposed Controller of Programmes and Director of Sales (Advertising Manager), Cyril Bennett and Guy Paine, were both holding similar positions in Rediffusion, the company which immediately preceded us in making their application before the Authority. Neither Bennett nor Paine came with us when we confronted Lord Hill, but we had been able to tell him secretly of their dilemma. It might have been fatal to their careers if their presence in our group had been betrayed to one of their existing colleagues. However, Cyril Bennett managed to get word to us as we waited in a nearby room that Rediffusion's application had not gone well and that in particular John Wills, the chairman, had made a bad impression. Morale was high as we entered the Authority's presence.

I remember little about the interview. I opened for our group and every other member of our team either spoke or answered questions. David Montague, the merchant banker, spoke for our financial backers. The terms which they had agreed were that 30 per cent of the shares (voting and non-voting) would be allocated to senior management such as programme producers, performers and other 'artistic interests'. David Frost had insisted that as co-founders he and I were to have 5 per cent each. No one shareholder was to have more than 10 per cent. We felt we had made a good impression on the Authority, but were on tenterhooks that night. When the telephone in Chester Square rang next day to tell us we had won the contract there was great rejoicing. We had no difficulty in meeting the Authority's request to include as substantial shareholders the *Daily Telegraph*, *The Economist* and the *Observer*. As a result, our board thus acquired three new directors, David Astor representing the *Observer*, Michael Berry representing the *Daily Telegraph*, and Sir Geoffrey Crowther, *The Economist*. The first two I knew well and I had a great respect for the third.

I did not intend to resign from the House of Commons but to wait and see how much time the chairmanship would take. There was no need to take any action until we had started televising the following year. In the meantime, however, it was made known to me that the Prime Minister, Harold Wilson, was of the opinion that no one who became the chairman of a television company should remain a Member of the House of Commons. When I consulted my Conservative colleagues, some of them were indignant. They pointed out that the chairmanship was not an office of profit under the Crown and that no Prime Minister had the power to deprive a Member of Parliament of his seat for such a reason. On reflection, however, I came to the conclusion that Harold Wilson was right. The chairmanship of a television company may not be an office of profit under the Crown but it is nevertheless an office, of which the incumbent administers a monopoly granted by the Crown, and an office which is particularly sensitive politically. Being obliged by the Charter under which he operates to ensure political impartiality across the broad spectrum of the programmes his company produces, any chairman who is an active party politician must be suspect. Even if his probity is unquestioned, he cannot be immune from the influences exercised by his daily duties in the House of Commons and cannot avoid arousing suspicion about the objectivity of his judgement. These suspicions may not only harm him personally but damage the interests of his company. I consulted the wise and benevolent Willie Whitelaw, Chief Whip for the Opposition, but he said that the decision was entirely mine and he would not attempt to influence me. He added that there was no immediate hurry and urged me to take my time. It was not until the summer of 1968, therefore, that I applied for the Manor of Northwood, one of the two ancient but non-existent offices which involved resignation of one's seat.

In London Weekend Television all went well to begin with. We rented an office in Cork Street near Burlington House, and settled down as a team. Later we moved to a high-rise building on the North Circular Road from which we were to go on the air. As part of our contract we had undertaken to build new studios on the South Bank of the Thames and our negotiations with the Coal Board Pension Fund produced the building which Londoners can see today to the east of the Hayward Gallery and Festival Hall. Our troubles only started when we began to broadcast.

One of the reasons I had chosen Michael Peacock to be managing director was that when I had known him as a young man at the BBC he had taken a decisive hold of whatever department he was running. But at London Weekend both he and his programme controller, Cyril Bennett, seemed to have made up their minds to give their producers a free hand. The results were disastrous. As our ratings decreased, advertising fell away and after six months we were facing a crisis.

The board decided that Peacock and Bennett must go and we were met at once with vigorous protests from the producers who no doubt saw their restraint-free holiday coming to an end. The board also began to look around for new money to tide us over what we all believed were just growing pains. When Rupert Murdoch, scenting a chance to get control of a London television station on the cheap, offered to become a major shareholder, we accepted his offer, as did the Independent Television Authority.

Murdoch has never been a sleeping partner and he set about at once reorganizing the company. He did a great service by bringing in his top sales director from News International who within a very short time reversed the trend in advertising revenue. But although Murdoch held no official position in the company other than that of a shareholder, he began to come into the office every day and poke his nose into every department. I was bombarded with complaints from all sides. Although his energy was infectious I warned him that if he continued to behave as though he were the managing director, he would not only provoke a revolt within London Weekend but run foul of the Authority, who had the right to approve or disapprove of all senior managerial appointments. He did not listen, and when the Authority duly reproved him in no uncertain terms he rang me up from Australia and protested that I had allowed it to 'crucify' him. When he returned he ceased to come into the office but made it plain to me that he was going to do all he could to get another chairman. Soon afterwards, John Freeman, who was our original choice as deputy chairman and had returned from New Delhi where he had been High Commissioner, took my place. As I had been a founder of the company, at the instigation of David Montague the board made me President until London Weekend's original contract expired.

It had been a disappointing and at times agonizing experience. As chairman I naturally had to accept the blame for a disastrous start to a company which had begun with such high promise – and which has since proved itself. Perhaps my greatest mistake was to allow myself to be too closely concerned with the day-to-day management rather than remaining a little aloof and keeping closer to the board. Forbidden by the Authority to play the part he wanted, Rupert Murdoch moved on to other, even more contentious fields. But before I left he did me a favour by buying my shares in London Weekend at a price which guaranteed me a pension. He is an impetuous but in many ways an irresistible character and I like to think there was an element of contrition in his decision. After all, it was not I who had incurred the wrath of the Authority.

Rupert's purchase bore unexpected fruit. I gave a proportion of the money to my three children with the idea that they should have a little capital with which to start an enterprise of their own early in their lives. Each embarked on a different venture, but at first none succeeded. Then, by pooling what was left, they backed a winner. My eldest son, Andrew, was working for an Iranian-Japanese bank in Tehran. Impressed by the number of office and residential buildings going up all round him and wondering what the occupants were going to put on their walls, he wrote to his sister Harriet, who was then in Paris, suggesting that they might start a business connected with pictures. Harriet knew nothing about business and did not take him seriously. However, all three children had spent hours looking at pictures and Harriet had earlier been to a school of painting and sculpture in Rome. Some months later, when she decided to go to Tehran and help Andrew arrange his flat, she remembered what he had said and discussed it with a friend, Richard Price, who was running a successful business selling British television programmes around the world. Being a collector of old maps, he took her in hand and began to teach her about them. They agreed to form a partnership. He would buy old maps of Persia, she would try to sell them in Tehran and they would split the profit. Hearing where she was going, Antony Spink and Richard Green, both well-known London art dealers, wanted to know if Tehran would be a good place in which to hold an art exhibition.

They offered to pay for her ticket if she would do the necessary research and advise them. She accepted.

Harriet went to Tehran with twenty maps and sold them all to the first man she approached. Within three months Richard Price had trebled his money. However, Harriet had learned that women, who are usually in charge of the decoration of houses, do not like maps and she telexed Richard to know if he would like to buy sixteenth- and seventeenth-century engravings of cities. He replied that he did not want to step outside maps. At that moment Randall joined his brother and sister in Tehran and began to work in an art gallery there. He had brought with him all that remained of the money I had given him, three thousand dollars, and pooled it with a similar amount that Harriet had left to buy their first book of seventeenth-century engravings. They sold it almost at once to Queen Farah Deba's office.

So began a business dealing in works of art which Andrew joined full-time a little later on, and which has grown to include paintings, rare books, particularly of natural history, sculpture, engravings and ancient documents. Like all such businesses, it has its ups and downs, but it has prospered enough to enable them to lead a fascinating life based on the principle that by buying in Europe and selling all over the rest of the world, they can meet a demand that is never-ending. The skill lies in buying the right things and finding the right clients.

51

The Himalayan Kingdoms

It was only in the last ten years of our married life that Virginia and I discovered the Himalayas. Some time in 1972 a friend brought Thondup Namgyal, the Chogyal of Sikkim, to our house in London and we learned about the little kingdom on the northern frontier of India which the Namgyal family had ruled for four hundred years. It lies between Bhutan to the east and Nepal to the west and its northern frontier with Tibet stretches across great mountain ridges at heights of between fifteen and twenty thousand feet.

The Lama of Lhasa established Buddhism as the state religion in 1641 and appointed a Namgyal to be the first King or Chogyal. The family not only maintained the faith, but Thondup himself was six times over a reincarnate and therefore the religious as well as the political leader of his country. His father, Sir Tashi Namgyal, had a treaty with the British Indian Government which guaranteed his position as Chogyal but allowed the British Resident in Gangtok, the mountain capital of Sikkim, to exercise the real power. Although this treaty protected Sikkim from foreign invasion while the British were in India, it proved to be something of a Trojan horse when, in 1947, the Indian government inherited British responsibilities, for it prevented Sikkim from following the example of Bhutan and becoming a member of the United Nations. A senior member of the Indian diplomatic service became Resident and from that moment the eventual absorption of Sikkim into the Indian Federation became only a matter of time.

Nevertheless Thondup Namgyal was still fighting to preserve his rule in 1974. He had been trained in the Indian Civil Service, was attractive, with a quiet sense of humour and a strong sense of family tradition. He regarded himself as guardian of the Buddhist faith in Sikkim. When he asked us in 1973 to come and visit him, it rekindled an old urge in me. Why not make some documentary films on the three Himalayan Kingdoms, Sikkim, Bhutan and Nepal?

I rang Bernard Delfont (later Lord Delfont), head of the film distribution department of Electrical and Musical Industries, who said at once that he would back me. When I explained that we would be a family team – because otherwise we were unlikely to get permission to enter Sikkim and to move about as freely as we wished – he saw no difficulties. In his office I was advised by his colleagues that provided an independent producer employed no union members at all, he did not have any difficulty in getting his films distributed.

The team consisted of myself and Virginia, my younger son Randall and Harriet. We went twice to Sikkim, once for a reconnaissance in 1973, and the second time to make films not only there but in Bhutan and Nepal. Thondup himself gave us an introduction to his cousin, the Queen Mother in Bhutan, and I made arrangements through the Nepalese Embassy in London to visit Nepal. Nowadays package tours visit all these countries annually, but in the early 1970s one needed a personal invitation from the ruler of each country to be admitted at all, and also the co-operation of the Indian government, through whose territory one had to pass to reach their frontiers.

In Gangtok we stayed in the Chogyal's guest house, which sits on the edge of a steep mountain dropping two thousand feet to a stream. We were looked after most attentively, taken everywhere by ADCs in jeeps and often by Thondup himself and his American wife, Hope. Our only difficulty was at breakfast. The Sikkimese rise early and the cook, anxious to please, made sure that we were never kept waiting by frying our eggs an hour or more before we got up which meant that they were always stone cold when we sat down at the table. In the Chogyal's Palace, meals – usually some sort of curry – were served on little tables put in front of our chairs in whatever room we happened to be sitting. The Chogyal had an excellent cellar and we drank claret from Haut Brion and Château-Lafite.

The Chogyal invited us to accompany him on his traditional 'progress' through the country. He said we could film as we went. It turned out to be the last progress any member of his family was to make.

Except for the road from the Indian frontier in the south to Gangtok, the roads in Sikkim were then no more than jeep tracks cut out of the side of precipitous mountains. Sikkimese drivers prided themselves on their skill, and when there had been rain and the mud track was slippery, would accelerate so as to make sure of skidding across any wet patch, the outer wheels of the jeep often within a few inches of a drop of a thousand feet or more. Where a landslide had washed the road away – an event which occurred regularly – the jeeps would stop and we would all pick our way across the mud on foot, to be met by other jeeps which had been summoned from higher up in the valley. At each stopping place we would be met by men in red or yellow pointed caps playing wood instruments and the Himalayan horn, which was so long it needed two boys to carry it and emitted a low but penetrating moan which echoed across the mountains. We would then proceed to an arbour of branches surrounded by white prayer flags where the Chogyal would sit and listen to petitions and complaints.

The complaints in that year were mainly political: how members of the Nepalese-Hindu party were intimidating the Lepchas, burning their houses and beating them up while the Indian police looked on passively. Thondup did his best to calm the people but was powerless as the Indian Resident was really in control. Before we left Gangtok, I interviewed the Chogyal against a background of prayer flags and, in the distance, the peaks of Kanchenjunga, third highest mountain in the Himalayas and sacred to the Sikkimese. When I asked him if being a reincarnate six times over made him feel superior to the rest of us, he said with a gentle smile, 'Superior, no. But perhaps a little wiser.'

The Nepalese-Hindu party won the election; Sikkim ceased to be a Protectorate and became a Province of India. In due course Mrs Gandhi deposed the Chogyal even from the post of constitutional monarch. But the methods of the new rulers became so unpopular that when their term of office was up, they were soundly defeated by a party which supported Thondup Namgyal. Thus, although Mrs Gandhi would not reinstate him, Thondup was able to travel around the country again as its religious leader.

His life was to end tragically. His second wife, Hope, left with her two children when she realized that Thondup was no longer ruler; his eldest son, Tensing, was killed in a car accident on the mountain tracks which many people thought had been deliberately planned, and Thondup himself died shortly afterwards. No doubt his spirit has now joined those others whom he venerated which inhabit the peaks of Kanchenjunga.

*

Although you can drive by jeep, and sometimes by car, from the same point on the Indian frontier to both Gangtok and Thimpu, the capital of Bhutan, the countries could scarcely be more different. Bhutan is six times larger than Sikkim and, with a population of a million, has at least five times as many people, the great majority of whom are of Tibetan descent. Yet the country gives the impression of being even more remote and medieval than its neighbour. Known for centuries as 'the Forbidden Kingdom' because of the physical and political difficulties of gaining access to it, Bhutan is a monarchy, which under the present King's father, Jigme Wangchuk, began to emerge from feudalism in the 1960s. Before he died in 1970, he succeeded in making Bhutan a member of the United Nations under the sponsorship of India and the Soviet Union.

But Bhutan is still dominated by Buddhist Lamas, whose religion the King is sworn to uphold, and of whom there are many thousands. In 1974, more than a quarter of the country's budget was spent on their upkeep and the great *dzongs* in which they live, which are part fortress, part administrative centres, and physically dominate the main valleys of the country. The Bhutanese are great builders, using local timber and never employing metal in their construction. Curiously, they have never evolved a chimney, so that the guest houses in which we stayed instantly filled with smoke when we lit a fire.

Although it was through Kesang, the Queen Mother and widow of Jigme Wangchuk, that we gained admission to Bhutan, I saw her only once. However, she introduced us to her son, the Druk Gyalpo, or King, and he not only enabled us to see everyone we wished but lent us the helicopter which Mrs Gandhi had given him. We were therefore able to film the jungle on the Indian border in the south-east and also the Dzong of Bumtang in the centre of the country, to reach which would otherwise have taken us three weeks on mules. Through the foresight of his father, the young King, who was then only seventeen, was out of the predatory reach of Mrs Gandhi and relations with India were close.

Randall filmed me interviewing the King and his enchanting sister, Princess Detchen, who at the age of nineteen was Minister for

Economic Affairs, in their offices in the great Dzong at Thimpu. He then filmed the King sitting on his golden Dragon throne, facing a small Buddhist shrine. When I asked the Princess if she did not feel rather young to be in charge of her country's economy, she smiled and said that she had been specially trained by her father but that of course she also had very good advisers.

We filmed the monks at the other end of the same vast building when they were engaged in electing a new head Lama, and on another day we filmed the King's birthday ceremony where a kilted pipe band played while soldiers performed a wild 'dervish' dance. On the great parade ground, which was one of the few flat places near Thimpu, the King provided a free meal of rice, meat and vegetables for many hundreds of his people. He also took part in an archery match against the Indian garrison, which Bhutan won, as indeed it should have, archery being the national sport.

The day we most enjoyed saw another such match between two villages. Both teams had consulted the astrologers before the match started and both were convinced that they would win. Prayer flags flew proudly behind the targets and the village people picnicked in the middle while the arrows flew overhead. Girls in Sikkimese dress swayed in long lines to the rhythm of stringed music, and when a target was hit everyone broke into loud cheers. If everything had not been so orderly and graceful it might have been a scene from *Alice in Wonderland*.

*

Our visit to Nepal was made separately. The country is the size of England and Wales, but except for a strip along the southern border with India, very little of it is flat. When some remote regions suffered from drought in 1973, the only means of getting the people adequate food was to fly out bags of corn and land them by parachute. Our visit in 1974 was the first of many, for, once having seen the Kathmandu Valley and trekked towards Anapurna from Pokhara, we returned several times. Kathmandu is an hour's flight from Delhi and as you near it the panorama of the Himalayas stretches out in front of you from Mount Everest in the east to Daulagiri in the west. On a clear day at thirty thousand feet, you can see almost a hundred miles either side of the aircraft.

The Kathmandu Valley, with the snow-capped mountains as its backdrop, a golden wheat harvest covering the fields and the red-brick and seventeenth-century towns with their towering pagodas built by the Malla Kings, is one of the sights of the world. We filmed the harvest being cut by sickle, the carvings on the eaves of the pagodas, some of them quaintly erotic, and talked to European and American hippies. It was easy to understand why Kathmandu attracted them. Besides the hospitable traditions of a country where to share is natural, marijuana grew wild almost everywhere and the cafés and bars in Kathmandu had signs up inviting the smoking of hash. It took the Nepalese a few years to learn that hippies could be over-demanding guests.

But the joy of Nepal is the trekking. There are still very few roads and the normal method of travel is on foot. Wheeled vehicles, even wheelbarrows, are uneconomic outside a town. Trails, designed specially for people who walk, lead all over the mountains and valleys. Every five hundred yards or so there is a resting post, a two-tiered rectangular stone platform, the upper tier to take the packs of the porters and the lower their buttocks. You see astonishing loads being carried: enormous water tanks for a house boiler, beds, wardrobes, mirrors, crates of books and papers and bottles, all slung on ropes which go around the porter's forehead and hold the load on to his or her back. Quite often, following or preceding them is an elegant Nepalese lady in a brilliant red or yellow sari carrying an umbrella-cum-sunshade, or a man in a suit and bowler hat.

Trekking has become well organized. It is possible to trek alone, with a knapsack on your back, stopping at the many rest houses in the villages. We stopped once at such a house when torrential rain had made camping impossible and dried our clothes round a fire in the middle of the floor. But our treks were organized by a company founded by a Colonel Roberts, one-time commander of a Gurkha regiment, Military Attaché at the British Embassy in Kathmandu, mountaineer and organizer of several of Chris Bonnington's expeditions to Everest and elsewhere, and an ornithologist who has a unique collection of Asian pheasants in his garden.

The company hired the porters and the Sherpas who controlled them. They pitched camp at midday and cooked us a meal, pitched again in the evening and cooked supper. While they broke camp at dawn they gave us porridge, eggs, sausages and bacon; we drank our coffee watching the snow on Machapuchere or Anapurna turn from rose-pink to gold as the sun rose. We crossed swinging rope bridges over torrents at which it was wiser not to look down, and walked through forests of rhododendron trees, many of them forty feet high. At Gandrung, where the stone houses had solid slate roofs and no chimneys, we camped in the courtyard. Every house had photographs of some member of the family in a British Gurkha regiment.

Nepal seemed the most stable of the Himalayan Kingdoms. For our film both Virginia and I talked to King Birendra, who had been to Eton. He was moving away from personal rule to a more Elizabethan form of government. He maintained an independent policy towards China, his northern neighbour, and not only traded but accepted Chinese investment. He also kept the road from Kathmandu to Lhasa open.

On our return to England we met with nothing but frustration. Although the films we made were commended by the members of EMI who saw them, our efforts came to nothing because the Association of Cinematograph, Television and Allied Technicians blacked them, alleging that we and EMI were in breach of their overall agreement with the film industry. After lengthy discussion the films were cleared for distribution, but by then it was too late. The whole policy of EMI towards documentaries had changed and there was no prospect of getting them shown in the cinema. Meanwhile Bernie Delfont, disappointed but still enthusiastic, had commissioned a further film on the Philippines. Before setting out, I went to see an official of the ACTT, agreed to take a professional cameraman who was a member of his union, and thought I had a firm agreement.

President Marcos and his wife Imelda both took part in the film and the President let us use his air force and particularly their helicopters. The film included sequences taken on the island of Corregidor, discussed the role of the Philippines in the Second World War, and had a section about the Stone Age group known as the Tasaday who live in the rain forest on Mindanao, the main southern island of the archipelago.

But we were still unable to get distribution in England. After protracted negotiations with the ACTT, one of their young men said to me, 'The truth is we don't want you to produce or direct films at all since you are not a member of our union.' He added, 'I would rather no documentaries were produced for the cinema than that any should be made except strictly according to our rules.' He has had his way. Documentaries are no longer shown in the cinema in Britain, and those on television are made almost entirely by the television corporations themselves, not always according to ACTT rules. Thereafter, the films I and my family made were for private companies and private showing.

EPILOGUE

From 1974 onwards, Virginia and I lived mainly in France, Spain and Italy. We knew we were going to be so much abroad making films that it seemed sensible to let our house in London and become non-resident. In France we rented an old vicarage in the village of Villeperdue, twenty miles south of Tours. The owners, the Count and Countess d'Espous, were already friends and lived in the small château of Boisbonnard, a few hundred yards away. It was a perfect arrangement: they only wanted use of the vicarage in the winter since it was a much easier house to heat than their own, and we only wanted it from April till October.

At one time we bought an old olive mill which stood on a steep hill across the valley from Ronda in Andalucia, southern Spain. It was romantic, with three hundred acres of olive trees and springs of water, and could only be reached on horseback. But we realized in time that it would cost us more than we could afford to make habitable and that we should never be there enough to justify the expense. We were lucky to sell it at a small profit to Señor Manuel Ulloa (later Prime Minister of Peru). His plans for the house were much like ours but I am not sure how far he ever developed them. Thereafter we rented houses in the Costa del Sol for two or three months a year and our children came to join us. In Italy we twice rented a house in Tuscany and the children gave us fabulous weekends in Venice.

However, throughout these years a shadow had fallen across our lives. Virginia was suffering from emphysema. She had given up smoking as soon as the disease was diagnosed but it had gone too far for her to recover completely. Her breath became shorter and shorter and although she continued to do almost everything she wanted to do, her exertions became increasingly painful to watch. Before we went for our last holiday in Spain in 1983, her specialist in London had told her that her breathing was at zero on the register and there was no more he could do. He warned her that she had only weeks to live and that death might be painful. Luckily the house we rented that year was the most beautiful of all and her favourite relations and many friends were around her.

Driving home we met Randall in Madrid and stayed the night. Virginia had difficulty in getting out of bed in the morning. Next day we set out for Bordeaux where we were to stay with Philippe de Rothschild at Mouton. She asked me to leave the main road and drive through the Sierra Guadarama, which she had known during the Spanish Civil War. The diversion, which took us along narrow, twisty roads, cost a lot of time, and it was after half past two when we reached Biarritz. The restaurant in the Palace Hotel was closed and we had a snack at a café. Virginia went to sleep on the long, straight, flat road across Les Grandes Landes; I had not felt sleepy, but near Arcachon, at about five-thirty in the evening, must have dropped off for a second. I woke at the first bump as our wheel hit the grass verge, and thought I could easily correct the car. But we hit a soft patch and the car turned over. The car ended the right way up and I was able to lift Virginia on to the back seat. In doing so I realized that something was wrong with my neck. I never wholly lost consciousness and asked a man who came to help whether Virginia was alive. He replied, *'C'est très grave.'* I saw her lying beside me in the ambulance and was aware when they took her away. She had been killed instantly by a brain haemorrhage. Mercifully I was only half conscious for much of the time in the Bordeaux hospital. I remember Mary, Virginia's sister, saying to me on the telephone from Holland that God had been kind to Virginia but less kind to me.

Before he operated on my neck Professor Le Rebeller, the head surgeon, asked me if I played golf. I said yes, but badly. 'After today,' he replied, 'you will play better because you will not be able to lift your head.' It took me some months to get rid of the collar round my neck and two years to get as near normal as I can be. The Professor, a brilliant and charming man, has proved right about the golf. What I have lost in length I have made up in accuracy. The memory of Virginia keeps me active and prevents me feeling sorry for myself, which she would have despised.

There are things which sadden and others which infuriate me, in particular the occasional decline of BBC's *Panorama* to a sordid imitation of *Private Eye*. But there are many reasons for feeling hopeful.

The technological revolution which has made it possible for several new newspapers, two of them national, to be published in 1985 and 1986, is not only a surprise but a fillip for democracy. In the end, the old newspapers, many of which I worked for, will benefit, as will those unions whose 'Luddite' leaders are still opposing change. My children's business continues to thrive. My elder son has followed the example of his younger brother and married a girl who worked with them all for a year. I now have two daughters-in-law, to each of whom I am devoted, and four grandchildren. My daughter Harriet, who was adopted as Conservative candidate to fight Ken Livingstone in Brent East in 1987, and made a sparkling début at the Party Conference in Bournemouth, has had a baby boy since the election.

I myself am retiring to a village cottage in Northamptonshire within whose thick stone walls I hope to welcome family and friends and from which I shall watch the scene with greater calm than would be possible in London.

NOTES TO THE TEXT

CHAPTER 4

1   As I write, I have next to me a letter
from Miss Ironside dated May 10th,
1959, saying how much she had enjoyed
having our daughter Harriet in her school
for the past three years. Reenie, as she
was called, was then more than eighty,
still teaching and still as alive and imaginative as ever.

CHAPTER 6

1   See *A History of Lords and Commons
Cricket* by Eric E. Bullus MP (Blades,
East & Blades Ltd., London 1963).

CHAPTER 7

1   Only full members of the Cricket XI
were allowed to wear white flannels. Boys
trying for a place wore grey flannels.
Members of the Cricket XI also wore
speckled straw hats instead of white ones.
The normal way of receiving flannels was
for the Captain of the XI to throw a
speckled hat to the boy concerned before
he left the pavilion at the end of a match.

CHAPTER 9

1   It was not possible to take gate money
in the Parks because they were open to
the public. The Christ Church ground
had a high wall round it and, as so many
people wanted to see the Australians, it
was worthwhile for the Oxford University
Cricket Club to charge for admission.
This they were able to do by courtesy of
the Christ Church Fellows.

CHAPTER 10

1   *Cosmo Gordon Lang* by J.G. Lockhart
(Hodder & Stoughton, London 1949).

CHAPTER 12

1   The name of the club denotes its
origin. Lord Willingdon had been playing
golf with an Indian ruler and at the end of
the game suggested they go to his club for
a drink. The ruler replied that he would
be delighted but that he would not be
allowed in. The Viceroy was so shocked
that he immediately founded a club open
to all races.

CHAPTER 16

1   This was not as certain as I thought.
Lord Rothermere actually died in 1936
just after I had left the paper. He had such
huge debts that Esmond had to sell the
family holding in the *Daily Mirror* to pay
them and only just retained a controlling
interest in the *Daily Mail*.
2   The enterprise would have cost
between two and three hundred thousand
pounds in the 1980s.

CHAPTER 17

1   My father never really left the Cloisters: the ashes of my father and mother
rest in the crypt of St George's Chapel,
Windsor, and there is a plaque on the
floor commemorating them. I once asked
the Rt Revd Michael Mann, who became
Dean in 1976, if he remembered my

father and he replied, 'No, but I walk over him every day.'

2 *The Flying Sword, The Story of 601 Squadron*, by Tom Moulson (Macdonald, London 1964).

CHAPTER 18

1 She described her visit in her book *Looking for Trouble* (Hamish Hamilton, London 1941).

2 *Operation Cicero* by L.C. Moyzisch. Translated by Constantine Fitzgibbon and Heinrich Frenkel. (First published in Britain by Allen Wingate, 1950.)

3 Air Chief Marshal Sir Edmund Huddleston, born in Australia in 1908. Commander Allied Air Forces Central Europe 1964 and C-in-C of all Allied Forces in Central Europe 1964–65.

CHAPTER 20

1 Now Sir Stephen Runciman, Fellow of Trinity College, Cambridge, Professor of Byzantine Art and History at the University of Istanbul 1942–45. Among many publications he wrote *The First Bulgarian Empire* and *The Fall of Constantinople*.

2 This episode was brought to life again in 1987 when a London newspaper reporter came across a recently released security file containing correspondence between Air Marshals Harris and Douglas setting out the elaborate preparations made in Britain for Hitler's reception in the event of Baur being able to make his landing. Although all contact with Baur ended when the British Embassy left Sofia in March, in London hope was kept alive until May.

CHAPTER 22

1 It was not until after the war that I learned that Cavan had been captured by the Germans while helping the

Resistance in the Balkans and sentenced to ninety-two days' solitary confinement. He survived the war but I never saw him again.

2 An excellent account of 'Wings' Day's experiences as a prisoner of war has been written by Sydney Smith, a former journalist and fellow prisoner in Stalag Luft III: *Wing's Day* (Collins, London 1968).

CHAPTER 23

1 Looking back I think this fear was exaggerated. There were at least three million foreign workers in Germany at that time and no German was surprised to meet Czechs, Hungarians, French, Yugoslavs, Balts or people of many other races. Provided you did not actually burst out into English (which happened to some escapers) you were not necessarily suspect. What mattered was to have valid papers and to know the procedures.

CHAPTER 24

1 Comte Pierre d'Harcourt was ordered by Vichy at the beginning of the German occupation to form a resistance cell in Paris. He was eventually betrayed by one of his own staff. He was tortured by the French militia as well as the Germans, spent two years in Fresnes, a Vichy French prison near Paris, and was then sent to Buchenwald, which he described to me as 'paradise' because he could mingle with other human beings. For twenty years he wrote for the *Observer* in London and died in 1982.

2 In the early years of the war, many British prisoners of war received private parcels, some of which came from generous Dutch or Belgian families who had not enough to eat themselves. Because of that and of the feelings of those who relied solely on Red Cross

parcels, private parcels were banned at the end of 1942.

CHAPTER 25

1 A 'ferret' was a German guard, usually armed with a torch and a screwdriver, whose duty was to prevent escape. He had the right to enter the camp at any time of the day or night.
2 Accounts of their escapes have been written by Eric Williams in *The Wooden Horse* (Collins, London, revised edition 1979) and by Oliver Philpot in *Stolen Journey* (Hodder & Stoughton, London 1950). Mike Codner was killed in Malaya.
3 A full account of this march, of its winter predecessor in Silesia and of our release is given in my book *Escape from Germany* (published in its original form by Her Majesty's Stationery Office in January 1985).

CHAPTER 27

1 United States Ambassador in London, March 1947 to the end of 1950.

CHAPTER 30

1 *Facing the Nation* by Grace Wyndham Goldie, p. 86 (Bodley Head, London 1977).
2 Irrigation poles were made of bamboo and were twenty or more feet long, with a primitive form of box which could be filled with stones at the short end and a sort of mackintosh bucket at the other end which dipped into the river. By adding to the stones in the box the bucket could then be levered up to deposit in the ditches behind.

CHAPTER 34

1 Later Lord Trevelyan. After leaving Iraq he became Ambassador to the Soviet Union. He retired from the Foreign Office in 1967 and became chairman to the Trustees of the British Museum in 1970.
2 Henry J. Heinz Jr. and his wife, Drue. 'Jack' Heinz, as he was generally known, was the son of the founder of the famous American food company which produces fifty-seven varieties of canned foods. He died in 1987.

CHAPTER 36

1 In a letter written to me in August 1985, David Henecker recalls that he and Virginia were talking to some people in the farmyard when dive-bombers appeared from the east. They just managed to run into the farm buildings before the first bomb exploded. 'I still remember the heat and blast coming into the room, and then removing quite a lot of plaster from Virginia's hair, the ceiling having collapsed.'

CHAPTER 38

1 James Bredin became Managing Director of Border Television in 1964. After retiring, he was employed by several companies as creator and co-ordinator of television archives.
2 *Independent Television in Britain, Vol. I* by Bernard Sendall (Macmillan, London 1982).
3 Geoffrey Cox, now Sir Geoffrey Cox, my successor as Editor, had to fight hard to preserve the budget of three hundred and fifty thousand pounds which I had successfully defended, when he asked for its renewal the following year. He succeeded and lived to see a budget more than fifty times as large within twenty-five years.

CHAPTER 39

1 Now Lord Wyatt, chairman of the Racecourse Totalisator Board. I am

indebted to his autobiography *Confessions of an Optimist* (Collins, London 1985) for much of what I have written in the next two pages.

CHAPTER 42

1 Now Lord and Lady Donaldson. Jack was Minister for the Arts in Harold Wilson's government and Frankie has written many books, including one about Edward VIII, which was a best-seller.

CHAPTER 44

1 It is interesting to note that General Buhari, the military dictator of Nigeria, has said recently that it is essential that the rule of the hereditary chiefs be maintained. If anyone other than the Emir tried to rule Katsina, there would be civil war.

CHAPTER 48

1 *Hugh Gaitskell* by Philip Williams, p. 546, footnote (Jonathan Cape, London 1979).

2 Under BBC rules, being on a list of candidates did not disqualify you from broadcasting. It was only if you were adopted as a prospective candidate for a particular constituency that you were debarred from appearing on the screen. The exposure was thought to give you an advantage over your prospective opponent.

CHAPTER 49

1 The Kaffir wars were between white settlers pushing east from Cape Colony and the Xhosa tribes being pushed west by increasing population. They lasted a hundred years, between 1779 and 1878. Both peoples were stock farmers, the whites (Boer and British) supported by the Cape Government, and Xhosas by a highly organized tribal system.

INDEX

428